Dreadful Conversions

DREADFUL CONVERSIONS

The Making of a Catholic Socialist

JOHN C. CORT

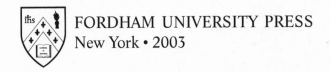

FORDHAM UNIVERSITY PRESS
New York • 2003

Library of Congress Cataloging-in-Publication Data

Cort, John C.
    Dreadful conversions : the making of a Catholic socialist /
John C. Cort.—1st ed.
        p.   cm.
    Includes bibliographical references and index.
    ISBN 0-8232-2256-X (alk. paper)
    1. Cort, John C.   2. Socialists—United States—Biography.   3.
Church and social problems—United States—Catholic Church.   I. Title.
HX84 .C67A3   2003
335'.7'092—dc21   2003002403

Printed in the United States of America
02 03 04 05 06   5 4 3 2 1
First Edition

To Helen Haye Cort

Who shall find a valiant woman? Far and from the uttermost coasts
is the price of her. . . . Many are the women of proven worth, but you
have excelled them all.

—Proverbs 31:10 (Douai-Rheims translation)

We are not particularly afraid of all these socialists, anarchists, infidels and revolutionaries. We keep watch on them and know all their doings. But there are a few peculiar ones among them who believe in God and are Christians, but at the same time are socialists. These are the people we are most afraid of. They are dreadful people. The socialist who is a Christian is more to be dreaded than the socialist who is an atheist.

—Police official in Fyodor Dostoyevsky's *The Brothers Karamazov*

Love in action is a harsh and dreadful thing, compared with love in dreams.

—Father Zossima in *The Brothers Karamazov*

A decent provision for the poor is the true test of civilization.

—Samuel Johnson in James Boswell's *Life of Johnson*

CONTENTS

ACKNOWLEDGMENTS

I am grateful to the following periodicals and publishers for permission to reprint bits, pieces, or large chunks of material that first appeared in their pages, usually in more or less different form or length: *America* for "Nine Years of ACTU" (April 6, 1946); *Commonweal* for excerpts from my column "The Labor Movement," from letters about the column during the year 1949, and from the articles "My First Hurrah" (November 7, 1958), "Eight Hundred Americans" (September 25, 1964), "People for Workers' Control" (February 15, 1974), "Why I Became a Socialist" (March 26, 1976), "My Life at the Catholic Worker" (June 20, 1980), and "How the Females Put an End to Male Oppression," (July 3, 1981); *The Sign* for "Kennedy for President" (August 1958) and "A New Road Back for the Workers" (September 1961); the *New Oxford Review* for "Discovering the Church in Harvard Yard" (November 1987); *Religious Socialism* for "A Boston Memoir" (summer 1993); and Times Books/Random House for material in Charles R. Morris's book *American Catholic: The Saints and Sinners Who Built America's Most Powerful Church* (1997).

For the publication of this book I am indebted mainly to Mary Beatrice Schulte, editor at Fordham University Press, and to James Fisher, the labor historian, who saw some merit in such an unlikely enterprise. I also am extremely grateful for help, criticism, advice, and encouragement from my late beloved friend and first agent, Herb Kenny; my present agent, Tim Seldes; Peter Steinfels, David O'Brien, Charles Morris, Sister Mary Emil Penet, I.H.M., and all my comrades in the Religion and Socialism Commission of Democratic Socialists of America; also Maurice Isserman, Jack Spooner, Curt Sanders, Tom Cornell, Gene Moore, Megan Maloney, and Charlie Sanphy; the three giants of the secular and Catholic left—the late Michael Harrington, Irving Howe, and Monsignor George Higgins; Fathers Ed Boyle, S.J., David Hollenbach, S.J., George Vartzelis, and Charles Oduke Onyango, S.J.; and especially my wife, Helen, and all my children and grandchildren, who have kept me alive and on my aging toes. A special thanks, finally, to Paul Buhle for a valuable suggestion as to arrangement of the material in this book.

ABBREVIATIONS

ABCD	Action for Boston Community Development
ACTU	Association of Catholic Trade Unionists
AFL	American Federation of Labor
CIO	Congress of Industrial Organizations
CLG	Catholic Labor Guild
CW	Catholic Worker
CWVs	Catholic War Veterans
DSA	Democratic Socialists of America
DSOC	Democratic Socialist Organizing Committee
HUD	Department of Housing and Urban Development
ILA	International Longshoremen's Association
ILGWU	International Ladies' Garment Workers Union
ISU	International Seamen's Union
IUE	International Union of Electrical, Radio and Machine Workers
MAW	Mothers for Adequate Welfare
MNCC	Model Neighborhood Citizens Council
NAACP	National Association for the Advancement of Colored People
NACSAC	National Catholic Social Action Conference
NCWC	National Catholic Welfare Conference
NMU	National Maritime Union
OEO	Office of Economic Opportunity
PSM	People for Self-Management
SDG	Self-Development Group
TWU	Transport Workers Union
UAW	United Auto Workers
UE	United Electrical, Radio and Machine Workers
VISTA	Volunteers in Service to America

PREFACE

The physical, philosophical, sentimental, moral, and spiritual confusions that orbit around the word *love* are infinite in their variety. It might be argued that how we sort them out and clarify them, or fail to clarify them, largely determines the shape of our lives. I begin therefore with my first amorous experience.

It was the summer of 1926. We were all over at the Hardies' cottage on Bluff Island for some kind of party. I was standing alone against the wall watching the dancing. More specifically, I was watching Flora Hardie dancing. She was a dark-haired girl from New Orleans, and as I watched her in the flickering light of the kerosene lamps, it occurred to me that she embodied all the qualities immortalized in the song that was that very moment spreading its jazzy questions and answers around the room:

> Isn't she cute? Isn't she sweet?
> She's gentle and mentally nearly complete.
> She's knockout, she's regal, her beauty's illegal,
> She's the girl friend.

I concluded that I must be in love with Flora Hardie. I had never been in love before, so this was an arresting thought. A powerful force within me was moving me toward a decision—a decision to ask Flora Hardie to dance.

> Take her to dance, take her to tea,
> It's stunning how cunning this lady can be.
> One glimpse of this vision would cause a collision,
> She's the girl friend.

On the other hand, certain countervailing forces and considerations palsied my will. One, I was only twelve years old, and Flora was seventeen.

> She is smart, she's refined,
> How can she be real?

> She has heart, she has mind,
> Shucks, the girl's ideal.

Two, she was much taller than I. Three, I did not know how to dance. And so I stood pinned against the wall, paralyzed by indecision. The record came to an end. I never asked Flora Hardie to dance, never saw her again after that summer, never even moped very much. After all, it is difficult to sustain romantic melancholy at age twelve.

Nevertheless, in some curious way—perhaps the combination of the song, Flora's distant beauty, and my hopeless longing—I conceived in my mind an impossibly idealized concept of the woman I wanted. The formula was simple: perfection. Or, as I later put it to myself, "a beautiful mind and a beautiful soul in a beautiful body."

Years went by, and it began to look as though I might be waiting for a long time. Came the summer of 1932. My oldest brother David, the family *literatus,* had sold his younger brothers on the virtues of the British novelists of that era—notably Aldous Huxley, Evelyn Waugh, and D. H. Lawrence. A more obscure but still influential author was William Gerhardi, who wrote a book called *Eva's Apples.* One day that summer I was sitting naked in the sun on the rocks of Little Huckleberry Island reading this novel when I came upon the following passage:

> Thus I prefer Eva to earnest women who can talk of Pessimism and Buddha but have no living and spontaneous form themselves. When an object like Eva shows no visible sign of containing a subject but appeals beyond all analysis, it may be taken that the divine spirit has found in her a happy home. She is God's art, perfect like a flower.

From the context it was obvious that this character was speaking for the author, so if the less-intellectual woman was good enough for Gerhardi, why should she not be good enough for me? Clearly, I had set my sights too high. I lowered them. As Thomas Aquinas said, love is an act of the will. I soon enough saw under my eyes a lovely girl with a sweet personality who also played the piano very nicely. And because my mother also played the piano very nicely, I was partial to piano players.

The people whom this lovely girl was visiting, friends of ours, asked me to escort her to a dance at the Thousand Islands Yacht Club. There was a moon that night and long rides across the silver river. I looked into her eyes and saw there, shining like onyx and carnelian, the divine spirit. I was gone.

While I was working up the courage to declare myself, she left the river and returned to Montclair. Something in her eyes as she stood on the train steps waving good-bye gave me hope, and I wrote and told her that I loved her. She wrote back that she loved me too.

When we had returned to Long Island, she asked me to her home for the weekend. There was another dance at some country club, and between dances we walked out and sat in the car, and I kissed her for the first time. I cannot say that I was disillusioned, not at least in her as a perfectly lovable and desirable representative of the human race. She was beautiful in a red evening dress, and I was crazy about her, but suddenly I was overcome by a strange sadness and knew what Shaw meant by his familiar warning: "There are two tragedies in life: one is not to get your heart's desire and the other is to get it."

Clearly there was a problem with the capacity of human love to satisfy the hunger of the heart for perfect joy. Or better, there was a problem with the capacity of the human mind to discover where perfect joy was to be found.

1

Dorothy Day and Peter Maurin

> Oh, no, the Depression was not a romantic time. . . . Have
> you ever seen a child with rickets? Shaking as with palsy.
> No proteins, no milk. And the companies pouring milk
> into gutters. People with nothing to wear and they were
> plowing up cotton. People with nothing to eat, and they
> killed the pigs. If that wasn't the craziest system in the
> world, could you imagine anything more idiotic? This was
> just insane.
>
> —Southern lady quoted by Studs Terkel in *Hard Times*

ON A SUNDAY MORNING in Boston I was coming down the steps of
the French church on Isabella Street when I saw a man holding up a
tabloid newspaper and crying out, *"Catholic Worker*—a penny a
copy." That was a price I could afford to pay, even on my reporter's
salary of $15 a week and trade ads. I bought a copy and took it home
to Pinckney Street on Beacon Hill.

It was the issue of December 1935, in the middle of the Great
Depression, a phenomenon of which I was almost totally unaware.
The economic system had broken down and was lying in pieces on
the ground. Approximately one-quarter of the labor force—14 million workers—was roaming the streets looking for work with no unemployment insurance. But I was employed on a little throwaway
weekly in Brookline, my head full of history, theology, books like
Evelyn Waugh's *Handful of Dust,* and dreams of love and marriage
to a Wellesley girl, topped off with illusions of becoming the first
successful playwright without talent.

I studied the paper. The front page featured a free-verse tract
headed "Easy Essay" and written by one of the staff, Peter Maurin:

> A Bourgeois
> is a fellow
> who tries to be somebody

by trying to be
like everybody
which makes him a nobody. . . .

A Leader
is a fellow
who refuses to be crazy
the way everybody else is crazy
and tries to be crazy
in his own crazy way.

A little weird, but intriguing. On the last page was an appeal for funds to support the paper and the House of Hospitality at 144 Charles Street in New York City. It was written by Dorothy Day, one of the editors, and started with mention of a reader's question as to "why we don't use efficient methods." Day responded:

> We choose to spend the salaries we might be making if we were business-like on feeding and sharing our home with the homeless and hungry. . . . We are willing to clothe ourselves in the donations of clothes that come in, we are willing to eat the plainest and most meager of meals and to endure cold rooms and lack of privacy. . . . And we feel too that the work gains by it. There is ten dollars in the bank, the rent isn't paid, the printer is trusting us. . . . We are quite frankly and unashamedly asking for bread.

Here was something to stir the mind and the imagination. Here was a group of people, obviously of some intelligence and sensitivity, down in New York City in the twentieth century, living a life of Christian poverty like any skinny, gaunt-eyed saint out of a stained-glass window and not ashamed to admit it either. I was further intrigued.

I had been converted to Catholicism while an undergraduate at Harvard, a fact that moved Arthur Schlesinger's wife, Marian, to exclaim many years later, "How positively bizarre!" All my friends and family were Protestants, Jews, and atheists. I was spiritually lonesome. So I visited the Catholic Worker (CW) center in Boston and thereafter began selling the paper in front of churches. I was impressed, and depressed, to see the grim, joyless faces on the people coming out of church. It didn't seem right. Because of the word *worker* in the name of the paper, we were denounced as Communists from time to time.

In April 1936 Dorothy Day came to Boston to give a talk in the dingy room of our headquarters in the South End. I was late for the meeting, and by the time I got there, she was speaking already. Suddenly, bang, without ever to that moment having given the proposition any serious thought at all, I decided to chuck my $15 a week, go down to New York, and work for room and board.

What was it about Dorothy Day that had such an effect? Certainly not physical attraction, although she was by no means an unattractive woman. In fact, the face was striking, the cheekbones high, and the eyes large and strangely slanted. She was tall and imposing in figure, but round shouldered and a bit stooped as though she were already feeling the weight of the burdens she had assumed. She was then thirty-eight years old—young, as I look back now from a snow-capped eighty-nine, but to me then, a mere boy of twenty-two, she was old.

She was not a forceful speaker in the usual sense. She spoke in a low, conversational tone, and the content of her talk was much like the articles I had read in the paper, personal and anecdotal, full of people, places, and events, with occasional quotes from the Gospel or a favorite saint or writer. She probably included one of her favorite quotes from *The Brothers Karamazov:* "Love in action is a harsh and dreadful thing, compared with love in dreams."

What moved me was something else, something that shone through the harsh and dreadful life she was living on behalf of the homeless and the hungry. I remember sitting in that dingy room and thinking, "This woman seems to be getting a lot of fun out of life, and I would like to get some of that for myself."

As much as anything, what attracted me was a quality of humor and laughter, but with a base deeper than the humor and laughter you might get from a good comedian. In one word it was a quality of *joy*. Not perfect joy perhaps, but close enough. Léon Bloy wrote once that "joy is an almost certain sign of the presence of the Holy Spirit." Whatever she had—fun, joy, Holy Spirit—it moved me.

After the meeting I went up to her and said that I wanted to join the CW organization and asked how I should go about it. I think she misunderstood me because she said, "Why don't you come down to the farm in July?"

That was nearly three months away, and anything could happen in three months. I might weaken and change my mind. With a little more nerve I might have argued with her and asked why I could not come sooner. Also, I was not a farm type. It was the action in New York City that appealed to me. As it was, I said yes, I would come down to the farm in July.

Shortly thereafter I was offered a job as the Esso reporter on Boston's station WBZ, which was going to triple my Brookline throwaway salary. This offer raised the stakes considerably. Something told me that if I really wanted the Wellesley girl, I should take that job and forget about the CW. Living on donations and cast-off clothes in a New York slum did not sound like the ideal setup for marriage to the daughter of a bank president, not in those days before the daughters of bank presidents learned to prefer slums, donations, and cast-off clothes. And my girl was no ordinary bank president's daughter, but a tall, bright blonde who danced like an angel and whose peers were soon to name her the Most Beautiful in the Class of 1936. This was high risk.

Something else told me I could have my CW fling *and* still win the girl. Also, what I really wanted was to be a playwright, not a radio news type, and what better place to pick up material and learn the trade than the Lower East Side of New York, a city recognized as center stage for all things theatrical, literary, and creative?

Such were the considerations that went back and forth in my mind during the time I waited for the arrival of July. In the midst of this struggle I went alone one night to see Hedy Lamarr in *Ecstasy,* one of the first of the erotic movies, but somewhat cleaned up for Boston's Watch and Ward Society, which was still watching in those days.

Ordinarily I would have enjoyed an erotic movie and the quick glimpse of Hedy swimming in the nude that the Watch and Ward had allowed to slip through, but that night I could not concentrate on the show at all. The debate on my multiple choices held my mind. To go or not to go? To be or not to be? And to be what? An Esso reporter or a skinny, gaunt-eyed saint? A bank president's daughter's husband or a playwright on or off Broadway? Or two or three of these options, all at once or in succession?

I settled for some vague, dreamy notion of the latter. There in front of Hedy I decided to pass up the radio job and stick with my first resolve. I was filled immediately with a great sense of relief. As I walked out of the theater and crossed Massachusetts Avenue, the moon came out from behind a cloud over the Christian Science Mother Church, like a sign of approval.

Dorothy's Credentials

Looking back, I think that one of the things that attracted me to Dorothy Day was the fact that her New York literary credentials were solid, and I was perhaps unduly impressed by both New York and literary credentials in general. Born in Brooklyn in 1897, the daughter of a sportswriter, she took to journalism with left-wing publications: the old Socialist *Call* and the original Communist *Masses.*

In 1916 Dorothy gravitated to Greenwich Village and the company of talented and radical Bohemians like the Communist Mike Gold, Max Eastman (in his pre–*Readers' Digest* incarnation), John Dos Passos (ditto), and Eugene O'Neill, who sometimes would recite *The Hound of Heaven* to her from beginning to end as they sat late over their drinks in a Village bar. She was engaged to Gold briefly, but he broke it off because he thought she was too flighty to make a good wife and mother.

Abbie Hoffman once told Dorothy that she was one of the first hippies, and she seemed pleased, although she had done her share of tongue clucking over the sexual and drug mores of the Hoffman breed. Dorothy could drink with the best and worst of the post–World War I generation. In his book *The Exile's Return,* Malcolm Cowley reports that "all the gamblers in a Greenwich Village bar admired her because she could drink any one of them under the table." Another friend of that period summed up her life: "Dorothy did some foolish things, but she was always protected by an armor of innocence."

As the child of an agnostic family that was typical of her father's class and profession, she had shown an unusual, if rather emotional, interest in religion. However, as she became involved in the fight for social justice, she began to identify religion and churches more and more with the status quo and turned away from them. She described her change of attitude in her autobiography, *The Long Loneliness:* "Jesus said, 'Blessed are the meek,' but I could not be meek at the thought of injustice."

After an assortment of jobs, a brief marriage, a traumatic abortion at the demand of a lover who then abandoned her, she wrote an autobiographical novel, *The Eleventh Virgin,* sold the movie rights to Hollywood for $2,500, bought a house on the beach in Staten Island,

and there settled down to a happy life with another lover by whom she had a child named Tamar.

This happiness seems to have led her back to God and religion. She was sensitive to the Marxist sneer that "religion is the opiate of the people," designed by the oppressors to make the oppressed forget their misery, but she could not accept this explanation of her conversion because she was far from being miserable: "no human creature could receive or contain so vast a flood of love and gratitude as I often felt after the birth of my child. . . . The final object of this love and gratitude was God."

She determined to have Tamar baptized a Roman Catholic and a year later followed her baby into the church. Her apologia for this decision was: "My very experience as a radical, my whole make-up, led me to associate myself with others, with the masses, in loving and praising God. Without even looking into the claims of the Catholic Church, I was willing to admit that for me she was the one true Church. She had come down through the centuries since the time of Peter, and far from being dead, she claimed and held the allegiance of the masses of the people in all the cities where I had lived."

Another thing appealed to her: "We all crave order, and in the Book of Job hell is described as a place where no order is. I felt that belonging to a church would bring order into [Tamar's] life, which I felt my own had lacked."

These developments led to separation from her lover, who was allergic to marriage, religion, and Catholicism in about that order. For Dorothy the next few years were therefore a period of struggle and suffering. Like me, she had no Catholic friends when she entered the church. She began writing for Catholic publications like *Commonweal*. With the arrival of the depression her concern for the poor sharpened. Sent by *Commonweal*, she went to Washington, D.C., to cover a march on the capital by the Communist-led Unemployed Councils. Watching the marchers, she felt a powerful impulse to do something for the poor and later entered a church to pray, "with tears and anguish, that some way would open for me."

When she returned to New York, she found waiting for her "a short, stocky man in his mid-fifties, as ragged and rugged as any of the marchers I had left." This man was Peter Maurin, a French peasant and what the Italians call a *filosofo vagabondo*, who eventually persuaded her to start publishing *The Catholic Worker*.

With $57 out of her own pocket she paid for the printing of 2,500 copies just in time for distribution on May Day in 1933 at the Communist parade and rally in Union Square.

The paper was an instant success. Within a few months circulation was 25,000. By the end of the year it was 100,000, and by 1936, about the time I joined the staff, it was pushing 150,000. The state of the Roman Catholic Church in the United States, especially among the younger clergy and laity, was ripe for a publication willing to tackle the scandal of unemployment and starvation in a country of immeasurable wealth—wealth in manpower, brainpower, and natural resources—and willing to tackle it not simply in words, which are cheap at any time, but by deeds and example in feeding the hungry, clothing the naked, and providing a home for the homeless.

THE POMPOUS STYLE OF THE HARVARD CONVERT

Between the time I decided to join the CW and the day I actually made it, I wrote a letter that appeared in the June 1936 issue of the paper, under the heading "Friendly Criticism from Future Worker." The pompous style of the Harvard convert is embarrassing to read now. The letter criticized *The Catholic Worker* for its doctrinaire stand against any and all wars and for one of Peter's designed-to-shock statements: "there is nothing wrong with communism." The letter also accused the editors of "a weakness for sweeping generalizations and a dangerous itch for martyrdom," adding, "People distrust those who are too eager to die, just as they will insist on their own right to die, however ignobly, for homes and families."

These objections were not the worst points in the world, but what I had done was to mark myself as a smart-ass critic who rejected pacifism, the distinctive dogma of the movement, and who was ready to tangle with Peter Maurin, Dorothy Day's and most of the staff's favorite guru. It was not the ideal introduction.

By that time the CW had set up a new House of Hospitality in a tenement house at 115 Mott Street on the Lower East Side of Manhattan, one block north of Chinatown and two blocks west of the Bowery in an area then known as Little Italy. The people were friendly, and there was never any sense of danger on the street, at least not for us.

One night several years later I was eating supper with friends in a restaurant on Mulberry Street just a block away when shots rang out, bullets ricocheted down the street, women started screaming in the high hysterical register that tells you mayhem is abroad, and we came out of the restaurant to find a man lying in the middle of the street, bleeding to death.

An assistant district attorney in our group immediately began asking questions, but even the little kids clammed up, staring dumb and unknowing into that outside face. When one started to talk, a man behind him clamped a hand over his mouth. I ran for a priest at the Franciscan church nearby, but it was too late for priests. In Little Italy, danger was for insiders, not outsiders, and it was very secret danger.

The twenty-room Mott Street building the CW occupied had been loaned by a pious lady who admired the movement, but not enough to fix it up to receive the poorest of the poor in proper style—those whom Peter called "the ambassadors of the gods," a title first conferred on them by the ancient Greeks because, in Peter's words, "people who are in need and not afraid to beg give to people not in need the occasion to do good for goodness' sake."

In the April 1936 issue of *The Catholic Worker,* a few months before we began to occupy the CW house, Dorothy had written a front-page story in the paper announcing the move to Mott Street. It was a warning to me of what lay ahead and included this passage:

> "There's a big rat like a kitten running around down here," called Mr. Rourke calmly from the cellar.
>
> "We have lots of rats," said Felicia, a neighbor's child. "When they come out in the room, we jump up on the bed. My father chases them with the broom and kills them."
>
> "It's funny when he catches them by the tail," said her friend Suzie gaily.

I learned that Suzie's gaiety is typical of the lighthearted contempt that familiarity with vermin can breed in what Maxim Gorki called the "lower depths." Eventually I was to become familiar enough myself so that the sound of rats running back and forth over the tin ceiling of the room where I was sleeping had an almost festive, friendly sound. It wasn't as easy to get used to the filth that accumulated if you didn't keep on top of it. No one seemed interested in cleaning the very popular single toilet on the first floor, right inside the front door. That was one dirty toilet. Finally I cranked up my courage and cleaned it myself. After that I knew that I could climb any mountain, ford any river.

PETER, MEDUSA, AND ST. BASIL

I remember nothing of my first twenty-four hours with the CW except the night. Sleep did not come easily. There were other kinds of vermin beside rats. I was sleeping, theoretically, in an apartment on the top floor with half a dozen other men. Peter was snoring in the bed next to mine. On this typical July night in New York, hot as any jungle, little or no air was moving in our building, separated from the street by a small courtyard and another tenement. The room was heavy with the smell of sweat, and after a little while I began to itch all over. I suspected bedbugs. I had no idea of how to deal with bedbugs and did not even know what one looked like, so sheltered had been my middle-class upbringing.

I just lay there in the dark, staring at a ceiling illuminated by the light of the great festering city outside, filled with a crazy kind of exaltation. The frustrated playwright in me immediately recognized a stage set worthy of Gorki or O'Casey.

Fortunately my sense of the dramatic was not tested by another night at Mott Street during that particular heat wave. The next day a group of us climbed into the back of an old truck and bounced across New Jersey to the CW farm in Easton, Pennsylvania.

The farm was not much, but it had a sensational view of the Delaware River winding through wooded hills, mile after mile of checkered fields on the fertile plain out front, and off to the left the twin cities of Easton and Philipsburg facing each other across the river. Dorothy confessed that when she saw the farm, she was so carried away that she failed to check on the water supply, and only after she had bought the place—it was April 19, the feast of St. Isidore the Farmer, so how could she go wrong?—she discovered that the spring nearby was not on the property and that the cisterns were just storage for the rainwater off the barn and the house. Most of the twenty-eight acres were woods, hillside, and rocks.

I expected that on our first day we would be put to work in the fields, which clearly needed help, but that was not Peter's way. This was not just a farming commune, but rather, in his words, "an agronomic university." One of the first objectives at Agronomic U was "to make scholars out of workers and workers out of scholars." Priority went to the former. After lunch we sat around the dining-room table in the farmhouse, and Peter led us in a round table discussion. His program was "Round Table Discussions, Houses of Hospitality, and Farming Communes." The table was more oval than round, and the discussion was more of a monologue. Peter sat at the head of the table and declaimed one "Easy Essay" after another in his thick French accent—for several hours.

Full as I was of my smart-ass Harvard distinctions, I was anxious to try an essay or two myself or at least ask a few loaded questions. No chance. From long practice on the debating fields of Union Square and Columbus Circle Peter had learned never to breathe between sentences. If by chance he did stop to breathe, he held up a finger to indicate that there was more coming, and if by some act of reckless bravado someone were to ignore the finger and interrupt before Peter was ready to yield the floor, Peter made a face that, like Medusa, was calculated to turn the intruder to stone. In *The Catholic Worker* someone once described Peter in the act of being interrupted by a visitor: "he made a face like a water buffalo about to sneeze." Take your pick, Medusa or a water buffalo. Either way it was pretty discouraging.

I make the joke now, but at the time I was in no mood for jokes. I was sore as hell. As the hours and the voice singsonged on, I sat there sweating in the summer heat, sphincter tight and teeth clenched in rebellion and resentment. The problem was generation gap, culture gap, idea gap—all kinds of gaps.

Later Peter and I became good friends. If you got him alone, he was a gentle, lovable soul who would listen to you patiently and give you his last pair of pants. And he rarely had more than one. It was an article of faith that he should rarely have more than one. "The coat that hangs in the closet belongs to the poor," he used to say, quoting St. Basil. This saying eventually became for me the best and shortest summary of the Catholic Church's concept of rock bottom justice as distinguished from charity.

Arthur Sheehan, Peter's friend and biographer, tells a story of a character who arrived at the CW some years later with a few potato sacks, a basket of papers, and a conviction that "Christ was only a criminal among criminals." He was full of bitter talk, but Peter, already old and ailing, sat up with him until dawn one night and on another occasion until four o'clock in the morning.

"You must be patient with these people," Peter explained. "If he talks long enough and gets it off his chest, he may be better." So Peter also had this side—a side of infinite patience and goodness.

It was difficult to argue with him when he said things like, "St. Francis thought that to choose to be poor is just as good as marrying the most beautiful girl in the world. Most of us seem to think that Lady Poverty is an ugly girl and not the beautiful girl that St. Francis says she is. And because we think so, we refuse to feed the poor with our superfluous goods. Instead we let the politicians feed the poor by going around like pickpockets, robbing Peter to pay Paul."

Maybe I did have to argue with (a) that "most beautiful girl" bit, which hit a little too close to home, and (b) the last bit, which was a reflection of Peter's anarchism, his profound distrust of every organization but the Catholic Church, from trade unions on up to the state, even the welfare state. This distrust grew out of his childhood experiences growing up in a medieval village in southern France, where the family's eighty sheep grazed on a communal pasture in a flock of three thousand. It developed during his life as a wandering loner, from teaching school in Paris to driving a team of oxen twelve abreast while standing on a three-tongued plow in the wheat fields of Saskatchewan.

The life of a wandering loner tells only part of his story. For ten years he was a Christian Brother and taught in elementary schools in and around Paris. During this period he was drafted and served as a soldier in the French army. At the age of twenty-five, before he took final vows, he left the Brothers and worked for a popular youth movement called Le Sillon (the Furrow), led by an extraordinary man named Marc Sangnier, who was trying to prove that democracy is the form of government most appropriate to Christianity and Catholicism.

Sangnier was about thirty-four years ahead of his time. His ideas are similar to those Pope Pius XII expressed in his Christmas Message of 1944, but in 1910 Pius X, a saintly reactionary, condemned the movement. A year before this condemnation, however, Peter had already wearied of the movement and taken off for Canada, lured by

Canadian government propaganda that good farms were to be had cheap in Saskatchewan. He decided to go back to the land. But Saskatchewan was not all the government's propaganda claimed it to be, especially when the winter wind blew across the prairie. Some of the settlers froze to death in their little shacks, and by 1911 Peter had had enough.

He headed south across the border and began the life of a hobo in the United States, riding the rails, sleeping in boxcars and flophouses. At one point he worked for a coke company owned by H. C. Frick, the antilabor tycoon. He was paid $1.50 a day and lived in an unused coke oven with a black coworker as a roommate. He once described the arrangement to Joseph Breig in a *Commonweal* interview: "The next-door oven was in operation, and the heat from it kept us warm. All you had to do was to crawl in and lie down, and you were at home. What did we sleep on? The bricks, I suppose. I think the Negro did all the cooking. Maybe that was what I liked about it. Also, he was a gentleman."

Peter ordinarily was reluctant to talk about that period of his life, but he did reveal that for ten years he was out of the church. Dorothy once asked him why, and he said only, "Because I was not living as a Catholic should." Something told her not to pursue the subject.

Then, in the mid-1920s he had a profound religious experience that changed his life again. By this time he was giving French lessons in such places as the art colony in Woodstock, New York. He had even been photographed in a natty suit. He stopped charging for the lessons and gave them for nothing or for whatever people wanted to give him. He wore cast-off clothing, and when one lady complained about his appearance, he replied, "I don't want to arouse envy."

He began reading more intensively, so intensively that Father Wilfrid Parsons, the editor of *America*, the Jesuit magazine, was later to describe him as the best-read man he had ever met. Peter was particularly attracted to European writers like Eric Gill, Nicholas Berdyaev, Peter Kropotkin, Arthur Penty, Hilaire Belloc, Jacques Maritain, Christopher Dawson—men who emphasized the values of freedom, religion, the land, craftsmanship and decentralized communities. When the Great Depression struck, it seemed to him a confirmation of all he believed about overorganized mankind, the evils of mass production, and the subordination of spiritual values to the demands of the machine and the lust for profit. Two of his early "Easy Essays" included these passages:

> Industrialization is evil
> because it brings idleness
> both to the capitalist class
> and the working class.
> Idleness does no good
> either to the capitalist class
> or to the working class.
> Creative labor
> is what keeps people
> out of mischief.
> Creative labor
> is craft labor.
> Mechanized labor
> is not creative labor. . . .

> The industrial revolution
> did not improve things;
> it made them worse.
> The industrial revolution
> has given us
> technological unemployment.
> And the best way
> to do away
> with technological unemployment
> is to place idle hands
> on idle lands.

In 1932 Peter met a redheaded Communist in Union Square, New York City, who told him that he ought to get in touch with Dorothy Day because "you think alike." He visited George Shuster, managing editor of *Commonweal*, who told him the same thing and gave him her address.

Actually, Dorothy and Peter did not really think alike. With her strong Marxist background Dorothy was intellectually and emotionally wedded to the struggle of the workers through the trade union movement. She once confessed to me that she was always uncomfortable with one of Peter's favorite plays on words, "Strikes don't strike me," and with one of the favorite nonsequiturs that usually accompanied it, "When the organizers try to organize the unorganized, then the organizers don't organize themselves." Also, she was not then an easy target for Peter's idea of the Agrarian Revolution.

She did, however, share his love for the poor and his faith in the Christian gospel, and she was searching for a program that she could reconcile with both. She did not believe Marxism filled the requirements. She also had lost the man in her life, and though she had large resources of her own, I think she did feel the need of a man's help and support. This is not to imply that she had any strong physical or romantic attraction to Peter. I never saw anything that would support such a notion.

THE HARSH AND DREADFUL THING

In a 1952 profile in *The New Yorker* Dwight Macdonald wrote of Dorothy that "her mind works by free association rather than logic. . . . She is more a feeler and a doer than a thinker." This description is a little unfair as well as overstated. She was a highly intelligent, literate person. In later years, she took to such thinkers as Martin Buber, Teilhard de Chardin, and Lewis Mumford, but most of her serious thinking she seems to have absorbed from novelists such as Dostoyevsky and Tolstoy or Englishmen as varied as Dickens and Orwell. That Dostoyevsky quote, "Love in action is a harsh and dreadful thing, compared with love in dreams," is a feeler-and-doer's quote that confirms Macdonald's perception, but it also refutes Macdonald because it is the observation of a sharp and penetrating mind. It might be said that it takes one to know one.

Two of Dorothy's complaints about Peter were that he had no great love for either Dostoyevsky or Dickens and that he did not share her love for music, which did run a bit to the romantic side. He was an abstract thinker, and to Dorothy he seemed, I believe, to make up for this lack in her own equipment. Peter was abstract, all right. John Cogley, a CW who later covered religion for the *New York Times*, told a story about him: "One night in a cheap hotel a young woman knocked on his door and asked, 'Want to have a good time, honey?' 'Come in, come in!' he cried, and when she did he inquired of her, 'Now, what would you say a good time means exactly? Let's discuss it.'"

Cogley did not record her response, which might have been interesting. In any case it seems Peter was living as a Catholic should by that time.

Despite the dramatic differences in their origins—a French peasant's farm for Peter and the mobile home of an American newspaperman for Dorothy—they in some respects had pursued similar odysseys before they met in her apartment on East Fifteenth Street. Both had been attracted to highly disciplined and restrictive organizations—Peter to the Christian Brothers and Dorothy to the Communist Party—and both had rebelled against these disciplines and experimented with very free lifestyles. Both had then returned to discipline, the spiritual discipline of the Catholic Church, with a minimum of temporal restraint. Both identified strongly with the life of the poor and had an almost mystical attachment to voluntary poverty, an attachment compounded of religious faith, their own experience, and compassion, or all three.

ERIC GILL, OWNING AND CONTROLLING

One of Peter's and the CW agrarians' great heroes was Eric Gill, the English artist and writer, and his *Autobiography* was practically required reading on Mott Street. I was and still remain deeply impressed by a line to the affect that "men work best when they own and control their own tools and materials." Everybody interpreted this statement as an argument on behalf of handicrafts and against the machine. I interpreted it as a principle that could be applied just as easily to industrialism and mass production.

So, it turned out, did Gill. We got a letter from him in December 1937. The first surprise was that the letter was written on a typewriter, which seemed inconsistent with his views about craftsmanship, but he explained this decision in the letter: "Some things are better made by machines than by hand. For instance, it would be ridiculous to make typewriters except by mass production; otherwise they would be absolutely prohibitive in price and the whole point of a typewriter is to save money and time. . . . The problem of the machine is one that should be dealt with by those who actually use machines. . . . The first thing to be done is for workers to recapture control of industry."

To me there were two principal ways for workers to recapture control of their own tools and materials and to make those changes in industrialism that were necessary to reconcile the machine with the demands of human personality. One was the long way around, by means of ownership and control of a state that was in turn democratically controlled by the workers. This method did not seem to be very practical. I was convinced of the truth of Lord Acton's aphorism about the corrupting effect of power, and surely there could be no greater concentration of power in the world than a U.S. government that owned and controlled the country's productive property. Freedom could not last in such a state. Democratic control could not last.

The practical method for gaining control, or even a meaningful share of control, I thought, was through the trade unions. Here again I clashed with Peter. His gentle but rugged individualism could accept the spiritual discipline of the Catholic Church but not the temporal discipline of a trade union. This contradiction was something I could never understand, either on Peter's part or on Dorothy's part: here was a bona fide radical who was antiunion but who, despite that, won the intellectual allegiance of a former Communist like Dorothy, who wrote some of her best pieces in support of the great organizing campaigns of the 1930s and 1940s.

She was to publish some wonderfully sharp reports after climbing through the windows of the General Motors plant in Flint to cover the sit-down strike and, later, after interviewing steel workers in the bar from which they marched a few days later, only to be cut down by the Chicago police in the Republic Steel Massacre of 1937.

My first thirty days on the Easton farm that summer of 1936 were enough to confirm me in some of my conclusions about agrarianism. Not that it was an unpleasant experience. At one point I slept in an abandoned pig pen, a tentlike structure with a tin roof, open ends, and a floor covered with fresh straw. When the sun came up in the morning across the valley, it shone on the straw and turned it to gold. I had the distinct feeling I was living in a palace.

On the farm there were workers and there were scholars, but not too many worker-scholars or scholar-workers. And there were others who could only be described as "ambassadors of the gods." One such was a former circus acrobat who on nights when there was a full moon sometimes could be seen doing cartwheels down the hill long after most of us had retired. Another man played the flute and seemed quite normal except that now and then his conversation took an odd turn. When introduced to him, a lady visitor asked if she might have met him previously. "Ah, yes," he replied, "I recall you as a nude on a mantelpiece."

Another guest on the farm was a handsome, clean-cut young man who we later learned was using it as a hideaway after pulling the heists that funded his heroin habit. I finally took him up to Bellevue Hospital for treatment. He was shaking like a leaf in a windstorm, and I absorbed an early lesson on the perils of addiction.

John Filliger, a seaman, was the man in charge of farming. He had grown up on a farm and was a good worker, but he had little help. Approximately six acres were planted, mainly in alfalfa, corn, tomatoes, and potatoes. We also had a horse and later a cow, chickens, and goats, but the farm never came close to being self-sufficient. Money had to be sent out from Mott Street to buy food. The place more accurately could be described as another House of Hospitality on the land.

Even though several months had elapsed since the purchase of the farm and it was the height of the growing season, we didn't have enough tools even to hoe the corn by hand, not to mention anything as sophisticated as a cultivator. I remember one warm afternoon crawling on my hands and knees down the long rows of alien corn, picking the weeds out with my fingers.

Fortunately I had company. Bill Callahan, managing editor of the paper, was crawling down the other side. Bill had studied Thomas Aquinas and was full of the Thomistic requirements for a just war. We spent the next few hours arguing about pacifism—on a CW farm a much more typical activity than actual farming. Bill stuck pretty close to the Thomistic line of argument and emphasized the killing of innocent noncombatants, an argument that has become even more plausible with the proliferation of nuclear bombs. Others at the CW would sooner or later quote Jesus: "I say unto you, do not resist evil. If a man strikes you on the cheek, turn to him the other. If he take your coat, give him your cloak also."

My answer was that Christ said to turn your own cheek. He did not say that you should turn your neighbor's cheek. If your neighbor cried to you for protection against attack, how could you refuse it? How could any government refuse it? It was impossible for me to think of a Christ who drove the moneychangers from the temple with a whip—an incident mentioned in all four Gospels—as somebody who was committed to nonviolence under any and all circumstances. So I remained a nonpacifist in a pacifist movement, a nonagrarian in an agrarian movement. Despite my dissents, Dorothy had a maternal attitude toward me and once referred to me as her "wayward son." She wanted to list me in the paper as a member of the staff, but other members objected so strenuously that I was never listed. It didn't bother me too much.

PERSONALISM, MOUNIER, AND PEANUTS OFF A TANK

Though often characterized as anarchists, Peter and Dorothy preferred to call themselves *personalists,* a term derived from the French Catholic intellectual Emmanuel Mounier, editor of *L'Esprit* and author of *The Personalist Manifesto,* which Peter wanted us to push as the answer to the *Communist Manifesto.* Peter translated Mounier's highly intellectual formulations into simple injunctions: don't tell anybody to do anything or not to do anything; do it yourself or don't do it, and your good example will gently but surely persuade others to go and do or not do likewise.

The trouble with this idyllic doctrine was that in the real world of Mott Street you could throw good example at some people forever and watch it bounce off them like peanuts off a tank. So a number of useful things did not get done—cleaning that popular toilet, for example—and some not-so-useful things did get done—that popular toilet again—because the people setting a good example were greatly outnumbered by the people setting a bad example or, more likely, just setting.

During much of my time at Mott Street I slept in a four-room railroad flat with nine other men, most of them guests off the Bowery. With no doors between rooms the place was more like a small, crowded dormitory. We also had Tex, a young seaman who joined us during the strike of 1936 and then decided, "What the hell, why go back to sea when I can get free eats and a bed right here?" Tex hardly ever spoke to anybody and never did any work that I can recall, but he could sleep like nobody I ever met before that time or since. He would go to bed at eleven or so, and at eleven or twelve the next day he would still be in bed, head buried under the covers, no sign of life. I figured he needed a psychiatrist. That and a little oxygen.

As it turned out, Dorothy informed me years later, what Tex needed was an operation for carbuncles on his backside. When he got it, he changed overnight into a productive citizen. A latter-day miracle.

The building had no bathtubs or showers. If we wanted a bath, we had to walk to the public baths some distance away and then face a pretty grim prospect, though not perhaps as grim as someone might face today. That scene hadn't yet developed. Some of us could count on CW fellow travelers who had apartments and would let us use their bathtub once a week. It was amazing how quickly I adjusted from a life of daily showers to the realization that no great harm would befall if I bathed but once a week.

Most of the men I lived with had long since resigned themselves to the realization that no great harm would befall if they bathed but once a month, once a year, or once a lifetime. Few of them made their beds, and fewer still bothered to take the broom that I left in a conspicuous spot and follow my example by sweeping up around their beds, not to mention that wider horizon beyond their beds that might encompass so expansive an area as the entire room in which they slept. The place grew ugly with the passing days and weeks. In addition, we had bedbugs, but bad. At one time or another we swept, washed, sprayed, and painted the apartment, but we could not destroy the bugs, which seemed to have dug themselves into the building and, like Tex, pulled the covers up over their heads. At night, they emerged to torture those of us who were delicate enough never to have learned how to sleep through a bedbug attack. One metal cot they assigned to me was so infested that I took it up on the roof and went over it with a blowtorch. To this day when I think about it, the rich aroma of roasting bedbug is there, sharp and acrid in my mind's nose.

Body lice were also a problem. I was a Third Order (lay) Franciscan at the time and wore a cord around my waist under my clothes as symbolic substitute for a habit. A louse got into the knot in the cord and sallied forth from time to time. When I went after him, he would bury himself in the knot, which was too tight to get untied. I finally got him by dipping the knot in boiling water. Somebody pointed out that Saint Benedict Labré, a favorite saint at the CW, would not have approved of this conduct. He had such a reverence for life and such a love of mortification that when a louse fell off his clothes, he gently picked it up and put it back on. I was not that kind of varsity material.

Given my middle-class hang-ups, there was no escaping the day when I would try to impose a minimum of order and cleanliness on my companions. As the one staff member on the floor I was understood to be in charge, whatever that meant beyond doing all the cleaning up. I therefore took it upon myself to post three typewritten rules that seemed like a modest minimum:

1. Everyone out of bed by 9:00 A.M.
2. Everyone is expected to make his own bed.
3. Everyone is expected to take turns sweeping up.

This plan backfired. My roommate, John Griffin, a Bowery alcoholic and a good friend who had absorbed more of the CW philosophy than most of our guests, objected to the rules and appealed to Dorothy, who was recognized as the court of last resort. In fact, we called her the Abbess. John thought the rules violated the principles of personalism. Dorothy agreed with him and told me to take them down. At the time I don't think I even argued with her, so great was her authority among us. What it came down to was that the CW was an extraordinary combination of anarchy and dictatorship.

Hard Work and Some Good Laughs

On the other hand, a great deal of hard work did get done at the Mott Street house, where about thirty men and women received bed and board and every morning another thousand or more were fed hot coffee and bread spread with apple butter, peanut butter, or cottage cheese. The breadline ran down Mott Street and around the corner onto Canal Street, with men gathering frequently before dawn and, in the winter, shivering in the cold. Men and women who came off the street did much of the work themselves; volunteers who came down to Mott Street did the rest because they wanted to help. They were young men and women full of enthusiasm—like Bill Callahan, Julia Porcelli, Marge Hughes, Joe Zarella, Jerry Griffin, Eddie Priest, Stanley Vishnewski—and some not so young, like John Curran and Martin O'Donnell.

Most of us took turns working on the breadline, which was a pretty depressing sight if we ever stopped to look at it. Fortunately we were usually too busy to do that, although we could see that many of those on the line needed a look in the eye, a word, some sign of human recognition, even more than the coffee and bread. It was on the line that I met the nice-looking man who said he killed an iceman when he found him making love to his wife. Grabbed an axe off the ice wagon and let him have it right through the head. Pleasant sort of fellow. I enjoyed talking to him, but the thought of that axe cleaving the iceman's skull still makes me wince. I don't recall that I asked the fellow why he wasn't in jail. That question may have struck me as getting too personal.

Many of the men appeared to be not far removed from the self-respect of men who worked at a steady job. Many certainly would not have been there if it had not been for the depression. Once we looked at them, it was impossible to be indifferent ever again to such abstract concepts as overproduction, underconsumption, the business cycle, supply and demand. I had been indifferent just a few years earlier, when I grew so bored with Economics A at Harvard that I quit the course at midyears.

In one of her books, *Loaves and Fishes,* Dorothy wrote that "John Cort thought he was coming to us to study and work with the problem of labor unions and he found himself 'running a flop-house,' as he said."

I am sure I complained. I'm the type. But she was wrong about why. I did not go down to Mott Street to work with labor, which began to interest me only after I had been there a few months. In fact, my first interest was worker cooperatives. I joined the CW, as noted, because Dorothy convinced me that I could get more fun out of life on Mott Street, New York, than on Pinckney Street, Boston. I could grant that Mott Street sometimes struck me as a flophouse, without the virtue of order that a flophouse must demand from time to time. But there was something there that held you. There were some good laughs, and things rarely got so disorganized that you couldn't stand it. The hungry did get fed, the naked were clothed, and the homeless were given a bed, with or without bedbugs. It *was* more fun than Pinckney Street. And I kept telling myself that I could still win Most Beautiful in the Wellesley Class of '36.

One of Dorothy's favorite Gospel narratives was the story of the two depressed disciples walking to Emmaus on the third day after the crucifixion and how Jesus joined them, but they did not recognize him. They came to an inn, and the disciples prevailed on Jesus to stay with them. During supper "he took bread, said the blessing, broke it and gave it to them. With that their eyes were opened and they recognized him." They went back to Jerusalem and told the other disciples "how they knew him in the breaking of the bread" (Luke 24:13–35).

Dorothy would develop this theme and explain how one's knowledge of Christ both in himself and in our poorest neighbors is enlarged and enriched by our breaking bread with them. She would make the obvious connection between this incident and Jesus' description of the Last Judgment in Matthew 25:31–46. Jesus, sitting on his glorious throne, admits the righteous to the kingdom of heaven because "'I was hungry and you gave me to eat, I was thirsty and you gave me to drink, a stranger and you took me in, naked and you covered me, sick and you visited me, in prison and you came to me.' Then the just will answer him and say, 'Lord when did we see you hungry and feed you, or thirsty and give you drink? When did we see you a stranger and take you in, or naked and clothe you? Or when did we see you sick or in prison, and come to you?' And the king will answer and say to them, 'Amen I say to you, as long as you did it for one of these, the least of my brethren, you did it for me.'"

Most translations describe these fortunate ones as "the righteous." Some of the older translations, notably the Douai-Rheims, call them "the just." I prefer the latter description for reasons that will become apparent further on in my story.

Meanwhile, these Gospel stories, as Dorothy realized and revealed them in her own pursuit of the works of mercy, provide a clue as to why that pursuit gave her so much pleasure, despite its hardship. Few people, few Christians, have demonstrated the ability to continue that pursuit, as she did, for so many years. I believe she was able to do so because she, in fact, could see the face of Christ in the least, the poorest, the most desolate and unattractive of our brothers and sisters. This was her gift, this was her message and her example, in word and deed.

2

The Labor Movement

A few hundred funerals will have a quieting influence.
—from an editorial in the *Journal of the New England Textile Industry* during textile strike of 1934

The democratic process on which this nation was founded should not be restricted to the political process, but should be applied to the industrial operation as well.
—Albert Gallatin, secretary of the Treasury, 1797

IT WAS DOROTHY who sold me on the labor movement—Dorothy, John L. Lewis, and books like Louis Adamic's *Dynamite*, still one of the most exciting works of U.S. history ever written.

Despite Peter's bias Dorothy realized that to ignore the unions during the mid-1930s would make as much sense as a radical movement ignoring the black revolution or Vietnam during the 1960s and 1970s. It would have been a ticket to oblivion. Labor was where the action was, where John L. Lewis and the Committee for Industrial Organization (CIO, later the Congress of Industrial Organizations)— aided and abetted by Communists, socialists, and every young radical off the college campus—were busy organizing the unorganized and raising the flag of freedom from the tyranny of the boss.

It is difficult to judge 1936 from the perspective of the year 2003. Most workers then were either on the edge of starvation, without paid work, and in despair, or they were grinding out their lives in factories and shops, overworked, miserably paid, and powerless to protect themselves from capricious discharge.

The summer of 1936, while I was still out at the farm, Dorothy was writing in the paper her justification for disagreeing with Peter's "strikes don't strike me." It is noteworthy that she expressed that disagreement in religious terms: "When men are striking they are following an impulse, often blind, often uninformed, but a good impulse—one could even say an inspiration of the Holy Spirit. They are trying to uphold their right to be treated not as slaves but as men. They are fighting for a share in the management, for their right to be considered partners in the enterprise in which they are engaged."

The next month, August, when I returned to Mott Street from the farm, the paper carried her report of her trip through the steel towns of Pennsylvania and of the "500,000 steel workers who have been unorganized, oppressed and enslaved for the last half century in the giant mills of the American Iron and Steel Institute."

She interviewed Lewis and his idealistic lieutenant John Brophy, who once was a hostile critic of Lewis in the Mine Workers and who told her of his "going through hell" when he tried to be both a Catholic and a socialist despite Leo XIII's and Pius XI's antisocialist statements.

She described a rally of steel workers on the picnic grounds at Braddock, Pennsylvania, and a speech given by Father Adalbert Kazincy, a legendary figure whom even the Communist leader William Z. Foster recognized as a great man: "He stood broad and straight in the broiling sun, head held high, as he told the men, 'Do not let the Carnegie Steel Company crush you. For the sake of your wives and children, for the sake of your homes, you need the union. Remember that man does not live by bread alone. So do not let fear keep you from organizing. I am speaking to you as men, as creatures of body and soul. Remember your dignity as men.'"

In the next issue I wrote a lead story that started off, "Stormy days for labor in town and country threaten this week as the AFL [American Federation of Labor] moves inevitably to a wide-open split and drought-stricken farmers in East and West cry for subsidy and higher prices."

The split in the AFL was over the issue of industrial unionism—organizing all the workers in a factory into one union—as against craft unionism—splitting them up into a number of craft unions. Lewis and a minority of AFL leaders favored the former as the only hope of organizing the millions of workers in the mass-production industries: auto, steel, electrical, radio, rubber, and so on.

When roused, Lewis was magnificent in battle. He looked like an angry lion, complete with shaggy mane. His rhetoric was alternately biblical and Elizabethan, and his insults withering. At one point in the climactic AFL convention of 1935, alluding to the appeal of the unorganized workers in the steel mills and auto factories, he asked the delegates to "heed this cry from Macedonia that comes from the hearts of men" and warned them that if they refused, "high wassail will prevail at the banquet tables of the mighty."

Later, when he had lost the key vote by a three to two margin, he dismissed William Green and the craft leaders as a group of "stately asses," adding that "the AFL has no head—its neck just grew up and haired over."

The day after the vote, when Big Bill Hutcheson of the Carpenters Union called him "a son of a bitch," Lewis flattened him with one punch in what I would nominate for inclusion in any list of America's more historic prizefights. Thus American labor came to be split, a condition that was to last until 1955.

But the workers were organized, and Lewis was their leader. Even his talent for abuse supplied a kind of catharsis for workers who had seen the lords of industry go unchallenged for so many years. After the Republic Steel Massacre of 1937, Lewis called Tom Girdler, president of Republic Steel, "a heavily armed monomaniac, with murderous tendencies, who has gone berserk." Girdler replied that before he would deal with Lewis and the CIO, he would shut down his plant and "raise apples and potatoes." Eventually he dealt. Somebody said, "It took a megalomaniac like Lewis to give a monomaniac like Girdler the name he deserved."

During the negotiations to settle the Chrysler sit-down strike Lewis was irritated by company president K. T. Keller's supercilious attitude. He said to Keller, "I am 99 percent of a mind to come around this table and wipe that smile off your face." Keller wilted visibly, and as he wilted, the backs of American workers correspondingly stiffened.

This was the class struggle in America at its most bitter and its most exciting. It was not a spectacle that anyone could describe as ideal from a Christian point of view, and Lewis was no Christian saint. To me he was the leader in a just war, and I never questioned for a moment which side I was on.

With Dorothy's encouragement I worked for a while in a piecework sweatshop making cocktail trays to bring in a little money and learn something of the life of industrial workers. I learned that a worker there had to turn out an awful lot of cocktail trays to make any money. I learned something about the pressure on a worker whose income depends on piecework. The most common words I heard in that shop were "I'm losing money" or "You're losing money" whenever anyone stopped to talk or stretch or blow his nose. I called the CIO and asked if they were interested in organizing the place, but they said no, it was too small. I told the boss I was quitting, and he offered me a job as foreman. He could not understand why I refused and tried to cheat me on my pay.

I went back to writing stories for *The Catholic Worker* about strikes and strikebreaking, criticizing one strike at a small plant in Manhattan as unjustified because the union had pulled the workers out without giving the boss a fair chance to negotiate, then accused the employer of refusing to negotiate, and topped it off by lying about the average wage, which was bad enough to justify strict fidelity to the truth. I wrote, with unctuous righteousness, "The poor and oppressed are not exempt from the moral law simply because they are poor and oppressed."

You can imagine how this went down with the Marxist left in Union Square, not to mention the official labor movement. You use the moral law to beat employers over the head with, not unions. For Marxists the moral law was whatever helped the workers. Their view was that maybe the business agent messed it up, but no friend of labor cuts the ground out from under a strike that has any justification at all. Though I came to appreciate this view better as the years went by, I remained fixated on aphorisms like that of the sainted French king, Louis IX: "Always be on the side of the poor man rather than the rich until you know the truth," implying that when you know the truth, you might have to switch sides. And clearly Bill Callahan at the CW impressed me with the conditions for a just war—similar to those for a just strike—laid down by that sometime dinner guest of St. Louis, St. Thomas Aquinas.

HOOKED BY THE SEAMEN'S STRIKE

My interest in labor was growing as I covered stories like these, but what really hooked me was the seamen's strike of 1936–37. *Fortune* magazine described American sailors of that period as "the true proletariat of the Western world, the homeless, rootless and eternally unmoneyed," men who have "no stake in the system beyond this month's voyage . . . have been all over the world and seen none of it beyond its dull ubiquitous Sailortowns . . . have become a part of it nowhere. Four out of five of them have no wives and three out of five have no addresses."

As much as anything, these men were rebelling against their own organization, the International Seamen's Union (ISU), AFL, run by a man called Emperor Grange. His method of opening a meeting was to take out a .45 revolver and lay it on the table.

Grange had negotiated a sellout agreement providing for $57.50 a month plus continuation of the shape-up, a kind of slave-market method of hiring waterfront workers. West Coast seamen were getting better wages and conditions, and West Coast longshoremen, behind the leadership of left-wing Harry Bridges, had even knocked out the hated shape-up and replaced it with hiring halls.

The East Coast seamen rejected the ISU agreement by a three to one vote. In March 1936, a big boatswain (pronounced "bo'sun") named Joe Curran, everybody's idea of what a tough seaman should look and sound like, had led the crew of the intercoastal liner *California* in a sit-down mutiny and told the International Mercantile Marine Company that the crew would not cast off lines from the San Pedro dock for the trip back to New York unless the men received the West Coast pay scale.

Frances Perkins, U.S. secretary of labor, called out of a White House dinner in her evening gown, phoned Curran where he was in a San Pedro butcher shop and persuaded him to cast off by offering her help in gaining the men's demands. Her help did not prove effective.

To the accompaniment of *New York Daily News* headlines ("Shades of *HMS Bounty*") the ship returned to New York, where twenty-five of the men, including Curran, were fired immediately, fined six days pay, and blacklisted by the industry. Curran and his supporters responded with a wildcat strike that pulled four thousand men off the ships and got him denounced and expelled by Grange's ISU. On October 30 some forty thousand maritime workers walked out on the West Coast in a struggle that revolved mainly around the longshoremen's determination to retain the hiring hall and the seamen's unions' determination to win a hiring hall for the first time.

On the East Coast a few days later Curran and the rebel faction in the ISU pulled another wildcat strike that brought out all the seamen, who were followed in turn by the Masters, Mates and Pilots, the Engineers, and the Radio Telegraphers Unions—a total of thirty thousand workers. The entire American waterfront was shut tight and would remain so for two months.

This strike brought to the front of the New York stage some of the most able and interesting Communists in the labor movement—men such as Blackie Myers, Tommy Ray, Charlie Keith, and the glamorous Jack Lawrenson, a handsome young Englishman from the Isle of Guernsey who appeared on the waterfront dressed in natty tweeds and once told Dorothy that he was a Catholic, "but a bitter one." He had run away to sea at thirteen and had spent fifteen years in the black gang (engine room). Like other strike leaders, he received living expenses but no salary. He was assigned to public relations but said his "real job was that of agitator."

In the earlier strike more than forty seamen had stayed at the CW, but when the second one broke, the Mott Street house was full up. In any case, Mott Street was a long way from the waterfront, and Dorothy was determined to help, so we rented a storefront on Tenth Avenue just south of Twenty-first Street, close to strike headquarters and just around the corner from the home of Joe Ryan, the corrupt leader of the East Coast longshoremen who was doing his best to break the strike in the interests of his friends the shipowners and the leaders of the old ISU.

The whole West Side of New York erupted in battles between seamen and what were known as goon squads, thugs employed by the shipowners to break the strike.

For the next few months we operated a kind of commissary for the striking seamen, where we kept four large coffee pots going from 7:00 A.M. to 9:00 P.M. and spread about fifty pounds of our staple peanut butter, apple butter, and cottage cheese on slices of bread. About a thousand men were fed daily in an operation that cost us approximately $50,000 in today's money, which Dorothy begged from the readers.

The strike leaders were charged with being Communists, which many of them were. Dorothy then infuriated Ryan by printing "Open Letter to AFL Union Leaders, Especially Joseph P. Ryan," on the front page of the paper, accusing them and him of "being, in effect, Bolsheviks themselves" for the following reasons: "In that they deny their brother they are denying Christ; in that they use armed guards and strong-arm methods to maintain their rule, they are endorsing the use of force; in that they are not trying to deproletarianize the worker, as the Holy Father advises, helping him to become an owner, to have a share in the management of the calling to which he is engaged, they are denying the right to private property."

This last charge was a little below the belt, considering the intense lack of interest American workers in those years showed in anything more than higher wages and shorter hours, but she could have thought of many worse things to say about Ryan. It was discovered later that he took bribes from employers and spent union dues lavishly for his own pleasure.

In the middle of the strike a meeting of the Central Trades and Labor Council of New York was held, bringing together delegates from all the AFL unions in the city. A minority of progressive delegates argued for AFL support of the strike. Ryan was president of the council and ran the meeting, however, his musclemen hunching up and down the aisles and glaring at anyone who said a kind word for the strikers.

The meeting broke up in near riot, with Ryan shouting encouragement to his goons to beat the hell out of the opposition. I was covering the meeting for *The Catholic Worker*. Filled with horror at the thought of impending slaughter and moved by some impulse more childish than childlike, I approached Ryan as he came down from the stage with the intention of appealing to him to call off his tanks in the name of God. I had heard he was supposed to be a devout Catholic.

"I'm from *The Catholic Worker* . . . ," I started off. Ryan stopped me. "You go back and tell Dorothy Day that she's no lady," he said, in what must have been one of the mildest insults she ever received. He pushed me aside with a look of crippling contempt. "Get away, get away from me." I got away.

Ryan was a strange one. Solidly built, tough, reasonably articulate, he could sometimes be seen at daily mass at the Church of the Guardian Angels, just a few feet up the avenue from our waterfront headquarters. He was reliably reported never to use any language stronger than "for Chris-mus sake" or "you son of a sea biscuit," which struck me as some kind of heroic restraint for a longshore leader. Harry Bridges swore like—what else?—a longshoreman and was reliably reported to be either a Communist or a fellow traveler so fellow-traveled as to be indistinguishable. But Ryan was a sellout stooge for shipowners; $15,000 a year salary (big money then) was only the beginning of his take. Bridges was the man who had licked the shape-up and would accept only $3,900 in salary. The difference boggled and bedeviled the mind.

There was certainly no love in Ryan's heart for the CW. I'm sure he thought of us as the worst kind of Communists, masquerading as Catholics and tricky enough to think up reasons for slandering patriotic Americans as Bolsheviks.

STORMY NIGHT ON TENTH AVENUE

At one point, when the rampaging of the goon squads was at its worst and one seaman had been found dead on the docks, a warning came from strike headquarters that we should expect a raid on our waterfront commissary, and around three o'clock one morning a large paving stone was thrown through the big storefront. In the next issue, Dorothy wrote defiantly: "We now have a new window—half the stone is used to bolster up our stove and the other half is used to keep the bread knife sharp, as we are slicing up 150 loaves of bread daily."

About the same time one of the seamen who had been staying at Mott Street, Joe Hughes, disappeared. Joe was a likeable guy whom I had worked with on the farm and laughed with a lot, and all of us were deeply concerned, figuring that Joe might well be down at the bottom of the Hudson River with his head in a bag of cement—the preferred method of human disposal on the New York waterfront.

Bill Callahan and Joe had been sleeping at the waterfront branch at the time he disappeared, but with Joe gone Dorothy sent me over to reinforce Bill. We had two cots that we set up in the back room of the store, positioned so that we could see the front door. There was also a door in the back and one that led out to the hallway of the tenement house above us.

As we checked the locks on the doors and got ready for bed that night, we were more than a little nervous. Outside, the wind was howling, and a driving rain fell on Tenth Avenue. Those were the days when freight trains rode up and down the middle of the avenue, and that night one of them would go clanking through the storm every now and then. It was a spooky scene, a great night for "Slaughter on Tenth Avenue," the title of a popular musical composition.

As we lay on our cots, waiting for the possible raid, Bill and I began to talk. From his articles in the paper and our argument on the farm, I knew he was a pacifist, but I was uncertain how far his faith in nonviolence went. The talk went something like this:

"Bill, we can't just let them break up this place. We've got too much invested here. What do you suppose it's worth?"

"Well, there's the stove and the food and the pots and furniture. Must be a few hundred dollars anyway, maybe a thousand." (To translate into current dollars you have to multiply by fourteen.)

"So what could we do to stop them?"

"We have a big monkey wrench and a small crowbar that we use to open the cases of coffee and the other stuff. We could use them."

"Okay," I said, "let's do that."

I was satisfied that Bill was not an extreme pacifist. We placed the wrench and the crowbar beside our cots and waited for what the night might bring. It must have been around midnight when a big black car drove up and parked right in front of our store. Four men got out.

"Bill, do you see that? They look like gangsters."

"Yeah, I guess this is it."

We jumped out of bed and grabbed our weapons. The men walked past our front door and entered the door of the tenement house. We could hear their footsteps coming down the hallway alongside our store. We figured they would make their attack through either the side or back doors. Bill and I crouched there, one alongside each door, waiting like wound-up springs, clutching the wrench and the crowbar.

We seemed to hear footsteps going up the stairs of the tenement. The footsteps receded. Quiet dropped over the building, and we could hear nothing but the wind and the rain. We stayed put, crouched and waiting, for another five minutes and then went back to bed. We figured the men must live in the tenement house. Anticlimax. The next day Joe Hughes showed up with nothing worse than a bad hangover. We had no trouble for the rest of the strike.

Dorothy on Nonviolence

Strangely, I don't remember if Dorothy had any comment on this incident at the time or thought that Bill and I were wrong to yield to the lure of violence and give up the idea of throwing ourselves nonviolently in front of the coffee pot and the peanut butter. I had thought that nonviolence was an article of faith with her that was almost as absolute as her faith in the Virgin Birth. But was it?

Occasionally, as in reporting strikes, she would cast a tolerant eye on some evidence of rough stuff, particularly if it were cast in a defensive mold. A few months after the strike for example, after she had climbed through the windows of the General Motors plant in Flint to visit the sit-down strikers, who were holed up in a forty-one-day siege, she wrote of their homemade clubs and "boxes of hinges and bolts ready to be used as missiles." Then she added, "These were their arms, and their preparations seemed pitifully inadequate to me in view of the machine guns and riot guns of the militia and the guards of the company."

Surely our poor little crowbar and wrench were just as "pitifully inadequate" against the probable guns of the possible goons. She did not approve of nonviolence motivated by a cowardly desire to save one's own skin, but here again it was difficult to imagine just the right degree of resistance: enough to prove we were not afraid, but not enough to hurt anybody.

Looking back, I must admit that a more symbolic and less physical resistance, however difficult to gauge, makes more sense to me. The odds were that such a resistance would have been far more likely to keep our skins in one piece than the strategy of thrashing about with the crowbar and the wrench. But I doubt that this kind of reasoning would have appealed to Dorothy Day.

Years later I had a chance to explore the question with her. I repeated the point I had made to Callahan as we crawled between the rows of corn—namely, that Christ said to turn your own cheek, but not your neighbor's cheek. I reminded her that she had made a similar distinction in her book *The Long Loneliness* when she was defending her support of the workers in what is frequently open class warfare. She had written, "We were ready to 'endure wrongs patiently' for ourselves (this is another of the spiritual works of mercy) but we were not going to be meek for others, enduring their wrongs patiently."

Before I could say it to her, she said to me, "I don't understand how you think." She added, "You should read Gandhi." And she gave me a copy of a beautiful calendar with many excellent quotations from his writings. I said I thought W. H. Auden, a devoted admirer of hers, had scored when he wrote, "Rather oddly, and to the dismay of some of her co-workers, when Castro seized power in Cuba, Dorothy Day abandoned her hitherto uncompromising position." And he quoted her, "'We do believe that it is better to revolt, to fight, as Castro did with his handful of men . . . than do nothing.'"

I also reminded her of her defense of the sit-down strikers at Flint in 1937. She replied, "Gandhi speaks to this question. He points out that nonviolence by reason of cowardice is no virtue. If a man can overcome his fear and cowardice, at least that's a beginning. Then you can reach him. In the case of Cuba, I was saying that it is better to fight than to do nothing out of cowardice."

She was tougher with the Berrigan brothers and others who had raided military establishment offices: "I believe in the Golden Rule, and if we bust up their offices, we can't complain when they bust up ours. Gandhi never used violence even against inanimate things."

What gives these inconsistent views some semblance of consistency is perhaps the conclusion that she was more tolerant of violence when the options were few, as in the case of the sit-down strikers and Castro, but less tolerant when the options were many, as in the case of the Berrigans.

MARITAIN ON LIVING WITH THE MASSES

During that seamen's strike of 1936–37 I spent a good deal of time at the waterfront CW branch, working there and talking to the seamen. I learned something of the hard conditions of life and labor on shipboard. I also came to respect the intelligence and learning of many of them; they already had spent much of their free time reading. We talked and argued about everything: capitalism, communism, socialism, fascism, anarchism, and religion. Among them was almost every shade of opinion, from left to right.

One day I walked over to the docks to watch the picketing. The whole business of strikes and picket lines was still so new to me that I actually was afraid to join the picket line for fear some of the seamen might resent a nonseaman appearing on their picket line. I did have the satisfaction of getting myself shoved along the sidewalk by the backside of a policeman's horse. The cops were busy clearing a path for scabs and trucks driving through the seamen's lines, with thugs riding on the running boards brandishing their guns.

I did not go home for Christmas that December. I spent the day on Tenth Avenue feeding strikers, but I cheated a little. After dining on bread, peanut butter, and coffee, I shattered the spell of ascetic self-righteousness by going out and buying a chocolate fudge sundae. I can almost taste it still. The flavor lies somewhere among pleasure, guilt, and self-pity.

About a month later the men voted to go back to work. They had proven to the world that they could tie up the waterfront and that the corrupt ISU no longer represented them. Temporarily the strike was a failure, but within a few months Joe Curran and his rebels had affiliated with the CIO as the National Maritime Union (NMU). The National Labor Relations Board held elections to determine who would represent the seamen, and the NMU won on fifty-two shipping lines, the ISU on only six. Within a year, the ISU was dead, and the seamen were working under new contracts and better conditions. And I was hooked, again.

Dorothy had hooked me to live in the slums of New York. The seamen's strike had hooked me into working in the labor movement. I don't know if I was falling in love with St. Francis's Lady Poverty, but I was much attracted to a quote from Jacques Maritain, the French philosopher, who was one of our intellectual heroes at that time and who used to visit the CW and encourage us in the work we were doing:

> The working-class has left the Church because the Christian world has left the working-class. That the masses may live with Christ, Christians must first live with the masses. The strength of the Socialists and Communists comes less from their ideology than from the fact that they live with the masses. . . . And it is necessary to bind yourself to them. You can live with a man without binding yourself to him. . . . To apply the social doctrine of the [papal] encyclicals effectively, there is one essential—to live with the masses.

This statement was actually more appropriate to Europe and especially to France, Maritain's country, than to the United States, where most of the working class in the Northeast was still at least nominally loyal to the Catholic Church, as Dorothy had noticed, but the part about living with the masses, with the workers, seemed to me to be impossible to deny if I wanted to be effective. And I did want to be effective.

Even my Wellesley friend could not shake me from this conviction. She did not really try, which was part of the problem. She had followed me to New York, which was encouraging, and found work as a Powers model and then as a schoolteacher. She respected what I was doing, but there had never been any promises, any commitment. I would go uptown to see her and meet what looked like another rival or rivals. They swarmed like bees. One night when I returned to Mott Street from one of these visits, a suitor filled with a sense of the hopelessness of his suit, I went up on the roof to be alone, and the self-pity welled up so strong that I wept. The tears ran down my face and dripped off my chin. I looked down and saw that they were falling into an abandoned flowerpot that was still filled with dried-up dirt. I began to wonder if the dirt, watered by my tears, would grow flowers. It could be the making of a nice miracle.

Then I began to laugh.

3

Flashback: Home

I WAS HOME on vacation from prep school and sitting by the window in an upstairs bedroom reading a novel by D. H. Lawrence. Something about Lawrence's revolt against the dreariness of industrial England found an echo in my own mind. I put down the book and looked out the window across the dead garden. The sun was setting somewhere behind Manhattan twenty miles to the west. The spring had been cold, and the trees were still bare. As far as I could see, the suburban community of Woodmere, Long Island, stretched out with a pool-table flatness in all directions. The red glow of the sunset did nothing to warm that scene, and it slowly dawned on me that I hated the place where I had been born and raised.

Many years later, when I was living in Manhattan, I had occasion to visit Woodmere. Coming from the hot, treeless canyons of New York, I thought, "This is a nice-looking place." All the gardens were in bloom, and the maple trees, arching over the quiet streets, formed green tunnels of shade.

I was the youngest of five boys. Our father, Ambrose Cort, spent his days as principal of an elementary school, later a junior high school, in Brooklyn and his evenings as a night school teacher of English and Latin, working overtime to support his family and put his boys through college. He was born in Iowa, the son of Susan Patterson and the Reverend Cyrus Cort, a big man with a beard who looked like God and was a frontier missionary of the Reformed Church. Shortly after Father's birth Grandfather took his family back to the small town of Greencastle, Pennsylvania, not far from his own father's farm, where he served as pastor of one of the seven churches, wrote some fair history and bad poetry, did a little farming, and raised five children.

One story about him, perhaps the first of many such stories, was of the time he visited a black parish in West Virginia, and the pastor introduced him with the words, "Our preacher today is the Reverend Cyrus Cort. He may have a white skin, but he's got a black heart."

The story I like least is the one about his writing proudly to Father that George Baer had praised a sermon he gave as a visiting preacher in Reading, Pennsylvania. Baer had been spokesman for the coal operators in the great anthracite strike of 1902 and shocked the country with his statement, "The strikers don't suffer; they can't even read." He also had protested that "the rights and interests of the laboring man will be protected and cared for not by the labor agitators, but by the Christian men to whom God in His infinite wisdom has given control of the property interests of the country." I have no idea what Grandfather said in that sermon, but if an arrogant fathead like Baer praised it, I fear it was nothing to be proud of. But then, what do I know? It may have been a sermon Grandfather could be proud of as long as he was not proud of the fact that Baer liked it. Or maybe this happened before Baer had proven that he was an arrogant fathead.

We liked to believe, not without encouragement, that Father would have gone far in the school system of New York City if he had not made so many enemies fighting the spoils system made famous by Tammany Hall and finally eliminated, or at least crippled, by Fiorello LaGuardia. That may have been true, for he was a good-looking man who had brains, charm, a fine classical training, and a formidable brand of self-assurance.

Father's favorite word with regard to raising his children was *responsibility*, and his second favorite was *obligations*, especially as in "obligations to society." Again and again he indicted one or more of us for "irresponsibility." In these moods he would refer to us as "great hulking boys who don't want to do anything but have fun and sit around on their backsides."

Hell Offended Him

At that time Father was not a believing Christian, though for most of his life, because there was no Reformed Church in our part of Long Island, he was a church-going Episcopalian and may have died a believer. He thought it was pretty vulgar of the Judeo-Christian God to pressure people to pursue virtue and avoid vice by holding out the hope of reward or the fear of punishment. He felt people should pursue virtue for its own sake. The idea of hell especially offended him, and even heaven seemed like a form of bribery. He believed in

God, but not the Christian God, rather a sort of force for good in the world that was slowly but surely working things out in the direction of a Better Day. Father believed strongly in progress and the League of Nations. As I write, I detect a patronizing tone that I should not be proud of. The thought occurs that in time I came to think well of Teilhard de Chardin's ideas, and what are they really but my father's optimism in a more sophisticated, scientific, and Christian vocabulary?

Father was a sort of twentieth-century deist, a humanitarian, and a Wilson-Roosevelt Democrat. Somehow his creed did not catch fire with my brothers and me. In due time, we all voted for Roosevelt, and some of my brothers might have described their beliefs in something like the terms Father used, but without his conviction. As time passed, it became increasingly difficult to believe in Inevitable Progress.

The phrase "obligations to society" in those days had for all of us a cold and clammy sound. What did we know or care about society? True, we wanted to have fun, and when we were not having fun, we, especially the three youngest, wanted to sit around on our backsides and discuss the possibilities for fun. Tension between Father and his sons was therefore inevitable.

David was our natural leader. He was by no means a great hulking boy, but light and quick, both physically and mentally. He eventually became a prolific author, foreign news editor of *Life*, and one of the lovers of Lillian Hellman, who was an occasional guest in the house. The second oldest, Bob, was the nearest thing to responsible and in any other household would have been regarded as a model son. Third was Ambrose Jr., who had the best memory, the best disposition, and a great capacity for puns and mugging. Then Paul, whom his football coach at Loomis School described as the most brilliant end who ever played there. He was also a brilliant dreamer. He and I, being closest in years, fought often, both physically and intellectually. Physically he usually won. Intellectually I did better until he succeeded in making me lose my temper. He usually succeeded. We also had a great deal of fun together.

Our mother, Lydia, was the daughter of John Painter, part owner of the Reading Stove Works, which employed about five hundred workers. He was therefore a capitalist. He died when Mother was a young girl, and I did not know what he was like. Mother was small and had a lovely smile. She was no intellectual, and if she had ideas of her own, beyond the value of Dr. Alfred McCann's diet, she kept them to herself. She knew it was impossible to challenge Father's dogmatic assertions, not to mention those of her sons.

When Paul and I argued about religion, Mother said nothing except to plead with us not to shout at each other, but I am fairly certain she was a believing Christian. She had the kind of simplicity and innocence that goes naturally with faith. She was also an excellent pianist and a graduate of the New England Conservatory of Music. Despite swollen, arthritic fingers in later years she continued to practice regularly, and the house was often full of the sound of her music. Her taste ran to the romantic. Chopin was her favorite, but as time passed Paul and I were able to persuade her to play a satisfactory amount of Bach.

Good music has a spiritual effect, and it was difficult for us not to be uplifted by it. The example of Mother's daily practice, the discipline, the careful preservation of skill, the business of style and feeling, the intimations of form and composition, all these combined to give us some sense of the creation of beauty and of the hard work that is essential both to create and to preserve that beauty.

In the early years our block consisted mostly of vacant lots. Local bigots picked one of these lots on which to burn a fiery cross one night in the Ku Klux Klan revival of the early 1920s. I doubt they were much concerned about blacks, who were a rarity, or about Catholics. Woodmere had no Catholic Church and few Catholic residents. Most likely the cross was aimed at the Jews, who were moving into the neighborhood in ever-larger numbers.

Anti-Semitism was a reality on the south shore of Long Island from my earliest years, and I am ashamed to admit that our own family was mildly infected by it. Of course, we said "some of our best friends," etc., and looked upon fiery crosses with revulsion. Nevertheless the prejudice was there, and I think we regarded the restrictive covenants, concealed or revealed, that existed in such neighboring communities as Hewlett Bay Park as not too bad an idea and secretly envied the upper crust WASPs who lived there.

Not only were certain sections of the area de facto barred to Jews, but the community also had Jewish country clubs and gentile country clubs, foremost among the latter being the exclusive Rockaway Hunt Club, as well as Jewish swimming clubs and gentile swimming clubs on nearby Long Beach. We belonged to none of the country clubs, but later joined a beach club that was predominantly Jewish. Whether we could have gotten into the gentile club I do not know, but it was too expensive in any case.

A mile south of our house was a bay full of marshy islands cut by narrow inlets from the sea. Clam diggers worked the flats. They were native Long Islanders, almost the only people who had any real roots in the place, and along with the store clerks the nearest thing that Woodmere had to a lower class. A kind of snobbery prevailed among us kids toward the *clam diggers*, a term we used to categorize not only them but also their children and anyone who came from native working-class stock. Some of the clam diggers lived in shacks, and many of them were poor, but I was never aware of them as poor. Their shacks were in a remote area, some of them accessible only by boat.

Almost all of the people who lived in Woodmere, including ourselves, seemed quite comfortable, even during the depression. At least as far as we were aware. Not until 1936, when I was twenty-two years old, did I have the slightest idea, the slightest awareness, of the conditions under which the poor have to live.

The Unknown Poor

On the train to New York we could see the slums of Jamaica as we passed through. At Thanksgiving and Christmas, collections were taken up in church for "baskets for the poor." But the poor themselves were always in the background, remote and unknown. Helping the poor was a kind of necessary fixture, like pumpkin pie or mistletoe that went with the holidays and contributed to that warm Dickensian assurance that we were not like Scrooge. We never saw the poor, and if we did, we would never have recognized them. If anyone was aware that Christ gave helping the poor a certain imperious priority in his scale of values, I was not aware of the awareness.

By this I do not mean that Father and Mother had no sympathy for the poor or did not teach us to have the same. They were Democrats, and they were Democrats for good reason, in spite of Tammany Hall and all it stood for, including corrupt Catholic politicians. Like most humanitarian liberals, Father believed that the way to help the poor was through education and political action, which would build a better world in which no one would be poor unless they were plain good for nothing or "irresponsible." According to his lights, which were considerable, he did his best to help them in that way.

Father cared a great deal about the League of Nations and was greatly upset by what happened to Woodrow Wilson and the League, especially in the U.S. Congress, after World War I. This outcome was something that lived in the house for many years and affected all of us. We took for granted as simple common sense the necessity of international law and an international government that would enforce that law and prevent war. Our countrymen's refusal to see it for so long was a personal grievance with the whole family.

Father was not a believing Christian, so I am not sure why he sent us to church or went himself. His Christian upbringing had given him a sense of obligation and responsibility, and no doubt he hoped that his sons thereby might find the same. Pascal's gamble was not so different: if it was true, you were a big winner, and if it was not true, you had lost nothing but a certain amount of dissolute fun that was bad for you anyway.

Mother played the organ briefly in our Episcopal church and also in a synagogue in Far Rockaway, where she took me once as a child. I peeked through the curtains in the organ loft and watched with awe and wonder as the rabbi conducted the service in a strange language. All the Cort males sang in the choir at one time or another, and I, in fact, continued to do so off and on, up to and through the present moment.

During the sermons of the Reverend Bumpus at Trinity Church, we choir boys spent most of the time talking to each other by means of a primitive sign language that required spelling out each word with our fingers. Ambie and Paul eventually were expelled from the choir for misbehavior at rehearsal. I should have been expelled as well, but I was better at concealing my misbehavior. We all went home and got into an argument that Paul finally ended by climbing on a radiator and preaching a sermon that dissolved us in laughter, on the text "Be kind one to another, forgiving one another."

What made more of an impression on me than anything I learned from the sermons of Reverend Bumpus or our Sunday school teachers was a time I had to stay in bed with the flu when I was about eight. Mother gave me a storybook to read, with pictures, on the life of Christ. Whatever it was about the words or the pictures, that day the story really gripped me. I wept bitterly over the death of Jesus, and I don't recall that his resurrection consoled me. I remember only how bitterly I wept.

Christmas and Easter were of course the religious occasions that impressed us most and not simply because of the vacations and the presents and the food and the general festivity. The singing of carols and hymns at home around the piano was not so much an expression of religious faith or feeling as it was of a fondness for singing good tunes, but even after most of us had ceased to believe in the truth of the words, I think we nevertheless were attracted to the vision of love and simple goodness that those words expressed.

> Oh, star of wonder, star of night,
> Star with royal beauty bright,
> Westward leading, still proceeding,
> Guide us to thy perfect light.

The atmosphere at home, however, was ordinarily not that of a believing Christian family. The two family leaders, Father and Dave, did not believe. They did not agree with each other except in this, that the ancient teachings of Christianity were outmoded by the advance of science and enlightenment.

That was the family and that was the place into which I was born—a fairly typical American place, except that it was the suburb of a highly untypical place, New York City, and a fairly typical family of middle class and mixed blood, except that we had no sisters and the blood was even more mixed than most, being compounded of German, English, Scotch, Irish, French, and Swiss.

THE RIVER

Two Greek philosophers who lived in the time before Socrates had one thing in common: they both looked upon life as a river. One of them, Heraclitus, said that the most important thing about the river was its variety, the fact that it was always changing. The other, Parmenides, said that the significant thing about the river was its unity, the fact that no matter how the water changed, it always remained the same river.

Father had summers off, and he made up for his hard winters by taking his family to a modest cottage on one of the Thousand Islands in the St. Lawrence River, a cool, clear, green-and-blue river—*the River*, a magical place of sun and wind and sailing and swimming and picnics and pretty girls who lived on remote islands and were therefore all the more desirable.

We loved the River even more than we disliked Woodmere. Woodmere was the real world; the River was the world as it should be, the Kingdom of Heaven on Earth. Some memories:

Perfect Content

We have just returned late from visiting friends on another island. Mother is playing the piano in the living room, and I have flopped on the bed in the downstairs bedroom, drowsy, watching the flutter of the kerosene lamp turned low in its bracket on the wall and listening to a Chopin nocturne through the half-open door. It is a moment of almost perfect content.

Jibing

I am about twelve and crewing for a stranger in a St. Lawrence skiff race. The St. Lawrence skiff is a long, thin rowing boat that steps a lateen sail and is steered without benefit of rudder by shifting one's weight fore and aft and manipulating the sheet and the centerboard. It is a fast boat, and our boat is faster than most; we are moving faster than usual because the wind is blowing hard. We are out in front of the fleet, sailing downwind and approaching a mark, bow to bow with Dr. Wally MacAdam, who always wins the skiff races. Dr. MacAdam jibes, which is the fast but more dangerous way to get around the mark. The stranger comes about, which is the slower but safer way. MacAdam wins again. I vow that when I race my own boat and face a similar situation, I will always jibe. That vow I have kept.

The Corts are jibing types. In that same race I look aft and catch an action shot of Dave in our boat jibing and tipping over simultaneously. His crew is Freddie Packard, a friend and house guest, also for many years an editor of *The New Yorker*. I treasure the memory of the shock and dismay on Freddie's urbane face as he prepares, with inexpressible reluctance, to enter the cool waters of the St. Lawrence.

Ann Harding, the Perfect Woman

Summer is ending, and Father has returned to his job in Brooklyn, leaving behind a somewhat more relaxed atmosphere in our cottage. We have just bought a secondhand motorboat that is so much better than the old boat that it is impossible to describe our joy. On a moonlit night we drive it into Clayton to see a movie: Ann Harding in *Holiday*, a pre-Hepburn version of Philip Barry's play, light entertainment behind a mask of pseudoserious intentions. A young self-made man is about to marry a rich socialite. She expects him to settle down in Daddy's bank counting money, but he wants to put in a year or two spending it, having fun, and seeing what makes the world go round. On this conflict they break up, and her younger sister, played by Ann Harding, catches him neatly on the rebound.

To me Ann Harding in this role is the perfect woman: beautiful, intelligent, amusing, and shining with nobility. The incredible part is that she is able to make the hero's desire for an extended vacation with pay seem like a form of heroic idealism, as if he said he wants to give the money to the poor and take off for a leper colony. I am deeply moved.

The next day I try to persuade the family that *Holiday* is worth seeing again. No one agrees. At supper I argue and plead, but at last shut up because I have decided what I will do. I pick up my dishes and take them out to the kitchen, but instead of returning I keep going out the back door, around the side, and down to the dock. The moon is full, and I can see clearly, but my hands fumble with excitement and guilt as I untie the new boat.

The alarm has been sounded, and Bob is running down to head me off. I step on the starter, and the engine comes to life. I begin backing out of the slip, but before I get clear the engine stalls. Bob is already on the dock, and I push furiously at the starter. At the last second it starts again, and I pull out and away, my heart pounding faster than the engine, Bob behind me yelling on the dock.

The night air is cool and fresh in my face, and the spray shines like bright silver in the moonlight. I rejoice in my iniquity. For a second time I worship at the shrine of my illusions and afterward buy an ice cream cone and go quietly home. I am grounded for the rest of the summer, but I don't care.

All One in the Same Road Gang

I am about sixteen. Every morning except Sunday Paul and I rise at five o'clock, eat, make our lunch, get into the skiff, row a mile to the mainland, walk a mile to the point where we meet the county truck, climb in the back with the others, and bump about five miles into the country, where we work on the road gang for nine hours a day at forty cents an hour.

Most of the day we spend in a quarry producing rock for the gravel machine. This job involves work with a pick, crowbar, and sixteen-pound sledgehammer. Backbreaking work, but I enjoy it. Man's work. With intense pleasure, we stop work to get a drink of water, or at noon when we have an hour to eat lunch—never did food taste so good—we stretch out on the grass in the shade of the trees, glorying in the luxury of rest.

When the whistle blows at the end of the day, we ease our aching muscles into the truck and bounce, walk, row for another hour before we are home. We swim in the cool river, wash up, eat a tremendous supper, and drop exhausted into bed.

I am surprised to find how much satisfaction there is in the simplest activities of life when your senses are sharpened by hard work: eating, drinking, getting clean, resting, sleeping.

We also get to know something about the proletarian community and that strong sense of comradeship that binds workingmen together. The others on the road gang are mostly old farmers or young fellows from the native population. A generation gap exists, and when an older man has to help one of the younger ones, he usually takes the occasion to point out, "This job takes a man, not a goddamn boy."

Paul and I notice that another gap, the moat of reserve that ordinarily would separate them from us as summer people, disappears almost immediately. No longer is there any native or summer folk, any bond or free, but we—at least we younger ones—are all one in the same road gang.

Years later I read the following in Omer Engelbert's *Lives of the Saints,* something I was never aware of when I was living on the River, rejoicing in the enjoyment of heaven on earth:

St. Lawrence was the first of the seven deacons attached to the service of the Roman Church. His duty was to assist the Roman pontiff when celebrating the holy mysteries, to distribute Communion to the faithful and to administer the possessions of the Church. Called upon to deliver these to the Emperor's agents, he refused and was laid upon a gridiron under which were placed half-lighted coals so as to prolong his tortures and make his death more painful. To his tormentors St. Lawrence said, "The meal is done, turn and eat. But the riches of the Church, which you seek, the hands of the poor have carried away to the treasury of Heaven."

Perhaps it was just as well that I did not know more about St. Lawrence. The thought of him on that gridiron might have dimmed my enjoyment of his river. In any case there was no danger that I would survive adolescence under the illusion that life was all, or even mostly, pleasure free of pain. My school days took care of that.

4

Flashback: School Days

A student may easily exhaust his life in comparing divines
and moralists, without any practical regard to morality or
religion; he may be learning not to live but to reason.

—Samuel Johnson, in James Boswell's *Life of Johnson*

FOR SEVEN YEARS I went to the elementary public school in Woodmere. In about the third grade I got into a fight during the lunch
recess. The older boys took us out into a neighboring field and stage-
managed the fight into a big event, with half the school crowding
around to watch. The fight itself was a draw, but what was memorable
was the crowd sweeping us out into the field, the fear in my throat,
and the surprise with which I realized that one minute I was nothing
and the next, because I was going to fight somebody, the whole world
was crazy to watch me. Of all the things that happened to me at that
school, it was easily the most memorable.

At the age of ten I went off to the Choir School of the Episcopal
Cathedral of St. John the Divine in New York City. I was one of forty
boys who sang for their breakfast, lunch, and supper, dormitory beds
in a fine building on the cathedral grounds at Morningside Heights,
and a better-than-average education from a faculty of four men and
one woman, not to mention musical training and the chance to sing
Bach's St. Matthew's Passion every Holy Week.

Religion flowed over and around me during the next three years,
but very little penetrated. I sat or stood or knelt in the cathedral, stiff
as a stick, looking neither right nor left, determined to beat out Bruce
Watson for the gold cross awarded for good conduct in the cathedral.
I would hardly say I was born again. I said my prayers, was confirmed
by Bishop Manning, and received Holy Communion.

Heywood Broun, the columnist who founded what later was my
union, the Newspaper Guild, was a good and intelligent man as well
as a socialist and, at the end of his life, a convert to Catholicism. He

once wrote that whenever he was uncertain about what position to take on a public issue, he waited for Bishop Manning to take a position and then took the opposite. You might reasonably conclude from this statement that the bishop thought of Christianity as a bulwark of capitalism and the status quo. If so, he was not unusual among Christian bishops, either then or now. To me at that time he seemed a nice man. Remote but nice.

As far as I was concerned, what went on in the cathedral had to overcome a more serious obstacle than Bishop Manning's views on politics or economics, about which I knew nothing and cared less.

Because we were required to kneel with stiff backs and stand for long periods of time and were fed a starchy diet that made most of us constipated most of the time, boys would faint sometimes during the services. I myself never blacked out, but once or twice I felt myself going and walked out before I went. I became very anxious about fainting and developed a phobia about the cathedral. The oppressive atmosphere of those great musty vaults was something that I entered reluctantly, as into a hostile land, and I never left it without a sense of relief as though a weight had been lifted.

My strongest religious experience came one day when I was poking around our school library and came across a copy of Dante's *Inferno* as illustrated by Gustave Doré. I was not so much interested in Dante's text as in the naked women in Doré's illustrations, but I could not look at the naked women without looking at the scenes in hell in which they appeared. A feeling of intense horror came over me as I looked. The pictures haunted me for weeks. No, I would not say that my experience of religion at St. John's was very warm or positive.

Eventually I became head prefect, captain of the baseball team, winner of the Track and Field Day Cup (one of the most thrilling triumphs of my life), and top scholar. I was a big frog in a very little pond, but big enough to win a full scholarship to Taft, a sizeable prep school for rich boys in Watertown, Connecticut, where the size and self-confidence of the frog were dramatically reduced.

THE HIGH ESTEEM OF JESUS CHRIST

The first year at Taft I did reasonably well and even appeared to be headed for a position of modest success. The second year disaster struck. I was the youngest boy in my class during that upper-middle or junior year, only fourteen when the year started. Some of my classmates were already young men, eighteen or nineteen. Some of them conceived the idea of holding a purity contest. Before I knew what was happening I was dragged into a room on the upper-middle class corridor and asked a set of twenty questions calculated to determine the extent of my purity. Some of the questions had nothing to do with purity, and others that did have something to do with it were not asked. To make matters worse, I had a memory failure and answered two questions incorrectly. It did not occur to me to lie. The result was that I wound up with a mark of one hundred, a perfect score.

"Hey, have you heard the latest?"

"No, what?"

"Cort got a hundred in the purity contest."

"No kidding. A *hundred.*"

My reputation was ruined. What had happened was not that I had gotten a hundred in the purity contest, but that I had gotten zero in the impurity contest. I had committed the unforgivable sin: I was inexperienced.

A few days later one of my older classmates began calling me "Jesus." When we crossed each other's path in the corridor or on the campus, he would see me, laugh, and yell, "Hiya, Jesus." I would reply "Hi" with a sickly smile and walk on, hearing behind me the spreading laughter.

Some of the less obvious hecklers called me "J.C.," my initials, but the leer that went with them made it clear that they meant "Jesus Christ." I had no defense against it. After all, it was not exactly a dirty name. It was worse. Against a dirty name I could have fought, but who could fight against "Jesus"? And yet it remained insulting. Such was the high esteem in which Jesus Christ was held in a U.S. prep school in 1928–29. Such was the high esteem in which J. C. Cort held him.

Of course, I might have fought anyway. One night about a year later, when the situation had become close to intolerable, I had a run-in with one of the toughest boys in the school, one of those who took a special pleasure in using my nickname. The fact that I was by then a senior and he was a class behind me made it even worse. We argued over something, I have forgotten what, and I went up to my room furious. I stood in the dark looking out at the campus, the blood pounding in my head and my throat dry, clenching my fists until the nails bit into the flesh. I wondered what would happen if I went downstairs and picked a fight. I told myself that if I got the better of him, it could put an end to the whole business of the nickname. I stood there undecided for quite a while. Whether cowardice or good sense prevailed, I do not know, but it was certainly no turn-the-other-cheek spirit. I did not go down. He was an excellent boxer and would probably have beaten my brains out.

I tried to compensate by sheer weight of activity. I made the hockey, track, and soccer teams, sang in the glee club and choir, played in the orchestra, took part in dramatics, wrote for the literary magazine, joined the debating club, stumbled through several debates, and envied the articulate poise of Bob Wagner, son of the man who wrote the Wagner Act and himself later mayor of New York. The Wagner Act, often described as the Magna Carta of U.S. labor, was later amended by another Taft alumnus, Senator Robert Taft, nephew of the school's founder and headmaster and the author of the much hated Taft-Hartley Act.

None of my feverish activity seemed to make any difference. I began to resign myself to being considered slightly strange. A group of students used to gather in Mr. Roberts's apartment after lunch and listen to his classical records. Sometimes a perfectly normal boy would join us, but most of us were misfits of one kind or another: quiet grinds, cripples, boys in delicate health, the ones with bad eyes, school butts, effeminate boys.

Our taste was by no means refined: a lot of Tchaikovsky, a good deal of Wagner, Brahms, Beethoven, and, the big favorite, Schubert's *Unfinished*—not the best or the worst source of beauty and comfort from the pain of our life in the school. Those "normal" boys who joined us did not dare to come very often because they knew that just to be seen going into Mr. Roberts's room to listen to music was enough to endanger their reputations. They knew that in that school any unusual interest in literature, art, music, or anything that smacked of high culture automatically was considered suspect, if not actually queer.

I venture to guess that this situation was fairly typical of most U.S. schools and even most U.S. colleges of that era. Parents who think that the faculty sets the tone of a prep school could scarcely be more naive. Those who set the tone are the best athletes and occasionally a boy with a particularly quick and witty tongue. The faculty are largely helpless.

From recent Taft literature I get the impression that high culture is doing better today. I hope that is true.

Taft in the 1920s and 1930s had some good men on the faculty. One was Wallace Fowlie, just out of Harvard, a good teacher of French, a good friend, and later a distinguished author and critic. There was also Mr. Stearns, who taught ancient history and inspired me with a love for everything Greek—the sculpture, the architecture, the literature, even the philosophers—so that when somebody asked me whom I would most like to meet in the next world, if there were a next world, I replied, "Socrates," without hesitation, although I knew almost nothing about him and had never read Plato. And Mr. Reardon, who taught history, changed the course of my life because he taught it so well that I liked it and remembered later that I had done well in it.

One day I sat in the library, bent over a copy of Tennyson, and for a few moments thought about committing suicide. Then the bell rang, and I had to go to class or lunch, something intervened, and life never seemed quite so lousy again.

To buttress my self-esteem I conceived the idea that happiness was a fragile thing that depended on tricky factors outside oneself, something that could be produced the way you produce a stage show—a matter of scenery, lighting, stage properties, and the right casting. Given proper support and a good production, I thought I could be happy, so I dreamed of life at Harvard, where I intended to go in part because so few Taft graduates went there (they went to Yale), or in New York City among the talented and amusing kind of people Dave knew. The trouble with me was that I had just blundered onto the wrong stage.

At one point I made a pathetic attempt to create my own stage set. A small, rarely used men's room in the basement of a new building had what I thought was a functional New York look, so I used to go there, sit on the toilet, and sing to myself "Love for Sale," a slightly risqué song from Cole Porter's *The New Yorkers*, a show someone had taken me to see. It helped.

I fancied myself as a New Yorker. I admired the type. I had visited Dave's place in Greenwich Village. I did not visit the slums or the dark factory lofts. Corey Ford, one of Dave's friends, took me to some prizefights in an armory, where we sat at ringside. While one heavyweight was being counted out, I put up my hand and held him so that he would not roll into my lap. We went to a famous speakeasy, and Ford introduced me to Marc Connolly, who had written *The Green Pastures*.

THE ROAD TO FREEDOM

I no longer believe that people or the state of their psyches can be determined by environment, but I think they certainly are conditioned by it. I was happier when I left Taft behind, my classmates overwhelmingly voting me as the student who "Takes Life Most Seriously" and the faculty dubbing me the student who "Does Most with the Least Work." I should have been more grateful to Taft. It knocked a good deal of pride out of me, and pride, as we know, is the deadliest of the seven deadly sins.

During the summer of 1931 I went up to Keene Valley in the Adirondacks to work for the Reverend Paul Austin Wolfe, the chaplain at Taft and later pastor of the Brick Presbyterian Church in New York. I think Rev. Wolfe was also happier away from Taft. On Sundays he sometimes preached in the Keene Valley church, and I was surprised by how much better his sermons were when he was facing a sympathetic congregation than when he was confronted by that captive sea of bored young faces at Taft.

At Taft Rev. Wolfe's preaching had had little effect on me, but at Keene Valley I began to be really interested in God for the first time since I was a child. Rev. Wolfe had a good mind, and I remember one night as we sat over the supper dishes, he really got hold of me. I have no recollection of what he said. I just remember sitting there and thinking to myself, "This religion thing is more important than I realized."

At the end of the summer I had an invitation to join Dave at Corey Ford's place in Freedom, New Hampshire. I liked and admired Ford. At that time he was doing book reviews for the original *Vanity Fair*, on whose staff Dave also worked, along with Clare Boothe before she became Mrs. Luce. Ford turned out hilarious parodies under the name of John Riddell. He was also active in the movement to repeal Prohibition and inspired me to write an article for the Taft *Oracle* on the Anti-Speakeasy League, a countervailing force to the Anti-Saloon League. Mr. Taft was a devout dry and did not like my article at all, but he let it run in the interests of free thought.

Rev. Wolfe drove me over to Lake Champlain, and around noon I started hitchhiking across Vermont and New Hampshire to Freedom, a few miles from the Maine border. On the trip I had my first serious conversation with a black man, and it occurred in an unusual way. My mind was set on reaching Freedom that night, but the driving public was not cooperative. The result was that at 2:00 A.M. I was still about ten miles away and, for lack of a ride, had just hiked twelve miles over a lonesome country road, carrying a fifty-pound pack.

I limped into West Ossipee, which was on a more substantial route where I thought there would be more cars. I was wrong and was about to conclude that the price of Freedom is eternal suffering, when I looked up the road and saw a car parked in front of a gas station. Its parking lights were on, and I approached with something like the anxiety of a starving fox confronted by a live rabbit. The car was ancient and battered, but real people sat inside it.

"Hello," I said, "Where are you bound?"

"Nowhere," said the driver. That stopped me for a second. I looked at the inmates—four men, three white and one black. They were easily the toughest-looking individuals I had seen all day or all summer.

"Well," I said, "in that case how would you like to drive me to Freedom for two dollars? The last two dollars I got on me," I added quickly, thinking that by the look of them they would take whatever I had anyway.

"Okay. Get in."

I got in the back seat next to a black giant, and we started off. The moon shone down through a large hole in the canvas top, and we drove slowly on toward Freedom, the driver sticking his head out around the windshield to see through the night mists because the wipers didn't work.

The giant took a long pull from a bottle and handed it to me. "Have a drink."

The bottle smelled like hair tonic. I studied the label by the light of the moon. It was hair tonic. "No thanks," I said, trying to make it sound as though I would have enjoyed a drop of hair tonic except that I happened not to be thirsty.

The men had driven up from Boston, it turned out, because the giant wanted to see his wife, who was a maid on a summer place in Chocorua, a few miles north. She had not been home earlier in the evening, and they were driving around killing time until the morning. The giant was a heavyweight boxer known in the ring as Sweet William. He was upset about his wife, and indeed it seemed that relations between them were rapidly approaching a crisis.

"I got a razor," he told me, "and I'm gonna slit that woman's throat from ear to ear."

I was struck with horror. The way he said it seemed evidence that he meant it. "Why? Why do you want to do a thing like that?"

"She's doin' me dirty. She's foolin' around with another man."

"How do you know?"

"I just know, that's all. She don't love me no more."

I tried to reason with him, but he wasn't listening. The next time he spoke his voice was choked with emotion. "You don't know how I love that woman. I'd go through hell for that woman."

I relaxed. It seemed, after all, that he loved her too much to kill her. A few minutes later he stiffened in his seat, however, and his voice became loud again with menace.

"I got a razor. I got a razor, and I'm gonna slit that woman's throat from ear to ear."

The other men paid no attention to him but talked among themselves or took an occasional pull at the hair tonic, and so we drove on through the mist and the moonlight, past the shining waters of Lake Ossipee. On the seat beside me the big black man fluctuated between love and hatred, between longing and a rage to kill, and I, fascinated and appalled, pleaded with him to be reasonable. He was still fluctuating and I still pleading when we reached Ford's house and parted forever.

JESTERS, JOYCE, AND PROUST

Also staying at Ford's were Tom Wenning, later drama critic for *Newsweek*, and his wife. Tom had been editor in chief of the Columbia *Jester* the year after Dave held that job, Ford in the previous year. The house was full of *Jester* editors. Wenning was a very likeable fellow. He told me that he had been a devout Catholic when he was my age, so devout that he kept a rosary in his pocket and said it when he was walking along the street. He had lost his faith at Columbia.

I liked and admired all of these *Jester* editors. They were great men in my eyes, and I hung on their words as though they were oracles. After a while, though, I grew depressed just reflecting on how great a gulf separated me from them. I was so slow and so stupid, they so quick and so clever.

We went swimming, played intellectual parlor games, admired the magnificent view, played Sibelius's *Valse triste* again and again on the Victrola, and one night took turns recording on Corey's new machine.

Dave recorded "Fantasia," a Chesterton poem that he knew by heart:

> The happy men who lose their heads,
> They find their heads in heaven
> As cherub heads with cherub wings
> And cherub haloes even.
> Out of the infinite evening lands
> Along the sunset sea,
> Leaving the purple fields behind,
> The cherub wings beat down the wind,
> Back to the groping body and blind,
> As the bird back to the tree.
>
> Whether the plumes be passion red
> For him who truly dies
> By headsman's blade or battle-axe
> Or blue like butterflies,
> For him that lost it in a lane
> In April's fits and starts,
> His folly is forgiven then;
> But higher, and far beyond our ken,
> Is the healing of the unhappy men,
> The men that lost their hearts.
>
> Is there not pardon for the brave
> And broad release above,
> Who lost their heads for liberty
> Or lost their hearts for love?
> Or is the wise man wise indeed
> Whom larger thoughts keep whole?
> Who sees life equal like a chart,
> Made strong to play the saner part

And keep his head and keep his heart,
And only lose his soul.

I looked at Dave with surprise as he recited this poem. At one time in his life this atheistic, hedonistic brother of mine apparently had been captivated by an expression of religious faith, if only by the beauty and arrangement of the words. But that reading was too simple. There was more to the poem than that. I knew enough Bible to catch the echo of "What doth it profit a man to gain the whole world and lose his own soul?" I knew Dave did not bother to memorize many poems. The poem and the tribute it implied lingered in my mind.

After a few days Dave and I went with the Wennings to visit another literary friend of theirs, Philip Wylie, at his home in Connecticut. Wylie was best known for short stories and books like *Generation of Vipers*, sometimes described as jeremiads. I once read that he measured every human activity by a moral yardstick consisting of two questions: "Do animals do it?" and "What would happen if everybody did it?" By this test he was able to eliminate suicide as a reasonable activity—which is, after all, something.

The house was full of people, especially after we arrived, and I must admit that I have no recollection of Wylie at all. In fact, everyone there was overshadowed immediately by a monumental argument that started between Dave and a man named Mark Goodrich, who wrote *Delilah*, a long novel about a destroyer, and who married the movie actress Olivia DeHaviland. The subject of the argument was: Who is the greater writer, James Joyce (Goodrich) or Marcel Proust (Dave)? The debate raged long after the rest of us had gone to bed.

The next day Wylie had us all out moving rocks around in a brook where he was building a dam. This work cramped the debaters' rhetoric somewhat, so without conscious intent they shifted the ground of their competition to another question: Who can move the bigger rock, Goodrich (Joyce) or Dave (Proust)? I noticed that Dave threw himself into the rock moving with violent enthusiasm, perhaps to prove that a preference for Proust subtracted nothing from his own machismo.

That afternoon I hitchhiked on to New York and home and was a little relieved to get back to the minor leagues with Ambie and Paul. With them I was neither a wit nor a muscular intellectual, but at least I did not seem like a brainless oaf.

5

Flashback: The Bizarre Conversion

> It is only the simpletons, the ignoble, the senseless—slaves
> and women and children—whom Christians can per-
> suade—wooldressers and cobblers and fullers, the most
> uneducated and common men, whoever is a sinner—or a
> godforsaken fool.
>
> —Celsus, quoted by Origen

"THE UNIVERSITY OF CHICAGO," a wit of the 1930s pointed out, "is a Baptist institution where Jews go to become Catholics." I don't know if that is still true about Chicago, but I doubt it. The economics department has the reputation of being the place where Baptists, Jews, and Catholics go to become capitalists. What I do know is that in the 1930s no one would ever say about Harvard that it was the place for anyone to go to become a Christian, much less a Catholic. That is why Marian Schlesinger's remark "How positively bizarre!"— though amusing—was by no means inappropriate.

At that time not a single course in the philosophy department dealt seriously with Thomism. The introductory course in philosophy jumped from Aristotle to Descartes, a jump of two thousand years during which, according to the department, there was no philosophy worth thinking about or even mentioning.

In addition, the elective system inaugurated by Charles Eliot tended to leave it to the students to elect those courses that would qualify them for the title of Educated Man, a sort of tacit admission that the faculty did not know what a proper education was. And so it happened, as Chicago's Robert Hutchins wrote, that chemistry majors could not speak to economics majors, and hardly anyone was speaking to God.

I was greatly elated when I first came to Harvard, which seemed to be everything that Taft was not. Within one day, however, I had lost my wallet and $59 (the equivalent of $800 in 2003) that Father had given me to start me off. I was plunged into depression, and so I began my own search for a truth that might give me something more durable to hold onto than $59 in a wallet.

At Taft Mr. Reardon had persuaded me to like history, and Wallace Fowlie to admire French literature. At the end of freshman year, therefore, I elected to concentrate in French history and literature, and someone in the bowels of the university assigned Paul Doolin to be my tutor, the one who under the system then in effect was to guide me through that field.

Doolin was then a man about forty whose dark suits and black ties, combined with black hair and moustache, gave him an austere, somber look that he shattered at intervals with sudden, violent laughter. He had been a fighter pilot in World War I and once asked me if I was related to the Marquis de la Cour, beside whose chateau he had made an emergency landing in the French countryside. He was still a belligerent, an active rebel in revolt against the ideas that dominated the university and the Western world: the ideas of romanticism and materialism, the ideas of William James's pragmatist, who, in James's words, "turns away . . . from fixed principles, closed systems and pretended absolutes and origins" and "turns toward concreteness and adequacy, towards facts, towards action, and towards power."

Doolin was a Platonist, a medievalist, and a disciple of another Harvard professor, Irving Babbitt, cofounder of the Humanist School with Paul Elmer More of Princeton. They did not want to close any systems or ignore any facts. They merely insisted on the reality and the primacy of another set of facts, the facts of the spirit.

The tutorial conferences were held in Doolin's barren study in Dunster House. One of the first was on the *Chanson de Roland,* which he told me to read. He said it was a great epic poem about a nephew of Charlemagne who died at Roncevaux in the Pyrenees fighting the infidel Saracens. It left me cold.

To understand why it left me cold, please recall the lovely piano player from Montclair with whom I had fallen in love during the previous summer. Not only was I in love; I was a romantic in love. I had accepted the gospel according to Wagner and Metro-Goldwyn-Mayer that the feeling of a man for a woman, and vice versa, is the most important thing in life. And here a supposedly great poem had no love interest at all. I complained to Doolin.

He took the poem apart and put it back together again. In the process I somehow felt that he was taking me apart as well and that somehow, somewhere I must find the way to put myself back together again. What he did that first day was to set me straight on the relative values of love, sacred and profane. He showed me that because a man like Roland died fighting for the love of God, he was not a lesser man than one who died fighting for the love of a woman. His opinion seemed to be that, other things being equal, Roland was a greater man. He almost made me see it.

Almost, but not quite. I rebelled. I rebelled against a course assignment I had been given to write a paper on the medieval history of Brittany. I could not see how that was going to help me make a living and marry Montclair. I told Doolin I wanted to transfer to the English department to prepare myself for a writing job. He talked me out of it. He also talked the history professor into changing my assignment to a paper on the romances of Chrétien de Troyes, which was more to my liking.

Chrétien was a twelfth-century French poet who worked mostly at "the court of love" run by an erotic old duchess named Marie de Champagne. One of the laws of this court was that true love was impossible between a man and a woman who had been joined in legal wedlock.

That such ideas had a following in the Catholic civilization of medieval France was a revelation to me. Granted, most medieval marriages were arranged; nevertheless, to say that married love was impossible was going pretty far. My eyes opened wider as I read into Chrétien's stories, which were perhaps the most popular reading of that time. I was impressed not so much by the sex in them, which is mild by modern standards, as by the ideology that he uses to justify it. This ideology is summed up in one scene where the hero, about to set out on a military campaign, takes his sword, sticks it in the ground, and places upon it a doublet into which some golden hairs from the head of his lady love have been woven. He then gets down on his knees and worships it. Hollywood never went that far.

Chrétien's most famous romance is *Tristan and Iseult*. King Mark sends Young Tristan, a handsome knight, across the sea to bring back Iseult, the king's betrothed. On the voyage home Tristan and Iseult by mistake drink a love potion that Iseult is supposed to take just before she meets King Mark. After that they cannot help themselves.

The appeal of this story to composers such as Wagner was no accident. He gave it some visceral music that I used to listen to up at the River, swinging in the hammock and gazing out across the water, dreaming of my love. Nor is it strange that it has attracted poets such as Edwin Arlington Robinson. The love potion's destruction of free will, the opportunity for Tristan and Iseult to enjoy all the melancholy zest of their forbidden passion yet escape the pangs of conscience and remorse—these things naturally appeal to the modern mind and heart.

When I read these stories in their crude originals, without benefit of Wagner, Robinson, or Twentieth Century Fox, they struck me as strangely unconvincing. But they gave me pause, they made me think, they led me to reexamine some of my illusions about the nature of life and love.

PLATO AND THE PLATITUDES

Doolin also got me reading Plato. Socrates and Plato were no great admirers of democracy, as I. F. Stone and Karl Popper have reminded us, and Plato's *Republic* is by no means a place where you would really want to live. You might say that as a philosopher he was a great poet. In any event he was the kind of poet I needed at the time. I was deeply moved by Socrates' apology before the court that condemned him, one of the great statements of religious faith and one of the great moments in the history of confrontation between faith and conformity:

> Men of Athens, I honor and love you: but I shall obey God rather than you, and while I have life and strength I shall never cease from the practice and teaching of philosophy, exhorting anyone whom I meet and saying to him after my manner, "O my friend, why do you who are a citizen of the great and mighty and wise city of Athens care so much about laying up the greatest amount of money and honor and reputation, and so little about wisdom and truth and the greatest improvement of the soul, which you never regard or heed at all? Are you not ashamed of this? . . . Wherefore, O judges, be of good cheer and know this of a truth—that no evil can happen to a good man, either in life or after death.

Plato takes us to Socrates' cell after he is condemned to death, and in the dialogue Crito urges Socrates to escape, but Socrates rejects that suggestion on the ground that it would be wrong, it would be evil, not to accept the verdict of his fellow citizens in a fair trial, that "doing wrong [is] always evil and dishonorable" and "we ought not to retaliate or render evil for evil to anyone, whatever evil we may have suffered from him." Crito leaves Socrates determined to "follow the intimations of the will of God."

The *Phaedo* is even more moving, as it brings together Socrates' closest friends in his cell on the day of his execution for one last discussion of the basic questions: Can the soul exist independently of the body? Is it immortal? Is there a heaven for the good, a hell for the bad, and a purgatory for the indifferent?

At last, having answered all these questions in the affirmative (everyone seems to take for granted the existence of God), Socrates concludes that "when the foolishness of the body will be cleared away, we shall be pure and hold converse with other pure souls, and know of ourselves the clear light everywhere, and this is surely the light of truth." So he lies down, drinks the poison, and dies.

What Plato and Socrates did for me that sophomore year at Harvard was simply to take the old Christian words and the old Christian concepts, dust off the accumulations of a thousand dull sermons, the associations of a thousand pious platitudes, and all the bigotry, hypocrisy, and general dry rot of two thousand years, and leave them shining with the intellectual glamour of ancient Greece.

It is surprising how fashionable the old Greeks have remained. Even those who sneer at everything that Homer, Socrates, and Sophocles stood for will generally not venture to attack head-on the highly moral and religious standards of that magnificent civilization except perhaps to remind us, rightly, that the whole magnificent thing rested on a foundation of slave and female labor.

I readily admit that as a young man I was sensitive to the canons of intellectual fashion. Most young men are. God was old hat, passé, to the men and authors I admired. At that time neither Evelyn Waugh nor Aldous Huxley had shown any interest in religion, and so with something akin to shock I discovered that a very respectable tradition stood on the other side of the debate between believers and unbelievers—that a powerful and persuasive body of philosophers, poets, and writers upheld the primacy of the spirit and upheld it with just as much passion, eloquence, and persuasive power as the moderns upheld the primacy of matter.

Whole phrases and even sentences of Plato sound as if they are echoed in the New Testament. Peter and the apostles' defiance before the Sanhedrin when they cried out, "We must obey God rather than men," calls to mind Socrates' ringing defiance in "Men of Athens, I shall obey God rather than you."

"When do wars and quarrels come among you?" wrote St. James, whose knowledge of Plato must be considered doubtful. "Is it not from this, from your passions, which wage war in your members?" Four hundred years before him Socrates said in the *Phaedo*, "For whence come wars, and fightings, and factions? Whence but from the body and the lusts of the body?"

This conviction of the duality of human nature and of the existence of a higher realm of ideas and ideals—God's world of absolute truth, absolute beauty, and absolute goodness—was what impressed me in Plato. No need to go along with his peculiar theory of reminiscence or the Gnostic/Manichean implications of his dualism. It was the general picture he painted with the skill of a great artist that created a reflection in the muddy waters of my own experience.

WHITEHEAD ON FIRE

Another man at Harvard who moved me was Alfred North Whitehead, the English philosopher, mathematician, and process theologian. I took one of his philosophy courses, which was well over my head. The only thing I can remember from the course is Whitehead insisting that every concept that passes through the human mind, even if it be the coldest mathematical formula, is received in the mind of the receiver with a certain emotional coloring or sets up a certain emotional reaction.

I struggled through his books and understood very little, but I still believe Whitehead was the most inspiring teacher I encountered at Harvard. He was a little old man with a cherubic face, a bald head, and a fringe of white hair that curled up in the back. He wore wing collars and usually a blue ascot tie that set off his bright blue eyes. He had a wonderfully cheerful smile, and he smiled a great deal.

Whitehead would sit behind his desk on the high lecture platform in Emerson Hall, his pink, shiny face barely visible to us students, and almost every day he would go into a kind of public rapture of love for the truth, a rapture he would pour out to us in a weak voice strained through a fearful British accent, gesturing excitedly with his hands. The old man was on fire, and in spite of everything—his voice, his accent, and the difficulty of his thought—he was able to communicate his fire even to slow students like myself so that we too caught something of his love and his determination that the truth should be discovered and made known.

Still another influence was C. H. McIlwain, the star of the government department. He was bald, too, but in a Yankee way, and his fire did not burn as brightly as Whitehead's, yet it burned nonetheless, with a low, steady flame that may have produced more heat in the long run. Although he taught political theory, he was also one of the few men at Harvard who knew and respected Thomas Aquinas. In fact, he knew and respected most of the Catholic authorities in the field, even when he did not agree with them, and he was quick to point out that the chain of theories that produced our modern notions of democracy, popular sovereignty, civil rights, and representative government runs back through Cardinal Bellarmine, Suarez, and Aquinas to the New and Old Testaments.

He used to say that the political theory of the Catholic Church is bounded on one side by the words of St. Paul, "Let every man be subject to higher authority, for all authority is from God," and on the other side by the statement of St. Peter to the Sanhedrin, "We must obey God rather than men." That lesson in political geography has stayed with me ever since.

In the French department Louis Mercier was the very picture of a middle-class Frenchman who had all of the virtues and none of the vices of that genre. He had a tremendous number of children, a strong faith in the Catholic Church, and a mission in life, which was to reconcile the humanism of Irving Babbitt with the teachings of Christianity.

His influence was mainly that of example. He was a Catholic, the real thing—and there were few in evidence at Harvard—a man not only of intelligence and faith, but of works, a good man and a happy man. I looked at Professor Mercier, and I thought to myself, "If a man like that can be a Catholic, then there can't be too much that's wrong with Catholicism."

Babbitt, Rousseau, and Romanticism

But mostly, next to Doolin, Irving Babbitt had the greatest influence on me, although I never even saw the man. He died during the summer of 1933, just before I was scheduled to take his course. His erudition was overpowering. Some of the students in his course used to conduct a betting pool. As they entered the lecture hall, they handed in their bets as to how many references he would make to assorted writers, philosophers, poets, and so on. The one who came closest picked up the money.

Nominally his field was French literature, but he was also at home in Greek, Latin, English, and German literature. He read Buddhist texts in Pali and in one of his books apologizes because he had to read Confucius in translation. His books range over the whole field of human thought, art, and history in much the same way that those of Spengler and Toynbee have done. He was a man of the world in the best sense.

I think I read all his books, although none of my courses compelled me to read any of them. I still remember the sense of excitement I felt as I sat in the Lowell House library reading Babbitt as he demolished popular fallacies. In the midst of the slaughter I could see some of my favorite dogmas going down, but I did not care. What was happening to me was a genuine conversion from one view of life to another.

Babbitt's favorite target was romanticism, which he described as a movement that had forerunners in the Renaissance, the Middle Ages (for example, Chrétien de Troyes), and even back as far as the Taoists of ancient China, but that had not gathered speed and momentum until the eighteenth century. At first it was a rebellion against the dried-up, rigid formalism of seventeenth- and eighteenth-century writers who almost killed imagination in the name of reason, morality, and good taste.

But Rousseau and his disciples, he maintained, were not content to fight for the legitimate rights of the imagination. They launched a counteroffensive along a wide front that sought to wipe out the wisdom of the ages and set up canons of morality based on a new concept of human nature. As Villers put it in a letter to Madame de Stael, "The fundamental and creative idea of all your work is to show primitive, incorruptible, naive nature in conflict with the barriers and shackles of conventional life."

In short, human nature did not fall, either through Adam's sin or by way of a basic weakness in its makeup, Reinhold Niebuhr's "inclination to injustice." It was naturally and completely good as long as it remained in the primitive state. Society and civilization ruined it. Too much law, too much reason, too much religion— especially formal, dogmatic religion. Our salvation therefore was to get back to simple, spontaneous, emotional living, to let ourselves go, to be more natural and uninhibited.

Babbitt's favorite quotes from romantic writers, taken from his basic work *Rousseau and Romanticism,* include Goethe in *Faust,* "Feeling is all" and "The devil is the spirit that always says 'no'" (Babbitt acknowledged, however, that Goethe later reformed and turned against the romantic notions of his earlier career); as well as Rousseau's "The only habit the child should be allowed to form is that of forming no habit," "The man who reflects is a depraved animal," and "Let us lay down as an incontrovertible rule that the first impulses of nature are always right."

Babbitt quotes another passage in which Rousseau speaks of his own "warmth of heart," his "melting feeling, the lively and sweet emotion that I experience at the sight of everything that is virtuous, generous and lovely." Babbitt adds that Rousseau "abandoned his five children one after the other, but had, we are told, an unspeakable affection for his dog."

To show the political effect of this glorification of feeling, Babbitt quotes a speech by Robespierre before the French Assembly at the height of the Reign of Terror:

> Yet virtue exists as you can testify, sensitive and pure souls: it exists, that tender, irresistible, imperious passion, torment and delight of magnanimous hearts, that profound horror of tyranny, that compassionate zeal for the oppressed, that sacred love for one's country, that still more sublime and sacred love for humanity. . . . It exists, that egoism of undegenerate men who find a celestial voluptuousness in the calm of a pure conscience and the ravishing spectacle of public happiness. You feel it at this moment burning in your souls. I feel it in mine. But how could our vile calumniators have any notion of it?

And so, off with their heads!

Babbitt refused to admit that virtue was either a passion or a feeling—voluptuous, ravishing, burning, or otherwise. He defined his terms, and the definitions he used were those common to the great moralists of all ages, starting with Moses and proceeding to Buddha, Confucius, Plato, Aristotle, and Christ. He insisted on the distinction between soul and body, between the law of the spirit and the law of the flesh, between the law for things and the law for humans.

Granted, human nature is a unity as well as a duality. Granted, since the time of the Gnostics, the Manicheans, the Jansenists, and the Puritans, we have had to struggle against false doctrine to the effect that the body is in some way evil or shameful. As St. Augustine put it, "It is not the bad body that causes the good soul to sin, but the bad soul that causes the good body to sin."

But this is not the same as saying, with Rousseau, that the instincts of the body are always true and trustworthy and more to be obeyed than the promptings of the mind and the spirit. Let me illustrate some of the confusion that Rousseau and the romantics sowed in the modern world, but also the human truth that can still shine through that confusion, with some quotes from Aldous Huxley's *Point Counter Point.*

Up until the time I read *Rousseau and Romanticism,* the Huxley book was easily the most influential book in my life. Propelled by David's enthusiasm, the Cort brothers had adopted it as a sort of surrogate Bible, and by the time I was seventeen, I had read it twice. The only really admirable character in the book is Mark Rampion, an artist-writer whom Huxley is supposed to have modeled on the personality of D. H. Lawrence. Rampion is contemptuous of Christ and Christianity and singles out for special contempt St. Francis, whom he calls "a disgusting little pervert . . . going about getting thrills of excitement out of licking lepers." He is also contemptuous of disembodied romantics such as Shelley, and in a passage that I greatly admired and often quoted he comments on the "Ode to a Skylark": "I wish to God the bird . . . had dropped a good large mess in his eye. It would have served him damned well right for saying it wasn't a bird. Blithe spirit indeed!"

Rampion (Huxley/Lawrence) is more of an earthy romantic. On one page he recommends "renunciation of mental self-consciousness and abandonment to instinct." A few pages later he says, "The moment you allow speculative truth to take the place of felt instinctive truth as a guide to living, you ruin everything." Having thus identified himself with Rousseau and the romantics, he then contradicts himself by saying something that identifies him with Babbitt and the humanists, namely: "A man's a creature on a tightrope, walking delicately, equilibrated, with mind and consciousness and spirit at one end of his balancing pole and all that's unconscious and earthy and mysterious at the other."

Clearly, if the tightrope walker were to follow Rampion's earlier advice and abandon himself to instinct, renouncing mental self-consciousness and speculative truth, he soon would be nothing but a splatter on the pavement.

Babbitt classified most people as living on one or more of three planes: naturalist, humanist, and religious. Rousseau was to him a romantic naturalist. For the scientific naturalists Babbitt had more respect because they at least believed in reason and discipline, if only in pursuit of physical phenomena, but he could be rough with them when they tried to set up science in the place of philosophy and religion, as he maintained John Dewey had done. He attacked them on the ground that they were not scientific when they denied the reality of moral and spiritual facts.

WHERE BABBITT AND PLATO WERE WRONG

On the positive side Babbitt was more difficult to follow. He seemed to feel that Christianity was "symbolically . . . but not literally true." His favorite characters were Aristotle and Buddha. He was not foolish enough to back reason exclusively against feeling and imagination. With Pascal he agreed that "the imagination disposes of everything." What he wanted was "the ethical imagination"—that is, an imagination at once sobered by respect for the universal and the ideal, yet intoxicated by the romantics' wonder for the new and the strange. This is a difficult formula, but Babbitt showed that it had been realized in the work of the classic authors—Homer, Pindar, Sophocles, Virgil, Dante, Shakespeare, and Milton.

The problem is: Can you fashion this formula into something you can live by? To rephrase Gilbert, of Gilbert and Sullivan fame, if you took the books of ten classic authors and ten classical moralists, boiled them over a slow flame for ten years, and removed the scum, would a happy little humanist be the residuum?

Babbitt himself did not seem to be sure. He distrusted the extremism of the religious mentality but still had to admit that "though religion can get along without humanism, humanism cannot get along without religion." At another point he emphasized "the nothingness and helplessness" of human nature and "its dependence on a higher power." He admired Christianity because he felt its essential virtue was humility.

Babbitt's view of the good life and the good person did suffer from coolness and an accent on the negative, however. He quoted with approval a comment by Edmund Burke on Goethe's identification of evil with "the spirit that always says 'no.'" Burke said that this criterion would throw out "ninety percent of the virtues."

This view was a far cry from Christ, who summed up the law and the prophets in two commandments, love of God and love of neighbor. Not "thou shalt not" but "thou shalt." Humility was not king, though it might be queen. The greatest of these commandments was love.

I recently went back and read Rousseau with more detachment than I had read him at Harvard. Somewhat to my surprise I found him to be an eccentric and highly inconsistent, self-styled "Christian" who despised Voltaire and the Encyclopedists for their unbelief and once described himself as "the only man in France who believes in God." His writing is full of sensible and corny bromides, together with some foolish statements such as those Babbitt seized on and some ringing prose that did much to prepare the ground for democratic government. For example: "It is plainly contrary to the law of nature, however defined, that children should command old men, fools wise men, and that the privileged few should gorge themselves with superfluities, while the starving multitudes are in want of the bare necessities of life."

The opening line of his *Social Contract* has a revolutionary clang to it, anticipating the closing lines of the *Communist Manifesto:* "Man is born free, and everywhere he is in chains."

One might concede that Rousseau's exaggerations as to the basic goodness of human nature served a useful purpose in persuading people to trust themselves with democratic process and to throw off the oppressive structures of monarchy. I concluded that Babbitt had been a little unfair to Rousseau, but I remained persuaded that he had a profoundly beneficial influence on me. His lucid distinctions and definitions were precisely what I needed at the time.

NOT BY GREAT BOOKS ALONE

One night I was sitting in my room in Lowell House reading one of those books called *The Making of the Modern Mind*, or some such title. There must be a dozen of them at least. Written in a crisp, dogmatic style, it gave readers the feeling that everything was pretty right and tight and simple as long as they stuck to reason. I put the book down and said to myself, "I will be a rationalist. I will believe what is clearly evident to my reason, and I will not believe what is not clearly evident."

The trouble was that Babbitt had made clearly evident to my reason that people cannot live successfully on that plane, but must either sink below reason to the level of their emotions or rise above it to the level of ethical insight and perception. The question was, How can I acquire ethical insight and perception? Babbitt's answer was, "By a study of the great books." But can a man live by great books alone?

Mark Twain said, "a classic is something that everybody wants to have read, but nobody wants to read." One day I was reading Dante's *Divine Comedy* in the Lowell House library. I was sitting in an easy chair and began to doze off, so I transferred to a hard chair at one of the tables. That kept me going for another half hour, but then my head was down on my hands, and I was gone. My head resting on the wrists cut off the circulation, and the pain woke me up. I shook myself. If I was going to sleep, I might as well go up to bed, but it was still afternoon. I got up and wandered into the fiction section, looking for something that would keep me awake. I picked up a modern novel, opened it at random, and found myself in the middle of an erotic passage. Suddenly I was sleepy no longer. I took the book up to my room and read it all night. When dawn came, I went out and sat on a bench by the Charles, still reading and occasionally looking up to admire the gulls flying over the river in the early sunlight.

I don't remember a single thing in that book or the title or the author. I would have stayed and finished it, but Wallace Fowlie came along on his way to early mass at the Anglo-Catholic monastery a little way up the river and invited me to go along. It was a beautiful chapel, done in the best of taste, and the service was simple and moving. I came out feeling refreshed, cleaner than when I went in, and persuaded of the difficulty of absorbing ethical insight from the great books, the comparative facility of going to church, and the even greater facility of getting absorbed in an erotic book.

Another example of my engagement with great books and one that is wet, or at least damp, with my own heart's blood: not far into sophomore year I received a Dear John letter. The lovely piano player had fallen for a young man who bore an uncanny resemblance to Joel McCrea, the movie actor. Being cast off in favor of somebody who looks like Joel McCrea is a painful experience. Moved by this pain and Doolin's promptings, I began to read Plato with more than usual attention. I sat at my desk in Lowell R-31, a volume of Plato before me, and I said to myself, "This is working. I feel better already. I am really beginning to rise from *phenomena* (appearances) to *noumena* (realities). I am going up the ladder of love from the less beautiful to the more beautiful. I am getting out of the world of shadows on the wall of the cave, out into the light of the sun and the real world of Ideas. I am progressing from the Many to the One."

The next summer I went back to our cottage on the River, and I told myself that if I saw my piano player again or I did not see her again, it was all the same. I was cured of my fever, and I went to bed one night on the small porch upstairs overlooking the river. The lights went out in the house below and in the neighbors' cottages. Darkness and stillness descended upon the river and upon my small porch. I fell asleep but soon was awakened by the sound of a motorboat approaching our dock, apparently bringing some of our neighbors home from a party.

I stared out into the dark to see who they might be. As the boat came closer and was illuminated by its own running lights, I recognized it. I heard the sound of voices saying good-bye, then, quite clearly, the sound of a girl's voice, and I knew that it was hers. I didn't even see her. I didn't even hear what she said. All I heard was the sound of her voice, but that was enough. Plato, Babbitt, Doolin, Dante, Sophocles, Shakespeare, Homer, Virgil, Buddha, Aristotle— all the classical poets, philosophers, and heavy-duty thinkers in the world might as well never have existed, might as well never have written a word.

None of them could save me. The only thing that could save me was another swig of the love potion. I fell for Sally, another tall, beautiful blonde. She was no more interested than Montclair had become, but she was easier to forget, and in forgetting her I forgot both of them.

The truth was that I was even more helpless than Babbitt had warned me that I was. And Plato was wrong when he identified knowledge and virtue—when he said that it was enough to know what is right in order to do it. Aristotle was correct in his simple comment on this statement: the facts are otherwise.

JESUS CHRIST, HONEST WITNESSES, HONEST MEMORIES

What do we have so far? We have a competitive, energetic, self-absorbed young man who was born with the capacity to enjoy a wide variety of experience. Although he seems fairly well adjusted, he has not recovered entirely from the humiliation suffered in prep school when a funny twist of fate subjected him to the indignity of being called "Jesus" by his schoolmates. This experience leaves him with a flaw, but also perhaps an advantage. If death is the final humiliation, which none can escape but few really anticipate, then those who have experienced some form of mini-death by way of an intense humiliation of this kind might gain some dividends in "ethical insight and perception." Possible.

His situation therefore might make him receptive to religion, but he is also aware of the contempt into which religion has fallen among most of the contemporary intelligentsia. By another twist of fate his path falls across that of a man, Doolin, who introduces him to other men, from Plato to Babbitt, who persuade him that religious faith is by no means contemptible.

Somewhere about this point he opens the Bible and reads the Gospel. He reads all four Gospels. He notes some inconsistencies and contradictions, but nothing that cannot be accepted as the understandable disagreement of honest witnesses or the understandable failure of honest memories. In fact, the retention of the inconsistencies and contradictions is a tribute to the honesty of the early church that set its seal of approval on those Gospels.

There are also many consistencies and agreements—notably, that a poor Jew named Jesus lived in Palestine and that this man had extraordinary powers of speaking and healing. "Powerful in word and deed." These powers attracted a following, especially among the poor. He claimed to have a special and unique relationship to God, and this claim, together with his denunciations of corruption in high places, brought down upon him the wrath of the Jewish and Roman power structures. He therefore was crucified, and, the central and most basic point of agreement among the witnesses, several days after his crucifixion he rose from the dead and appeared to his disciples in a form that seems to have been alternately tangible and intangible.

The internal evidence has credibility. The evangelists write like conscientious reporters. The detail is realistic—it has the ring of reality, of truth—and much of it is unflattering to the founders of the Christian community. For example, it highlights Peter's denials and the apostles' mental and spiritual lapses. The zeal and missionary success of those same fallible men, revealed in the Epistles and the Acts of the Apostles, give further evidence of the strength of their conviction that Christ rose from the dead, appeared to them, and remains alive.

While our Harvard undergrad is thinking about this, he is going to Christ Church on the Cambridge Common and singing in the choir, for pay, for the nice middle-class and upper-middle-class Christians among whom he was born and raised. He begins to listen a little more attentively to the sermons of the rector and of various visiting preachers who are of the liberal Episcopal persuasion. He gets the impression that these preachers do not take too seriously the teachings of the creed that all of us recite together during the service. The folks in the pews, in effect, are encouraged to pick and choose those teachings that suit their fancy, a sort of cafeteria Episcopalianism. The young man thinks that this approach does not make much sense, that a proper church ought to have some teaching authority that commands respect, that is recognized as having the right and power to teach with authority and is not afraid to use that authority. And while he is thinking along these lines, he is taking a course entitled "The Intellectual History of the Middle Ages."

PREDESTINATION: AN INTELLECTUAL HEADACHE

Although the philosophy department offered no course in the thought of Thomas Aquinas or of any medieval philosopher, the history department was not quite so prejudiced, making available such a course taught by Charles Taylor, master of Adams House, a tall, lean, hawk-nosed man who himself looked like a medieval knight.

Taylor introduced us to Augustine, and Augustine introduced us to his own concerns about predestination and free will, based largely on his reading of St. Paul's Epistle to the Romans. We discussed these subjects in class, and I proceeded to contract an intellectual headache that lasted for about a week. It revolved around the question, "If God knew from the beginning of time (recognizing that with God there is no time) that Johnny Jones was going to shoot his dear old mother on the night of November 21, 1933, how could it be maintained that Johnny was free not to shoot his dear old mother?" Or, "If certain people are predestined by God to be saved and others to be damned, must we not, as Calvin did, deny free will? And doesn't that make God basically unfair and irrational?"

Of course, if we read St. Paul carefully, it becomes evident that my headache sprang from a misunderstanding of what concerned him, for he was not so much dealing with the salvation or damnation of individual Jews, but rather with their predestination as a people fated, in the main, to reject Christ as the Messiah.

At any rate I was worried about some legitimate questions. In this mood I went to Widener Library and consulted the *Catholic Encyclopedia*. Just why or how I came to do this I do not recall. I read two articles signed J. Pohle, a Jesuit professor of dogmatic theology at Breslau (later Wroclaw) University. One of the articles was on grace, the other on predestination.

I have a vivid memory of the experience, including just where I was sitting, facing west at one of the tables in the big reading room near the windows that look out toward Memorial Church. When I came to Pohle's statement that the Catholic Church teaches that all are given sufficient grace to be saved and that "grace is condemned to unfruitfulness only in the event of the free resistance of the will," I stopped reading the article on grace. That was enough for me. My sense of fairness was satisfied.

In the article on predestination Pohle distinguished between the Calvinist view and the Catholic view by way of two Latin phrases that I found peculiarly clarifying as well as reassuring. He wrote that Calvin believed in *praedestinatio ante praevisa merita* (predestination before foreseen merits), a teaching that effectively negates free will, whereas the Catholic Church holds to *praedestinatio post praevisa merita* (predestination after foreseen merits). He quoted St. Ambrose, "He did not predestine before he foreknew, but for those whose merits he foresaw he predestined the reward."

Thinking about this statement, I conceived a pleasantly anthropomorphic image of God as a man sitting in a balloon suspended over the River of Life. Because, however, this figure is not a man or a woman, but God, and because with God there is no time, no past or future, but everything is present, God sees and knows simultaneously everything that has happened, is happening, or will happen on the river. God knows the speed and direction of all currents, the location of all rocks. God knows the size and capabilities of all boats that proceed down the rapids of the river and, most important, precisely how the free will, intellect, nerves, and muscles of the men and women who guide their individual little boats will react to the rocks and whirlpools of the river as well as to the assistance (grace) that God gives them. Then, knowing all that, God predestines how they will come out, whether they are wrecked along the way, get stuck on a sandbar, or arrive safely at the mouth of the river and float serenely into the Sea of Paradise.

My headache was gone. I walked out of Widener Library into the Yard, not with a sense of having been born again but with a profound sense of gratitude to the Catholic Church for having produced a book like the *Catholic Encyclopedia* and a theologian like J. Pohle and two Latin phrases that could preserve my faith in the fact of my own freedom, on the one hand, and the basic intelligence and decency of God, on the other.

Out of that gratitude I went to St. Paul's Church and asked to see a priest. A pleasant young man, Father Greene, proceeded to instruct me in the Catholic faith. When I informed my family, Father was so upset that he wrote an angry letter to the dean of Harvard complaining about Doolin and told me that if I insisted on being received into the Roman Catholic Church, he would insist on withdrawing me from Harvard. This ultimatum rather appealed to my sense of melodrama, but I felt I should at least inform Father Greene. He in turn asked the pastor, a Monsignor Hickey, for guidance and the monsignor advised me to wait to become a Catholic until after graduation.

Being then more receptive to the counsel of monsignori than I have since become, I agreed and did not officially become a Catholic until after graduation in June 1935, when I was received at the altar of a church on Pineapple Street in Brooklyn Heights. My witnesses were the housekeeper and the sexton, who put down his broom for a few minutes to stand beside me.

6

The ACTU and the CIO

> The first and immediate apostles of the workers must
> themselves be workers.
>
> —Pope Pius XI, *Quadragesimo Anno*

IN 1948 Kermit Eby, research and education director of the CIO, resigned with a double-barreled blast at both Communist and Catholic factions in that organization. He said: "There are two extremes or poles of power attraction in the CIO, the Communist pole and the ACTU [Association of Catholic Trade Unionists] pole. Both receive their impetus and inspiration from without the CIO. Both believe the control of the CIO is part of the larger struggle for control of the world."

Eby's general conclusion was the familiar "a plague on both your houses." This raising of the ACTU to a kind of equality of evil with the Communist Party was far more flattering than we in the ACTU ever deserved. The ACTU never controlled or exercised dominant influence in a single CIO international union. (Most U.S. unions have locals in Canada and therefore call themselves "internationals.") During the 1940s the Communist Party controlled or exercised dominant influence in fifteen internationals with approximately 1.4 million members. With a few more votes they might have gained control of the United Auto Workers (UAW) with 1 million members, the largest union in the CIO, and then would have been in a position to take over the CIO itself. At that time the CIO had thirty-nine internationals and claimed 5.4 million members.

"Control of the world"? I don't recall anyone mentioning that objective at our meetings. "Receive their impetus and inspiration from outside the CIO" was maybe closer to the truth. I suppose this could be said of anyone who became active in the CIO for any reason other than self-interest, anyone whose activity was in some way motivated by Christianity, Marxism, Leninism, socialism, vegetarianism, or any other *ism*.

I was one of the founders of ACTU, worked for it full time for five years, and wrote for its national newspaper for about twenty. If a man as knowledgeable as Kermit Eby thought we were "a pole of power attraction" comparable to the Communist Party, perhaps it is incumbent on me to explain how this perception came about and how much, or how little, truth there was to it.

Garry Wills once tore me apart because I dared to pontificate on the meaning of a papal encyclical without having read it in the original Latin. He had a point. At the CW we were not that scholarly. Dorothy thought it would be useful for me to teach a class in the latest labor encyclical at the CW's Workers School, so in November 1936 I began meeting with a few zealous souls on Tuesday evenings in our storefront on Mott Street.

I started each session with a passage from Pius XI's *Quadragesimo Anno,* published in 1931 on the occasion of the fortieth anniversary of the first labor encyclical, *Rerum Novarum,* by Leo XIII. Although I was dealing strongly from ignorance, I did have the use of a good commentary by Father Raymond Miller that appeared in the Redemptorist magazine *The Liguorian.* I stayed at least a month ahead of the class.

In the first issue of *The Catholic Worker* in 1933 Dorothy had written that the purpose of publishing the paper was "to popularize and make known the encyclicals of the Popes in regard to social justice." Peter described our goal as "making the encyclicks click," misspelling the word, though it may have been intentional.

Our view of papal statements was not so sophisticated as to question the inconsistency of lauding certain documents while brushing aside others, such as Pius IX's reactionary *Syllabus of Errors* or Leo XIII's, Pius X's, or Pius XI's conservative positions on certain subjects. At that time few of us, and certainly not I, would have questioned the antisocialist stands of all four.

We were pragmatic about it. Not cynical, but pragmatic. We acknowledged the popes as our spiritual fathers. Fathers could be wrong, so wrong that they must be ignored, but ordinarily the father's authority should be respected and especially when he agreed with us. On the social and economic questions that concerned us, the popes agreed with us more often than not, or we with them more often than not. Also, we were not unmindful of the fact that many Catholics, in

particular the clergy, looked on papal statements as highly authorita-
tive. Monsignor Reynold Hillenbrand, the brilliant young rector of
Mundelein Seminary in Chicago, which was turning out more progressive priests than any other seminary in the United States, told me
once that he thought papal encyclicals were pretty close to infallible.
Ergo, we at the CW used pro-labor, anticapitalist statements in the
encyclicals for all they were worth, and sometimes in our use we
leapfrogged over logical argument and factual evidence into lazy appeals to authority.

THE ENCYCLICAL AS CLUB

When we were dealing with antilabor pastors or prelates, or even
with nonunion Catholic workers, the encyclicals, rolled up into one
or two handy quotations, made a club useful for either offense or
defense, and they were especially valuable when we were being attacked as "Communists," which was fairly often.

Quadragesimo Anno was not the most exciting reading in the
world. Like most papal documents, it tended to be abstract and
marked by a kind of Pollyanna optimism and defensiveness about
things Catholic that might be called looking at the church through
purple-colored glasses. For example, in discussing the departure of
many Catholic workers to the ranks of socialism, Pius XI lamented
that some Catholics "out of greed for gain do not shame to oppress
the workingman [and] even abuse religion itself, cloaking their unjust
imposition under its name." He nevertheless insisted that "the whole
history of the Church clearly shows . . . that these appearances [of
taking sides with the wealthy and being little moved by the sufferings
of the poor] were undeserved and unjust."

The whole history of the church clearly shows nothing of the kind,
although the record is not as one-sided as most Marxists have maintained. What it shows is a record of behavior that was too often identified with the interests of the rich and powerful, not only in the past
but today, right now, when the administrators of Catholic universities
and hospitals hire expensive lawyers to help them bust unions or to
deny their employees the right to join unions and bargain collectively,
rights that the popes' statements have affirmed repeatedly.

Also, Karl Marx's radical statements in the *Communist Manifesto* preceded by forty-three years Leo XIII's radical statements in *Rerum Novarum*. It is true that in 1848, the date of the *Manifesto*, Wilhelm Emmanuel von Ketteler, a German aristocrat who was bishop of Mainz, condemned capitalism and defended trade unions against the criticism of those pious conservatives who said that they were nefarious instruments of atheistic revolutionaries.

"The air we breathe," the bishop said, "remains God's air, though breathed by an atheist. It is the same with unionism—it is essentially Christian and rests upon the divine order of things, though those who favor it most do not see the finger of God in it."

He remained a loyal friend of labor and the poor and even consulted Ferdinand Lassalle, the German socialist leader, on how best to establish workers' cooperatives, which were Lassalle's favorite kind of socialism. By the measure of both words and deeds, Ketteler can be described accurately as the first Catholic socialist bishop. For his pains, however, he did not receive Marx's gratitude or even his civil respect. Marx wrote, "Whenever they see fit, these dogs (for instance, Bishop Ketteler in Mainz, the clerics at the Düsseldorf Congress, etc.) flirt with the labor question." If Ketteler's support for labor and the poor was no more than "flirtation," it would be interesting to know Marx's definition of a full-scale marriage.

I learned that the workers did have their champions in the church during the nineteenth century, but they were few. When Leo finally spoke out in 1891, he struck some blows that had a solid impact against the capitalist system. He denounced "the inhumanity of employers and the unbridled greed of competitors" and added, "The whole process of production as well as trade in every kind of goods has been brought almost entirely under the power of a few, so that a very few rich, and exceedingly rich, men have laid a yoke almost of slavery on the unnumbered masses of nonowning workers."

Forty years later, in *Quadragesimo Anno*, the encyclical I was teaching in that CW storefront on Mott Street, Pius XI decried "the power and economic domination that is concentrated in the hands of a few" and called attention to the fact that "this accumulation of power is the *characteristic* note of the modern economic order" (emphasis added).

I used to quote passages like these when I was lecturing to Catholic audiences, without identifying them, and ask the people whether they were Catholic or Communist statements. Invariably I got unanimous or nearly unanimous votes in favor of Communist statements. Which proves something about how seriously they were regarded in those echelons of the church below the rank of supreme pontiff.

Unlike Marx, Pius XI denied that the wage contract was essentially unjust or inevitably exploitative, but he recommended that it be modified by a contract of partnership so that the workers could share "in the ownership or the management or the profits." He proposed that the economy be organized and governed by representatives of labor, management, and government—a kind of industrial democracy.

Thirty years later John XXIII was to go further in demanding structural changes in the economy, but in 1936 Leo XIII and Pius XI were enough for us at the CW. We felt confident that through them the church had condemned the basic principle of capitalism—namely, production primarily for profit rather than for the satisfaction of human needs, the dubious notion that the greed of the few can be trusted safely to promote the welfare of the many. In these popes' support for trade unionism, I saw a signpost that pointed the way for me personally.

CHAMPIONS AND CRITICS

The fact that in the United States labor also had its Catholic champions and capitalism its critics encouraged us further. Cardinal Gibbons of Baltimore had made a special trip to Rome to stop a condemnation of the old Knights of Labor, as proposed by Archbishop Corrigan of New York on the ground that it was a secret society.

Gibbons wrote to Cardinal Simeoni in the Vatican, quoting Cardinal Manning of England, another friend of labor: "In the future era the Church has no longer to deal with princes and parliaments, but with masses, with the people." And Gibbons shrewdly added, "To lose influence over the people would be to lose the future altogether." Not the loftiest motive for defending the poor, but irrefutable.

When the Great Depression struck, even the aristocratic Cardinal O'Connell of Boston, recalling his roots in a textile worker's family in Lowell, was moved to indignation: "The greedy capitalist, the tyrannical boss has had his brutal day." The conservative Cardinal Hayes of New York protested that the capitalist system was "built upon a foundation of selfishness."

The more progressive Cardinal Mundelein of Chicago, an FDR supporter, added a note of mea culpa that anticipated the laments made by certain Latin American prelates of a later day: "We were too often drawn into an alliance with the wrong side. . . . Our place is beside the poor, behind the workingman."

Pius XI had said to Canon Cardijn, founder of the Young Christian Workers, "The great scandal of the nineteenth century was that the Church lost the working class." He was referring primarily to Europe. Down on Mott Street in 1936, we had reason to hope that, for the Roman Catholic Church in the United States at least, our efforts were not too little and too late.

When I started teaching my little class at the CW, I noticed a passage in *Quadragesimo Anno* that dealt with the popes' support of trade unions: "Side by side with these unions there should always be associations zealously engaged in imbuing and forming their members in the teaching of religion and morality so that they in turn may be able to permeate the unions with that good spirit that should direct them in all their activity."

At this time there was nothing like this connection between unions and religion in the United States and had not been since before World War I, when for a few years Father Peter Dietz of Cleveland had persuaded John Mitchell and other top labor leaders of the AFL to join him in organizing the Militia of Christ for Social Service.

In the fall of 1936 Dorothy wrote in the paper, "The president of the Edison Electrical Workers Union is a good friend of the Catholic Worker and has been holding occasional round-table discussions with the editors on the subject of organization."

The man she refers to was Marty Wersing, a bespectacled, solid young labor leader who was to have a big impact on me, the CW, and the labor movement. She quoted him: "There are 40,000 Edison employees [in New York City] and the membership of the union is comparatively very small. . . . Most of the utility workers are Catholics, and their indifference to organization means that the most active members in the union are apt to be Communists, who have made a religion of their devotion to the trade union movement."

"SAVE THE TRADE UNION MOVEMENT"

In this same article Dorothy concluded: "Christ our Brother started with twelve men. Let us not lose sight of that fact. A few strong and ardent Catholic men can save the trade union movement in this country. Join your union and see that it is a workers' union and not a company union. Work for it. Study the history of the labor movement, not only here in America, but all over the world."

Encouraged by the pope, by the Abbess (that is, Dorothy), and, perhaps even more to the point, by a real live labor leader who knew what was possible in the real live labor movement, I began thinking about the possibility of a new organization that might include women as well as men. Then came the seamen's strike, and I was convinced that something should be done. We invited union members that we knew, and on a Saturday afternoon, February 27, 1937, eleven of us met around the kitchen table at the CW and organized something we decided to call the Catholic Association of Trade Unionists.

Joining Marty, Bill Callahan, and me were another utility worker, the level-headed Ed Squitieri; Mike Gunn, a fiery little Scotsman from the Brushmakers Union; Joe Hughes, the seaman we worried about that stormy night on Tenth Avenue; Larry Delaney, an engaging young redhead from *Life* magazine and the Newspaper Guild; as well as two carpenters, a teamster, and a young Italian from the International Ladies' Garment Workers Union (ILGWU) whose names are lost in the mists of time.

Marty was the only one who held any official position in a union, and his local was small and without a contract, so we bore little resemblance to Father Dietz's organization of top AFL officials. The group assigned Marty and me to draw up a provisional constitution. I was just smart enough to know how ignorant I was, so I sat down at a typewriter and told Marty to start dictating, and thus we defined the purpose of the organization:

To bring to Catholic workingmen and women a knowledge of the social teaching of the Catholic Church as laid down by Leo XIII and Pius XI by

    A. Enrolling into this Association all Catholic trade unionists.
    B. Promoting unionization among unorganized Catholic workers.

   C. Applying Catholic doctrine to the problems of the trade union
   movement.

   What the last objective meant was not entirely clear to us. The
next Saturday afternoon the group met again and picked a committee
consisting of Marty, several others, and me with instructions to digest
the two labor encyclicals and other expressions of Catholic social
teaching, such as the writings of Monsignor John A. Ryan, the American church's foremost economist, whom the anti-Semitic radio priest,
Father Charles Coughlin, had sarcastically tagged with the title
"Right Reverend New Dealer." Ryan had written *Program of Social
Reconstruction,* which the U.S. bishops adopted in 1919. James B.
Carey, secretary of the CIO, described this extraordinary document
as "a more radical program than that of the CIO." Of its eleven major
recommendations ten were voted into federal law, mostly during the
New Deal era of Roosevelt in the 1930s. The only one not voted into
law was "participation of labor in management and a wider distribution of ownership in the stock of corporations."
   Our committee labored and brought forth a program we called
"The Rights and Duties of the Worker." The next issue of *The Catholic Worker* included a report—which, judging from the melodramatic
language, I probably wrote—that "the founders of the Catholic Association of Trade Unionists intend to steer a straight course between
reactionary, corrupt forces in labor and the rising tide of United
Front revolutionaries. . . . It is not the purpose of the Association to
foster a dual union movement. Members of all bona fide trade unions
are eligible for membership, whether AFL, CIO or otherwise."
   In short, the intention was not to create Catholic unions, but to
provide a religious and educational organization for the Catholic
members of existing unions, an organization that was going to take
on the capitalists, the Marxists, and the racketeers and make the
world safe for Catholic social theory, all at once and immediately.
   Shortly afterward I went uptown to the Catholic Chancery to inform Cardinal Hayes's chancellor of our existence as a new Catholic
organization. He was Monsignor Francis McIntyre, who later became
the ultraconservative cardinal archbishop of Los Angeles, so conservative that he banned *Commonweal* from the seminary and churches
of his archdiocese. To me in 1937 he was friendly, suggesting only
that we change the name to Association of Catholic Trade Unionists

so that it would not sound like an official organization of the Catholic Church. Otherwise, he had no comment.

Because we expected to be making trouble, I could not object to his suggestion. Thus, we became the ACTU rather than the CATU. We had to admit that it made a better acronym.

RIGHTS AND DUTIES

The first meeting in April approved the program. Whose idea it was to shape the program in the form of rights and duties I do not remember. Again, this approach was off the beaten track of U.S. labor history, which has been strong on rights but weaker on duties. The program went like this:

Basing our stand on the papal encyclicals, the writings of other recognized Catholic authorities and the basic principles of common sense and justice, we believe that:

The worker has a right to—

1. Job security.
2. An income sufficient to support himself and family in reasonable comfort. [*Reasonable comfort* was a common phrase in Catholic social theory. Presumably it was to contrast with the "unreasonable comfort" of the rich and greedy.]
3. Collective bargaining through union representatives freely chosen.
4. A share in the profits after just wage and return to capital have been paid.
5. Strike and picket peacefully for just cause.
6. A just price for the goods he buys.
7. Decent working hours.
8. Decent working conditions.

And that the worker has a duty to—

1. Perform an honest day's work for an honest day's pay.
2. Join a bona fide union.
3. Strike only for just cause and after all other legitimate means have been exhausted.
4. Refrain from violence.
5. Respect property rights.
6. Abide by just agreements freely made.

7. Enforce strict honesty and a square deal for everybody inside his union. [We later changed this statement to "strict honesty and democracy inside his union."]

8. Cooperate with decent employers who respect rights to bring about a peaceful solution of industrial war by the setting up of guilds for the self-regulation of industry and producer cooperatives in which the worker shares as a partner in the ownership, management or profits of the business in which he works.

Several things are noteworthy about this list, other than the weak grammar and the sexist language. (At that time the labor movement was a very sexist place. It remains so, but far less now than it was then. At least we included the word *women* in our preamble.) In the list most of the rights are nouns, and the duties are verbs that involve doing or refraining from doing something. The word *guilds* was a synonym for what Pius XI had in mind in *Quadragesimo Anno* and was identified more accurately as vocational groups or industry councils. The idea was to make it possible for workers to share, through their unions, in the control and decision making both at the level of plant and industry as well as at the level of the national economy. Communists and others labeled this idea corporatism and fascism, a charge that I deal with in detail in chapter 9.

Finally, the reference to "producer cooperatives" was inaccurate because in a true cooperative the workers, operating on a one-person-one-vote basis, share democratically in the ownership and control of the enterprise. Simple profit sharing should in no way have been confused with a producer or worker cooperative, which, incidentally, was the favored form of enterprise among Christian and Lassallean socialists before Marx.

In his early *National Review* phase Garry Wills questioned our dependence on two sentences of *Quadragesimo Anno* to support the workers' right to a share in the profits. While dismembering me in his book *Politics and Catholic Freedom,* he pointed out, correctly, that the Vatican's English translator had translated those two sentences incorrectly. Some years later, however, in the encyclical *Mater et Magistra,* good Pope John XXIII gave us some *post factum* support not only for the right to profit sharing, but also, in the case of the more prosperous "large- and middle-size productive enterprises," for a right, as "a demand of justice" *(iustitiae officio),* to "some share in the enterprise." He added that one way to meet this demand of justice was that "workers gradually come to possess a share in the ownership of their companies." The Latin, Garry, is *"opifices in partem possessionis sensim veniunt suae cuiusque societatis."* This "share in the ownership" would ensure, of course, a share in the profits "after just wage and return to capital have been paid," as our Right No. 4 clearly stated, naturally implying that there is a limit to a "just return to capital," a limit that Thomas Aquinas explicitly defined when he wrote that "profit-making can become justifiable, provided this is meant to fulfill some necessary and worthy purpose" (*Summa Theologiae* [Blackfriars, 1972], 38: 229]). I don't have the Latin for this, but the Dominicans at Blackfriars include some pretty good Latin scholars.

Wills also questioned the moral duty to join a union, as have many conservative Catholic priests, nuns, and laymen before and after him, especially in the administration of Catholic hospitals, schools, and universities. The ground for this plank was the obligation imposed by the mandate of social justice, which requires that each one of us contribute what is necessary to the common good, as distinguished from distributive justice, the virtue of giving to each whatever is his or her due.

The argument then revolves around the question whether union membership is or is not necessary to the common good. The encyclicals were ambiguous, even though they were very clear on the worker's *right* to join a union. Eventually the Canadian bishops appeared to resolve the issue by declaring that union membership is an obligation under ordinary circumstances. Actually, in the real world of 1937 it made little difference whether workers had a moral right to a share in the profits or a moral duty to join a union. The questions more relevant then were simpler questions, such as, Do workers have a right to a living wage? Should this right come before excess profits? What are excess profits? What is a living wage? What is reasonable comfort? Do workers have a right to join a union? Should government protect this right?

The ACTU had a full work schedule trying to deal with these questions. We agreed on one thing: it was not enough for us to sit around the kitchen table at Mott Street. We began publishing our own weekly newspaper, *The Labor Leader*, first in mimeograph form and then as a printed tabloid, the first newspaper in the country devoted exclusively to labor news and Catholic social teaching and commentary. Here we began to diverge from the CW and Dorothy's leadership, whose interests went beyond the labor movement to agrarianism, pacifism, liturgy, spirituality, and so on. In fact, within a few years, as the labor movement picked up members and power with the onset of World War II, Dorothy's interest in the union movement did tail off a bit, though she retained her devotion to *la causa* of the United Farm Workers.

THE POPE ON A PICKET LINE

We also began looking around for opportunities to prove that we meant what we wrote in the paper. We did not have to look far. Saleswomen—many of them little more than girls—at the Woolworth stores in New York had gone on strike. Heywood Broun wrote about it in one of his columns, calling attention both to the miserable pittance given to the women—for some, less than $10 a week for six days on their feet—and to the fabulous fortune of Barbara Hutton, the Woolworth heiress. Barbara, or "Babs" as she was more commonly known to the American public, was young and beautiful then, and her face and love life were printed and reprinted in U.S. newspapers everywhere.

A New York society columnist, feeling that Broun had been unfair to Ms. Hutton, came to her defense, pointing out that she was really a nice person and, to the columnist's personal knowledge, had given $11 million to charity.

Down at the ACTU we discussed the strike, voted to support it, made up some crudely lettered signs, and went uptown to picket the big store on Fourteenth Street, just a brick's throw from Union Square, the favored hangout of New York radicals. One of our signs informed the world, "BABS GAVE $11 MILLION TO CHARITY, *BUT* 'THE WORKER IS NOT TO RECEIVE AS ALMS WHAT IS HIS DUE IN JUSTICE'—POPE PIUS XI."

This was probably the first time the pope had appeared on a U.S. picket line, so the sign made something of a stir, even for the jaded lefties over in Union Square. The quotation, incidentally, was not from *Quadragesimo Anno,* but from an encyclical that Pius XI had just published, whose Latin title is *Divini Redemptoris* and whose English title is *On Atheistic Communism.* I once analyzed this encyclical and found that one-quarter of it is devoted to the evils of communism, and three-quarters are devoted to the evils of capitalism and what should be done to correct them. It might well have been entitled *On Atheistic Capitalism.*

The Woolworth women, however, lost their strike. We did not have to look far for another strike to support. A few hundred yards away from the Fourteenth Street store, the women at Grant's 5&10 decided to have a sit-down. That was the year that the sit-down strike was sweeping the country. The success of the sit-down at General Motors in Michigan—owing largely to the restraint exercised by Governor Frank Murphy, a reader of *The Catholic Worker*—led to similar strikes in all sorts of unlikely places. One of our members, an Edison lineman named Bill Kennedy and a member of Marty Wersing's union, sat down on top of a fifty-foot utility pole on the main street of Flushing, Long Island—becoming a sort of latter-day Simeon the Stylite. Simeon, however, outdid Kennedy both in the height of his pole, sixty feet, and in the length of time he spent aloft, thirty-six years.

The ACTU's peculiar contribution to the Grant strike was for me to borrow a car and take the Catholic women to mass on Sunday morning, then sneak them back in again. This strike was more successful, winning a union contract and a 10 percent raise for most of the women.

The Supreme Court eventually outlawed the sit-down strike, and its vogue faded in labor circles. Some people maintained that it was a violation of the ACTU plank to respect property rights, but we did not look upon property rights as that simple or absolute. In fact, men such as Monsignor Ryan and Bishop Michael Gallagher of Detroit agreed with us, defending the morality of the sit-down in situations where workers were entirely dependent on their jobs and employers could afford to pay living wages but would not, thanks to their autocratic control and abuse of their property.

A Good Show, an Awful Hour, a Razor's Edge

The ACTU also got involved in several strikes called by the Newspaper Guild, the union that Broun had founded a few years earlier. One of these strikes was at the *Long Island Daily Press.* The editorial employees had decided that if the printers could make more money than the reporters by just reproducing in print what the geniuses in the city room had created, then there must be some good reason, and maybe the reason was the fact that the printers had a union but the geniuses did not. So they joined the Newspaper Guild and voted to strike.

The printers were sympathetic and assured the Newspaper Guild that if its members could put on a good show on the picket line, blocking the entrance and making it look dangerous for the printers to go to work, then they would stay out, and the paper would be unable to publish.

So we came out from New York to help put on a good show. The picket line numbered several hundred, and as it charged up against the front door of the plant to block the way, I was at the point of the lance and found myself pressed against the large stomach of a policeman in whose eyes I could read one word—*terror!*—as he fought to keep from being pushed bodily through the glass door. In the midst of this violent scene I suddenly was moved with compassion and began pushing back against the crowd with him to ease the pressure.

In any case it was a good show. The main questions in dispute were referred to an arbitration board on which sat a friend to both me and the ACTU, a wonderful priest named Father William Kelly, who was my confessor for many years. Thanks in part to him the strikers won a good settlement.

Another Newspaper Guild strike that year was at the *Brooklyn Eagle,* also a daily newspaper. It lasted for more than three months, and on at least ten occasions delegations from the CW and ACTU, sometimes ranging up to twenty members, crossed over the bridge to picket with the strikers. Bill Callahan, Marty Wersing, and I spoke at their meetings, and several Brooklyn priests supported them, including a prominent Coughlinite, Father Edward Lodge Curran, whose support was very helpful.

I remember the Brooklyn strike largely because of Joe Applegate, a great character and a tough little reporter who looked and sounded as though he had stepped out of Hecht and MacArthur's *Front Page.* On several evenings, as people were coming home from work, he and I and a wistful but gutsy striker named Peggy O'Reilly, who looked a little like Dorothy Gish, traveled around Brooklyn with a U.S. flag and a folding chair to stand on and held meetings on the street corners to tell people about the strike and urge them not to buy the paper.

Applegate always wound up his talk with the same peroration, which he had read somewhere in a book: "My friends, this strike is the greatest blow to be struck against the forces of tyranny and injustice since the French Revolution, when the poor people of Paris beat with bare hands against the iron gates of the Bastille and in one awful hour made satisfaction for centuries of kingly crime." As he worked himself into one final and awful frenzy, Peggy and I stood in the crowd, silent with admiration and wondering if the poor people of Brooklyn enjoyed his performance as much as we did. I don't remember how that strike came out, but I think the strikers won a Pyrrhic victory, with the paper closing sometime later.

Then there was the Gem Razor strike in Brooklyn, involving eight hundred workers, which was a kind of model for us. A little CIO union there needed help. The ACTU voted to support the strike, and we arranged for Father William Brennan, a local curate, to speak to the strikers, who were mostly Catholic. He gave a rousing talk, and we picketed with them and distributed copies of our paper, *The Labor Leader*. Copies of *The Daily Worker*, the Communist Party paper, also were distributed, and, in fact, we were concerned about Communist influence in the local that was running the strike.

Father Brennan and I went to see management and tried to talk them into granting what seemed to us the very modest demands of the strikers. When one striker and his family were evicted from their home for failure to pay their rent, we secured lodging for them through Catholic Charities.

The plant was shut tight, but after five weeks there was talk of management starting a back-to-work movement. At the next strike meeting the local union president announced the move and said, "If they try to open the plant, all of you have to be ready to get out on the line and break the goddamn neck of any goddamn scab that tries to go to work."

Being present at the meeting and hearing these words, I asked myself, "How can you reconcile this with Worker's Duty No. 4?" If the union were going to adopt a policy of organized violence, how could the ACTU go on supporting the strike? So I stood up and asked for the floor. I detailed the different kinds of assistance the ACTU had given the strike and explained that we probably would have to withdraw our support if the union started beating up people.

I also made the somewhat more dubious statement that violence was "a highly impractical and ineffective strike tactic." At any rate the threat to withdraw support worked. Another union leader made a motion that the union go on record as opposed to violence, "both individual and collective." A veteran organizer from the Mine Workers, whom John L. Lewis had sent up to help out, spoke in favor of nonviolence, and the motion passed unanimously.

Fortunately my theory of strike strategy was not tested. A few days later management gave in, and the thing was over. We had helped eight hundred workers get a decent contract and stop plans for wage cuts. One of the most promising leaders of the local, a young man named Joe Flynn, the one who had made the motion against violence, joined the ACTU and brought in several others with him. The only catch in the whole story is that within a few years the local came under Communist domination anyway.

NONVIOLENCE AS STRIKE STRATEGY

The Gem Razor strike did highlight the question, Is violence a necessary tactic in conducting an effective strike? Or did Dorothy Day and Gandhi have something important to contribute to strike strategy?

The issue is simply stated: sooner or later, especially in the earlier stages of organization, a striking union has to decide what to do when management tries to run the plant despite a strike and invites workers through the picket lines. If a worker believes that he can get into the plant without serious danger, the chances of preventing the plant from operating are not so good. That is the case for violence in a nutshell. Very simple.

The case for nonviolence is more complex and difficult to state without ultimately resorting to an appeal to notions such as faith, not to mention hope and charity. All these notions are difficult to express in terms that are understandable and appealing to someone who sees his job and perhaps his whole life being threatened by a scab.

Cesar Chávez is the only top labor leader I can recall from my years in the labor movement who adopted nonviolence as a basic principle and tactic. On at least one occasion, he almost ruined his health by a prolonged fast whose main objective was to discourage the use of violence by members of his union, the United Farm Workers. For Chávez, of course, nonviolence was an easier gospel to preach because the success of his strikes depended so much on public support and the boycott of nonunion grapes, wine, lettuce, tomatoes, and other fruits and vegetables. It is also worth noting that Chávez was a man of deep religious faith and that one of the last occasions on which Dorothy was arrested was on a Farm Workers picket line, where she was photographed in a wide straw hat and sun glasses, looking old and fragile.

For myself I can testify only that during my nearly twenty years of working actively in the labor movement, observing and sometimes participating in many strikes, on the one occasion when the use or nonuse of violence was a clear-cut issue, the act of faith paid off. Conversely, I might add that I do not recall a strike that I had anything to do with or was in a position to observe closely where the use of violence clearly made the difference between winning and losing.

The reason for that is also simple: the amount of force available to the employer is almost always superior, far superior, to that available to the union, so it makes sense to conclude, "If we're going to lose the battle of force anyway, why not take advantage of the weapons of nonviolence, the weapons of the spirit? What have we got to lose?" For the weapons of the spirit do have firepower in terms of public support, in terms of persuasion, in terms of a certain spiritual energy that sometimes can be stronger than goon squads and baseball bats. But still ultimately an act of faith. Not demonstrable by scientific proof.

FROM BROOKLYN SHIPYARD TO STOTTSVILLE TEXTILES

The ACTU supported about a dozen different strikes, mostly by new CIO unions. During a shipyard workers walkout in Brooklyn I spoke to the men in an open lot just off the waterfront and pointed out, as *The Catholic Worker* had, "the superiority of persuasion over violence and abuse when arguing with scabs." As I said that, a somewhat dazed and incredulous expression fell over the faces of the men who stood around the soapbox from which I addressed them. But neither violence nor nonviolence availed, and the men were forced to return to work without the union recognition for which they had struck.

On another occasion I took the train up the Hudson to Stottsville, New York, in answer to an appeal from the CIO's Textile Workers Union. Some five hundred members at Atlantic Mills, a subsidiary of the mighty Juilliard chain, had walked out because management refused to arbitrate a 12.5 percent wage cut or to sign a union contract. Shortly after the strike began, the local priest had spoken against the union from his pulpit at Sunday mass, which was the reason why the Textile Workers had appealed to us for help.

In his remarks the priest had said, "Strikes and unions are a detriment to the country. . . . The CIO is imbued with Communistic tendencies. . . . If a union is necessary, why can't we have a local union formed and controlled by our own men and women?" In other words, a company union. It turned out that the superintendent of the mill was a parishioner. So too were most of the workers, but their influence was not as weighty, it seemed, as a single superintendent's.

After talking to the union leaders, I went to see the priest, Father Daniel Horan, in his rectory. He received me cordially, listened attentively, gave me dinner, invited me to spend the night at the rectory, an invitation I gladly accepted, and arranged for me to see the superintendent the next day.

That night I spoke to a crowded meeting of the strikers and told them what men like Archbishop Edward Mooney of Detroit, Bishop Robert Lucey of San Antonio, and Monsignor Francis Haas had said in defense of the CIO. Bishop Lucey: "But now in the providence of God a better day has dawned for the teeming masses of the people. By enormous effort the CIO is lifting labor from its lethargy. Literally millions of semiskilled and unskilled wage earners are enrolling under the banner of organized labor."

I quoted the popes in support of the worker's right and need to join a trade union to win a wage that would be enough to support a family "in reasonable comfort." I stressed the advantage of a strong national union as against a weak local organization whose leaders would be dependent on the boss for their livelihood.

The response was good. As I spoke, looking down at those anxious faces, I could sense a kind of lightening of the atmosphere as the Catholics present began to realize that they could stop worrying about any conflict of loyalty between their union and their church.

The next morning I went to see Superintendent Boyer at the mill. My reception was not as enthusiastic as that by the workers or as cordial as that by Father Horan. Mr. Boyer had "nothing to say for publication." He obviously knew what I had said to the workers the previous night, and he was not pleased. Did it make a difference? Hard to say. The strike wound up with an agreement to submit the wage cut to an impartial arbitrator, which under the circumstances had to be considered a victory for the strikers.

SCULLY, DONAHUE, AND FATHER MONAGHAN

Several months after our little group met in the CW kitchen to organize the fledgling ACTU, I received a phone call from a lawyer. It was Ed Scully, a warm-hearted cynic with a game leg and now the first in a long line of graduates of Manhattan College, a Christian Brothers institution, who were moved to join us at the ACTU and do something about social injustice. Brother Justin, an extraordinary teacher and motivator, had motivated most of them to do so. They included George Donahue, John Sheehan, John Harold, Norman McKenna, Joe Conlon, and Vic LoPinto.

Ed introduced me to Danny Loughlin, a truck driver who had gotten Ed interested in fighting the common practice of paying drivers "under the hat"—namely, at less than the union scale, the difference being split with a union official on the take.

Through Ed I also met George Donahue, an embattled checker on the docks, a member of a corrupt local of the corrupt AFL International Longshoremen's Association (ILA), the personal fiefdom of Joe Ryan, the pious friend and beneficiary of the shipowners.

Ed, George, and Danny became devoted ACTU members and leaders and remained so for more than thirty years, as long as there was an ACTU to which they could be devoted. Ed later helped to organize the Catholic Labor Defense League, an organization of young lawyers who gave free legal aid to men and women who, like George and Danny, were trying to free themselves from exploitative employers or union leaders or both.

We needed a chaplain. I asked Dorothy if she knew any New York priests who were sympathetic to labor. It is significant that after eight months at the CW I should still have to ask such a question. She recommended Father John Monaghan, a professor of English at Cathedral College. I went to see him. What he lacked in size he made up in quickness of mind and tongue. He looked a little like an Irish leprechaun—a leprechaun possessed with a remarkable capacity for eloquence, laughter, compassion for all who suffered, and contempt for all persons and things that were phony, stupid, or unfair. His description of the Irish West Side waterfront where he grew up could serve as a description of life on the other side of the Hudson, the side immortalized in the film *On the Waterfront:*

> The present West Side docks are a jungle: matted growth of good trade unionism with graft and sabotage. In the open, families. In the undercover, beasts of prey. Some children of the old Irish dockers are still there, good, but poorer than their fathers in spirit and professions. Every people under heaven mingles in the daily shape-up and some of them look spit up from hell. Every one in the shape-up is coarsened by the all-covering racket that operates by the connivance of management, labor leaders, politicians and police. The saloons are now hangouts where the men talk from the side of the mouth about deals, cutins and dames. Shifty eyes X-ray the stranger at the bar. In these saloons the men drink to watch, to wait or to forget.
>
> In and out of this jungle slink men, bodily different, face-shaped the same. The young wolf-eyed, the old rat-faced. These men don't fight; they hunt in packs and kill in the dark. They kill for the racket, for the slick, softening brains who often eat at Cavanaugh's and sometimes pass the exclusive barriers of the Downtown New York Athletic Club.

Not a pretty picture.

ANOTHER IDEA: THE LABOR SCHOOL

Over the months our numbers increased. We moved from the CW to 191 Canal Street, just around the corner and a floor above the headquarters of a Chinese Communist organization. Ade Bethune, the CW artist, painted on the wall a magnificent mural that ran the length of our meeting room and showed Christ the Worker hand in hand with the workers of the world—white, black, brown, and yellow. Unfortunately, we could not take it with us when we moved again in 1938 to larger quarters a few blocks uptown at the corner of Lafayette and Spring Streets, this time over an Italian Tammany Club out of which came Carmine DeSapio, the man who ran New York some years later. The building also boasted a likeable, unkempt janitor, Rocky, whom John Sheehan of the Arrow Collar profile, another of our Manhattan College lawyers, once described as a man who "gets up in the morning, throws a little dirt in his face, and is refreshed and ready for the day."

Even though the labor movement then was a hopelessly male world, as I've noted, fortunately a few young women were willing to help us build the ACTU, march with us on picket lines, do tedious office work, sing with us, dance with us, and marry us. There was the inseparable duo from Metropolitan Life—Maggie McGarry, who married George Donahue, and Anne Prange, the shy, lovely blonde who became a nun and died young; Mary Berry, bulwark of the Utility Workers; Angie Leibinger Conlon, who mothered the distinguished conductor James Conlon and my godson Philip, a good Canadian radical and trade unionist; Lucy Squitieri; Dorothea Harold; Helen Haye Cort; Mary and Nina Conroy; and many others.

The ACTU idea spread rapidly through the country as the labor movement grew along with the growth of the war industry and more prosperous times. By 1940 we had ACTU chapters in New York, Detroit, Pittsburgh, Philadelphia, Chicago, Boston, Cleveland, San Francisco, and Oklahoma City. Most of them were doing similar things: urging Catholics to join unions, supporting strikes, and defending the CIO from the attacks of employers, Coughlinites, and the more intransigent AFL types.

An even more successful and contagious idea was the Catholic labor school. With the help of Father Ignatius Cox and his fellow Jesuits at Fordham, we had started a school in Fordham's downtown branch high up in the Woolworth Building. We charged no admission fee and opened the school to members of all religious faiths or none, although we required that applicants be members of a trade union. Courses included labor relations, labor history, labor ethics, parliamentary law, and public speaking. By the end of the term in June 1938 more than 340 students had enrolled, representing sixty-one different unions and including 81 students who held official positions in their unions. I know because I was the registrar.

The school was, I believe, another first of its kind in the United States and was typical of hundreds of similar schools that followed it in Catholic parishes and colleges all over the country. At one point there were nineteen parish schools in the New York archdiocese, eleven in Brooklyn, and forty-one in Detroit, to mention only three dioceses. By the late 1940s more than thirty dioceses had labor schools going. Jesuit colleges and schools were particularly active in this field, and the argument still goes on as to whether Father Phil Carey's Xavier Labor School on Sixth Avenue or the ACTU school was the first of its species.

This network of schools was a significant factor in developing a union leadership and membership in the United States that, by and large, tended to take its ideology from Catholic social teaching rather than from some branch of the Marxist left, which over the same period was making its greatest gains in U.S. labor history. These gains were most impressive in the CIO. We spent a great deal of time defending the CIO from charges that it was Communist dominated and a certain amount of time worrying lest it become so.

COMMUNISTS AND COUGHLINITES

Charges of Communist influence in the CIO came from many sources, but none gave us more trouble than those from Father Charles Coughlin and his fanatical followers. Through his mastery of the radio and the rabble rouse, this man had become the single most influential voice in the United States, with the possible exception of Roosevelt, and the single most influential voice among American Catholics, with the possible exception—and I stress possible—of the pope.

In the summer of 1937 Father Coughlin was telling Americans that no decent Catholic could belong to the CIO because it was a tool of Moscow teeming with atheistic Marxists who took their orders from "the Communist Central Committee of the United States." At the same time his followers in Michigan were organizing Christian unions that they called Workers Councils for Social Justice.

That was the summer that Antoine Allard, a visitor to the CW and the son of a Belgian baron, offered to pay my way to Paris to attend a congress of the Jeunesse ouvrière chrétienne (Young Christian Workers). Dorothy asked me to stay home, and I agreed. It seemed to us that the whole future of the U.S. labor movement might be hanging in the balance and that even small efforts to clarify the issues might be important in determining the outcome.

In *The Catholic Worker* for July 1937 I did a piece whose lead was, "What is the difference between the ACTU and Father Coughlin's new Christian unions?" The answer was in the headline "ACTU Prefers to Be Inside, Not Outside" and in the subhead "Why Surrender U.S. Labor Movement to Marxists Without a Struggle?" One paragraph read: "Granted there are Communists in the CIO. Granted the CIO makes mistakes in tactics. In general, however, we contend along with Monsignor Ryan and Monsignor George O'Toole [another labor priest] that the Communists constitute an insignificant minority. In the vast majority of CIO unions the leadership is not Communist, the tactics are sound, and the workers are getting the benefit of real union organization." The phrases "insignificant minority" and "vast majority" in that statement were stretching it a bit, but not as we saw it at the time.

FASCISM IN JERSEY CITY

Wherever Father Coughlin's influence was strong, which included most of the industrial centers of the Northeast and Midwest, we ran into trouble and the CIO into violent opposition. The *Brooklyn Tablet,* a Catholic diocesan paper edited by a Coughlinite, Patrick Scanlan, was particularly influential and was sold in Catholic churches all over the East Coast. It was a continual source of confusion and wild charges directed at the CIO, the CW, and the ACTU.

Nowhere was this kind of opposition stronger than Jersey City, across the Hudson River. There Mayor Frank Hague had established a political fiefdom that dominated both church and state, including the state's governor, Harry Moore, who was Hague's protégé. "The church" included both Catholic and Protestant clergy and even Jewish rabbis. CIO organizers and supporters, including several U.S. congressmen, were allowed neither to speak nor to distribute literature in any public place. It was worth their lives to try.

The economic realities that glued this machine together included: the average woman worker in a garment shop in Hudson County was then making $10 to $13 for a work week ranging from forty to forty-eight hours, and some as little as $4 a week for forty-six hours. In

New York across the river the union scale was $35 to $40 for thirty-six hours. William Carney, CIO regional director, reported, "Among the unorganized workers in the tobacco, bag-making, soap and needle trades, wages of $3, $4, and $5 a week are no exception." The dollar was worth more then, but still!

Hague's empire required a high tax rate to sustain his huge and padded payroll, a tax rate reported to be the highest in the country for a city of that size. Industry complained that it could not afford to stay in Jersey City and raise wages, too. Hague's salary was $6,520, but he was able to maintain a fourteen-room apartment, a $125,000 summer home, a cook, two maids, a nurse, a chauffeur, and a gardener, plus he took trips abroad nearly every year (multiply 1930s dollars by fourteen).

On January 6, 1938, the local chamber of commerce showed its appreciation to Hague for keeping the CIO out of Jersey City by sponsoring a rally in the armory, beneath great banners that exhorted the twenty thousand people present: "Time to Strike Against Red Invasion . . . Drive Communism Out of Labor . . . Patriotic Rally Against the Red Menace to America." An overflow crowd of fifteen hundred stood outside in the rain and listened to the speeches over loudspeakers. The president of a local fireworks company had donated rockets that were bursting in air as I arrived to cover the rally for *The Labor Leader.*

The press table was directly in front of the platform. I was sitting at one end, and as I looked past the crowd of visiting newspapermen and women, mostly from across the river, I could see the huge figure of Heywood Broun sitting next to Dorothy Parker right below the speaker's lectern.

The president of the chamber of commerce said, "We here in Jersey City have practically no labor trouble. . . . The mind and hand of the rowdy is rarely seen here." The president of the New Jersey AFL sat behind him and did not blink. Neither did a phalanx of Roman collars, ministers, and rabbis on the platform. The Democratic governor, introducing Hague, said, "The leaders of the CIO are men who believe neither in the law of God nor the laws of men. They are men who have injected themselves into the ranks of labor not to improve the conditions of the workers but to destroy industry and business and change our American form of government."

Finally Hague rose to speak. The ovation was overpowering. His appearance was that of a well-dressed Irish undertaker, diamond stickpin in a sober tie, stiff white collar supporting florid jowls, topped by a look of shrewd and calculating gloom.

Said he: "The leaders of the CIO are enemies of our government. They are for the destruction of American freedom and the setting up of a Communist nation." As he went on, the charges grew even wilder. At one point he claimed that "every organizer in the CIO is a Communist." In referring to his troubles with newspapermen, he said, "When they follow the Newspaper Guild, they follow the Communist Party."

At this point a Newspaper Guild reporter sitting on the other side of Broun yelled out, "Nuts!" After the rally ended, Broun lumbered up onto the platform in an effort to challenge Hague's remarks about the Guild, of which he was then president, but Hague had departed already.

Irony of ironies: Broun—one of the brighter and more useful men of his generation, as well as one of the funniest, a socialist but never a Communist—must have been appalled by this display of native American Catholicism at its worst. And yet, within the year, he had become a Catholic convert. Within the following year he was dead. And the final irony: of all the wild and crazy things Hague had said, perhaps the least wild was his reference to the Newspaper Guild. Broun was surrounded by Stalinists in the guild leadership, and after his death the Communist Party did in fact control the international union, at least for a few years, and the big New York local for a few more, as I discuss later in the book.

FIRST CAUSES AND THE U.S. CONSTITUTION

The next day the CIO filed suit in federal court in Newark, charging that Mayor Hague had interfered with fundamental rights guaranteed by the Constitution. A few months later the U.S. Supreme Court ruled that several of Hague's local ordinances were unconstitutional, and four of us, backed by a vote of the ACTU membership, took to the streets of Jersey City in the first distribution of Catholic literature supporting the CIO and attacking Hague. We handed out copies of The Catholic Worker, The Labor Leader, and ACTU leaflets.

At one point, as George Donahue and I were working different sides of the street, I saw several cops approach him. I crossed the street to join them and got in on a weird conversation. Apparently the cops were not aware that the Supreme Court had declared Jersey City's antilittering ordinance unconstitutional. This was how our exchange went:

COP: You can't distribute that stuff here. You're littering the street.

DONAHUE: Number one, the Supreme Court has ruled that your antilittering ordinance is unconstitutional. Number two, we can't help it if people drop things on the street. If anybody is littering the street, they're littering the street.

COP: Yeah, but you're the first cause of their littering.

He kept repeating that phrase, "first cause," which he apparently had picked up from some legal case. The conversation began to sound like a discussion of metaphysics, at which point I joined in.

CORT: If you're going to talk about first causes, then God is the real first cause because God made man.

SECOND COP (figuring to expose our Catholic pose):   Why did God make man?

CORT (letting him have it straight from the Baltimore Catechism):   God made man to know Him and love Him and serve Him and be happy with Him forever in heaven.

THIRD COP: That's funny. I thought that God made man to break the law so we could have a job.

We stood on the sidewalk and laughed, and suddenly Frank ("I Am the Law") Hague seemed farther away. In the middle of the fascist state of Jersey City, with a little help from the Supreme Court, humanity in the form of a wisecracking Irish cop had broken through the wall of humorless repression.

The cops went off to call headquarters and check our claim about the Supreme Court. They did not return, and we completed our distribution without difficulty.

Others were not so lucky, nor was I on another occasion. The CIO and its friends began to organize public meetings in Jersey City to bring their message to the public. Norman Thomas spoke for the Socialists in Journal Square and was pelted with eggs. A news photographer, in fact, took an extraordinary photo of an egg making a direct hit on Thomas's noble brow.

Two liberal Congressmen, Jerry O'Connell, Democrat of Montana, and John Bernard, Farmer-Labor of Minnesota, offered to come and speak for the CIO, an offer that moved a local official of the Catholic War Veterans (CWVs) to announce that eight hundred CWVs armed with rubber clubs would greet the two Congressmen if they should attempt to speak in Jersey City.

George Donahue, speaking for the ACTU, wrote to the national commander of the CWVs, protesting against the man's remarks: "Please turn that over in your mind for a few seconds: two representatives of the sovereign people of the United States being threatened with violence by a responsible official of a Catholic organization for daring to attempt the exercise of their constitutional right of free speech!"

A few weeks later the CIO tried to organize a rally in a park called Pershing Field. Congressman O'Connell began a speech but the police had to rescue him as the crowd closed in with shouts of "Kill the bum! . . . Throw him out! . . . Run the dirty Red back to Russia!" The mob then beat up the assistant regional director of the CIO, Sam Macri; he lay on the ground for an hour and a half waiting for an ambulance, with a broken jaw and a concussion of the brain serious enough to make him unaware of who he was or where he was.

The next day I went to Jersey City and distributed copies of *The Labor Leader* with a front-page headline that read: "Jersey Catholics Misled by Hague's Communist Scare." I picked Journal Square, outside the exit to the Hudson Tubes, the subway line from New York. I was scared but hopeful that I would be safe in such a public place, with cops clearly in evidence. I was wrong.

I had been distributing only a few minutes when a young man jumped me from behind and pinned my arms to my side. At the same time two others grabbed about two hundred copies of *The Labor Leader* out of my hands. In the scuffle I fell to the ground. By the time I was on my feet again, they had run away, and a crowd had gathered around me. The police were nowhere in sight. Seeing the crowd, I made a short, angry speech.

"Those guys," I said, "must be afraid of the truth. The papers they took are the publication of the Association of Catholic Trade Unionists, an organization supported by many priests and bishops throughout the country. It is not a Communist organization. It would be a terrible thing for the country if the Communists were the only ones opposing Hague's dictatorship. We want it known that a Catholic organization, among others, is opposing both Hague and communism."

That day I really learned, right down in my gut, about fascism and the Bill of Rights.

One final story about Jersey City. While we were looking for some Catholic leverage that we could use, the thought occurred to us that the pleasant Jesuit who served as president of Fordham University, with whom we had a good working relationship in the operation of our labor school, had been head of St. Peter's College in Jersey City previously and had a solid reputation in that community. He seemed like a liberal man and a natural ally.

As executive secretary of the New York chapter of the ACTU, I wrote to him, asking for assistance. Unfortunately, in the same letter I felt constrained to suggest that we also discuss another matter—the grievances of the Fordham groundskeepers and maintenance men who were trying to organize a union and had called on us for help. After all, Fordham and the ACTU were jointly running a labor school, and the labor school was teaching Catholic social ethics about the right to organize and receive living wages, etc., etc.

In reply I received a terse telegram from which all trace of pleasantness had fled away. It informed me that the president could give us no help in Jersey City and that if there were an appropriate body with which Fordham's labor relations should be discussed, he failed to see that "your little organization" was such a body. Our association with Fordham did not long survive that telegram. What did survive was the unhappy conviction of the truth of the Gospel mandate "Physician, heal thyself." Or to put it even more bluntly with St. Basil, quoting Plato: "This is the last extreme of injustice: 'To appear to be just without being so.'"

THE ACTU TACKLES COUGHLIN IN DETROIT

An even more direct confrontation between the ACTU and Father Coughlin occurred in Detroit in 1939. A lively, articulate group of Catholic unionists had organized a Detroit ACTU during the spring of 1938, led by Paul St. Marie, president of the Ford Auto Workers local, and by Paul Weber, a sharp newspaperman who was president of the Detroit Newspaper Guild. Almost immediately they won the support of Archbishop Mooney and began organizing labor schools in parishes of the city, which was the home of thousands of major auto plant workers who were members of the new CIO union, the UAW. Here, over the next ten years, a major struggle for control would unfold between the Communist Party and an anticommunist coalition behind Walter Reuther, a struggle that was to determine the shape of the U.S. labor movement for years to come.

In the fall of 1939 the Detroit ACTU began to publish its own newspaper, *The Michigan Labor Leader* (later called *The Wage Earner*). By this time twenty-seven parish labor schools functioned in and around Detroit, and thirty-five parishes had their own "captains" to organize parishioners into the ACTU. With its well-edited paper (mainly Weber's accomplishment), a network of labor schools, and organization at the parish level, the Detroit ACTU was ready to tangle with Father Coughlin.

On Sunday, November 11, 1939, the radio priest, operating from his headquarters in a Detroit suburb, had devoted his talk to an all-out effort to break the strike that the UAW had been leading at Chrysler. On the following Wednesday the UAW organized a rally in Cadillac Square in the heart of Detroit. About forty thousand auto workers, of whom maybe half were Catholic, cheered Monsignor John Mies as he took issue with Coughlin and encouraged the crowd to stick by their union. Mies was a labor priest who had loaned his parish school to the ACTU for its headquarters. That same night the ACTU sponsored a radio talk by one of its chaplains, Father Raymond Clancy, who proceeded to refute Coughlin's arguments point by point.

The back-to-work movement was a flop, and the strike went on to a successful conclusion. Coughlin was through as a serious threat to the organization of industrial workers in the CIO. I think it can be said with sober objectivity that the ACTU played a significant role in turning back that threat, both in the East and the Middle West.

In any case the CIO was on its way, and we rejoiced in its success. In Peter Maurin's words, the organizers were organizing the unorganized. American capitalism would never be quite so bad again.

7

Racketeers and Kennedys

Unions by their very nature are easily affected by the virus
of bureaucratic rule. Unions tend to be monosocial (like
a parish church), to be combative (like an army), to be
administrative (like a government agency), to be market
oriented (like a business). Taken together, these traits form
a strong natural bent toward the one-party system.

—Gus Tyler, education director, ILGWU, AFL

THE AFL gave the ACTU trouble in the 1930s, 1940s, and 1950s—
and vice versa. We at the ACTU ordinarily urged Catholics to join
AFL unions as readily as CIO unions, especially when they were the
only ones in the field. But if the problem of the CIO was Communist
influence, the problem of the AFL was racketeer influence. That
problem occupied a great deal of our time and attention during the
early days.

The power of the racketeer rested on the gun—the gun and the
goon squad. Union goons pushed me around and hassled me on several occasions, but what I remember best about guns and goons was
something a truck driver, a member of the Teamsters Union, told me
in a conversation in our ACTU office on Lafayette Street.

He described an occasion when a member of a West Side mob
shoved a pistol into his ribs one dark, rainy night under the old Ninth
Avenue El and told him to cease and desist from criticizing his local
leadership. Somehow the man communicated to me almost the total
terror of that dark night. Fighting against guns was not easy. Communists you could beat with superior organization and hard work, but
against racketeers these tools were rarely enough. As almost everybody knows, racketeering got its big push during Prohibition, when
the bootlegger was the folk hero of half of America, aglow with the
Hollywood glamour of Jimmy Cagney, Edward G. Robinson, and
George Raft. Not content with rumrunning and speakeasies, the

mobs moved into legitimate business, and by 1930 the underworld either controlled or influenced some twenty-five industries in and around New York City. When Prohibition was repealed in 1933 and the liquor business became legitimate, unemployed gangsters moved into other industries. Special attention was given to the unions, whose power to strike gave the mobsters a handy weapon to extort bribes from employers.

Sometimes one mob would take over from another by the simple application of superior force or terror or both. When Morris Manna and Barney Brown grabbed the longshore local in Jersey City, they simply walked in and ordered Slim Lucey to sign his resignation and open the safe. Lucey signed, but as to the safe he said, "I'm not going to do it." It was costly courage. They hit him in the face with a gun butt, knocking out seven teeth, and then held his feet in a fire of newspapers for several minutes.

GEORGE DONAHUE AND COCKEYE DUNN

George Donahue got the ACTU involved on the Hudson River piers. George was solidly built, with the face of an unsuccessful boxer and a combination of brains, guts, and Irish rhetoric not found on the docks every day. He had earned the ill will of the mob that controlled his longshoremen's local by bucking the efforts of Johnny (Cockeye) Dunn, later executed in Sing Sing for murder, to get control of the platform men and checkers in inland terminals. One day a goon squad including three ex-convicts came down to the pier where George was working. One of them said, "Mind your own business, or I'll blow your head off and throw you in the river."

George replied, "You'll never blow my head off. It would take a good man to shoot me, and you're a louse."

They proceeded to work George over and left him unconscious on the pier. A lesser man would have taken the hint, but that night George went to his local meeting, told what happened, and was cheered by the 150 men present, who then voted overwhelmingly to support him.

Alarmed by this threat, the mob arranged to have George fired from his job and then further arranged that he should not find another job on the docks. He got one of his assailants, Flounderfeet

Baker, sent back to jail for violation of parole and brought charges against those others whom he could identify, but the men were acquitted when a boss loader testified in court that George had started the fight—a minor example of how the mob not only controlled unions but infiltrated management as well.

The quality of George's courage can be estimated from a few facts about Cockeye Dunn, who eventually controlled sixty piers in the Greenwich Village area. George was a checker. Control of checkers was particularly important to the mob because only the checker could make out the phony receipts that made it possible to hijack entire truckloads of goods off the docks. In this scam the checker gives the truck driver a shipment receipt signed with a fake name, and the gang loads the shipment on another truck and drives it away before anyone can put it on a ship. Months later when the consignee in Hong Kong complains, the original truck driver produces his receipt, and the checker says, "Sorry—no such person works here."

Malcolm Johnson, a reporter for the *New York Sun* who did an important series of articles on waterfront crime, wrote that "the men on the docks credited Dunn with having committed or instigated 37 murders before he was finally nailed for the killing of Anthony Hintz, a hiring boss who refused to take orders."

Buster Smith, an ex-convict who controlled Pier 59 at the time, described the manner of Dunn's takeover of the loading racket at the pier. Dunn killed two members of Smith's gang and wounded Smith, which was persuasion enough for Smith to move on.

Several years later, when Smith appeared in a bar on the waterfront after a stint in jail, Dunn and a friend walked in and shot him. With just a hint of righteous indignation, Smith told the police, "They thought I was going to try to muscle in on them at the docks. I didn't have no such idea, but they didn't wait to find out. Just shot me. That's the way Dunn worked."

Dunn was part of the Joe Ryan machine. A longshoreman present at a meeting of Ryan's own local, which Ryan himself occasionally chaired, wrote an account of the meeting in a letter to the June 1938 issue of *The Labor Leader*, the ACTU paper:

> The meeting was called for the purpose of installing that old slave driver, Mickey Maher, as stevedore [hiring boss] on Pier 58, over the protests of the men who had worked under Mickey for years on Pier

61. The meeting was called on a Saturday afternoon and everyone was there, including the gorillas.

One man, Harry Fay, took the floor and protested. A short while later, when he left the hall for a minute, he was pushed around by the gangsters. He came back to the meeting and denounced Ryan and company. There are quite a few others who are not blessed with Harry's courage; they took a lumping and remained quiet. . . .

Ryan must be a first-class diplomat, for his strong-arm squad consists of men who have earned degrees from Sing Sing, Dannemorra and Clinton Prisons, and some are members of the New York Police Department. They work in the closest harmony with him.

If a member has too much to say, Johnny Dunn, Hawkey, and Flounderfeet Baker immediately surround him to shut him up, while Puggy Reece [member of the New York Police] looks on to see that the boys don't forget their lines. You know, Dunny and Hawkey were delegates of the Rock breakers Union at Sing Sing and since they were let out of it, it is whispered that no less than four people have gone to their eternal rest.

How long supposedly red-blooded men are going to tolerate this bullying by Ryan and his gangsters I do not know. I do know that before long there is going to be trouble, and it is not going to stop with dumping his gorillas into the river.

Despite these macho and anonymous threats of counterviolence, Cockeye Dunn had little trouble for eleven years. From the figure of only four murders it is evident this account was written early in his career. There was no trouble for Ryan for fourteen years, until 1952, when the New York Waterfront Commission dug up information that led to his indictment on fifty-one counts of accepting bribes from employers and using union funds for his own purposes.

At one point theft on the New York docks was estimated at $140 million a year, more than three times that in all other ports combined. Most of the rackets and thievery revolved around and depended on power that came to the mobsters through their control of hiring bosses, many of whom were ex-convicts themselves. These bosses in turn held their power over the men through the infamous shape-up, the system whereby men gathered around the hiring boss at the pier head twice a day and waited for him to select those who were to work for the next few hours. In short, what you saw in On the Waterfront was pretty close to the truth.

A Future Bishop Blasts the Shape-Up

Organizing opposition to Ryan and his gangster friends was not easy. Even George Donahue, who had worked on the docks himself, was regarded as an outsider and a dangerous man to be seen with. One, he was a college man. Two, he did not live on the West Side; he lived in Brooklyn. Three, he had managed to get himself beaten up and fired. And four, he had violated the "D 'n' D" (deaf and dumb) code by calling the cops, getting Flounderfeet Baker put away, and hauling several others into court.

Also, the ACTU made mistakes. We called a public meeting too soon, and practically nobody came, which compounded the mistake and scared those who did come.

We knew there was little hope of making progress as long as the shape-up continued, but in the summer of 1938 a labor priest who had grown up in Red Hook, the waterfront section of Brooklyn, and who had served in waterfront parishes, wrote a book called *The Waterfront Labor Problem,* in which he blasted not only the shape-up but also the union leaders and the employers who allowed it to continue. Father Edward Swanstrom later became a bishop and national director of Catholic Relief Services.

Even waiting for the book to be published was too much for us. We took the printed announcement of its impending publication by Fordham University Press, made a news story of it, and wrote big banner headlines across the front page of *The Labor Leader:* "PRIEST HITS SHAPE-UP EVILS IN BOOK ON LONGSHOREMEN." Subhead: "Finds Union Heads and Employers Have Failed to Aid Situation." Sub-subhead: "Says Port of New York 'Entirely Lacks System of Organizing Longshore Work.'"

The problem then was to get this information into the hands of the longshoremen. A college student at the CW, Tom Sullivan, helped me pass out copies of the paper along the West Side docks. We should have stuck together, but to speed things up he took the bars on one block while I was covering the next. I went into one bar and almost immediately got jumped by a Ryan man who wrestled the papers out of my hands and went out the back door with them. I might have made another angry speech to the men at the bar who were watching with what seemed to be amusement or indifference, but I was more scared than mad at this point. After I got outside, I began to think that I had not behaved very well, that I could have put up more of a fight. I went back into the bar looking for the papers, searched the trash barrel in the men's room, asked the bartender if he knew what the guy had done with them. He did not. He was D 'n' D.

A few days later I went out distributing again. As I was walking along the waterfront under the West Side Highway, I began to wonder what it would be like if a hostile longshoreman sneaked up behind me and sunk his loading hook into my back. Most longshoremen carried their own hooks with them, and many sharpened the points so that the hook could be used as a weapon as well as a tool. The imagined sensation of a hook in the back became so intense that I almost panicked. Fortunately, the feeling was never more than imaginary. The men took my papers without comment and without further incident.

Father Swanstrom himself attempted to distribute circulars advertising his book at the 1939 ILA convention at the Hotel Commodore in New York. Ryan's Catholic piety did not stop him from ordering the sergeant-at-arms to take the circulars away from the priest. He also asked the hotel management to put Father Swanstrom out of the building.

One day, shortly after we organized the ACTU, I called Ryan on the phone to ask him something. I forget the question, but I remember the answer. When I identified myself and said, "I'm from *The Labor Leader*," he said, "I lead sixty thousand longshoremen. What labor do you lead?" At that point, as the president of Fordham had reminded me, the New York ACTU chapter had less than one hundred members, so I was hard-pressed for an honest answer.

In those days there was not much we could do to stop Ryan. Through fear or preference he had the longshoremen. We did not, or not enough of them. The CW had hurt him by helping the seamen knock out his allies, the corrupt leaders of the old AFL seamen's union, and thereby helping to diminish his power and influence on the docks. But the CW had left the waterfront and retreated to Mott Street when the seamen's strike ended. The ACTU stayed on the docks, organizing and educating both seamen and longshoremen. We were a presence at least, a reminder to the men that a trade union could be more than a racket, that it even might be an instrument of freedom and justice, an expression of democracy and a better life.

The ACTU Makes Some Headway

Came the war. With the departure of most of the ACTU militants into service and me into a TB hospital, our presence on the docks was diminished seriously, but a nucleus remained and continued the fight. In 1945 Ed Scully and the Catholic Labor Defense League took the leaders of Local 895 into court. Local 895 was another key West Side local controlled by Dunn that had gone twenty years without an election. When we finally forced them to hold one, the mob won it by the simple expedient of stuffing the ballot boxes. Ed persuaded the judge to throw out the election and run an honest one under court supervision. ACTU members, led by a smart longshoreman, John Dwyer, won several key offices. No longer were the members afraid to come to our meetings. For one in St. Veronica's Hall five hundred men showed up.

A few years later, after a series of costly wildcat strikes, the Waterfront Commission began investigating. It revealed that Ryan had taken more than $15,000 from employers for which "he did nothing" and that ninety-eight other ILA officials had accepted similar sums for a total of $182,214 (multiply these figures by 7.5 for 2003 value). Ryan explained that employers contributed this money to a fund to fight communism, but he was at a loss to explain why such a fund would pay him $460 for a cruise to Guatemala, $1,332 for golf club dues, $220 for shirts, or $478 to bury his sister-in-law. His attempt to explain is worthy of inclusion in an anthology of doubletalk: "In these troubled times we're out fighting these Commies. We had to take money from the international treasury, and then I had to pay some of these expenses at the international treasury, like the trip to Guatemala, as you say, where I was reimbursing the international treasury for money we had taken out at a particular time." This was too much even for the AFL.

The decision to act represented a sharp and painful break with tradition. In 1940, after David Dubinsky of the ILGWU had proposed to the AFL convention that the executive council be given "summary power to order the removal of any [union] officers convicted of any offense involving moral turpitude . . . or using their official positions for personal gain," Joe Fay, a vice president of the Operating Engineers, slugged Dubinsky for his pains in a bar outside the convention hall. Fay rightly saw himself threatened by any such policy and was soon to be convicted and jailed for extorting large sums of money from New Jersey building contractors. He was about twice Dubinsky's size.

We used to run articles about Fay in *The Labor Leader*. Fay read one of these articles aloud to a union meeting and then protested with a very injured air that it was a terrible thing for a Catholic organization to call him a racketeer, and him "a Holy Name man."

Vacuous William Green, AFL president, also had opposed the Dubinsky move, but more politely, on the ground that it was a violation of the sacred autonomy of AFL affiliates. So ignorant was Green of what was happening in his own organization that he had stood on the platform and challenged critics to "show any racketeering in the AFL." The delegates overwhelmingly defeated the Dubinsky resolution. The AFL, with most of its crusaders and idealists having defected to the CIO, had sunk to a new low.

THE AFL INTERVENES

In 1952, however, Green died and was succeeded by George Meany. Whatever Meany's subsequent failings, William Green's style of fatuous hand wringing in the face of public scandal was not one of them. Meany demanded reform of the ILA, the ouster of all ex-cons, and the elimination of the shape-up. When the ILA refused, he asked the 1953 convention to expel it. The vote was better than one hundred to one. The AFL then chartered a rival longshore union to contest the ILA's hold on the waterfronts of the East Coast, the Gulf, and the Great Lakes.

I rejoiced in *The Labor Leader*: "This is the chance we have waited for, from the very first days, over 16 years ago, when we started fighting on the waterfront against the rule of the mobs. It will challenge all our courage, all our faith, all our ingenuity and resourcefulness, all our imagination." I might have added a few other qualities, for even more were needed.

The AFL gave powerful support to the rival union, in money and men. The showdown came in New York. Cochairman and general organizer of the AFL drive was ACTU's John Dwyer, with George Donahue hired on as consulting strategist. The mob, however, was not idle. The body of Mike Brogan, who was close to the ACTU and

John's friend, was found floating in the Hudson River near Pier 32, where he worked. Brogan was a leader on the pier who had expressed support for the AFL union.

Strange developments occurred. John L. Lewis's Mine Workers had broken with both the CIO and AFL, and in looking for friends Lewis loaned $400,000 to Ryan and his beleaguered union. Several locals of Harry Bridges's West Coast union, also looking for friends and a toehold on the East Coast, sent money to Tough Tony Anastasia, kingpin of Brooklyn's ILA mob, a very interesting development that brought together the Stalinists and the Mafia. *The Daily Worker* was the only newspaper in New York supporting the ILA gangsters, apparently figuring the Communist Party had a better chance for ultimate control in a mob-ridden union than in one led by ACTU types.

The first Labor Board election, held in December 1953, saw nearly twenty thousand longshoremen in the port of New York cast their ballots. The ILA won by several thousand votes, but the board threw out the election on the grounds of violence and intimidation at the polls. The ILA also won the second election, but by the narrow margin of 9,407 to 9,144. A shift of 134 votes would have thrown it the other way.

Brando and Malden Too Late to Help

A few months later the movie *On the Waterfront*, starring Marlon Brando as the rebel longshoreman and Karl Malden as the priest, was showing in New York theaters. The priest role was based almost totally on the character and work of Father John Corridan, S.J., assistant director of the Xavier Labor School, who since 1948 had been working with Father Carey and the ACTU, training and encouraging reform elements on the docks.

In one scene the mob kills a rebel longshoreman, and Malden makes an angry speech to the men standing around, a speech copied almost word for word from Father Corridan, who once told a group of dockworkers:

> You want to know what's wrong with the waterfront. It's love of a buck.
> . . . Christ is in the shape-up. . . . He stands in the shape-up knowing
> all won't get work and maybe he won't. . . . Christ works on a pier, and

his back aches because there are a fair number of boys on the pier. . . . They don't work, but they have their rackets. . . . Christ goes to a union meeting. . . . Sees how few go. Sees how many don't speak. Sees a certain restraint. At some meetings he sees a few with one hundred and fifty dollar suits, diamond rings on their fingers, drawing a couple of salaries and expense accounts.

On the Waterfront was a powerful movie—it won eight Academy Awards—and made a head-on assault on the waterfront code of D 'n' D that had protected the mob for so many years. The year 1954 was still in the era of the happy ending, however, so the picture was not entirely true to life. When Budd Schulberg wrote the book afterward, reversing the usual procedure, he more realistically had Terry Malloy, the Brando character, wind up in a New Jersey lime pit, like Peter Panto, the Brooklyn rebel against Anastasia's control. He gave Johnny Friendly, the mob leader, a one-year sentence for perjury, which was a little stiffer than the sentence given to Joe Ryan—six months and a $2,500 fine.

There were other unrealities. None of the mobs ever tried to break up our meetings at St. Veronica's. The rough stuff was reserved for less-public and less-sanctified places, times, and characters. Nevertheless, I have often thought that if they had only been able to speed up production and get that movie out a few months earlier, it could have swung the election the other way. All it had to do was switch 134 men out of 9,407.

A Bitter Comment

I was bitter about the defeat and in that bitterness wrote a piece for *Commonweal* that asked why "the men voted again for the old mob, for corruption, murder, chaos, more wildcat strikes, lost wages, thieving leaders, entanglements with Bridges," etc., etc., and went on:

> Why? It baffles you. It baffles me. The AFL's strategy was not letter-perfect, but it was good enough to win. It should have won. If it proves anything, it proves that the corruption goes deep, into the men themselves. I know that all the better labor writers have maintained that the men themselves are clean and decent, simply the victims of a pack of jackals who feed upon their unprotected vitals. I always hoped that was true myself. I can't believe it anymore. True, there is the group loyalty,

the old waterfront loyalty resenting the intrusion of outsiders. But there is more than that. Too many of the men like to do a little pilfering themselves, hanging around the fringes of the mob to pick up whatever crumbs are falling, admire the mob leader as the kind of man they would like to be themselves if they only had the guts and the brains.

You can't say now that the men didn't know better. They were given the facts—by the papers, by radio and television, by their own friends. They knew from their own experience what the ILA meant. And still they voted for it. I think they voted for what they wanted. Why they wanted it I don't know. Blame the system, blame the low state of religion, blame the long infection of the years, blame anything you want. It can't last. I have too much faith in human nature to believe that.

But it did last. The AFL tried again in 1956 and lost by a larger margin. Having then exhausted its reservoir of moral energy, the AFL—now become the AFL-CIO—readmitted the ILA at its 1959 convention on the inaccurate assumption that the union had done penance and purged itself of sin. And who was now its president? Teddy Gleason, the man who got George Donahue fired back in 1937 and smoothed the way for Cockeye Dunn.

Philip Taft, the labor historian, commented at the time, "The federation has demonstrated that it will intervene in cases of flagrant corruption, but its willingness to allow the ILA to rejoin demonstrates that its standards of ethical practice are not extremely high." Taft, incidentally, was one of the few labor historians who wrote about the ACTU with sympathetic accuracy.

And yet, by another route, my childlike faith in human nature was justified. New York and New Jersey, by action of their legislatures and with the support of the federal government, stepped in and virtually took over the docks with the creation of the New York Waterfront Commission. The pierhead shape-up was effectively abolished, the loading racket wiped out, and employment regularized, with most of the casuals being eliminated so that the regulars could make a decent living. Average earnings rose from $2,356 in 1953 to $7,000 in 1967. The commission banned seven hundred unsavory characters from the docks because of criminal records.

The longshore defeats of 1954 and 1956 marked the low point of my faith in democracy. But where industrial democracy failed, political democracy intervened and rescued the more sensible minority from the stupidity and cupidity of the majority.

SHEEHAN & HAROLD AND A PAIR OF MURDERS

More often than not the only way anyone could fight the racketeers was to take them into court, which required lawyers who were not only smart but willing to work for nothing because the odds were that their clients would never have the money to pay. Fortunately, we had such lawyers. Besides Ed Scully, there was the handsome John Sheehan and his partner, John Harold, a young man with the face and figure of a boy but a mind superior to far more experienced attorneys.

Among the cases that Sheehan & Harold worked on in the 1940s and 1950s, with some background assistance from the rest of us, included:

Local 32E, Building Service Employees, AFL. This was a local of 3,500 apartment house superintendents in the Bronx. Their homes went with their jobs, which made them even more vulnerable than the usual union member because only union members could work, and if they were expelled from the union they lost both their jobs and their homes. The local president, Tommy Lewis, would tolerate no opposition, it being his practice to expel members of our ACTU committee from jobs and homes for violation of such by-law provisions as the following: "Members shall not join in any movement that will obstruct, retard, impede or impair the progress of this organization, that may impair the morale of the AFL, *or any American institution,* our international or our local union, are subject to expulsion" (emphasis added, faulty syntax in the original).

Unfortunately, Tommy Lewis also had a smart attorney and more money than we had to pay for appeals to higher courts when he lost in the lower. He was stopped only by an ex-convict who killed him but who himself was killed by police while he was trying to escape, so that the motive for the murder was never clear.

Local 456, Teamsters, AFL. Sheehan & Harold gave legal assistance and helped John Acropolis, a truck-driving grad student at Manhattan College, to organize a rank-and-file committee. It produced the first honest leadership in a union that Acropolis once told me was "totally under the hat—no enforcement of wage scales, no meetings, no financial reports, most of the contracts allowed to expire—a racket, not a union."

After John Acropolis and friends ousted the racketeers, they were forced to call strike after strike to persuade the employers that Local 456 was no longer a racket. It was a long fight, but they tripled the membership, held regular monthly meetings that brought out an average attendance of one thousand workers—a truly miraculous figure for a local meeting—and got all the members up to scale. Though an ACTU member, John was not a Catholic. He was Greek Orthodox, but he told me, "The Catholic Church, through labor priests, labor schools, and ACTU, is doing more to help working people than any other organization I know of."

On August 26, 1952, somebody fired two bullets through John's head at point blank range. He was found in the doorway of his apartment, having apparently just opened the door for a visitor. A policeman who knew John gave his personal opinion that he was murdered "because he could not be bought." In describing the funeral, *The Labor Leader* reported, "The church was packed with weeping men, men who knew Acropolis, knew him for a man who had died for them." The case was never solved.

Local 42, Hat, Cap, and Millinery Workers, AFL. The rank and filers, a group that called themselves the Blockers Movement and whom we called "our Jewish chapter," came to us in 1943 with various complaints. Their union meetings were irregular and infrequent. Officers were elected by a show of hands, and those who voted wrong found it difficult to find jobs. Opposition leaders were expelled or suspended.

John Harold persisted and won an agreement, dictated by Judge Goldberg, for regular meetings, secret ballot elections, and elimination of job discrimination. The Blockers Movement won sixteen of twenty-three offices at the next election. They wrote us, "Our debt to the ACTU would be impossible to weigh."

Local 88, Masters, Mates, and Pilots, AFL. The president of this local, C. T. Atkins, was an ex-convict, a thief, and an embezzler who took the election ballots out of the designated post office box, counted them, declared himself and his friends the winners, then expelled from the local all the opposing candidates, who had been meeting at the ACTU, and forced them out of their jobs. It took Harold six years to get a similar court-ordered agreement for a fair election that swept Atkins and friends out of office.

Local 272, Garage Washers and Polishers, Teamsters, AFL. Strong-arm men beat up three of our members in the union hall after the vice president of the local, one Harry Jacobsen, told them that "any-one going down to the ACTU should have his skull opened."

One of our members, Richard Bergel, was battered so badly that he had to have two operations and wound up totally blind in one eye and blind enough in the other so that he could not work. Two members were expelled from the union for no other crime than attending ACTU meetings. John Sheehan went to court to get them reinstated, but his appeal was unsuccessful. The men were putting in fifty-four hours a week for low wages, and the union had already hit them for $70,000 in assessments on top of their union dues.

Fracas at the Opera House

In the spring of 1941 I went uptown to deliver copies of *The Labor Leader* at a meeting of this local. With me was Bill Evans from the CW. The paper had a good story about some of the shenanigans going on in the union. The meeting was being held in a picturesque old hall in midtown Manhattan called the Central Opera House. From the street floor a broad staircase went straight up and up about three stories into the hall.

After we had been distributing the papers for a while, the goon squad came down, jumped Bill and me, grabbed our papers, and retreated with them into the hall. Realizing that to pursue them was an invitation to a concussion, preceded or followed by a quick trip down those stairs, I went off to get a cop and with him climbed the stairs.

Harry Bessler, the local president, said to the cop, "You can't come in here. This is a union meeting." The cop backed off and left me there alone. I thought the man was known to this gang and probably in on the take. Bessler then said to me, "Come up here without the cops, and we can do business with you. What are you looking for—money? We'll take care of you."

Bessler's remark, on top of the theft of our papers, infuriated me and, perhaps encouraged by the operatic setting, I bellowed like a Wagnerian tenor, "You couldn't buy me off with a million dollars!" It was such a corny performance that I was ashamed to mention it when I wrote up the story for *The Labor Leader.*

Although the cop indeed may have been in cahoots with this gang, it wasn't necessarily true. Thirty years later, while preparing a college course for police officers on the administration of criminal justice, I learned that the Fourth Amendment of the Bill of Rights did in fact make it illegal for the cop to enter that hall without a warrant unless he himself had witnessed the crime and was in "hot pursuit." The Bill of Rights, which in Jersey City had come to the rescue of the forces of light and truth, in this case came to the rescue of the forces of darkness and corruption. So it goes with democracy, and I would not venture to say that it is not a necessary price to pay.

WE APPEAL TO CONGRESS

Laws to take care of murder and mayhem were on the books, if one could find the perpetrators and get them convicted. No federal law and virtually no state law, however, protected the right of ordinary union members to stand up and speak their minds, criticize union officials, and run against them in a fair election. To what extent could American citizens be said to be free if they could not be free to speak and act in those matters that involved their jobs and everything that depended on those jobs? And yet we did not want government to move in and take over the unions or interfere with their legitimate functions. What to do?

During the 1940s public anger increased at union abuses like those I've mentioned, partly as the result of exposure by the ACTU and by other organizations and individuals, but perhaps mainly as the result of strikes during the war, in particular the coal strikes that John L. Lewis directed and orchestrated with full brass section.

The result was the Taft-Hartley Act of 1947. The ACTU shared the labor movement's dislike of Taft-Hartley largely because it gave a green light to state legislatures to pass antiunion laws called right-to-work laws that had nothing to do with the right to work and everything to do with destroying union security. We also disliked Taft-Hartley because it made it possible for antiunion employers to smother organizing drives with firings, legal red tape, and time-killing appeals.

One thing many of us liked about Taft-Hartley was its provision that no one could be fired from a job, under a union shop, by reason of expulsion from the union for any cause other than nonpayment of dues.

All of us at the ACTU, however, agreed that the Taft-Hartley remedy was half-baked. What was needed was legislation to protect the union member from unjustly being expelled from his union. Therefore, at the New York ACTU in February 1949, after a series of meetings and discussions, we passed a resolution calling on Congress to give the National Labor Relations Board "the power to review cases of union discipline when these cases involve expulsion from membership or other major penalty."

Although we sent copies of our resolution to all members of the labor committees of the U.S. House and Senate, I can recall only one reply, from Representative Andrew Jacobs, Democrat of Indiana, who had been a labor attorney and had some appreciation of the problem. Ten years would pass before Congress really addressed itself to finding a solution. Meanwhile, most of its members were interested in listening to only two viewpoints on labor: either it could do nothing wrong, or it could do nothing right.

A HANDFUL OF KIDS

In a book published around 1956, *Labor USA*, Lester Velie wrote with only slight exaggeration that "neither the old AFL nor the newly merged AFL-CIO paid any attention to the sweetheart contract racketeer and his underworld allies until a handful of kids, some barely out of their teens, took them on."

The handful of kids included a new generation of ACTU zealots who succeeded the Sheehans, Harolds, Scullys, Donahues, and Corts of the 1930s and 1940s. The latter mostly had gone on to careers that took them away from ACTU work. Lawyers and college students, this new generation included young men like Norman DeWeaver, John McNiff, Dan Schulder, Bob Mozer, and Tom Rizzo. At one point in 1957 they were processing twenty-five cases before the National Labor Relations Board and four injunction actions before state courts, all on behalf of thirteen hundred black and Spanish-speaking workers who were being exploited under racket union contracts. Many of these involved a mobster named Johnny Dio, a friend and ally of the notorious racketeer Jimmy Hoffa, president of the Teamsters.

In 1953 the New York ACTU began training bilingual teachers and organizing labor schools in a number of church parishes in Spanish Harlem and the Bronx to service the large number of Puerto Rican and black workers in New York City.

During the AFL-CIO's second and perhaps most historic convention at Atlantic City in 1957 DeWeaver took a delegation of racket-ridden workers down to the Jersey boardwalk and picketed the convention. The picket line helped to focus the attention of the delegates on their corrupt affiliates, some of whom, including the mighty Teamsters, that very convention expelled from the house of labor.

In that same year DeWeaver, who had succeeded to my old job as ACTU executive secretary, put together a body of testimony that Mc-Niff took down to Washington and presented in public hearings before Senator McClellan's labor committee. McNiff's photo and testimony appeared on many newspaper front pages throughout the country, and members of the committee—including such diverse types as Senators McNamara, Goldwater, McClellan, and Kennedy—praised him lavishly.

Kennedy said to him, "I think your testimony, perhaps more than any other, dramatizes the close tie-up between corrupt employers and racketeers who move into the labor movement and exploit the worker." McNiff's testimony must have had its effect on the final action of Congress in what became the Landrum-Griffin Act of 1959, which, after the Wagner Act and the Taft-Hartley Act, was the third most important action of Congress in the field of labor. The Landrum-Griffin Act originally was the Kennedy-Ives bill, and the Kennedy brothers, John and Robert, were its major architects.

A BROTHER ACT

When I first met Robert Kennedy in 1940, he was a fresh kid who sat at my table at Portsmouth Priory, a Benedictine monastery and prep school in Rhode Island. The prior, a kind man named Gregory Borgstedt, a convert like myself and fellow alumnus of the Cathedral Choir School at St. John the Divine, had given me shelter for a few months while I was convalescing from tuberculosis and working on a bad labor novel. I did a few odd jobs around the school, and one of them was to take a table of students at dinner and try to maintain some semblance of order.

I was not very good at maintaining order, and the kids were not very good at keeping it, Bobby being one of the worst. I can recall food flying through the air at one point. I felt a little like another Portsmouth monk, the gentle Father Placid, who, in reporting a bad scene in his classroom during which students had thrown horse chestnuts at him while he was writing on the blackboard, hastened to assure Father Gregory, "But I want you to know that none of them hit me."

My own scene grew so bad that after one riotous dinner I took the boys across the hall to the common room and gave them a pompous little lecture on what it means to be a gentleman. It seemed to strike some subterranean layer of shame or pity, and they were a little better for a few days.

Nineteen years later I broke bread with Bob Kennedy again, this time at an ACTU communion breakfast in New York. He was there as recipient of the ACTU's Quadragesimo Anno Medal for his work as counsel of the Senate McClellan Committee in exposing corruption and racketeering in the labor movement. I was there as toastmaster.

In introducing him I took a perverse pleasure in reporting my previous experience with him at Portsmouth Priory. I added, "I have been watching his table manners closely during the breakfast, and I am happy to report that they have greatly improved." Kennedy's smile was a bit strained, but he was gracious enough to say that he would relay this information to his mother, and he knew that she would be very pleased to hear it.

Bob Kennedy's presence as counsel for the Democratic majority on Senator McClellan's labor committee probably was not unrelated to his brother John's membership on the committee. There is no question that he did an effective job. The exposure of labor abuses was getting much press in those days, and the committee had attracted some high-powered senators, including Barry Goldwater, Sam Ervin, and the infamous Joe McCarthy.

I got to know John Kennedy after we moved to Boston in 1950 and I became the executive secretary (business agent) of the Newspaper Guild of Greater Boston, CIO. When the *Boston Post* got into financial difficulties, John Thompson, president of our local, and I went to see Kennedy, then a young Congressman, in his apartment up on Bowdoin Street across from the State House. We wanted to check out rumors that his father, Joe, was going to buy the paper. He denied the rumors but assured us that he would let us know when and if it did happen. The conversation was friendly, but I remember saying to Thompson as we walked down Beacon Street, "That's a very cool customer." Kennedy's coolness struck me as unusual in light of the stories I had been hearing from friends as to what a dashing, charismatic character he was.

THE CAUTIOUS LIBERAL

I saw Kennedy around town from time to time, usually at labor meetings or at Americans for Democratic Action affairs. Then in 1958 I interviewed him for a profile I did for *The Sign,* a national Catholic magazine. The interview was also in the Bowdoin Street apartment. I arrived on a Sunday morning, and he asked me to wait while he went to mass at the Paulist church around the corner on Park Street. I had already been, so I waited. He returned after only a few minutes, and I was a little worried that he might think that the interview was more important than the mass. In the light of subsequent developments it seems possible that that was exactly what he thought.

In interviewing Kennedy I was concerned, by reason of my own bias and my own hopes for him, to show that he was a good liberal. I remember the feeling of effort as I tried to draw liberal statements out of him. He gave a few but kept throwing in modifiers like "with restraint," "not with any intent to destroy our economic system," and "due regard for the national security." He seemed distracted, ill at ease, and shortly thereafter I found out why.

I asked him, "How did it happen that you, the son of a rich man, developed a sympathy for the poor?" I felt him beginning to focus for the first time. He said, "My first political office was the job of representing the people of this congressional district, and this district includes a lot of poor people. It seemed to me then, and now, that the democratic system cannot survive unless the government does something to redress the balance in such things as substandard wages or housing, which were very important factors in this district."

At this point in his career Kennedy was chairman of a subcommittee of the McClellan Committee and had been given the responsibility of drawing up legislation to correct labor abuses. He clearly had his eye on the White House and the middle road that might lead to it in 1960. Meanwhile, he knew that if he were going to make it, he could afford to alienate neither labor nor those Democrats and independents who wanted to see some restraints on labor dictators and racketeers. He was walking a very tight rope.

Bobby had made that rope even tighter. He wrote a report for the McClellan Committee that was more one-sidedly critical of labor than Kennedy would have liked, but in loyalty to his brother Kennedy signed it. The only other northern Democrat on the committee, Pat McNamara of Michigan, not only refused to sign but resigned from the committee in protest. AFL president George Meany attacked the signers of the report and charged them with having "gratuitously insulted the entire labor movement."

The day before my interview of Kennedy, Al Hayes, the prominent president of the Machinists Union, renewed the attack on Kennedy and other "so-called friends of labor" and compared them with Juan Perón, the ousted dictator of Argentina.

On the day of our interview a Sunday *New York Times* story reported Hayes's attack on Kennedy. I had not seen the article yet, but Kennedy had, and it was the reason for his distraction. While we were talking, the phone rang, and the senator went into another room to answer it. Having to make a phone call myself, I picked up a phone in the room where I was sitting, not realizing it was an extension of the phone Kennedy was using. Before I could put the receiver down, I heard him say, "Did you see where Hayes kicked the shit out of me?" I did not use this quote in the *Sign* piece.

The amazing thing is that within a few weeks Kennedy was a labor hero again as he and Lyndon Johnson led the successful fight on the Senate floor to prevent Senator Knowland and the Republicans from attaching much more restrictive amendments to what was then known as the Kennedy-Ives bill. He eventually was able to get the bill through the Senate by an eighty-eight to one margin and keep it free enough of bad amendments to move George Meany to admit it was "worthwhile." In short, he had accomplished the near miracle of simultaneously putting his name on a bill that regulated unions and still managing to remain, in most quarters, "a friend of labor."

The more conservative House killed the bill, but it returned in 1959 as the Kennedy-Ervin bill after the House tacked on more restrictive amendments. Unable to remove these amendments in the Senate, Kennedy and Ervin took their names off the bill and let Landrum and Griffin have the honor. Final passage depended on a conservative coalition of Republicans and southern Democrats.

But not all of that bill was bad. Contained in it were, in essence, recommendations that the ACTU had made to Congress in 1949, ten years earlier, giving the government the power to review and reverse disciplinary action against union members by their officers where such action did not provide for a fair trial. It also contained recommendations that a national ACTU convention in 1957 had made to give the Labor Board power to enforce honest procedures in the negotiation and enforcements of contracts and the holding of elections.

Not every violation of these provisions has been punished or corrected, but several noteworthy acts of enforcement have occurred. One invalidated the crooked election in the United Mine Workers in 1969, which resulted in victory for the reform candidate, Arnold Miller, and some retribution for the murder of an earlier reform candidate, Jock Yablonski, on the orders of the union president at that time, Tony Boyle.

CONVERSATION WITH JIMMY HOFFA

In 1955 I read an interview with Jimmy Hoffa Sr. that Murray Kempton did at the AFL-CIO merger convention that year. I had known Kempton since the 1940s, when I was managing editor of *The Labor Leader* and he was covering labor for the *New York Post*. He used to call me nearly every week and milk me for leads on what was happening.

In this interview Kempton told how Hoffa, leaning against the wall and surveying the convention, remarked contemptuously, "This place is full of guys who are satisfied to go on making a hundred and twenty bucks a week for the rest of their lives."

Twenty years later I happened to be at a conference at which Hoffa was speaking about the injustices that convicts suffer in federal prisons. Because he had been released recently from one by special act of President Nixon, who was repaying the Teamsters for support, he knew whereof he spoke.

After the meeting I introduced myself to Hoffa and interviewed him briefly on the way up to his room. I said I was an old friend of Kempton, which was a mistake, because his opinion of Kempton was not good. I reminded him of his remark to Kempton at the merger convention, which intrigued me at the time as an expression of the vaulting ambition of the trade union hustler:

CORT: Do you still believe that?

HOFFA: Sure, I still believe that. The labor movement died that day. It became just a business.

CORT (startled):   You mean the crusade, the idealism went out of it?

HOFFA: Yeah.

CORT: What were you sent up for? [I actually had forgotten.]

HOFFA: Mail fraud and jury tampering.

CORT: Do you think you were the victim of a bum rap?

HOFFA: Of course. Bobby Kennedy rigged the court. It's just like now. They can't stand anybody with power down in the precincts, power with the people. They don't care about Fitzsimmons.

Fitzsimmons was Hoffa's colorless successor, and Hoffa resented the fact that the terms of his parole did not permit him yet to run for his old job, which he generally was favored to regain without difficulty.

The striking thing about this exchange, however, was the complete reverse twist between his interpretation of the remark about the $120 and my interpretation. Hoffa remembered it as an indictment of business unionism. I remembered it as an indictment of humble but honest porkchoppers by a big business unionist who really saw the possibilities of cashing in. And yet I am persuaded that such is the complexity of human nature that his interpretation may have been closer to the truth, at least as far as the remark reflected the confusion of his own self-image.

Some years later Hoffa disappeared, probably the victim of some complicated struggle over control of the Teamsters. In 1998 his son, Jimmy Hoffa Jr., was elected president, replacing a reformer, Ron Carey, who could not resist the temptation to dip his hand into the union treasury to finance his own reelection. The federal government invalidated Carey's election and declared Carey ineligible to run again, smoothing the way for Junior's succession to one of the most powerful posts in the U.S. labor movement.

The ACTU deserves some credit for that series of events, as I have somewhat shamelessly and repeatedly implied, but I would not have it otherwise, sorry though I may have been to see Hoffa Jr. elected. Perhaps there may be in him something of his father's spin on that ancient remark about the $120. We can only hope, and we believers pray, that it might be so. Meanwhile, there remains the indomitable Ken Paff and the Teamsters for a Democratic Union to keep an eye on Junior just in case.

8

Flashback: Time to Think

> If you want to live forever, get yourself a good incurable
> disease and take care of it.
>
> —Cardinal Mercier

AT THE CW we had corn flakes for breakfast, and we did not know
as much as later generations about how we were being cheated on
nutrition. Lunch was usually soup and bread, and dinner some kind
of stew. The CW stews are thicker now. Times were harder then, and
stews thinner. The days were full of activity and the nights full of
meetings, and it seemed essential that you make them all. I believed
that the fate of the labor movement, the nation, and the world hung
in the balance. Even if controlling the world was not on our agenda,
saving it was still hard work. I lost weight.

In the fall of 1938 I developed a cough and ignored it for longer
than was wise. Father Monaghan sent me to a friend of his, a chest
specialist with an office on Park Avenue. After the X-rays and the
check-up, the doctor said to me, "There are indications of tuberculosis in your chest."

I said, "You mean I might get TB if I'm not careful?"

"No, I mean you've got it. There's a cavity in the apex of your right
lung about so big," making a circle with his thumb and forefinger.

Those were the days before drugs had been found that could handle the TB bacillus. The usual cure was to lie on your back for months
and years or have a few ribs cut out or have air pumped into your
chest cavity, in both of the latter cases to collapse the diseased part
of your lung, render it immobile, and give it a chance to heal. When
the doctor thought your condition had stabilized, he would let you
return to work by easy stages. Then you tried to do too much, re-
lapsed, went back to the hospital, and started all over again. Frequently you died. They told us that advanced TB, which was what I
had, could never be cured. It could only be "arrested." That is still
true, drugs or no drugs.

I spent about five and a half of the next twelve years on my back, had pneumothorax treatments (the air-pumping remedy) for about four years, and had so many hollow needles stuck between my ribs that my chest wall turned to something near the consistency of leather. I tried five times to make it back to normal life without success.

The first hospital I went to was a place in the Bronx run by an order of nuns, full of men who were dying. Many of them were alcoholics from the Bowery, men whom I had served on the breadline at the CW. The city gave the nuns a certain amount of money to take care of them while they were dying, but it was not enough to make it possible for them to die in style, and the nuns could not raise enough to make up the difference. It was called "a terminal facility," from *terminus*, Latin for "end of the line."

I spent more than three years there, in three different installments. I was one of the few who made it out. Onions helped me make it. The food was so bad that I had to ask my friends to bring me raw onions to kill the taste. Stories out of the kitchen consisted mostly of the following types of conversations:

"Sister, these spareribs smell bad."

"That's all right. Just keep boiling them. The smell will go away."

I can testify that Sister was wrong. Some men died slowly, with grace and even a touch of humor. Some died quickly, in panic and tears. Others died at every conceivable tempo and style in between. Every couple of months we would gather in the big wards and receive the last rites, not because we were all at death's door, but because the chaplain was afraid of TB, afraid to give a man the last rites when the man was actually dying, coughing blood and contagion, so to ease his conscience he gave us all the holy oils at the same time. He was a big, red-faced man, healthy as a horse, and a terrible case of miscasting.

When my roommate was on the way out, I had to phone Father in his house across the street and plead with him for five minutes before he would come over and say a prayer over Eddie, careful all the time not to touch him or to stand too close.

Some of the nuns were great, but some of them looked upon themselves as sergeants and upon the patients as malingering privates. The porters and orderlies were mostly off the Bowery. They received room and board and $30 to $35 a month—that word was *month—*

which even in the 1930s was terrible money for work in a contagious boneyard, hardly enough to get bombed on their day off. Turnover was high. Even so, it was better than the old folks' home down the road, run by another order of nuns, which was popularly known as the Five and Ten because they paid porters $5 a month and orderlies $10 a month, plus keep (remember to multiply these dollars by fourteen for 2003 dollars).

Fortunately for me I liked to read. Many men just lay on their beds and worried about those little bacilli that were eating holes in their lungs, which just accelerated the process, until they could stand it no more and went over the wall and got drunk, staggered back after a few days, which further accelerated the process. So it was good that I liked to read and could even write and get what I wrote printed in *The Labor Leader, The Catholic Worker,* or *Commonweal.* I'd even write letters to the *Tablet* proving that the editor was all wet about the CIO, and he might print the letter, but only at the price of printing a long comment after my letter in which he further compounded and embroidered his previous misstatements.

WHY THIS MONSTROSITY OF WANT?

I knew that I was weak in economics, having dropped the course at midyears because it was so boring, so I took the opportunity to read up on what Carlyle inaccurately called "the dismal science." Inaccurately not because it isn't dismal but because it has no legitimate claim to be called a science. It involves morality; it involves justice as much as it involves anything that is subject to scientific inquiry. I began to learn this distinction as I pursued my reading.

The question that haunted me was: How did this monstrosity of want come about in the midst of plenty? How did it happen that so many millions of men and women could not find work in a country so rich in resources, brain power, and energy, when there was such an obvious need for their labor and for the products their labor could provide? Something was terribly wrong.

I was sitting, or lying, at the end of a decade that C. Wright Mills described in *The New Men of Power* as follows: "If everyone who was working in 1929 had continued to work until 1939, each one could have taken a vacation for one year and two months, and the loss of national income would have been no greater than it actually was. In terms of the total of all the goods and services available to the people, the free enterprise system was set back 33 years. The average citizen had about as much available to him in 1932 as he had in 1899."

That was the rotten reality. What was the solution? For that, I turned to a book called *Economics and Society* by a Catholic priest, John F. Cronin, a disciple of Monsignor Ryan and John Maynard Keynes. In his chapter on the business cycle Father Cronin gave this Keynesian explanation of the problem:

> Classical economists [maintained] that it made relatively little difference who received the income [from production]. If it went to the poorer classes it was spent directly. If it went to the wealthier classes it was spent indirectly by means of capital investment. . . . The attitude behind such theories is not confirmed by recent studies, such as the Brookings Institution's analysis of *The Distribution of Income in Relation to Economic Progress.* . . .
>
> *When the poorer classes receive a relatively larger portion of the national income, they spend more and thus increase the demand for the products of industry. This increased demand provides an incentive for new capital investment to supply these wants. The savings of the wealthy are then put to practical use.* (emphasis added)

Not the whole story perhaps, but a major part of the story. From my reading I conceived the notion that justice was the best economist. If government recognized and enforced the right to a job, and if every worker received that decent living wage that justice requires, then the economic machinery would run smoothly because it would always have enough gas in the cylinders. If industry failed to provide jobs and decent wages, then—another Keynesian solution—government must provide them even if it must operate on deficit budgets until full employment is restored, and those who can afford it must provide the taxes to make up the deficit.

CHASING RUNAWAYS IN PENNSYLVANIA

In the summer of 1941 the doctor told me I was well enough to take a job as an organizer for Dubinsky's ladies' garment union, the ILGWU, AFL, better known as the ILG. They sent me to Pennsylvania in pursuit of runaway sweat shops that were trying to escape union wage scales in New York City.

Years later, working for the Peace Corps in the Philippines, I met Paul Jacobs, a delightful character also working for the Peace Corps. Like me, Paul had been an organizer chasing runaway shops for the ILG. This was not easy work because a garment manufacturer needed only his sewing machines, and, when ILG organizers threatened him, it was a simple matter for him to pile the machines in a truck in the dead of night and run away to some more elusive location. To prevent such flight, the ILG was not above employing a few characters with more liberal views about the use of force than sensitive souls like Paul and myself.

One of these characters, Paul told me, caught up with an employer who was in the very act of loading his machines for a quick getaway. The ILG man, a well-muscled specimen, grabbed the employer by the necktie, pulled him up close, and said, "Mr. Goldberg, don't move the shop. Because if you move the shop I'm going to have to take out your eyeballs and eat them like grapes."

Mr. Goldberg did not move the shop. At least not on that occasion.

I was assigned to a strike in the little town of Lititz near Lancaster, where my father and grandfather had attended Franklin and Marshall College. This was the land of the Plain People: the Amish and the Mennonites. The Amish were mostly farmers, but the Mennonites lived in the towns, and the women in their little white caps worked in the garment factories. We had trouble with them because their ministers told them that the only organization they could belong to was their church. The pragmatic men who ran the ILG finally edged aside this roadblock by agreeing that those who had religious scruples need not sign a membership card as long as they paid dues.

Being Plain People, many of the workers were suspicious of us city slickers from New York. I made this impression worse by wearing a new hat and a pinstripe suit that I had bought with the first decent paycheck of my life. One prospect made critical reference to this attire as I stood in her doorway trying to sell the union. With an injured air, I responded that I had paid only $17 for the suit. This was true, but as I looked at her face, I could hear my defense through her ears, and I almost disbelieved it myself.

My boss was a charmer from the ILG staff and an excellent pianist and composer of catchy songs. When he wasn't playing his songs for me, we were likely to be arguing about organizing tactics. When we signed up 75 percent of the workers in a local shop, for example, I objected to his announcing that we had signed 87 percent. These arguments culminated at a lunch meeting with three or four of the big brass from New York. We sat around a big table in a good restaurant, and I tried to persuade them that the lie was not an effective organizing technique. They looked at me with friendly amusement as if I were a nice boy who would maybe be better off at home with mother.

They were mostly socialists, or former socialists, who had forsaken Norman Thomas because Roosevelt had given them most of the things they were looking for. Hitler's or Stalin's big lies appalled them, but little lies in the interests of organizing a few workers into a good union? Objecting against them was carrying scrupulosity to ridiculous extremes.

In any case I was not around very long to bug them with my scruples. The TB bacillus was bugging me again. The strike still unsettled, I had to return to Nassau County Sanatorium, out in the potato fields of Long Island, where I spent the next year and a half. Having acquired a decent salary, I had thought that I was on the road to matrimony with Wellesley's Most Beautiful, but that road ended here. There were tears of self-pity again, but this time no laughter.

A PRIESTLY IDEA DIES ABRUPTLY

On the rebound I played with the idea of becoming a priest. It came to me after reading two books, one after the other: Franz Werfel's *Song of Bernadette* and Jan Valtin's *Out of the Night,* the autobiography of a German Communist, which shamed me with its account of the sacrifices that Communists make for their faith. The idea died abruptly one day when a good-looking young woman walked through the ward, and I decided that I needed one of those for my very own.

Also on the rebound I fell in love with birds. When I got well enough to go out for walks, it became boring just to walk, and they did not allow the female patients to walk at the same time as the males. One patient in the ward, our bookie, was too sick to go out, but he had a little bird book and a pair of four-power field glasses. The first day I went out with the glasses, I got a good look at a scarlet tanager sitting in a bright green bush, and my heart turned over inside me. This new love helped me to forget the old.

Another thing I learned in that sanatorium was a lesson about state ownership and private ownership. Outside the window of my ward I could see where the potato fields came up to the sanatorium grounds. The county owned one field that prisoners from the county jail tilled under the direction of a foreman with farm experience. A farmer owned the field right next to it, and he and his family worked it themselves. The contrast between the two fields, both having the same kind of soil and producing the same crop, was dramatic. The county field was weedy and poorly cultivated, and the yield small. The private field was beautifully cultivated, free of weeds, and the yield tremendous.

Private ownership often serves as a screen behind which workers are exploited for the benefit of people who are not the owners, but only the managers of private property. But there is a fundamental truth, a fundamental dynamic, to Eric Gill's aphorism, "Men work best when they own and control their own tools and materials," and he might have added, "and their own land."

The drive for personal profit, in cash money, is powerful indeed, but it perhaps is equaled by another kind of profit, the psychic income that comes from seeing and feeling the fulfillment of your own personality in the work you are doing and the product or service you are providing, so that the product and the work become an extension of your own personality and even, for such as believe, a participation in the creativity of God.

The problem and the trick are to devise ways and means of getting ownership and control into the hands of those who are doing the work while at the same time retaining the advantages of technical progress and efficient management.

BEAUTIFUL MIND, SOUL, AND BODY

I left the sanatorium in 1943 and worked for *Commonweal* for a few months before breaking down again. One night as I was doing volunteer work at the ACTU, I noticed another volunteer, a senior from the College of New Rochelle, a Catholic women's college, standing with her back to me, working at a table directly in my line of vision.

I said to myself, "That is a great pair of legs." It sounds crude, it is crude, but let's face it: that is how great romances often begin.

That volunteer was Helen Haye, the realization of my adolescent ideal, "a beautiful mind and a beautiful soul in a beautiful body." Fortunately, she did have one weakness: she was foolish enough to think that I was worth bothering with.

By December 1943 I was back in my original resting place, the hospital in the Bronx. Discouraged by the slow, uncertain benefits of bed rest, I signed out and went on pilgrimage to the shrine of St. Anne de Beaupré in Canada. There, a solitary pilgrim in the dead of winter, I looked with hope at the great piles of discarded crutches, climbed on my knees up a long flight of stairs, prayed to God, Jesus, Our Lady, St. Anne, and all the saints. No immediate cure was forthcoming, but who knows? The fact that I am sitting here, sixty years later in reasonably good health, pounding this word processor, seems to be miracle enough. It just took a while.

I went back to New York and tried the Gerson diet, an experimental treatment that involved eating great quantities of apples, vegetables, and a soup cooked in a sealed pot and made of potatoes, tomatoes, leeks, celery knobs, and parsley roots. My brother David took me in for a time, then I moved to a nursing home on Eighty-fourth Street, a cheerless place where one night, with a total lack of heroism or the most elementary consideration and in violation of every Hollywood cliché, I asked Helen to marry me if I could ever get myself into shape. Foolishly, but gratifyingly, she said yes.

But the Gerson diet was not working, and in a sweat of fear that I was heading down the long decline into terminal TB, I returned to the hospital in the Bronx and two more years of bed rest.

LIFE ON THE HORIZONTAL

The following are excerpts from letters to Helen:

July 10, 1944

Father Ed Bergin came to see me. It was hot, and he took off his coat, collar, and shirt and sat here gabbing in his undershirt, smoking a cigar. He's a fine fellow, good sense of humor. In his parish, about two hundred out of five hundred are black. He says that in the school white

and black children like each other fine, especially in the early grades.
Then as they grow up the parents start talking to them, the white kids,
and turn them against their black friends. He says it's sickening to
watch it happen.

July 26, 1944

I deserve a spanking for letting myself get into an argument with Matt,
my Coughlinite roommate, about the Bretton Woods monetary conference. He's one of the best-natured, even humorous fellows you could
want to know, but when he gets started on money, it's like all hell
breaking loose. [Money and international Jewish bankers were an ob-
session of Father Coughlin.] A verse of the black poet, Countee Cul-
len, is most apt, and I hereby adopt it as my theme song:

> All day long and all night through
> One thing only I must do—
> Quench my pride and cool my blood,
> Lest I perish in the flood.

In its October 20, 1944, issue *Commonweal* printed a piece that
Ed Skillin, its publisher, asked me to write on the subject of the CIO
Political Action Committee, the first of the controversial PACs. The
committee, along with its chairman, Sidney Hillman, had become
one of the major issues in the presidential campaign. The Republican
candidate, Governor Thomas Dewey of New York, had charged that
Roosevelt "is indispensable to Sidney Hillman and the Political Action Committee, to Earl Browder [chairman of the U.S. Communist
Party]." Dewey's running mate, Governor Bricker of Ohio, went even
further in saying that the New Deal had "abdicated its cause and its
leadership to the Browder-Hillman axis." Republican billboards and
newspaper ads announced, "It's your country. . . . Why let Sidney
Hillman Run It?"

My article made these points: (1) that Sidney Hillman, president
of the Amalgamated Clothing Workers, CIO, was a former socialist
and anticommunist whose economic philosophy was closer to the
pope's than to Karl Marx's; (2) that he was a Jew born in Russia, a fact
that gave impetus to much of the attack on him, which was marked by
"bigotry, malice and dirty, smirking innuendo"; (3) that anticommunist members retained firm control of the CIO and its Political Action
Committee; and (4) that

in PAC the CIO is doing nothing more nor less than the ancient AFL practice of "rewarding friends and punishing enemies." The difference is that the AFL did it inefficiently, halfheartedly. . . . PAC, on the other hand, has really done a job, and it is this simple fact that so infuriates the opposition. And so the howl went up. It is a howl so loud, so expensive and so dishonest that if there were no other argument on the face of the earth, it would be obvious, for that one reason alone, that an organization like PAC is indeed necessary to protect labor's skin from such powerful, unscrupulous forces.

A MINOR CAMPAIGN DOCUMENT

October 18, 1944

John Brubaker [*Commonweal* advertising manager] came to see me last night and brought news that bucked me way up in the air. PAC liked my piece so much they want thousands of extra copies. Only figure he remembers is "five thousand for Chicago alone." Since paper shortage makes that impossible, they asked for permission to reprint.

November 3, 1944

Last night was very exciting. Matt [the Coughlinite] was home, and Steve and I were lying here in the dark listening to Roosevelt's speech and then immediately afterward Hannegan and the quote, the same quote that Quentin Reynolds used Wednesday night on the same network. [Robert Hannegan was chairman of the Democratic National Committee, and Reynolds was a writer and radio commentator. The quote was from my PAC piece.] It was quite a thrill and I didn't sleep much afterwards. To think that a sick pipsqueak like me has had the luck to give birth to a minor campaign document.

Roosevelt won big, and the resentment and vituperation from the Coughlinites was quick to follow. They had made defeat of Roosevelt a virtual crusade. Matt was incensed by my role in Dewey's defeat and life in Room 8 became unbearable.

December 26, 1944

Today you see before you a very happy man. Yesterday I was transferred from Room 8 to Room 9, where I am most comfortably ensconced with Ed Bingham, a wonderfully quiet and uncontentious roommate. A big black cloud has lifted and sunshine floods the plain.

There is an insightful saying that "no good deed goes unpunished." In 1996 a friend doing labor research sent me two pages from *Labor Will Rule*, a biography of Sidney Hillman by Steve Fraser, published in 1991. In a chapter about that same campaign of 1944 Fraser writes: "In *Commonweal* John Cort boiled biography and history into a single digestible clump, arguing simply that Hillman's Russian and Jewish origins were enough in themselves to prove he was a red." I sent Fraser a copy of the original article, and he called to apologize and express his amazement that he could have made such a mistake. I think I may have been even more amazed than he.

January 25, 1945

Speaking of religiosity, the other night I went to sleep with a gassy stomach and had a nightmare that was, I believe, a gift from God. Stop laughing and listen to me. I dreamt that I was going through a kind of quick purgatory, directed by some agent of God whom I didn't recognize, which involved the most excruciating pain—mental, physical, and spiritual—that I can remember ever having endured. I woke up, lay half awake for a few minutes, and went back to sleep, and the dream resumed exactly where it left off, something that almost never occurs with me. The purgatory then proceeded to a climax wherein the devil (I know he doesn't belong in purgatory) appeared before me, pointed at me, and, without even speaking, unleashed such an overwhelming blast of pure evil that I fell down in a semiconscious faint. I remember nothing of his appearance but the face, which was thin and basically handsome, but contorted with hatred and this positive fury of evil. I thereupon rolled down an incline and found myself looking through a long tube that apparently led to hell. Fortunately, the tube was too thin for me to get into, and I heard a voice from the other end say, "Not him." Blessed sense of relief! I had exactly the feeling of complete passivity in a completely strange world that the dead must feel before they reach Paradise—if they ever do. I can't express the horror and the terror that I felt at the idea of going to hell. I think I really knew in my mind and soul and body what it is like—the hopelessness, the loss, the pain, the darkness, the despair.

Finally, a priest and three other men came with a stretcher and carried me away, but they had only gone a short distance before I woke up again. I lay in the quiet and the dark and I could almost feel the devil in the room with me. I prayed hard and after about an hour got back to sleep, clutching my rosary.

Involved with French Labor

During 1944, before the end of the war, Helen and I became active in organizing the Committee of Catholics for Post-War Cooperation with French Labor, working along with our friends from the French Resistance, Joseph Botton and Paul Vignaux, both of whom were officials of the French Christian unions. Helen was treasurer, and I was secretary. In a letter to the advisory board I wrote:

> Things are moving fast in France. The Communists have established themselves in control of the main labor federation, the CGT [Confédération générale du travail], formerly controlled by the Socialists. However, the outlook for the Christian unions and the progress made so far have been even better than we hoped. The main obstacles to further progress are the absence of leaders who were deported to Germany and a rather desperate lack of working funds. About the first we can do nothing. About the second we can and must do a great deal.

Eventually we raised about $25,000 to get the French Christian unions going again. Within a few years they had replaced the Socialist force ouvrière as the major barrier to total Stalinist control of the French working class. By the 1970s they had established a reputation, in many industries, as more militant than the Communists, notably in such episodes as the Lip factory affair, where workers took over a watch factory after the owners had sold out. Around 1970 they changed their name to the French Democratic Labor Federation, as we had urged them to do during the war, and began working closely with the French Socialists. By 1981 they were the main support of the Socialists among the working class and contributed substantially to François Mitterand's election and the Socialist Party takeover of the National Assembly.

February 10, 1945

> Have just been reading *The Daily Worker* and its report of the London conference to organize a new World Federation of Trade Unions. I don't know when I've been so excited about anything. The issue has been joined and so far the Communists seem to be winning, with R. J. Thomas [UAW president] running a little interference.

The Communists did not control the new federation, not exactly, not yet, but the AFL's refusal to join and the CIO delegates' ignorance and naïveté allowed them to gain control, mainly through the election of a French fellow traveler, Louis Saillant, as general secretary. Another factor was the refusal to admit the Christian unions, a refusal the CIO supported because the Christian unions wanted to retain their own international organization.

May 2, 1945

Hitler and Mussolini dead in the same week! The speed with which the world is being rearranged leaves one dazed. . . . The Communist Party was a big success in the French elections.

May 5, 1945

Botton was here for two hours, and we spoke French the whole time, which left me exhausted. He talked to Saillant in Washington a few weeks ago. Saillant claimed that he was not a Communist and that he wasn't afraid to say so when he disagreed with them, although he didn't mention when he had said so. He also made the extraordinary statement, "the Communists are very strong in France; you cannot criticize them."

DEATH: INDIVIDUAL AND COLLECTIVE

July 18, 1945

It is difficult to think of us when Ed's death agony is so powerfully present in the room. Not that he's in terrible pain right now. Please God the worst is over. This morning I'll remember as long as I live. About 9:45 he got this attack of stomach gripes and just writhed in agony on his bed, moaning and crying out with pain. It was heartbreaking to watch and try to comfort him. I didn't do very well. It seemed like 15 or 20 minutes before the rattled nurse could call up the doctor and get instructions for medicine and a hypodermic needle. After that he was better, but very weak. I sent a telegram for his brother to come. I can't remember ever seeing him come to visit Ed, although he lives no farther away than Brooklyn. Poor Ed, such a lonely life he's had. So quiet and unassuming. He always wanted to go it alone, but when you're dying, it must get awfully lonesome. I know he wants to see his brother. It must be tough to die among strangers.

July 19, 1945

Ed died last night about 9:15. About 8:40 the night nurse helped Ed sit up to take some medicine because he said, "I'm weak as a kitten."

About 8:50 I came back from the bathroom, said, "Good night, Ed," and he said, "Good night." Usually I say, "Pleasant dreams," but I couldn't say it last night, so I said, "God be with you," and he answered, "Yeah," but he said it in such a way that I was much reassured, as though he really wanted God to be with him. Earlier I hadn't been too sure. A few minutes later he was coughing hard, as though something was stuck in his throat. I thought he was in pain, and I reached my hand up to turn on my bed light, but just then he stopped, and he must have seen me reach—it was still light outside a little—because he said, "It's all right." Those were his last words, and you could do far worse for last words. A few minutes later his brother and the night orderly burst into the room, switched on the light, and there was Ed, his mouth open, dead. His brother missed him by ten minutes at most. I wonder if he will ever forget that terrible sight.

July 27, 1945

My new roommate, Eddie Calder, unlike the former Ed, likes to talk. I learned today he once belonged to the Ironworkers Union and worked on the Empire State Building in the girder stage. He says that nearly one hundred men were killed—mainly as the result of criminal violations of law by the contractor, all hushed up. But he saw one man fall nine stories and survive. He landed on a pile of sand.

August 1, 1945

Another friend is dying—Harry Harkonish, the young Ukrainian Catholic I may have told you about. I just went over to say good-bye to him. He had his family there, with lit candles. He wished me luck and said, "Pray for me and forgive me for everything." What, I don't know, for he was always extremely polite and thoughtful. Poor Harry, or perhaps I should say, "Lucky Harry." He smiled at me. A fine, peaceful, Christian death. Not like Ed, dying alone in the dark. He was impatient to go.

August 8, 1945

The atomic bomb hit me at first as a sensation that intrigued the mind and the imagination. Only slowly did it reach the heart and the conscience. It is now making me sick indeed. So the Russians are in it. The world is moving so fast it makes you dizzy. Please God, make the Japanese quit and put an end to this horrible slaughter.

Despite my protestations, my former roommate Ed Bingham's death agony dropped out of mind many years later, as memories do that are too painful to recall, until I reread the letters excerpted here. I remember more clearly Eddie Calder's less dramatic death as he drifted into delirium from a combination of TB and meningitis, and how the mechanical skill of his right hand, of which he was so proud, went on expressing itself in delicate, intricate movements as he played with the bell cord beside his bed, long after his mind had gone and he could speak no longer.

BACK IN THE LAND OF THE LIVING

In the spring of 1946, when the doctors decided that they had been misreading my X-rays for eight months, they sent me out into the world again with approval to work. During these eight years of recurring illness I had learned something about patience and resignation to the fact that the world might well survive without me. I was not entirely convinced, but some light was beginning to dawn. I also had learned something about economics, something about life and death, and something about how lucky I was not to be dead myself.

Commonweal took me back and, determined to keep me well, set me up in a fine furnished room overlooking Central Park. In the evening, as I looked from my window, ecstatic to be back in the land of the living, the apartment houses on Fifth Avenue, lighted up on the other side of the park, seemed like enchanted cities or fairy castles rising out of a forest. In this mood I wrote a piece for the magazine in which I quoted Aldous Huxley's remark that "modern cities are nothing but great garbage heaps," but added, "If this is true, then New York City is surely one of the greatest, most fragrant, most wonderful and exciting garbage heaps of them all."

Helen and I were married during the summer of 1946 and went to live in an apartment more in keeping with my economic status, a tenement house on East Twenty-first Street, which my father once described as "that uncomfortable rabbit warren." The bedroom was so narrow that we had to put the twin beds end to end. There was barely room to sit down in the bathroom. From the living room we looked out on a magnificent view of a factory wall twenty feet away. If we wiped the windowsill clean, the grime was thick on it again before the next sunrise. But the rent was $30 a month, there was plenty of heat, and if it ever failed, we supplied our own. We had everything we needed, everything we wanted.

Having proved, with a good wife's help, that I could survive on the street, I returned to the ACTU that same year, to the dingy office at 226 Lafayette Street. My job was managing editor of *The Labor Leader* for $40 a week, to which I could add a few dollars doing labor pieces for *Commonweal.*

My brother Ambrose used to come and have dinner with us on Sunday evenings, and afterward we would listen to Fred Allen on the radio. On one of these evenings, as I was working at the desk, dummying up the pages of the ACTU paper, Ambie said to Helen, "I can see that John is happy. He's combining three things he loves— journalism, labor, and religion." And he could have added a fourth thing, marriage to a good wife.

Good wife, good life. Our first child, Barbara, was born, and then our second, Nicholas, and we knew the joys of parenthood. There were still, however, some hard times ahead.

9

The ACTU and the Stalinists

> The Christian opposition to the Soviet Union and commu-
> nism must not be identified with the capitalistic opposition
> that now generates so much emotion in the United States.
>
> —John C. Bennett

I RETURN NOW to the subject that so concerned Kermit Eby noted in chapter 6: the struggle between "two poles of power attraction in the CIO, the Communist pole and the ACTU pole," and his ominous comment, "Both believe the control of the CIO is part of the larger struggle for control of the world." Let me be frank. Not during the 1930s, but in the period after the war, the way things were developing, some of that thinking was in my own mind, I have to confess. I used to say that what happened to the CIO would determine what happened to the labor movement, what happened to the labor movement would determine what happened to the country, and what happened to the country would determine what happened to the world. Not exactly what Eby was saying, but there was a similarly heavy portentousness about it.

For many years after the war—that is, from the 1950s into the 1980s—a kind of malaise spread regarding the idea of being anticommunist. Without going so far as to be pro-communist, many liked to describe themselves as anti-anticommunist. Anyone who talked much about communism in those days still tended to be suspect among those of liberal and generous mind.

After the horrors to which Senator Joseph McCarthy introduced us, it is not difficult to understand why. But there was a time, well before McCarthy, when those of liberal and generous mind suffered no malaise, no squeamishness whatever, at the idea of being anticommunist. Of course, it helps to be old enough to remember what life was like in the labor movement of the 1930s and 1940s.

When I returned to the ACTU in 1946, the situation was different from that of the 1930s. With the support of Roosevelt and some help from labor shortages created by the war, the CIO had won the fight for union organization in the basic industries. The AFL, using the employers' fear of the more militant CIO, also made great gains in membership. William Green actually told his organizers to sell the AFL to workers and employers as "an American organization as against a foreign-controlled organization," meaning the CIO.

One way or another the workers did get organized. From a weak movement of 3 million members in 1935, U.S. unions had exploded to more than 14 million members in little more than a decade and had become a major element in the economic and political life of the country. In fact, you might say that the history of this country since then can be summed up in reactionary forces' successful effort to reduce the labor movement from a major element to a minor element. Its membership has been held to about the same number, but the labor force has increased so much that the percentage of union membership has shrunk from 35 percent to approximately 15 percent. A large part of this reduction occurred during the presidency of Ronald Reagan, who was at one time a New Dealer and a prominent union official in Hollywood. He discovered that there was more profit to be made from antiunionism than from pro-unionism.

THE KERNEL OF TRUTH

William Green's lie contained a kernel of truth, however. Stalinists had gained control or dominant positions in a number of CIO unions. Some of these unions had grown to impressive size. The United Electrical, Radio and Machine Workers (UE), for example, had grown into a powerhouse of more than half a million members. We at the ACTU figured thirteen unions as strongly anticommunist with 2.5 million members, fifteen unions pro-communist with 1.4 million members, and eleven unions doubtful, or somewhere between pro and anti. Of these in-betweeners, the UAW, a crucial battlefield, represented 1 million members. At various times the Communist Party and friends had been close to gaining control of this union, which would have given them a good shot at taking over the CIO itself, or at least of holding veto power over anything the CIO might want to do or say. The threat was real enough. Early in the game, various

Stalinist leaders realized the counterthreat that the ACTU posed to them. Catholics were estimated to be somewhere between one-third and one-half of the membership of U.S. unions, and the percentage was higher among the top and secondary leadership. Anybody who could begin to organize this mass into a cohesive opposition to Stalinist influence was somebody to be cut down as fast and hard as possible.

"Redbaiting clerical fascists . . . Cardinal Spellman's stooges . . . tools of Rome"—these were some of the epithets the Communist press threw at us. One top leader of the UE, James Matles, told his members that Jim Carey, former UE president and CIO secretary, was "the puppet of outside forces vastly more intelligent, subtle, and patient than himself," meaning the ACTU and the Catholic Church—a flattering statement, however inflated. Carey had been ousted from the UE presidency when he broke away from the party line during the Nazi-Soviet Pact in 1941.

The movement to free the UE from Stalinist control originated at the ACTU when 13 members from five different locals in the New York area were brought together by an ACTU communion breakfast in 1946. It soon expanded to include a broad coalition of socialists and assorted independents and eventually backed a Jewish candidate for UE president, Harry Block, against the Irish Catholic fellow traveler who had succeeded Carey. Block did not win, but he came close enough to give the Communist Party a good scare. This kind of ecumenical effort impressed observers such as Philip Taft, the labor historian, and Michael Harrington, another alumnus of the Catholic Worker, class of 1951, who had left the Catholic Church, become a Socialist leader, and in 1960 published a study of this anti-Stalinist movement in the UE in the academic journal *Labor History*.

HARRINGTON GIVES ABSOLUTION

Prior to the 1960 *Labor History* publication the ACTU opened its files to Harrington, and he reprinted a confidential memo of May 23, 1947, from ACTU headquarters to priests who were active in the labor movement. It read: "The ACTU has to be careful that it will not give the appearance of advancing the intra-union fortunes of its Catholic members. On this it has to be above suspicion." Harrington added that he had found no evidence that this policy "was not scrupulously carried out."

He also was impressed by something I wrote in *The Labor Leader* for February 1947, which criticized the anti-Stalinist leadership of a UE local in Bridgeport, Connecticut, for expelling 27 members for "communism." I wrote that in taking this action "the local leaders made a big mistake," adding, "It was not only a violation of the UE constitution, but was, we believe, wrong in itself. Under the maintenance of membership contract these workers had to be discharged from their jobs. Even if they were all Communists, we still believe that no union should take the terrible responsibility of throwing men out of work for membership in a party that the U.S. Supreme Court and Congress still recognize as legal."

An ironic footnote is the fact that the UE executive board suspended the Bridgeport local for this action, charging that the local had expelled the members without notification or trial. *The suspension of the local, however, was also without notification or trial.*

Harrington concluded, "The key to the UE struggle was not religion, or even the political issue of communism: it was the ability of each side to convince the workers that they could deliver decent wages, hours and so on." In a sense he was right because, as noted, the anticommunist slate led by Harry Block lost the election. The UE leaders, perhaps the most competent in the Stalinist faction, had done a decent job in delivering decent wages, hours, and so on. But in the larger CIO struggle the issue was in fact communism. In most cases the workers were ready to cast off Stalinist leadership whenever they had anything like a reasonable expectation that the alternative would do a competent job.

The Case for Anticommunism in the 1940s

In any attempt to analyze what communism looked like to the American worker of the 1940s it is important to distinguish between reality and what the military-industrial complex overlaid on reality in terms of an exaggerated picture of the situation and some of the more frigid expressions of the Cold War mentality.

No one could say exactly to what degree American workers saw communism in religious terms, to what degree in political terms, and to what degree in economic terms, the latter including communism as an economic system akin to the Soviet system as well as communism identified with the success of American Stalinists in winning economic gains for the workers.

I would guess that the religious aspect has been underestimated. Whenever Dorothy Day's former Communist friends asked her to accept "the outstretched hand" that the party offered Catholics during the Popular Front periods of 1935–39 or 1941–45, to join party fronts, or to cooperate with the party in any important undertaking, she always turned them off with a line that became a sort of refrain with her: "Lenin said that atheism is an integral part of Marxism." Usually that was the only reason she would give. For her it was enough.

It was enough for many others who did not share the intensity of her faith or her intellectual concerns about Marx and Lenin. A young, tough-talking New Yorker named Jim Conroy joined the Communist Party in 1940 and became the top official of a UE local, where he remained until the party line took a sharp turn to the left after the war. He then resigned and joined the ACTU because of the party's "unprincipled attacks upon the pope." The party then knocked him out of his UE job, and when he tried to return to his job in the shop, the UE lied to his former employer that the CIO had barred Conroy from employment in a union shop.

In the 1940s even more Catholic workers went to mass than do now, and most of them believed what they heard and read about the antireligious aspects of communism. Most of them took it seriously. They also took seriously the political aspects of communism: dictatorship, purges, suppression of both civil liberties and dissent. They had seen how Stalin signed an agreement with Hitler in 1939, stabbed Poland in the back, and attacked little Finland. They had seen how this agreement with Hitler turned American Communists completely around, from being pro-Roosevelt to anti-Roosevelt, to the point where they would dump a union president such as Carey for remaining pro-Roosevelt and would start and prolong strikes that kept planes and munitions from reaching the enemies of Hitler. These workers had seen then how party members did a reversal again when Hitler attacked Russia in 1941, so that they supported the war and Roosevelt with fanatical enthusiasm, signed and enforced no-strike pledges and piecework contracts, denounced John L. Lewis, whom they had formerly worshiped, broke strikes if necessary to keep the planes and munitions moving to Russia, and clamored for a second front before anyone was ready for it, all in order to relieve the pressure on the Soviet Union. American workers were not stupid. They could read. They could think.

A MAJOR OBJECT LESSON

Let me support my statements of the previous paragraph with a quick review of the North American Aviation strike in California in the month of June 1941, shortly before Hitler tore up the Nazi-Soviet Pact and attacked Russia. The strike is worth reviewing because, in the context of the times, it offered for me, for the ACTU, and for most of the more knowledgeable noncommunist leaders and members of the labor movement the single most persuasive lesson as to the meaning and significance of Stalinist control of unions.

North American Aviation produced the planes that England, Canada, and the United States needed to train student pilots. Its continued operation was extremely important to England's battle for survival against Hitler's blitz. Wyndham Mortimer, a competent and dedicated Stalinist, was then the West Coast director of the UAW and had organized the plant, where the workers' genuine discontents culminated in a vote for a strike on May 24, 1941.

However, the director of the UAW's aircraft division, Richard Frankensteen, was at that point in his anticommunist phase. He secured agreement from the local negotiating committee that there would be no strike until efforts to resolve the dispute had failed. R. J. Thomas, UAW president, then also in an anticommunist phase, and Philip Murray, CIO president, both joined Frankensteen in telling the workers to remain at their jobs pending the outcome of negotiations.

The National Defense Mediation Board proceeded with hearings in Washington, D.C. Although the country was not actually at war yet, there was a consensus that our fortunes were bound up with those of Great Britain, which stood almost alone against the Nazis. Not sharing this consensus was Elmer Freitag, chairman of the local negotiating committee, who was so anxious to see mediation fail that he turned his chair around and sat with his back to the government and company representatives. Another member of the local's committee simply got up, walked out, and disappeared.

Back in California Stalinist agitation succeeded in stampeding the workers into a strike, in violation of the local's constitution, international and CIO instructions, and the pledge of the local's negotiating committee. Top Stalinist leaders in the CIO—Harry Bridges of the West Coast longshoremen; Phil Connelly, head of the California CIO Council; and Milton Kaufman, a top officer of the Newspaper Guild—publicly urged the strikers to stay out and other workers to support them.

Frankensteen had to leave the bargaining table in Washington, D.C., and fly out to California, where a meeting of the strikers, orchestrated by the party leadership, booed and hissed him and denied him the mike. He persevered, however, and eventually got the workers back into the plant. Mediation continued and in the end won the workers the best aircraft contract in the country.

Walter Reuther, already a rising star in the UAW, characterized the strike as a Communist attempt "to sabotage defense production and discredit the Roosevelt administration." A few days later Hitler attacked Russia and strikes became, in the eyes of the party and its union friends, the worst kind of treason.

Pushing into the Vacuum

The end of World War II arrived in an atomic explosion that lit up the landscape of future wars with a horrible clarity. Stalin pushed into every vacuum that the defeat of Germany and Japan presented to him. Mao Tse-Tung, a loyal disciple, took over the vacuum that was China. The war-ravaged nations of western Europe also appeared to constitute such a vacuum. Common sense, plus a decent respect for human suffering, dictated that Truman should respond with the Marshall Plan, an outpouring of money and supplies to feed the people and rebuild the shattered economies of that region.

Stalin was unhappy with the Marshall Plan, but why? Why did he instruct his minions in the U.S. labor movement to oppose it tooth and nail? What other reason makes sense but that he wanted those western European countries to remain as weak as possible so that he could move in on them?

His followers quickly won control of the major labor federations in France, the Confédération générale du travail, and in Italy, the Confederazione Generali Italiana del Lavoro. Using that control, they were able to organize powerful Communist parties in both countries, parties that made it difficult for the majority parties to govern. The future of Europe was at best cloudy, and both the clouds and their consequences for the United States did not seem to us in the ACTU to be just the manufactured phantasies of "a Cold War mentality," even if reactionary capitalists and militarists and politicians used the situation to promote their own agendas. We were anticapitalist, but we were not anti-American.

By 1946 No Qualms

During the war the ACTU had been comparatively quiescent, although it continued to publish its newspapers in New York and Detroit and maintained most of its other chapters. In New York many of its leaders—Donahue, Wersing, Sheehan, and Harold among them—were in the armed forces, and I, as noted, in one hospital or another. But by 1946 most of us were back, either organizing at the ACTU, working for some union, or practicing labor law. We had established ourselves as outspoken defenders of labor, of the CIO, and of honest, democratic trade unionism over against the racketeer element in the AFL. We had paid our dues, won our badges of credibility, and had no qualms about taking on the Stalinists, who were, of course, far more numerous, better organized, better disciplined, and much better funded.

C. Wright Mills estimated the strength of the Communist Party in the late 1940s at approximately 60,000 members, most of whom, I would guess, were union members. In the labor movement the party's influence over American workers extended to much larger numbers. In 1945, for example, the party claimed only 840 members among marine workers, but its members and friends controlled the following marine unions with approximately 170,000 members: the East Coast seamen (the NMU), the West Coast longshoremen (International Longshore Workers Union, ILWU), and the Fishermen, Inland Boatmen, and West Coast Marine Cooks and Stewards. That is a ratio of about one to two hundred.

I doubt if the ACTU ever had more than 6,000 paid-up members nationally, and its members could not be said to control or dominate any international unions and controlled very few local unions. But we did have powerful allies, both within the labor movement and the society at large, notably the Catholic Church.

Mills pointed out that "anyone who has watched a successful CP [union] revolt knows that the CPs are not for rank-and-file democracy any more than the vested interests they replace." This truism may not be self-evident to nonunion observers, even when they are convinced that the Soviet Union was no democracy. From my observation the Communists did not use murder as a common tactic, like Stalin or Cockeye Dunn. Nonhomicidal violence, yes. Character assassination, yes. Economic strangulation, yes. False witness, yes. Violation of union constitutions, yes.

I could set down factual evidence of eleven examples of such tactics from our experience and observation in such unions as the Transport Workers, Office Workers, Bridges's West Coast longshoremen, UE, Retail Drugstore Employees, Local 3 of the Retail and Wholesale Employees, and the NMU, but will limit myself to a few of the more interesting ones.

QUILL AND HIS BLACKTHORN STICK

Michael Quill, president of the Transport Workers Union (TWU), was a colorful character. Born and raised in Ireland, he had seen members of his family jailed by the Black and Tans, and by the age of fifteen he was carrying a rifle in the Irish Republic Army, or so he said. He had a game leg that was said to be a casualty of this latter career, though his enemies gave less-glamorous explanations, and he often carried a blackthorn stick. He had come to this country in 1926 and a few years later went to work for the subway in New York as a gateman, twelve hours a day for six days a week. Douglas MacMahon, a confessed Communist who was secretary-treasurer of the TWU, revealed years later that Quill was a member of the party when Mac-Mahon met him in 1934 and paid dues until 1948, at one point being elected a member of the party's national committee.

After his break with the party Quill himself told Philip Murray that in 1947 and 1948 he and the UE's James Matles and Julius Emspak, its secretary-treasurer, attended secret meetings with William Z. Foster, Gene Dennis, and John Williamson, all top party officials, to plan the party's strategy in the CIO.

Quill once told me, during an interview in his office, that he was a practicing Catholic and that he had no illusions about its being possible to be a Catholic and a Communist at the same time because "the party is against religion." At this point he was still denying membership in the party.

September 1939. At the TWU convention in Atlantic City Quill blasted ACTU members in the union as "rats and company stooges" despite our record of active support of the TWU against the transit companies and several rival unions. ACTU member John Gallagher asked for evidence, but Quill gave none. Later, when time came for election of officers, no nominations were permitted from the floor in opposition to the official Communist Party slate presented by the nominating committee.

Years later I had lunch with John Sheehan, who related with a good deal of amusement his recollections of that convention. He reported that Father Charles Owen Rice, ACTU chaplain in Pittsburgh, was there, but as an old friend of Quill, whom he had gotten to know and like in connection with the cause of Irish freedom. This was well before Father Rice began to worry about Stalinist influence in the CIO, and in any case he did not believe that Quill was a Communist. He even spoke to the delegates in support of Quill and in criticism of his opponents, much to the dismay of our members at the convention. It was a classic example of the poor communication and coordination between ACTU chapters. John Sheehan was sitting up in the balcony and observing the convention when one of the Communists from New York fingered him and identified him as an ACTU attorney and general troublemaker. One of our members on the floor defended John and said he was attending the convention not as an attorney but as a correspondent for *The Labor Leader.*

Quill, who was in the chair, looked up and said, "Ah, by night a bed, by day a chest of drawers," and made much too much of inviting John to come down and sit at the press table. Thirty-six years later John was still able to laugh. Especially thirty-six years later.

One old Irishman said about Quill, "Don't cast your vote for Mad Mike Quill—he never worked and never will." Not true. Quill worked hard, or at least he talked hard. Another Irishman said more truly, "Ah, dear Lord, listen to the man—all he has to do is open his mouth, and the thunder pours out."

September 1939. Quill was running for reelection to the New York City Council and speaking from a soapbox in front of the car barns of the Fifth Avenue Omnibus. A driver named John Walsh was warming up the engine of his bus nearby, and the roar of the motor drowned out Quill's speech for a time. Intentional or not, God knows. Quill was overheard to say to his supporters, "A few of you fellows take care of that man." That night as Walsh was leaving the home of a friend, five men waiting in a parked car waylaid and beat him up.

September 1940. John Sheehan was assaulted and ejected physically from the union trial of Patrick Reilly, ACTU member, on the orders of James Fitzsimon, secretary of Local 100, the big New York local that was firmly under Communist Party control. John was there to defend Reilly, who was up on charges of "circulating false rumors" that the local spent $3,125 to bring home from Spain 25 members of the Abraham Lincoln Brigade.

Although a *Daily Worker* article confirmed that the TWU pledged this money, Reilly was expelled from the union anyway and, because union membership was a condition of employment under the union shop, lost his job on the Fifth Avenue bus line. Taft-Hartley outlawed this type of abuse seven years later.

Sheehan & Harold argued Reilly's case, without fee, up through the courts and won at every level on a judicial finding that the union trial was "unfair and arbitrary." State Supreme Court Justice William Collins ruled that Reilly was punished for "being a member of the opposition and not for slandering the union," adding, "Unionism is harmed if its members are hushed by threats or intimidations or fear, if fair and reasonable criticism is suppressed."

The final decision reinstating Reilly in his job with back pay ($3,654) did not come, however, until sixteen months later; meanwhile, Reilly, a seventeen-year employee who was campaign manager for the anti-Stalinist slate in the local elections, was conveniently out of the way. The Reilly slate, led mainly by ACTU members and Father Carey's students at Xavier Labor School, had polled 8,000 votes against the Stalinists' 12,000 and was clearly a threat the next time around. The Reilly ouster and similar tactics used on other members effectively crippled the opposition until after the war.

(Incidentally, no one should infer from the previous account that the ACTU was pro-Franco. Many of us, like Dorothy Day and *Commonweal*, were both anti-Franco and anti-Loyalist; some were pro-Franco, and some were pro-Loyalist. We had no official position.)

The Reilly decision inspired an interesting letter to *The Labor Leader* (February 17, 1942) from a Jewish trade unionist, Joseph Regelson, whom ACTU had helped as well. Regelson was a member of a CIO drugstore employees local that he described, accurately, as "a Communist-led outfit." After congratulating ACTU on the Reilly decision, he added:

> I too received a two-year suspension from union activities and had to resort to Supreme Court action to win vindication from a packed committee who acted as my inquisitors, indicters, jurors, judges and executioners. I was never permitted to cross-examine my accusers. . . .
> As a Jewish trade unionist I can attest to the non-sectarian nature of your action and your principles. I have found the ACTU the foremost, most consistent and most fearless of all who are conducting the fight for the betterment of trade unions in the interests of their rank-and-file members.

FATHER DROLET ON COMMUNIST PARTY TACTICS IN THE NMU

August 1947. Father Jerome Drolet was an outstanding labor priest who fought for striking workers repeatedly in the New Orleans area. He wrote a letter to the NMU convention, at which a struggle was taking place between the Communist Party and anticommunist factions. The letter called attention to the following events:

Two New Orleans Communists, state chairman Irving Goff and Ray Tillman, a TWU official, ordered a black stenographer in the NMU office, Dorothy Morris, who was apparently a party member, to send a wire to the NMU convention charging that two former NMU port agents, Harry Alexander and R. J. Sullivan, were guilty of racial discrimination.

Ms. Morris, a party member of conscience, refused to send the wire on the ground that the charges were untrue. Bill McCarthy, acting port agent in New Orleans and former chairman of the party's waterfront branch in New York, then discharged Ms. Morris. *Goff and Tillman meanwhile sent the wire anyway and signed Ms. Morris's name.* Fortunately, several hundred black members of the NMU in New Orleans sent a statement denying the racial charges against Alexander and Sullivan, and the convention's trial committee cleared them completely.

Target for Mud in the Newspaper Guild

September 1947. My own experience as a member of a Stalinist-led union was confined mainly to the Newspaper Guild. One night I was attending a meeting of the New York local's Representative Assembly, to which I was a delegate from *Commonweal.* I had organized a newspaper guild unit there in 1943 and was active, along with Larry and Kay Delaney of *Time-Life* and Bob Stern of the *Herald-Tribune,* in an anticommunist coalition that included socialists, social democrats, Actists, and plain ordinary trade unionists.

On this particular occasion two Irish Catholic leaders of the Newspaper Guild local had just announced their switch from the Stalinist to the anti-Stalinist camp. Neither of them showed up for the meeting. Jack Ryan, however, did show up. Ryan was a competent, tough, and loyal party comrade, the brother of a nun, and the chief officer of the local, which was one of the party's prize possessions in the labor movement, having 6,500 members in the news and opinion center of the country.

Ryan proceeded to make a long and angry attack on the two deserters and on the ACTU, which he blamed for their disaffection. At one point he claimed that a priest had told one of them that he had to make the statement or he would be read out of the Catholic Church, a story that turned out to be a total fiction.

When Ryan mentioned the priest, I could not resist interrupting, though I was clearly out of order, and I asked him, "Jack, could you tell us the name of that priest?" He said no, he could not, and then turned his attack on me personally, indicating that I was the Svengali, the Rasputin behind the whole business. Boos and angry shouts erupted from his supporters in the hall. Several of them, sitting in front of me, turned around and cursed me, and the hatred in their eyes struck me like a physical blow. It was a scary experience, particularly because at that point I had never had a serious conversation with either of the two men who had jumped over the wall, and I was as surprised as anyone by their jump.

The experience, however, was even scarier for the Communist Party. A few months later the two men headed a slate that defeated the Stalinist slate led by Ryan and a woman from the *New York Times* who described herself as "a Catholic and a Republican," which I have no doubt she was.

In a union like the New York Guild it would have been folly to bring people up on charges for opposing the Stalinist leadership in the crude ways that were successful in other unions. The whole operation was too close to the media and instant exposure. Therefore, the tendency was to use more gentle techniques such as character assassination and social ostracism. ACTU members had to be ready to take "Red-baiting clerical fascist!" thrown at them from time to time.

While the ballots were being counted during that crucial election, I happened to walk past one of the tables at Guild headquarters where counting was going on. A friend of mine sitting there told me later that a young woman beside him, whom I did not know, said as I walked by, "I wouldn't sit at the same table with that man." I began to notice that even friends edged away from me at Guild meetings. Some of the mud had obviously stuck.

CELLS, JEUNESSE OUVRIÈRE CHRÉTIENNE, *COMMUNIDADES DE BASE*

The Newspaper Guild experience calls to mind a running debate that went on at the ACTU about the best technique for developing union members and leaders who would not simply be anticommunist but positively effective in the direction of honest, democratic trade unionism. After all, one of our students at the Fordham labor school learned all about parliamentary law and public speaking and then used what he had learned to help the racketeer leaders of a Teamster local to frustrate a rank-and-file movement for reform.

We had the schools, our papers and other kinds of literature, and an occasional communion breakfast or retreat. There was also the ACTU cell within individual unions, often as part of a broader coalition organized to oppose undesirable leadership. Being a convert and coming out of the highly pietistic atmosphere engendered by Dorothy Day at the CW, I was an often painful advocate of a more religious approach. I remember one meeting at ACTU headquarters when, trying to gain a cheap advantage, I had the bad taste to point to the crucifix on the wall and work it into my argument. Larry Delaney rose in indignation and said, "There goes Cort sounding that phony religious note again."

I was impressed by the methods that the Jocists of Europe and French Canada employed. Canon Cardijn had founded the Jocists, the Jeunesse ouvrière chrétienne (in this country the Young Christian Workers), in Belgium back in the 1920s, and it had grown to be an international movement of millions with offshoots among students, intellectuals, farmworkers, and married couples. They emphasized spiritual development, study of the Gospel, small group meetings, and a technique of "see-judge-act."

This technique worked as follows: meetings would start with Bible study and proceed then to (1) examine, analyze, *see* some situation in the members' everyday life that might not square with the Gospel, (2) *judge* that situation in the light of the Gospel, and finally (3) resolve to *act* in some specific way to change the situation so that it might be brought more into conformity with the Gospel. This was not too different from the Marxists' cell technique, except in the all-important matter of the values applied to the life situation. It was also a precursor of the *communidades de base* in Latin America, as promoted by the exponents of liberation theology.

In ACTU inner councils I was continually harping on the need for something closer to the Jocist approach, pointing out that the kind of work we were doing required a high degree of moral stamina and dedication. Most of the members were reluctant to push a religious approach that could turn off workers who might otherwise cooperate with us for the secular goal of better trade unions. So most of our cells, where we had them, concentrated on union issues and a kind of natural-law morality that was acceptable to Catholic, Protestant, Jew, or atheist.

In the Newspaper Guild, however, I had a chance to try the Jocist technique. A group of us, all Guild members, met with one of the ACTU chaplains about once a month—usually Father Thomas Darby or Father John Byrne—and read a passage of the Gospel and talked about how it applied to our working lives. I believe it made us better trade unionists and better Christians, but the experiment was not duplicated elsewhere in the ACTU.

CURRAN AND QUILL JUMP SHIP

During those years—1946 to 1949—Joe Curran kicked free of the
Stalinist traces, carrying with him popular leaders such as Jack Lawrenson, Charlie Keith, and Hedley Stone. At the 1947 NMU convention, which I covered for *The Labor Leader,* Curran was determined
to let the Communists talk themselves out. At one point Keith made
a motion to close debate, and Curran ruled him out of order, which
he was not. The debate droned on and on. The convention lasted
three and one-half weeks, probably the longest in U.S. labor history,
and nearly bankrupted the union.

I marveled at how Curran had developed in the ten years since I
had watched him chair the first NMU convention in 1937, when he
was still a raw, rough seaman. He had grown in sophistication and
savvy, but still not enough to know that too much talk can be just as
lethal as too little.

As I listened to Keith and Lawrenson argue brilliantly with their
former comrades, I thought, "Where are the Catholics, where are
the Christians? Is there nobody to stand up to these Stalinists but
former Stalinists?" We did have some good men in the NMU, Joe
O'Toole and a few others, but when it came to public debate, they
were not in the same league with the products of Communist training. It was evident that there was a long way to go before Christianity
might be an ideological force that could compare with Marxism on
the U.S. waterfront.

In 1948 the Communist Party challenged Curran directly by running Blackie Myers against him, and Myers was crushed by a better
than two to one margin. The Curran faction won control of the national council for the first time. Curran was to remain president for
more than twenty years, until he retired with a pension so large and
a tendency to dictatorial tactics so oppressive that it threw a cloud
over all he had accomplished to make American ships decent places
to work.

Mike Quill was the next to jump ship. His former comrades now
became "irresponsible left-wing crackpots." His tactics in fighting
them were about as rough as his former tactics in fighting the ACTU,
so much so that we felt compelled to rebuke him in *The Labor
Leader* for his "haphazard use of strikes, strong-arm tactics, suspen-
sions without trial," and so on.

Nevertheless, in December 1948 Quill carried the Chicago TWU convention by 473 to 186 over his old friend, Austin Hogan, and the party was through in the TWU. To replace the party leadership, the convention elected other officers, including ACTU members, Xavier Laborites, and former Stalinists.

THE STRUGGLE FOR THE UAW

The struggle for control of the UAW went on for years and featured a kaleidoscope of shifting alliances during which the Communists backed at one time or another Walter Reuther, R. J. Thomas, Dick Frankensteen, and Dick Leonard, all of whom they had opposed at various other times. Their strongest and steadiest friend was George Addes, a self-proclaimed Catholic who was elected secretary-treasurer repeatedly until the final victory of the Reuther forces.

Reuther, who knew communism at first hand from two years in a Russian auto factory, set his face firmly against the Stalinist faction in 1937. From its founding in 1938 the Detroit ACTU supported him as part of a coalition of socialists, Schactmanite Trotskyists, and assorted anticommunist groups, recognizing him as the most intelligent, articulate, energetic, and reliable of the available leaders.

As I've noted, the Detroit ACTU was strong, with firm support from Archbishop Mooney, an excellent weekly newspaper, a talented editor and leader in Paul Weber, a network of forty-one labor schools, and, as early as 1941, more than 2,500 members, most of whom were also members of the UAW. This count may not seem like a great number, but it should be noted that the Communist Party had only 1,000 members in the UAW and yet came close to controlling it. Paul St. Marie, one of the ACTU's more prominent members, served several terms as president of Local 600 at Ford, which, with 90,000 members, was probably the largest local union in the world. Another effective leader was Tom Doherty, secretary of the big Local 7 at Chrysler.

Several things are noteworthy about the UAW story, in addition to the Communist Party's effort at North American Aviation to sabotage Great Britain's battle against Hitler in 1941. Although the tactics used were not as blatant as at North American, a similar intention appeared to be a factor in the Allis-Chalmers strike at Milwaukee and a General Motors wildcat strike in Flint, both in the same year. By 1943, however, when the Stalinists wanted an all-out effort to produce war material for the Soviet Union, they pushed hard for the introduction of piecework provisions in UAW contracts, having already inserted them in UE contracts. Piecework has always been beloved by employers and hated by most employees because pay depends so much on production, and the pressure to produce becomes unbearable, as my experience taught me in the cocktail tray sweatshop. The Reuther faction and the ACTU fortunately defeated this effort at the 1943 UAW convention in a three to two vote.

During the war Reuther was a vice president and director of the General Motors Division. After the war he was the strategist in the great General Motors strike of 1945, whose major demand was a substantial raise without any increase in the price of cars. Truman had made it clear that he would stop any raises beyond the Little Steel formula unless they could be granted without price increases. When General Motors said no to this, Reuther demanded that the company open its books and prove inability to pay. President Charles E. ("What's good for General Motors is good for the country") Wilson said no even louder to that and continued to say it to a Truman-appointed fact-finding board.

Paul Weber in *The Wage Earner* and I in *Commonweal* and *The Labor Leader* applauded Reuther's bold strategy. Weber wrote, "Reuther has performed a great public service" by getting people to question the assumption that "labor must concern itself only with rates of pay, not with the factors of prices, profits, and production that determine labor's *actual* pay" (emphasis in original). We recognized Reuther's effort as a historic attempt to extend the area of collective bargaining to those decisions that really determine the fate of American workers. This is a goal that still has not been realized, with sad effects for the nation and most especially for the autoworkers, as stupid decisions by management lost hundreds of thousands of jobs to Japanese and European automakers.

At any rate, when we at the ACTU compared this kind of labor leadership with the Stalinist policy of "What's good for the Soviet Union is good for American workers," we had no question whatsoever in our minds as to why we preferred Reuther.

Wilson did not open the books for either the UAW or the federal government, but Reuther got a decent settlement after a long and bitter strike during which the UE undercut the UAW by accepting a poorer offer for 30,000 workers whom it represented in General Motor's electrical division. This betrayal and ACTU's increasing support helped Reuther defeat R. J. Thomas by a razor-thin majority at the 1946 convention, but it was not until the 1947 convention that he was able to consolidate his control.

As Irving Howe and B. J. Widick point out in their book *The UAW and Walter Reuther*, this convention "turned out to be the decisive event in the gradual destruction of Stalinist power in the CIO."

THE ADMIRABLE PHILIP MURRAY

I admired Philip Murray so much that when our seventh child was born, Helen and I named her Alice Murray Cort. He was also the man who played the key role in the final departure of the Stalinist unions from the CIO, but the former fact did not depend upon the latter. The latter, however, has been the cause of hindsight judgments by elements of the American left, including the Christian left, that have cast a shadow over his place in labor history. I believe he deserves better.

The first time I saw Murray was around 1940 at a New York TWU convention in Madison Square Garden. I was at the press table down front; close enough to get a good look. The thing I remember is the wonder I felt at the modesty of the man. Humility is such a rare quality in an important leader, and Murray by this time was a national figure. Opinion polls of the 1940s showed that he was easily the most admired labor leader in the United States, yet he spoke as one who regarded himself as the least and the lowliest.

In 1942 he came to an ACTU communion breakfast in New York and, encouraged by Father Monaghan's warmth and wit, spoke for more than an hour. He talked about the CIO's Industry Council Plan, a wartime proposal for the organization and democratization of U.S. industries under tripartite councils representing labor, management, and government.

About the plan he said, "Once a bright young man charged me with sovietizing America. Another time an individual charged that I had taken the plan—body, boots, and britches—out of the encyclicals." In reporting this comment, *The Labor Leader* added, "Actually, he said, the Industry Council Plan really follows the plan laid down in the encyclicals almost completely." Even more actually, the plan came out of Pius XI's *Quadragesimo Anno*, the encyclical I taught at the CW in 1937.

Murray's roots were deep in the labor movement. He had come to the United States as a boy of sixteen from Scotland and went to work immediately in the coal mines near Pittsburgh. Two years later he punched a foreman when he caught him cheating the miners in the weighing of the coal that determined their pay—another kind of piecework. A strike followed, and the miners voted Murray president of the new Mine Workers local. Clearly there was more than humility in the young man, then only eighteen years old. Within four weeks the strike was broken, and the hungry miners, minus Murray, returned to the pits. Deputy sheriffs escorted him out of town with the cheerful parting words, "Don't ever come back." Reminiscing years later, Murray said, "I never had a doubt in my mind since then what I wanted to do with my life."

What he did was to become vice president of the Mine Workers under Lewis, then he became president of the Steelworkers, the man who organized the open-shop fortress of the steel industry, and finally in 1940 president of the CIO when Lewis lost his foolish gamble on Wendell Willkie, telling the American workers, "If you reelect Roosevelt, I'll quit as president of the CIO."

When Murray took over the CIO in 1944, he inherited from Lewis a staff that included a Stalinist editor of the *CIO News* and several Stalinist lawyers, one of whom, Lee Pressman, he even allowed to function as secretary of the resolutions committee at CIO conventions. Of course, during the war, after Hitler attacked Russia, there were really no issues that would lead Murray and his hired hands on a collision course.

In 1946 and 1947, however, they had the Marshall Plan and Stalin's hostile reaction to it, from which came the Cold War, the organization of the Progressive Party by U.S. Communists, and their successful wooing of Henry A. Wallace to be that party's presidential candidate in 1948.

ARCHBISHOP CUSHING BELONGED THERE

The Boston convention of the CIO in November 1947, a few weeks before Reuther's final victory in the UAW, was notable for several reasons. One, Archbishop Richard Cushing welcomed the delegates with one of the strongest pro-labor addresses ever given by an American bishop, greeting them with the words, "I belong here." Two, Murray still felt so unsure of his position vis-à-vis the Stalinists that he felt compelled to continue his policy of trying to reconcile the two camps. He persuaded the anticommunist bloc to go along with a resolution on foreign policy that failed to mention the Marshall Plan, an ambiguous statement that the Communists could support. The convention also ducked the question of Wallace and the Progressive Party, leaving it to the executive board. Murray was obviously playing for time, waiting to see how the UAW convention would turn out.

Reuther's victory was the turning point. Murray, from the careful compromiser of Boston, felt strong enough two months later, by January 1948, to warn all CIO affiliates not to endorse any party or candidate until the board had an opportunity to vote later that month. Anticipating a negative vote, the Communist Party opened fire on Murray for the first time. George Morris, head of *The Daily Worker* labor desk, wrote on January 12, "From what I know of Wallace's supporters in CIO ranks it is a foregone conclusion that they will not obey Murray's injunction."

Having decided to open fire on Murray and the national CIO, the party guns also opened up on the CIO's Industry Council Plan. In fact, they did the ACTU the honor of calling it "the ACTU Industry Council Plan." In another January column Morris attacked the plan as "fascism" and as simply an American application of "Mussolini's and Franco's 'corporate state.'"

Morris had forgotten that party chairman William Z. Foster had written in 1942 a pamphlet entitled *Labor and the War* in which he said, "The Murray Plan of industry-labor-management councils in the various industries offers a practical means of speeding up production by giving labor a real voice in war industry." But by 1948 a real voice for labor had become fascism and Mussolini's corporate state.

At the ACTU I welcomed the Communist attack, noting in a *Labor Leader* piece that "the fight against the CPs in the CIO has been too much on a strictly organizational plane. Now it moves onto the plane of ideas and policy where it belongs."

The CIO executive board voted thirty-three to eleven to oppose the Wallace candidacy for president and to support the Marshall Plan by name. The issue was clearly joined. By the time the CIO met in convention the following December in Portland, Oregon, Wallace and the Progressive Party had been wiped out, and Truman had narrowly edged Dewey for president. Wallace received 1,116,390 votes, or just 2.3 percent of the total.

Reuther and Emil Rieve, president of the Textile Workers, urged Murray to support a move to lift the charters of the Stalinist unions. He rejected this advice, content with resolutions condemning the Wallace candidacy and supporting the Marshall Plan. Wild applause greeted his charge that the Stalinists had "wanted to drive Truman out of the White House" and that "they did not care whether Dewey was elected or the devil was elected."

So discredited were the Communists that they were able to muster only 47 votes, as against 537, to oppose the anti-Wallace resolution. They did not even venture to oppose the Industry Council Plan when it came up again for discussion and approval. Or perhaps somebody at party headquarters reminded George Morris about Foster's pamphlet.

The last act of rejection came at Cleveland in 1949, when the convention, on Murray's recommendation, voted to expel the UE and the Farm Equipment Workers and to empower the executive board to expel any other unions that were proven to be Communist dominated. The key resolution opened with the words, "We can no longer tolerate within the family of CIO the Communist Party masquerading as a labor union." The board set up trial committees that sat in judgment on ten other indicted unions. Only one, the Furniture Workers, escaped expulsion on the grounds that its president, Morris Pizer, meanwhile had led a revolt that freed the union from Communist control.

ACTU supported this action. Were we wrong? I think not. Not under the conditions that prevailed in 1949. Since then the Communist world has split, fragmented, and finally imploded, with only China, Cuba, and Vietnam still claiming loyalty to the name of communism. In those days, however, the Soviet bloc stretched unbroken from the Pacific to the heart of Europe. Yugoslavia did not break away, really, until 1949, and even little Albania remained loyal for another ten years. There was no Euro communism, and all the Communist Parties in the world marched in lock step to a cadence dictated by the man in the Kremlin.

It came down to this question: Did a labor federation have either a legal or a moral obligation to make it easier for the Communist Party to gain control of unions in various industries so that it might be able, in the hour of the Soviet Union's need, to use that control for the Soviet Union's benefit? We thought not, believing that the historical record of performance proved that such control was so used and had become a clear and present danger to the CIO, not to mention to the country. The CIO was still locked in a struggle both with the AFL and the employers for the allegiance of American workers. Therefore, the libertarian argument had to yield to the law of self-preservation. When two of the ousted unions appealed to the courts, we agreed with Judge Simon Rifkind's decision that a labor federation should have the freedom to set its own conditions for membership within fairly broad limits.

FATHER RICE, THE REPENTANT CRUSADER

Monsignor Charles Owen Rice is an extraordinary man. Probably no priest in the United States during the 1930s and 1940s spent more time and energy working and fighting in behalf of organized labor. Born in New York, he had lived for part of his life in Ireland, where he acquired a musical brogue, enthusiasm for Irish independence, and a profound sympathy for the poor and exploited.

Inspired like me by Dorothy Day and the CW, he joined with Father Carl Hensler and Monsignor George O'Toole, two other Pittsburgh priests, in organizing the Catholic Radical Alliance. They operated St. Joseph's House of Hospitality, which at one time was feeding more than eight hundred a day and sleeping anywhere from three hundred to eight hundred. Father Rice marched in picket lines, spoke at union meetings, blasted both capitalism ("a mess [that should] be changed from top to bottom") and Catholic supporters of capitalism ("traitors to Christ"), and in 1938 started a Pittsburgh chapter of the ACTU.

On June 6, 1937, these three priests had traveled to Youngstown, Ohio, at the invitation of the CIO Steelworkers, who were on strike at a Republic Steel plant. One week earlier, ten strikers had been killed and one hundred wounded in the infamous Republic Steel Massacre at the Chicago plant. In 1981 Father Rice reminisced about this strike and that trip to Youngstown. I quote at length because what he says shows the quintessential Father Rice and because this event probably was just as important to U.S. labor history as Father thought it was:

> They wanted us because the whole local establishment had been mobilized against them: politicians, police, newspapers, businessmen, professional men and clergy, including a couple of highly vocal Catholic priests. . . . Our visit did not win the strike, but it definitely helped to win the hearts and minds of workers to the union side. The anti-union clergy had been getting away with murder until we challenged them, quoting the popes' encyclicals as proclaiming the worth of trade unions and the dignity of labor. . . .
>
> Our foray did more than influence the workers. It was a factor in changing the Church and its reputation from anti-labor to pro-labor. Priests all over the country began sounding off on the union side and supporting the CIO, but ours was the most dramatic and effective action. It got national attention. I was a fledgling priest, only three years ordained. I've been flying since. Those local priests, who were loudly pro-company and anti-union, were furious and counterattacked, but we creamed them. (*Pittsburgh Catholic*, September 4, 1981)

More than any of us, Father Rice, in spite of fighting for labor and creaming its enemies, attracted the most bilious vilification from the Stalinist camp in the CIO. Being close to Murray, who was a fellow Pittsburgher and loyal Catholic, Father Rice was often given credit for turning Murray against the Communist wing. He was also active with the anti-Stalinist element in the UE locals around Pittsburgh. Some years ago, however, I read that he regretted this activity and, in particular, that he regretted his cooperation with the House Un-American Activities Committee, which most of us looked on as an enemy of organized labor.

Shortly after reading about my old friend, I happened to be in Pittsburgh and dropped in on him. I found him in the rectory of a beautiful Gothic church in a black ghetto. He was thinner, more ascetic, and gentler than the firebrand I remembered. I asked him about his change of heart. He said, "Too many thieves and charlatans replaced the Commies." He also mentioned that he had been turned around by Michael Harrington's piece about the ACTU and the UE in *Labor History*. When I got home, I looked up the piece and read it for the first time, but to my surprise found nothing in it that would justify Father's dismissal of his anticommunist activity as "all that negative crap."

Harrington wrote from a socialist point of view and had no illusions about the Communists in America being anything but "the pawns of Russian foreign policy," as he had described them elsewhere. I found his piece objective on the whole, tending to exaggerate by a little the ACTU's lack of cohesion and to disparage the value of the ACTU a little, but no more than I might expect from a man who felt that workers should be meeting in socialist groups rather than in Catholic ones.

I could only conclude that Father Rice was perhaps too quickly impressed by the change in intellectual fashion, which has changed again in more recent years and moved him to a more balanced viewpoint. Our conversation did move me to look more closely at the ACTU's role. My conclusions did not change dramatically. Not that our conduct was always above reproach. Sometimes a kind of childish petulance marked our efforts, a certain mean-spirited quality, and doubtless from time to time an exaggerated concentration of energy and concern.

I picked four issues of *The Labor Leader* at random from the period November 1949 to March 1950, the height and climax of the anticommunist campaign in the CIO. I found 6.4 percent of the reading matter devoted to this subject. Because in the perspective of history this campaign was probably the most newsworthy thing happening in the labor movement at that time, the thought occurred to me that maybe we underplayed it.

DIFFERENCE OF OPINION IN THE CEMETERY

Kermit Eby was not alone in regarding the ACTU as an organization that took its orders from a hierarchical network of priests and bishops that ultimately owed its allegiance to Rome, not to American workers. One way to clarify this viewpoint is to take an example of a difference of opinion between the New York ACTU and its own cardinal-archbishop, Francis J. Spellman—namely, regarding the Calvary Cemetery strike of 1949.

At the time the cardinal seemed to have a good opinion of the ACTU, perhaps influenced by our anticommunist activity. He was giving us $3,000 per annum out of his own funds. As one of two full-time employees on the staff—the other was Roger Larkin, our solid executive secretary—I was especially conscious of this largesse, which paid for my salary plus another $1,000. It therefore became a serious business when in January 1949 the ACTU and its chaplains became involved in support of a strike of approximately 250 workers at Calvary Cemetery, in defiance of Cardinal Spellman. He characterized the strike as "an anti-American, anti-Christian evil and a strike against the church." We characterized the strike as justified, and not simply because John Sheehan and John Harold were attorneys for the union.

At one point in the strike I stood with a group of the cemetery workers on the sidewalk of Lexington Avenue near St. Patrick's Cathedral. We were waiting for the main body of strikers, who were attending a union meeting to decide what their response would be to telegrams the cardinal had sent each one of them, with the exception of the negotiating committee, summoning them to a meeting in a hall across the street from us.

We saw the cardinal, a short man with a quick, firm step, come around the corner and go into the hall. Finding no one there, he came out and crossed over to speak to us. With him was a man holding an umbrella over him to shield him from the snow. The cardinal said, "It's time for the meeting to start, men, and I'd like you all to come into the hall."

He went back across the street, but nobody followed. He came back again, the man still holding the umbrella. "I said the meeting is about to start, men. Please come into the hall."

He started back. Nobody followed. The cardinal turned and saw that nobody was following. He stopped in the middle of Lexington Avenue. The man and his umbrella kept going, and the cardinal stood in the middle of the street and the falling snow. Fortunately for him the lights were red, and for a moment there was no traffic. I wondered at the tenacity of the man, standing there, pulling at us with his eyes, like a bulldog, teeth clenched on the seat of our pants. I decided it was not for nothing that he was cardinal.

The men could not stand to see the cardinal publicly humiliated or themselves publicly humiliated by him—I'm not sure which. They followed him into the hall. I followed too, but was turned away because I had no telegram.

After several months of suffering on the part of the strikers, bitterness and acrimony on the part of all, the cardinal backed down, improved his offer and settled the strike. Of course, the $3,000 he gave to the ACTU was cut off immediately. It was a serious blow, but a cheap enough price to pay for proof that *The Daily Worker* was wrong when it maintained that the ACTU was simply the stooge of the hierarchy in the U.S. labor movement.

THE DEATH OF THE ACTU

With the expulsion of the Stalinist unions it is probably true that some of the yeast went out of the CIO and in some areas vacuums were created into which moved the "thieves and charlatans" Father Rice had deplored. On balance, when the good and bad are weighed, it was my judgment then and remains my judgment today that the good tipped the scale.

In 1969 another long and bitter strike was conducted jointly, in an unusual display of cooperation, by the Stalinist UE—by then reduced to a shadow of its former size and power—and its AFL-CIO rival, the International Union of Electrical, Radio and Machine Workers (IUE), which had done most of the reducing. The strike was against General Electric and the reactionary antilabor policies of its president, Lemuel Boulware. James Matles, the UE's most effective leader, spent Christmas week visiting picket lines at General Electric plants in Indiana and Ohio. I was impressed by the UE's willingness to work with the hated IUE and, almost more, by the Christmas picketing. I doubt if Christmas meant the same thing to us, but even so. Not all of that yeast was bad.

In its November 1959 issue *The Labor Leader* ran a house ad under a big black head: "WANTED: People to Save a Life, the Life of the ACTU." It said that "anticipated income will not see our New York Chapter into the New Year" and appealed for financial support.

That was the last issue of *The Labor Leader.* The chapter itself kept going into the 1970s. *The Wage Earner* died in 1964, but by that time it was no longer an ACTU paper, the Detroit chapter having disaffiliated in 1956 over the question of taking stands on controversial issues, the kind of thing that both the New York ACTU and the Detroit ACTU had been doing in the 1930s and 1940s. Because the New York ACTU also included the national office, and the national director was always a member of the New York chapter—George

Donahue, Vic LoPinto, and Frank Andolina all served in that position—there was a tendency to feel that the action of the New York chapter compromised the other chapters. The Detroit chapter became the Detroit Catholic Labor Conference; the Boston chapter became the Catholic Labor Guild (CLG); the Chicago chapter became the Catholic Labor Alliance, ably led by Ed Marciniak, Bob Senser, and Father Daniel Cantwell. For many years the alliance published an excellent paper called WORK.

We New York types did have a way of getting into trouble, sticking our noses into other people's business, embarrassing both enemies and friends. We were aggressive, self-righteous, and critical. And we made mistakes. Yet . . .

The grain of wheat, falling into the ground, dies. Like a good grain of wheat, the ACTU fell into the ground and died after some thirty-odd years. Other wheat sprang up in its place. About the time the ACTU was fading, a New Yorker named Herman Benson founded the Association for Union Democracy, which over the past thirty-odd years has been giving invaluable help to rank-and-file movements in many of the same unions with which the ACTU was involved.

Of the hundreds of Catholic labor schools the ACTU started, only one remains, a highly successful one run by the Labor Guild, formerly the CLG, of Boston and by one of the last Jesuit labor priests, Father Ed Boyle. Labor education has been taken over by the unions themselves and by colleges and universities, but it is a secular education that could use a few courses in labor ethics. Such a course might help to persuade union reformers to avoid Ron Carey's fatal error in the Teamsters Union, when illegal use of union funds not only destroyed his promising career, but stopped cold the surge of optimism for all labor that followed the popular success of the United Parcel strike.

However, it seems that a more permanent surge exists behind and below that one. The religious community has come alive in the National Interfaith Committee for Worker Justice. A dynamic young woman named Kim Bobo, a kind of Protestant Dorothy Day, has brought together, at last count, sixty-two organizations in thirty states into an ecumenical coalition that has not been afraid to take stands on controversial issues, supporting strikes, organizing campaigns, and, in short, putting different sects—Catholic, Protestant, Jewish, and Muslim—on the line in favor of social justice and the rights of labor.

The coalition has stood firmly on that line, even when it runs through the administration of religious schools, universities, hospitals, and nursing homes, reminding them that the employment of union-busting attorneys is consistent with no religious faith that is worthy of respect.

Waking as if from a long sleep, the academic community, both faculty and students, also has come alive to the fact that it has the power to stop paying big money for products made by children for starvation wages in distant sweatshops, products covered with the names and logos of their colleges and universities. And this awareness is beginning to make a difference. It might even mean that U.S. unions such as the Union of Needletrades, Industrial, and Textile Employees may still have a chance to win decent contracts in factories making the 15 percent of our clothing that is still manufactured in this country.

The election of John Sweeney and a more militant leadership at AFL-CIO headquarters have also encouraged the academics. Labor and the academy are actually talking to each other once again. There is evidence that labor's decline has bottomed out and that the AFL-CIO may yet become strong enough and smart enough to challenge the power of Big Money to dominate and exploit the U.S. economy and U.S. politics.

Reactionaries who rejoice at the decline of labor's former strength and liberals who mourn might do well to think again. Their joy and sorrow are premature. Two nuggets of ancient wisdom should give them pause and hope respectively. The first is Lord Acton's aphorism, "Power tends to corrupt, and absolute power corrupts absolutely." The power of Big Money and of those who wield it is in many areas approaching the absolute of corruption, and that kind of corruption inevitably sets in motion countervailing forces that will not rest until they stop it. The second is the simple saying, "In union there is strength." For all its crazy excess "the Battle in Seattle" against the myth of the all-powerful, all-knowing World Trade Organization in December 1999 was probably a fair indication that said forces, stumbling toward each other into some kind of union, are already in motion.

HIGH MINDS AT DIFFERENT LEVELS

Sometime in the 1950s I was attending an ACTU national convention in Cleveland and sharing a room with Joe Dever, novelist and union activist, on the sixth floor of an ancient hotel in a low-rent section of that city. During the night while we slept, a visitor took advantage of our failure to check the lock on the door and stole all our money.

The next morning, downstairs in a hall of the same hotel, Joe and I were listening to a convention speaker, one of the more solemn labor priests. Working to a climax, he proclaimed, "What we need is more high-minded individuals at every level."

Joe leaned over and whispered, "Especially on the sixth floor." The story can serve to mark my passage from ACTU crusader to the more pragmatic world of a full-time local union business agent, a world where one better learn to check the door locks.

10

The Virgin Business Agent

"Cort thinks he's a virgin until he's had a strike, and he's
determined to lose his virginity."

—Boston Newspaper Guild member

THE SUMMER HEAT in New York was rough on tubercular types. The
summer of 1949 was rougher than usual, and the doctor sent me back
to the horizontal. This time I went to a sanatorium run by the Sisters
of Mercy in the Adirondacks, an excellent facility, very different from
the hospital in the Bronx. Helen took Barbara and Nicholas to her
parents' home in upstate New York, where, realizing she was preg-
nant again and might well be losing her gamble on my recovery, she
struggled with a temptation to despair.

Eight months later the doctor said I could go back to work as soon
as Helen had her baby. Much to her doctor's surprise, the baby
turned out to be two babies: Paul and Rebecca. Meanwhile, the
ACTU told me they could not afford to take me back, and, physically,
I could not afford to go back to the frantic rat race that was life in
the New York labor movement.

Fortunately, a *Commonweal* reader who was an officer of the Boston Newspaper Guild, Frank O'Donnell, wrote and asked me to
come to Boston to do a temporary job as negotiator for the local with
three of the Boston dailies. I did, leaving Helen and the children in
Baldwinsville and living on the backside of Beacon Hill in a cheap
hotel that was also favored by strippers from the Old Howard bur-
lesque theater around the corner.

After seven months I was hired on a more permanent basis as
executive secretary (business agent) of the local. I was able to bring
my family to Boston and settle them into an apartment in a working-
class district of the city in Brighton, fifty yards from the Cenacle
convent grounds. A few years later, thanks to Helen's father, we were
able to buy a house on top of the hill on which the convent stood,

right next to the sisters' fence, commanding a great view of the city and an indigo bunting's nest.

The house was fine, but the yard was full of broken whiskey bottles and abandoned bedsprings. The kids from the neighborhood used it as a shortcut from the main street below to their homes on the hill. To enclose our yard I built a chain-link fence, effectively blocking the shortcut, or so I thought. A few days later I looked out the window and saw two kids scrambling over the fence and coming through the yard. I charged out of the house bellowing like a wild bull. We had never owned real estate before, and despite my training at the CW, here I was fighting for the right of private property, *my* property, like any feudal lord. I shocked myself with the force of my reaction.

Another aspect of primitive instinct was revealed during those first days in the house, which had a fireplace, the first we had lived with since our marriage. It was summer, and we had no occasion to use it until one cold, rainy Sunday. I built a fire and sat in front of it all day, transfixed by this ancient symbol of hearth and home, which seemed to unite us with our ancestors and with the ancestors of all people everywhere who had ever been cold or lonely. As St. Francis put it,

> Glory be to thee, my God,
>   for our brother fire,
> by whom you illumine the night.
>   He is beautiful, and joyful,
> and strong, and full of power.

FROM FASCIST TO COMMUNIST, QUICKLY

The first few days on the Boston job I was scared stiff. Although I had been working in and around the labor movement for fourteen years, I had never had the major responsibility for negotiating a union contract, and this situation was a tough place to start. The Boston Guild had no Communist problem. What it had was a bad case of company unionism. Too many of the members wanted the Guild to roll over and play dead for management.

Our big unit was at the *Herald-Traveler*, a rich Republican newspaper run by Robert Choate, a Boston Brahmin. The contract had no arbitration clause, except on certain kinds of discharges, so we had no way to enforce it. We negotiated for 550 employees, and the remainder of the plant was represented by fourteen AFL unions—I repeat, fourteen. Everyone assumed that these unions would not respect our picket lines if we were so foolhardy as to go on strike, so we were unable to get a vote from the membership even to threaten a strike because they did not trust their own leaders not to call a strike if they were so reckless as to give us that power. The result was a piece of cake for management.

What I said in negotiations was therefore less relevant than what I said to the membership. I immediately set about stirring up class war and resentment by putting out leaflets highlighting the generous profits the company was giving itself and comparing the wages unfavorably to Guild scales in other cities of comparable size. Many members were so pro-management that they resented the leaflets more than they did the management, and the word began to go around that Cort was a Communist. After years of being tarred as a fascist in New York, only two hundred miles and a few months away, this attitude was almost refreshing.

During negotiations at another Boston paper I was pushing for a joint production committee that would eliminate waste and make the paper more profitable. I said, "We don't agree with Karl Marx that labor and management have nothing in common. We want to see a bigger pie so we can get a bigger slice of it."

A man from the *Herald-Traveler* who was on our negotiating committee but not paying attention heard only the words *Karl Marx* and nudged the Guildsman next to him, "Did you hear that? I told you Cort was a Commie." This was the level of union sophistication that I had to deal with.

My second objective was to build some kind of united front with the craft unions, who had more power to shut down papers than we did. If nothing else, we had to sow the seeds of doubt in the publishers' minds as to whether the crafts would support us in the event of a strike. I therefore set out to organize a joint council of newspaper unions, playing up our common failure to win either pensions or health and welfare plans.

This approach worked out well; I had planted the seeds of doubt, which led to a bargaining session at the *Herald-Traveler* during which, as I wrote Helen, "I started dropping hints about strike action if they did not accept arbitration. So they began to get sore again, and I got sore. My voice began to break and I almost lost control, I was so fed up with the whole damned thing. Everybody feels we could not get a strike vote, but who knows? Anyway, judging from their reaction, we gave them a scare."

This pathetic picture of the virgin business agent threatening strike action, his voice breaking betimes, was an accurate indication of the power balance at that point. It would be six years before we could persuade the membership at that paper, or at any paper in Boston, to back up our demands with a strike vote.

Meanwhile, the Korean War forced up the cost of living, and the publishers had to respond with raises. They also gave way on pensions and on health and welfare plans. To that extent I enjoyed a measure of success. In 1957 we finally got the strike vote at the *Herald-Traveler*, thanks to the leadership of a dauntless reporter, Bill Wells, and an equally dauntless dispatcher, Leo McCusker, and won ourselves a contract we could enforce. We never did have a strike, although we were on the street several times in support of mailer or printer strikes.

I remained a virgin, but with no regrets. Any union leader who thinks he has to have a strike to prove his machismo is a fool. But the strike vote, or the threat to strike, is essential to effective bargaining. Without it the union leader is just in there with his hat in his hand, begging for crumbs. Without it he is not so much a virgin as he is a eunuch.

TRYING TO SAVE THE FOX FROM EXTINCTION

The *Boston Post* had once been the paper with the largest circulation in New England. It also had been one of the few Democratic newspapers in New England. The Newspaper Guild had more than three hundred members there who were naturally anxious to see it survive.

After years of dwindling circulation and revenue, a slightly mad financial genius named John Fox bought the paper in 1952. Fox had sold a controlling interest in Western Union in order to buy the paper, a fact that should justify my calling him slightly mad. He operated out of offices high up in a building he owned on State Street, where his sense of melodrama required that a guide go before anyone scheduled to meet him, unlocking doors as that person approached the inner sanctum. Sometimes he received us sitting in a thronelike chair in a room that included a grand piano, albums of old 78 rpm jazz records, a huge safe whose open door revealed a stuffed fox and stacks of paintings, and walls festooned with peeling paint.

Fox once told me that President Eisenhower was illiterate. He sounded as though he meant literally illiterate, so I questioned him further. He said, "Yes, literally illiterate. He can't read." I said, "How do you suppose he got through West Point?" He said, "Oh, that's no problem."

Fox enjoyed the fun of publishing a paper, reading his own prose in print, and throwing his weight around in the furious bear pit that was Massachusetts politics. Although he was a Harvard man himself, having worked his way through by playing a pretty good piano in a jazz band, he could not stand proper Bostonians like Choate, or they him. At that time the *Boston Globe* was too pure to dabble in politics, and Hearst was Hearst, more national than local. There seemed to be room for another kingmaker.

But Fox was faced with some difficult economic facts. His competitors had morning-evening combinations, whereas the *Post* was just morning, which gave the competition an edge in selling ads. And the craft unions had made the publication of newspapers an expensive luxury. The pressmen's requirement of eighteen men on a certain press contrasted, according to my information, with a requirement of nine men on the same kind of press in New York. My guess was that the press could probably be run with four men or less. The printers insisted that when an ad came in already made up in mat form, a typographer must sit down and set up the same ad in "bogus type," which was then thrown away just so that nobody would lose any work.

Like so many American workers, they could not forget the nightmare of the Great Depression, and their fear of unemployment was so great that they insisted on contract provisions that were slowly but inevitably forcing unemployment on them again, as well as making it more difficult for us to get decent wages for the editors, reporters, and advertising and business personnel who had come late to the realization that they needed a union.

Shortly after I came to Boston, I introduced into negotiations a proposal that I thought was in keeping with the need for greater economy and efficiency on the newspapers. It also happened to be in keeping with Pius XI's call for workers' sharing in management and profits. I proposed, as noted earlier, the creation of "a joint production committee."

The federal government had encouraged the organization of such committees during World War II. At one point they had numbered more than three thousand and had made a significant contribution to the production of bigger and better quantities of war material.

Part of my interest stemmed from reading *The Dynamics of Industrial Democracy* by Clinton Golden and Harold Ruttenberg, which had been published in 1942, early in the war, when the national mood was more receptive. Golden had come out of the Mine Workers and was a vice president of the Steelworkers, one of Murray's trusted lieutenants and also one of the finest and most intelligent men to reach the top ranks of U.S. labor. Ruttenberg was research director of the Steelworkers and another very bright man.

A SENSE OF EXCITEMENT

Years later I reread Golden and Ruttenberg's book and found myself reading with the same sense of excitement that marked my first look at it. In my opinion few things so good or so relevant to what ails us now, today, have been written since then, certainly not by anyone who knows workers and the labor movement as well as Golden and Ruttenberg knew them. I also think it should appeal to any representatives of management who are smart enough and decent enough to know what is good for themselves, their workers, their company, and their country.

As a Catholic, I still find it exciting that two union officials of that caliber, neither of them Catholic, were saying in 1942 what Pius XI had said in 1931—namely, that workers should be sharing in the management and profits of the enterprise in which they are employed, as well as in the management, through their union representatives, of entire industries and of the national economy as a whole.

Phil Murray and John Brophy had been pushing the latter point, with support from the entire CIO, through the Industry Council Plan, but they had been relatively silent on the former. Golden and Ruttenberg were saying that economic democracy should be extended beyond the usual union contract at the plant level as well, and that when it is, it can be both dynamic and profitable for both labor and management.

From the book I put together the proposal for a joint production committee and then sold it to the Boston Guild's leadership and membership. We proposed that the committee, representing equally the Guild and management, should meet every two weeks and discuss members' suggestions on "how to improve production and increase efficiency." Further, "management and labor shall share equitably any benefits resulting from the committee's work through regularized employment, better working conditions, increased earnings, lower costs, and other feasible ways." (The proposal was a bit weak on ways and means of sharing equitably, a weakness later corrected by the Scanlon Plan, named for another Steelworkers official.) Also: "No employee shall lose his job as a result of any improvement adopted. . . . Management shall seek the consent and understanding of the committee before introducing production changes."

Without consulting the national Newspaper Guild, we made our proposal to all three papers with whom we had contracts in the negotiations of 1951. I had been corresponding with Ruttenberg, and I wrote him: "Hearst was rather bored by the idea. The *Post*, which desperately needs it, gave us some blather about 'management prerogatives,' and the *Herald-Traveler* at least pretended to appreciate our attitude, but preferred an idea of their own, which is to call key people in from time to time for a friendly lunch in the company dining room. The *Post* is going slowly to the wall, and I hope we can beat some sense into them in the coming negotiations."

My hope was in vain. Mrs. Grozier, the publisher's widow who then owned the *Post*, was too insulated from the operation to know what was going on. Her hired hands, who knew, did not have the intelligence to use their knowledge. Fox bought the paper, and before I could try out the proposal on his hired hands, it ran afoul of the national Guild. The officers ordered us to withdraw the proposal on the ground that we did not have the Guild's ideal union security and job security provisions.

We replied, "Where is union security and where is job security if the paper folds? We don't like to be obvious, but if the paper folds, there is no union and no jobs—period. The Guild is supposed to be a smart union, but it seems that we are still slogging along under the old schooner rig in an age, not of steam, but of diesel engines. The dinosaur was a powerful beast once. It died out because it could not adjust to changing times."

We appealed to the Guild convention in Los Angeles. I presented Boston's case, and the attack began. The low point was a speech by my counterpart in St. Louis, a competent and respected professional who said, "We don't want any holding hands with management. What we need is more militancy, not less." I had trouble keeping my temper when confronted with this kind of insulting stupidity. When it came to a vote, we were decisively defeated.

Some time later I sounded out Fox informally to get a feel for his receptivity to the idea. There was none. As one of his spokesmen put it, "We may run this paper into the ground, but at least we'll be the ones who do the running." Smart. And they did. It died in 1956.

On June 19, 1972, the *Herald-Traveler,* no longer rich, sold out to Hearst, which merged three newspapers into one. The city is down from seven dailies in 1950 to two in 2003. In New York, during my lifetime, the *World, Herald-Tribune, PM, Mirror,* and *World-Tele-gram* have followed the sinking *Sun* over the horizon. Since 1954, the year the Los Angeles Newspaper Guild convention turned down the Boston Guild on production committees, approximately eighty newspapers have either merged or folded under Guild contracts, leaving thousands out of work. Many more have failed that the Guild never managed to organize. More and more relentlessly monopoly has been fastening its death grip on the vocal chords of American free speech and free press.

Some Guild members turned out to be too intelligent to let this go on happening without some kind of response. I called the international office, at this point part of the Communication Workers, and learned that committees similar to the one I proposed in Boston had been operating successfully at the *Minneapolis Star and Tribune* and also at the *St. Paul Pioneer Press.* They call them "voice committees" because they give the workers a voice in how their jobs are organized.

Other U.S. unions, including some of the largest in some of the largest corporations, are beginning to smarten up. Sometimes they are called "quality-of-working-life committees." Their members are coming to see that the old, narrow view of collective bargaining is passé, and they are finding ways to prove that a more participatory way of working pays off in job satisfaction, job security, and cash money. Some employers are also smart enough to notice that it pays off for them in reduced absenteeism, tardiness, turnover, waste, and strikes, as well as in improved productivity, quality, and profits. But why should noticing that take extra intelligence?

Among the unions and companies displaying that kind of intelligence are the UAW at the Ford Wayne Stamping Plant and Rockwell International, the IUE at Lockheed Martin, the Machinists at HR Textron and John Deere Horicon Works, and the Steelworkers at LTV Steel, Hennepin Works.

Now all we need, as John Paul II suggested in one of his encyclicals, is to extend the principle of worker participation upward. Why not give workers seats on the board of directors, joint ownership of the company, shared responsibility for planning the economy and for providing jobs at decent wages for all? Why not make it easier for producer cooperatives to succeed? Why not?

GAP BETWEEN RELIGION AND LIFE

Herewith something lighter, but also heavier—a story from my more frequent duties as handler of Newspaper Guild grievances on the job. This incident involved two young women, whom I will call Pretty and Plain because their appearance was a significant factor in the grievance. Pretty got sick, and when she came back to work, she asked her boss for an easier job until she could recover her strength.

The boss asked Plain if she would take Pretty's job for a while on a temporary basis. Plain said okay, she would, so the two switched jobs. Pretty got along fine in Plain's job and fully recovered her strength. But Plain, who was a high-strung, delicate person, didn't like Pretty's job at all, and it began to affect *her* health. She went home sick and told the boss she would not come back until she was restored to her old job, as he had promised she would be.

But the boss wanted Pretty where she now was, which was working close to himself. He obviously enjoyed that proximity. He didn't care if this situation affected Plain's health. Management had the right to assign employees where it wanted them, and if Plain didn't like it, she could go somewhere else, and so on.

Plain complained to the Guild, and I went to work on the case. Under the contract management did have the right to assign. All we had was an appeal to justice. The boss had promised Plain's job back when Pretty recovered her health. He was now welshing on that promise.

It was obvious that if Pretty would agree to go back to her old job, we would have a stronger argument. In fact, all she had to do was go back for a couple months. Another job was opening up then, and both women could have the kind of jobs they wanted.

I went to see Pretty, but on company time and company property. That was my first mistake, although this practice was customary in handling grievances at that paper. I said to her, "Look at this as an act of charity, something you can do to save Plain's job and save her health." That was my second mistake. I should have said, "Look at this as a question of justice. Plain helped you out when you needed help. You owe her." I guess I assumed she could see that for herself.

To my appeal for charity she responded, "No, charity begins at home. I have to think of myself first."

This bald-faced expression of selfishness triggered something wild and reckless inside me. Before I could stop myself, I hit her with the dread C word. I said, "Are you a Christian?"

"Yes," she said, "I'm a Catholic, a good Catholic. I went to communion yesterday and today, and I'm going again tomorrow. My conscience doesn't bother me."

I broadened my appeal from charity to something more serious and binding. I said, "I think you have a moral obligation to do this for Plain. If you don't think so, go to some priest in whom you have confidence and ask him."

"No," she said, "I don't have to ask a priest. I know the difference between right and wrong."

At this point I might have said, "Pretty, you don't have the vaguest notion of right and wrong. Your conscience is not clear. It is a murky quagmire of moral confusion and self-deception. Here you are committing a serious sin against both justice and charity—objectively if not subjectively, materially if not formally, as the theologians say— and you can only tell me what a good Catholic you are. In this context your attendance at daily mass and communion is almost a sacrilege, a blasphemy."

As it was, I said none of this. Finally, as a great concession, she promised to think it over for twenty-four hours, and I left. It was a polite, friendly parting. I am partial to pretty young women myself, and I don't make a habit of abusing them.

Pretty did not keep her promise to think it over for twenty-four hours. She went to the boss and told him everything I had said. The boss told the Big Boss, another Catholic, and the Big Boss went through the roof.

The shop steward, still another Catholic, said to me, "This time you've gone too far. The Big Boss wants to bar you from the building. He says he won't stand for you intimidating the employees and bringing religion and talk about priests into the building, where they have no place. And I agree with him."

The Guild shop chairman, still another Catholic, agreed with the shop steward. He said to me, "If you told me to go see a priest, I'd bust you in the nose."

So it seems that I did indeed make a big mistake. It seems that the Bible, the popes, and bishops are wrong. It seems that religion doesn't have anything to do with real life, after all, and certainly it has nothing to do with industry and the relations between worker and employer or between worker and worker—or so all these Catholics told me. But somehow I could never bring myself to believe them.

11

The Miracle of Good Pope John

> The peoples have, as it were, awakened from a long torpor.
> They have assumed in relation to the state, those who gov-
> ern, a new attitude—one that questions, criticizes, dis-
> trusts. . . . Taught by bitter experience, they are more
> aggressive in opposing the concentration of dictatorial
> power that cannot be censured or touched, and call for a
> system of government more in keeping with the dignity
> and liberty of the citizens. . . . If we consider the extent
> and nature of the sacrifices demanded of all citizens. . . .
> the democratic form of government appears to many as a
> postulate of nature imposed by reason itself.
>
> —Pope Pius XII, Christmas Message, 1944

SHORTLY AFTER going to work in Boston, I wrote to Ed Marciniak:
"The situation here is really shameful. Millions of Catholic workers
and not one labor school. The Catholic Labor Guild is a sewing
circle."

I began signing up members in the CLG and organized them into
a caucus. We asked for a new election of officers because one was
long overdue, but the chaplain refused to hold an election or even to
call a meeting to discuss it. At this point he was telling his friends,
"John Cort is a Communist from New York who is trying to take over
the Catholic Labor Guild for the Communist Party."

When a year went by without a meeting or election, we appealed
to Archbishop Richard Cushing. He asked a friend of mine, Father
Dan McColgan, a professor at the seminary, to investigate and make
a report. Father reported, and Matt Marley, Gus Goslin, Joe Dever,
and a few others went with me to the chancery on May 4, 1952, to
get the archbishop's answer from the chancellor, Monsignor Walter
Furlong, a man with a bushy head of white hair and a very direct
manner of speaking.

He ushered us into a sort of boardroom, where former bishops of the archdiocese looked down on us from the walls, and I began to talk in a rambling, incoherent way. Monsignor Furlong stopped me. "We had Father McColgan's report," he said, "so today I happened to see the archbishop, and I asked him what he thought we ought to do. 'It's very simple,' the archbishop said to me. 'Just write [the CLG chaplain] and tell him he's through.'"

It was one of the more delightful moments of my life. I wrote a friend: "One surprise followed another. Furlong is fantastic and a bird-watcher to boot, showed us all over the place, and loaned me a bird book. Father McDonnell, our man, will probably be appointed chaplain [and he was]. . . . Furlong is all for lay initiative and clergy in the backseat. Joe Dever said, 'My whole anticlerical world is collapsing.'"

Within weeks we elected new officers and got a good labor school going. The school and the CLG, under Father Ed Boyle, are still going strong today, fifty years later.

POPE JOHN EXPECTED ME IN ROME

Sometime early in 1961 I received in the mail a small leaflet whose front cover read: "Roma, May 15, 1961—World Meeting of Christian Workers. 1891—*Rerum Novarum*—." On the back cover was a picture of the pope over the words, "His Holiness Pope John XXIII expects us in Rome!"

I knew at once I had to get there, but how? I persuaded the CLG to elect me a delegate, but it had no money, and neither did I. I tried other sources of funding without success. On an impulse I picked up the phone and called the archbishop, by then Cardinal Cushing. We were friendly, but I knew that if you caught him in the wrong mood, he could bite your head off. I got him on the phone and asked if I could see him.

"What do you want to see me about?"

It sounded like the wrong mood. I swallowed hard and launched into the deep. "Well, next May they're having a congress of Catholic workers in Rome to celebrate the seventieth anniversary of Leo XIII's *Rerum Novarum*."

"You want to go? I'll send you. Come and see me Thursday." I hung up in a pleasant state of shock.

I went to see him Thursday, and he said, "I'll give you a thousand dollars. You've got to go jet. It's the only way." Jets were new then, more expensive and much faster than the old prop planes. I had barely recovered from this good news when he added, "Anybody else you want to go? I'll give you another thousand." The cardinal was both a great fund-raiser and a great spender, as his successor, Cardinal Humberto Medeiros, learned to his sorrow.

I thought of suggesting Helen, but it seemed a little selfish. "I'm sure the Labor Guild would be happy to send another delegate."

And so it came about that George O'Brien, a conductor on the Boston subway, and I came to represent the United States at the World Meeting of Christian Workers. I've always felt a little guilty about that $2,000, a much more sizeable sum then than now, because I think the cardinal overestimated my influence with the Boston press and thought he was going to get better coverage by being kind to me. Or am I that easy to be kind to?

SAD SAINTS IN FIVE LANGUAGES

Rome was a revelation. The fountains alone filled me with enthusiasm. Most of the sessions were held in a large building in the suburbs, where we also lived, the Domus Mariae, a place more accustomed to conferences of bishops and other religious types. Excellent meals were served at small tables, with a carafe of white wine on each table. The waitresses were young and pretty, and George was so smitten by ours that he urged me to ask her to come to the United States and marry his fourteen-year-old son. Fortified by the wine, my Berlitz Italian was able to convey this proposition with such appeal that she stood by our table for ten minutes giving it consideration. Her major problem seemed to be the question, "Can I bring my mother?"

Approximately three hundred delegates from forty-two nations were at the conference. They represented organizations similar in nature to the ACTU and the CLG—those from Europe being larger, better funded, and better organized; those from Asia, Africa, and Latin America, most of them, even smaller and poorer than ourselves.

The Congress languages were English, French, Spanish, Italian, and German, and we quickly learned some of the difficulties attached to simultaneous translation, particularly when done by linguistic amateurs, and the consequent difficulty of developing international cooperation and goodwill. Even the Spaniards found it difficult to understand the Spanish of the South Americans. The poor English priest who was handling the English translation had to wait for the Spanish to be translated into French before he could put it into English. Small wonder that meaning got lost.

One of the sessions featured five speakers, all of whom spoke in French in the same vein—very spiritual, very vague, very sad, and, after three days of similar speeches, very exasperating to our practical and optimistic American minds. One Swiss carpenter in particular, tall, thin, and lugubrious, looked and sounded as though he had spent more time in a seminary library than a carpenter shop. When the floor was opened for discussion, I rose to my feet in an advanced state of suppressed frustration.

A few moments earlier, ten French bishops had entered the hall and taken seats down front. I pleaded for something a little closer to the language of the workers and the Gospel—something shorter, simpler, more concrete, more to the point. "Most of the speeches so far," I said, "have been marked by profound sadness. It is true that there is anguish and suffering in the world, particularly among the poor, and we must be deeply concerned about that, but the impression I get from the speakers is that we Christians, far from trying to overcome this suffering, have been overcome by it."

I closed with a French quote from St. Francis de Sales, "*Un saint triste est un triste saint*" (A sad saint is a poor saint). One of the French bishops smiled and nodded in agreement, but the reaction of the French-speaking laymen was less favorable. I think they put my comment down as one more bit of evidence that the Americans are a nation of boorish materialists lacking in most of the finer feelings. It was more kindly received by the U.S. delegation, which included such friends as Bob Senser of Chicago, Fathers Bill Kelly and Joe Hammond of Brooklyn, and Father George Higgins of Washington, D.C. Repetition of the slogan "A sad saint is a saint sad" became the occasion of loud and unseemly laughter in gatherings off the floor.

The upshot of the meetings was the adoption of a provisional constitution of a new federation of Catholic organizations engaged in the social and labor apostolate, to be called the World Movement of Christian Workers. There was a general feeling of optimism, which I shared, but tempered somewhat by the more sober remark of one of the movement's leaders: "Well, we may have our new international, but I don't think it's going to stop the march of communism."

CLUE TO HOPE UNREALIZED

At one of our sessions Amintore Fanfani, leader of the Christian Democratic Party and premier of Italy, spoke to us. I was impressed. He spoke with force and eloquence in the language of the social encyclicals. He called for a fight against the evils of poverty and injustice and for "a life both free and prosperous, dynamic and just, in no way burdened by the traditional faults of capitalism, yet never confused by the false lures of communism."

To me at the time Fanfani was a symbol of hope for Italy. Looking back now, however, past an endless series of economic and political crises, I have to conclude that this particular hope was never realized. I got a clue as to why one night when Romeo Maione took me to a large meeting of the Italian Catholic Action, an organization whose members formed a powerful bloc within the Christian Democratic Party.

Maione was an interesting young man, a big, tough-looking type who was at that time the international president of the Young Christian Workers and one of the most zealous, attractive Christians I have ever had the pleasure of knowing. Raised by Italian parents in Montreal, he was equally fluent in English and French as well as Italian, thereby solving the problem of simultaneous translation.

Cardinals, bishops, and priests heavily laced the meeting we attended. Most of the laymen were dressed in fine black suits and looked very bourgeois indeed. They were having their own celebration of the encyclical anniversary. The proceedings were entirely in Italian. A prestigious prelate spoke and was warmly applauded.

I noticed Maione scowling during the speech and leaned over to whisper, "What's he saying?"

Maione whispered back, "Reactionary crap."

The Christian Democratic Party, unfortunately, was never able to free itself entirely from the influence of this conservative crew, finally breaking up in the 1990s, its members going all over the political spectrum, from far right to far left, and the government finally winding up in the hands of an impressive former Communist named Massimo d'Alema and still later in the hands of Silvio Berlusconi, a rightwing billionaire who seems to own half of the Italian media.

THE WORKERS RETURN FOR POPE JOHN

The most memorable part of our week was the meeting in St. Peter's Square with Pope John. I never got closer to him than a hundred yards, but it was close enough to see and feel something of the quality of that extraordinary man. I had been disappointed when he was elected pope three years earlier, a corpulent old man of seventy-seven whom few of us in the United States had ever heard of. But it had not been long—probably those first dramatic visits to the prisons of Rome—before I realized that this "fat old man" was just what the poor old church had been waiting for.

Back in the 1920s Pius XI, as I noted earlier, had lamented to a visitor that the scandal of the nineteenth century was that the church had lost the working class. On that Sunday afternoon in 1961 it almost seemed as though the workers had returned to the church. From a platform erected before the portal of St. Peter's, Pope John looked out across a sea of workers, nearly one hundred thousand, come to him from the four corners of the earth.

Was it an answering look of love or simply of awe and wonder that I saw in the faces of those hard-handed, leather-faced workers who stood around me, many of whom had traveled on buses for days or hitch-hiked from distant lands to reach the Eternal City, to take part in the parade from the Coliseum, scene of the martyrdom of the early Christians, to stand and sing the credo with Pope John in St. Peter's Square?

The pope, reading in Italian in a strong, clear voice and punctuating his sentences with vigorous gestures of his right hand, told of his concern for "the misery and hunger in which millions upon millions of human beings are now struggling" and promised us a new encyclical, within a matter of weeks, in which he would bring the social teaching of the church up to date. This encyclical was the highly progressive *Mater et Magistra.*

He also called that day for "the recognition and respect of a moral order that is valid for all, which recognizes its foundation in God, the protector and defender, the distributor of goods, riches and mercy, and the terrible avenger of injustice and inequality from whom no one can flee."

The crowd knelt, and the pope gave us his blessing, shook hands with the attending cardinals, and, as a band played Gounod's *Processional,* walked down through the rows of papal guards in their colorful uniforms, down through the cheering crowd of workers in the square, past the black- and brown-skinned Africans and Asians, past the blond Germans and Scandinavians, past the French and the Brazilians, and past at least one American who felt the tears gathering behind his eyes.

The sense of the past is strong in Rome, the feeling of history and the passing of centuries, the long view. You see it in the ruins of ancient Rome, in the medieval helmets and halberds of the Swiss Guards, in the ancient pageantry of St. Peter's, even in the scarlet vestments of the cardinals.

One young delegate standing with me, a recent convert from the Communist Party of Denmark, was a little shocked by the splendor of it all. He found it difficult to reconcile this splendor with the poverty of the proletariat. I tried to explain to him something of the function of ceremony and symbol in the life of the church, but did not tell him that behind my loyal explanations I shared some of his misgivings.

The sense and weight of the past returned again the next day when thousands of the worker-pilgrims crowded into the basilica for the celebration of a special mass by Cardinal Cento, who spoke to us in six languages and told us that when he was a young seminarian he had seen Leo XIII himself, an old man of ninety, in this same basilica during the Holy Year of 1900. "His face was emaciated," the cardinal said, "like parchment, but his eyes still shone with an effulgent brilliance."

In recalling how Leo had cried out against "the almost servile yoke" that a small group of very rich men had fastened upon an immense multitude of proletarians, Cardinal Cento reminded us that "five years before the promulgation of the encyclical *Rerum Novarum* in 1891 an industrialist told the Belgian Labor Commission, 'Industrial science consists in obtaining from a human being the greatest possible amount of work while paying him the lowest possible wage.'"

"Alas," the cardinal added, "the god of certain capitalists was none other than the golden calf."

Pope John's Contribution to Democratic Process

Pius XII's Christmas Message of 1944, with which I opened this chapter, might be viewed with some cynicism because he might be charged with jumping on the winning bandwagon after being somewhat less than forthright with Hitler when it might have made a difference. Not so in the case of John XXIII, who in terms similar to those of Pius XII, points out in his other great encyclical *Pacem in Terris* that "it is in keeping with the innate demands of human nature that the state should take a form that embodies the threefold division of powers corresponding to the three principal functions of public authority." From the context it is clear that the pope refers to the division of power in the legislative, executive, and judicial branches characteristic of democracies. He says further that people have "a right to choose who are to rule the state, to decide the form of government, and to determine both the way in which authority is to be exercised and its limits."

For Catholics, of course, the great question then and now is, "If the 'innate demands of human nature' require democracy in the government of states and the conduct of industry, why should they not require at least some measure of democracy in the government of a church?" This question has become even greater and more relevant in the wake of the sex abuse scandals within the church that came to light in the United States in 2001 and 2002.

I believe Pope John was conscious of this basic question when, only ninety days after his election, he decided to convene the Second Vatican Council. From that moment it was inevitable, as he threw open the Vatican's windows to the modern world, that the Catholic Church itself must feel the winds of democracy blowing through those ancient halls and respond to them. For what was the council itself but an instrument, an expression of democratic process? It is ironic but also reassuring that, in responding to those winds from the modern world, the church was only returning to the apostolic tradition of the Council of Jerusalem described in the fifteenth chapter of the Acts of the Apostles.

BACK TO ROME IN 1967

In 1967 I had a chance to witness something of the development of the laymen's role in the democratization of the church at the national and international level, an opportunity that revealed some of the promise as well as the perils that lay in the path of that development.

At the time I was president of the National Catholic Social Action Conference (NACSAC). When the American bishops invited the organization to send somebody to Rome for the Third World Congress of the Lay Apostolate, I was chosen to go. Before we took off for Rome, approximately fifty of us, representing most of the major Catholic lay organizations in the United States, met at a pleasant retreat house in Bethesda, Maryland, for a weekend of getting our heads together.

There were several representatives of the Curia present, one of them being an Italian bishop and another a laywoman from New Zealand, Rosemary Goldie, said to be the first woman ever employed by the Curia in an administrative capacity. She had been the organizer of the first two lay congresses in 1951 and 1957. Also present were men and women representing the Washington, D.C., offices of the American bishops and the really big lay organizations.

It soon became evident that two schools of thought prevailed among us. One wanted us to go along with whatever Rome and Washington might decide, particularly in respect to the structure of a permanent international organization of the laity. The other wanted the laity to have the deciding vote in this matter. To non-Catholics this issue may seem an incredible thing to be arguing about, but to Catholics, even in the postconciliar world of 1967, it was still a hot topic, so strong remained the dominance of Rome and the hierarchy.

I made a modest motion "to petition the Holy See that the provisional structure of the international body of the lay apostolate to implement the documents of Vatican Council II be developed and approved by the Third World Congress of the Lay Apostolate." Matt Ahmann, president of the National Catholic Committee on Interracial Justice, and Mike Woodruff, president of the U.S. Young Christian Workers, were among those who spoke in favor. We recessed Saturday night with the outcome still very much in doubt. Late that night, during a few delegates' bull session, Pat and Patty Crowley, copresidents of the Christian Family Movement, swung over to our side. The next day we won the vote by about two to one, and the international committee planning the congress subsequently endorsed our petition.

Most of the meeting in Rome was held October 11–17, 1967, at one end of the Via della Conciliazione, the Street of Reconciliation, which runs from the Tiber River up to St. Peter's Square. The name of the street was appropriate for the occasion. Paul VI had arranged for the congress to meet at the same time that he had called the first meeting of the Bishops' Synod in the Vatican at the other end of the street. His intention was to mobilize the entire body of the church, laity and hierarchy, to begin to implement the ideas of Vatican Council II.

It was a noble concept, but as a gesture of unity or reconciliation not entirely successful. In some ways the lay congress was more impressive than the synod, although we had only a week, as compared with the synod's month, to deal with all the problems in the church and the world. The congress included 2,987 people—both men and women from every walk of life—from 103 countries and eighty international organizations as well as hundreds of national organizations. The synod, consisting of approximately two hundred bishops, represented only one sex and one profession.

No real dialogue developed between the synod and the congress, but at one point during the week a delegation of twelve lay leaders, including four women, walked up the Via della Conciliazione and made an official visit to the synod. A U.S. magazine published a picture showing them sitting at the front of the hall facing the bishops in a sort of historic confrontation. The photo shows Romeo Maione, who meanwhile had been elected president of the laity's key body, the Assembly of Heads of Delegations, sitting there with one finger pressed against his lips as if to suppress an irresistible desire to say something.

Spokesperson at the time, however, was the woman who happened to be chairing the congress that day, Eleonore Shields, president of the U.S. National Council of Catholic Women. She greeted the bishops and read a strong memorandum from the congress requesting a role for the laity in "the establishment of future directives" and the right to elect our representatives to new "structures" and councils at all levels of the church, from the parish and the diocese on up to the

Curia, thereby assuming our "proper responsibilities as members of the people of God."

This bold language, however, came to very little. At a great mass in St. Peter's Paul VI spoke to us—the synod of bishops behind him, the ambassadors in their braided uniforms looking on, and all around him the representatives of the Catholic laity of the entire world. Dorothy Day was one of a hundred delegates chosen by the steering committee to receive communion from the pope's own hand, a wonderful thing for me to see. But the pope's remarks were rather negative and discouraging.

He spoke about the danger of creating two "parallel hierarchies, two organizations existing side by side." In view of this statement the assembly decided to limit itself to a respectful request that the Holy Father "enlarge the composition of the Council of the Laity [a body of twelve lay leaders whom he himself would name] in accordance with democratic processes so that it may be truly representative of the multiple cultures, organizations, and forms of the lay apostolate in all parts of the world."

THE LAITY ON BIRTH CONTROL

The congress took a number of progressive positions on such subjects as war and peace (including a slap at U.S. involvement in Vietnam), racism, poverty, and the responsibility of the rich nations to stop exploiting and start helping the poor nations. Our lack of weight was perhaps best illustrated in the resolution of the hottest topic to come before the congress: the question of birth control.

In this matter we actually had more freedom than the bishops, whom the pope had told once again, as at Vatican Council II, not to discuss the issue at all. The word was out that Paul himself was getting ready to issue an encyclical on the subject. The word was also out that a special commission of fifty doctors, theologians, sociologists, and assorted laymen and women, including the Crowleys, which the pope had established several years earlier to advise him, had voted overwhelmingly in favor of easing the ban on artificial means of contraception.

As I was sitting in a workshop on economic development chaired by Tom Melady, then of Fordham, and the brilliant English economist Barbara Ward, someone introduced a resolution on birth control that included these words: "There is need for a clear stand by the teaching authorities of the church which would focus on fundamental moral and spiritual values, while leaving the choice of technical means for achieving responsible parenthood to the parents, guided by medical and scientific advice."

During the discussion it occurred to me that this wording would imply that the church had no business speaking out against abortion or sterilization, which were also technical means of limiting the size of families. When I pointed out this problem, the words "acting in accordance with their Christian faith" were inserted after "parents." This rewording appeared to bring the teaching authority of the church back into the determination of technical means, and in a sense it did. I can testify that the delegates' intention was that parents would be free to select their own method, short of such techniques as abortion and sterilization.

In the final vote this wording passed the Assembly of Heads of Delegations by a count of sixty-seven for, twenty-one against, and ten abstentions. This outcome was better than the necessary two-thirds, even if the abstentions were counted as negative votes. The entire congress approved the vote at the closing session in the presence of a large delegation of bishops from the synod.

Paul VI, however, was not moved by this advice or by that of his own commission or by that of a smaller theological commission that he also appointed, a group that started out leaning toward the traditional view but wound up with a fifteen-to-four majority in favor of liberalizing the church's position. He appointed still another commission that gave him advice he could accept. In July 1968 he issued the encyclical *Humanae Vitae*, affirmed the old teaching, and set off a chain reaction of discontent that continues to this day.

Dorothy Day used to quote an old Spanish proverb that "every baby is born with a loaf of bread under its arm." For ourselves and our ten children Helen and I always found that to be true. Christ said, "Take no thought for the morrow, what you shall eat, what you shall drink or wherewithal you shall be clothed. . . . But seek first the kingdom of God and his justice and all these things shall be added unto you" (Matthew 6:31–33). This proverb also expresses a profound truth, but sometimes it is difficult to believe that the only reason so many people are hungry is that they are not seeking first the kingdom of God and his justice. Maybe the kingdom of God and his justice involves using some more reliable means of limiting the number of our children if we find that we cannot feed them.

That's one popular—very popular—view of the matter, and it was my view in 1967. On the other hand, the richer people of the world like to absolve themselves of all responsibility for the poorer people of the world by saying, "If these poor people only had the intelligence to use birth control, they wouldn't need our help, so why should we blame ourselves for their suffering or do anything about it?" So birth control becomes the great cop-out, as well as the great facilitator of fornication and adultery. Meanwhile, Amartya Sen, the 1998 Nobel laureate who has been president both of the American Economic Association and the International Economic Association, assures us that "there is, in fact, no serious evidence . . . that population is beginning to outrun food production. . . . Food output per person has been steadily upward." Further, Sen says that "population growth is declining" and "is expected to go steadily down until the size of the world's population becomes nearly stationary." Food experts also assure us that "the world today produces enough grain alone to provide every human being on the plant with 3,600 calories a day. That's enough to make most people fat" (qtd. in Frances Moore Lappé and John Collins, *World Hunger: Twelve Myths*).

The problem therefore is simply one of a more equitable distribution of food, work, and money, and on this topic "the kingdom of God and his justice" have a great deal to say.

For Catholics who know their Bible, it is difficult to forget that Jesus Christ, in several chapters of John's Gospel, promised that "the Holy Spirit whom the Father will send in my name will teach you everything" (14:26) and "will guide you to all truth" (16:13).

Catholic tradition, at its most liberal, still holds that the pope plays a role in the Holy Spirit's guidance. Errors and contradictions in minor details of the Gospels make it evident that Jesus' promise does not apply to minor details. But birth control is not a minor detail. It is clearly a major detail, as are such other controversial matters as abortion and homosexuality. True, the church has changed its position on such questions as slavery, usury, capital punishment, and repression of heresy, which also might be described as "major details." The problem may come down to such questions as "How major?" and the further question of timing. If the pope cannot bring himself to approve a change, the more conservative view of the promises in John's Gospel is that the Holy Spirit does not want him to do so. However, this view of the matter is the less popular one, but I must confess that it is the view toward which I have been tending in old age, without, however, any claim to infallibility. It is also the view that Dorothy expressed more confidently in *On Pilgrimage* (1999 edition, p. 228).

AN EXCHANGE WITH CARDINAL WRIGHT

Early in 1970 Cardinal John Wright returned from Rome to Boston for his mother's funeral. By then, in his position as head of the Congregation of the Clergy, he was one of the growing numbers of non-Italian members of the Curia. We had become good friends while he was bishop of Worcester, so he called and asked me to visit him at the Copley Plaza Hotel. We had a pleasant talk during which he asked me to gather some information for a study he was making of lay organizations in the United States.

I sent him a sizeable packet of material and a letter that read in part:

> Virtually all lay organizations are suffering a decline, both the old and the new, both the relevant and the irrelevant. The one major exception is the parish council. Its rapid expansion is enough to make up for other discouragements, for it is involved with the real nitty-gritty, namely, power in the Church.
>
> I agree that one can go too far with the democratization bit. The Church is not a democracy in the usual sense of that word. But it seems reasonable that, with changing times, the Holy Spirit may want to express itself through the mind and experience of the faithful as well as through the mind and experience of the Holy Father. And the times they are certainly a-changing.
>
> I agree with Pius XII when he said that there is something in the democratic process that corresponds to human nature. That is our conviction deep down beneath the fear and the laziness that we are most human, most alive, and most divine when we are given the opportunity to govern ourselves. Our first efforts, like those of the adolescent, are usually marked by disaster, high comedy, low tragedy, and great gobs of unbearable boredom. As we learn the trick of it and learn how to protect ourselves from disaster and to some extent from unbearable

boredom, then things pick up and increasing quantities of energy and wisdom are released.

If we are made in the image and likeness of God, then should it not follow that sometime in this life it would be the will of God that we should share in the self-government of God? And if we are to follow this impulse to express what is divine in our nature, isn't it also natural that this drive should extend outward to the self-control of a really democratic society?

The same principles do not precisely apply to the government of a church as apply to the government of a nation. Okay to that. But still I think the point remains.

One thing I can report with confidence from where I sit, or struggle, in the war on poverty [by this time I was an antipoverty official] and the whole mix of government innovations in the delivery of public services: the idea of participation in decision making is sweeping all before it—participation of the poor in antipoverty agencies, participation of tenants in the operation of public housing projects, participation of parents, faculty, students in the control of schools and colleges. The union movement has of course already won the right of participation for workers in industry. [Thirty years later, by 2003, however, that victory had become much less obvious as antiunion employers became more and more aggressive and successful.]

We live in a participatory age. And the Church cannot escape it. It hangs in the air we breathe. You might call it pollution. I call it oxygen mixed with the fragrance of spring flowers and just a touch of skunkweed.

In response the cardinal thanked me warmly for my help and added, "I sense that in philosophical and related matters we have grown miles apart, but perhaps in practical conclusions we would find ourselves more nearly at one, if not, indeed, entirely so. I do not do my thinking in terms of 'power,' and I never did."

I did not respond at the time, but looking back now, I think I might have been tempted to write, "Your Eminence, you never had to do your thinking in terms of power because you had it."

The question of power in the church remains—power to govern and power to teach, to teach as one having authority. I became a Catholic because I recognized that the authority to teach and govern is essential to a church that is going to be faithful to the Gospel of Jesus Christ.

How to reconcile a reasonable authority, both to govern and to teach, with exalted democratic feeling as expressed in my letter to Cardinal Wright is not the easiest or the simplest job in the world. How difficult and complex it is may be judged by contrasting the tone of my letter, written in 1970, with the tone of my comments about major and minor details, written thirty-two years later. I am not a disciple of either Hans Küng or Charles Curran, and I am not happy that so many Catholics are. There has to be a via media, a middle way.

The parish councils are alive and well and since 1989 have been made mandatory in our archdiocese, but they are only advisory. If there is a serious disagreement between the pastor and the council, the pastor or the vice chair, who is an elected layperson, may appeal to the regional vicar or bishop or both to mediate the disagreement. In our parish one such appeal, based on a very legitimate grievance, met with no relief. Actually, this event occurred before the councils were made mandatory, and the pastor still had the power to operate without one. In this case he did not like the results of the annual election and simply abolished the council. The old ways die hard.

Since the pontificate of John XXIII, many church officials, from the Vatican down to the parish, have made attempts to turn the clock back to the old ways, to slam shut the windows that John opened to the modern world. That this effort cannot succeed permanently I have no serious doubt. Pope John made it impossible. Vatican Council II, under his inspiration, made it impossible. For that miracle, together with his other saintly qualities, it is difficult not to believe that he has earned canonization. And from late reports, it appears that by the time this book sees print he may already have done so.

Afterthought: The shocking developments of 2001 and 2002 have served as a kind of electric charge to efforts to make the church more accountable to the laity and the lower clergy. I have included an appendix giving some of the major documents and events in this effort over the years, during and since Vatican Council II, because they have affected my current parish, St. Thomas Aquinas, in Nahant, Massachusetts, and this archdiocese, formerly headed by Cardinal Bernard Law.

12

First and Last Hurrahs

> Democracy is a charming form of government, full of variety and disorder.
>
> —Plato

AS THE YEARS went by, I began to go stale, get burned out, in the Newspaper Guild job. Contract succeeded contract, and every contract involved the same arguments with the same publishers, almost word for word—more money, shorter hours, union shop, arbitration, job security, pensions, health and welfare benefits. We organized a few more papers in Dedham, Waltham, Malden, Medford, Haverhill, and Lowell—places where they were paying experienced reporters $60 or $70 a week, less than half what Guild reporters were getting. Winning decent money and conditions for these people was a rewarding experience, but there were not enough of such experiences.

One day I was sitting at my desk in our office at 40 Boylston Street, and the boredom and frustration grew so thick and so oppressive that I started pounding the desk with my fist like a man going berserk. I did not regret the years with the Guild, twelve in all. It was good and necessary work that brought in enough money to feed the growing number of mouths in our household, and the mouths were wonderful to behold and even to hear. But it was obvious that I needed a change.

I began to look toward the political arena. Early in the 1950s I had joined Americans for Democratic Action and was one of the very few Catholics who were active in it. I got to know and like Sam and Roberta Beer. Sam was chairman of the government department at Harvard and at one point head of the Massachusetts branch of the organization. We had worked together in the campaign against Senator Joe McCarthy, and I had solicited Catholic names for an anti-McCarthy ad in the *Globe,* not the easiest job in the Boston area. Both of us were concerned about the chasm that yawned between the Catholic community of Boston and the secular liberal community centered at Harvard—not to mention the additional chasms between the Catholic, Protestant, and Jewish communities.

These chasms were illuminated one night around that time when I was speaking as a Catholic representative on an interfaith panel at the Arlington Street Church, which was trying to build bridges over the chasms. When the Protestant and Jewish speakers and I had concluded our pious expressions of goodwill, the floor was opened for questions and comment. An angry-looking man rose in the back and declared, "Let's face it—we all hate each other's guts."

It was pretty funny, but, to be honest, I don't remember if anybody laughed.

Sam Beer didn't hate anybody's guts, but he confessed to me that he did not know where Boston College was located, even though it was one of the largest Catholic universities in the United States and he had lived only a few miles away from it for more than twenty years. This lack of knowledge did not make him different from the average Harvard professor, however. What made him different was that he decided to find out where Boston College was located, with a view, as he put it in a letter, "to discuss those issues with regard to which social advance is hindered by religious differences, and second, to help remove prejudices on each side about the other, especially among liberals on both sides."

Beer had no Boston College friends on whom he could try this radical idea, but I did, so in 1955 we set up a meeting at our house, a kind of neutral No Man's Land between the two camps. By coincidence our house was one of the few in the Boston area from which both Harvard and Boston College were visible.

Among those from the Harvard side attending that first meeting were Arthur Schlesinger Jr., the historian; Seymour Harris, head of the economics department; Louis Lyons, curator of Harvard's Nieman Foundation and a popular news commentator; Stan Miles, senior tutor of Dunster House; and Dean Clark, professor at the Medical School and director of Massachusetts General Hospital. On the Boston College side were Father William Kennealy, S.J., dean of the Law School; his successor as dean, Father Robert Drinan, S.J., the future Congressman; Don White, associate dean of the Business School; Ed Hirsh, head of the English department; Paul Heffron, head of the history and government department; Dick Sullivan, professor of law; and Bill Daly, professor of history. I am ashamed now to note that it was an all-male group. Even Helen, no shrinking violet, was reluctant to join us in the living room. Academe, like labor and politics, was even more male dominated then than it is now.

As things turned out, we did have some things in common, mostly an interest in social justice and civil liberties. I think all of us were Adlai Stevenson Democrats. What we had in disagreement we proceeded to explore. At the end of the meeting we agreed to take up the items of difference *seriatim* at subsequent meetings.

As our guests headed for their cars, three of the Catholics stood out on the sidewalk discussing what had happened. One of them said, "That was a surprise. I expected Beer to ride herd on the discussion all night, but he hardly said a word. And Schlesinger has the reputation of being a terrible revolutionary, but I found him as reasonable a man as you could want to meet."

Difficult as it may be to believe in the year 2003, Schlesinger once had the reputation, among Catholics in particular, of being "a terrible revolutionary." In the 1950s Catholics and many others considered even the Americans for Democratic Action to be a dangerously radical organization.

What the Harvard men were saying about their new Catholic friends that night I don't know, but apparently the experience was not too unpleasant because most of them kept coming back at approximately six-week intervals for the next few years. Among the subjects discussed were censorship, federal aid to education, adoption problems (a perennial headache around Boston then), freedom of the Catholic press, anti-Catholicism as the anti-Semitism of liberals, tensions between Jews and Catholics, Catholics in politics, belief in God as essential to social cooperation, and, of course, birth control. It is interesting that nobody thought abortion was a controversial subject at that time.

One highlight of these meetings was an appearance by Father John Courtney Murray, the Jesuit theologian who did more than any single person to change the Catholic Church's stand on religious freedom. His topic was, at his own suggestion, "How much unity do we need, how much pluralism can we stand?" A most impressive man was the consensus. One member pointed out that it took a good man to hold the floor without interruptions after the group had passed the two-beer mark, but that night, whenever Father Murray spoke, all present listened in silence and respect.

A similarly impressive man was Paul Tillich, the German Protestant theologian, who was then teaching at Harvard Divinity School. At one point, in reference to his concept of God as "the ground of our being," I asked him, "Professor, does this God as the ground of our being have anything in common with the self-conscious God of the Gospels?" Tillich looked at me as if I were pretty stupid to imagine that it might. I have forgotten his precise answer, but the general impression was "not much."

Tillich's theology always brings to mind a story that the late James Luther Adams, a Tillich scholar himself and a much-loved member of the Harvard Divinity School faculty, told me. It seems another apocryphal Gospel was discovered that included the following exchange between Jesus and his disciples: After Jesus asked what people were saying about him, he asked the famous question, "But who do you say that I am?" Peter replied, "Thou art the eschatological manifestation of the ground of our being, the *kerygma* manifested in the conflict and resolution of the humanizing process." And Jesus looked at him and said, "What the hell is that?"

Many years later, during a late-night bull session at a Christian-Marxist dialogue conference, another theologian who knew Tillich told us that Tillich had once said that when he spoke to intellectuals about God, he used terms like "the ground of our being," but when he got down on his knees at night to pray, he said his prayers just as his mother had taught him. I felt better about Tillich after that but remained confused about what he in fact did believe about God or the Gospels.

We spent one evening with Governor Paul Dever discussing the conduct of Catholics in Massachusetts politics. More than one of us, from both camps, were surprised and pleased to find such a well-read, urbane egghead on the shoulders of a prominent Irish Catholic politician.

An important guest was Leo Pfeffer, national director of the American Jewish Congress, speaking on the separation of church and state and on the persistence of anti-Semitism in the Catholic community as well as in other communities.

Cardinal Wright, then bishop of Worcester, also visited us one evening. I had broken the ice by persuading him to have dinner at our house and meet Schlesinger. I was considerably to his left in the political spectrum, but I remember that as we sat in his study, lined with books about Joan of Arc, he told me he thought Adlai Stevenson's speech to the American Legion in 1956 was one of the finest speeches ever made in the history of U.S. politics. I agreed. But the next minute he was telling me why he favored Dwight Eisenhower's reelection.

On the night he came to dinner, a torrential hurricane had flooded the Boston area. Schlesinger was flying in behind it from Chicago, and the bishop's car plowed through the washouts on the road from Worcester. It was a wild night. The storm clouds, sweeping out to sea, raced across the face of the city below us. When the bishop arrived, I took him out on the back porch to show him the view.

Most observers suspected that he wanted to be archbishop of Boston one day. I could not resist the temptation. I said, "All this will I give thee if falling down thou wilt adore me." He would have been justified in throwing me off the porch, but he laughed. He was a good laugher.

The dinner and the conversation were pleasant, but poor Schlesinger was scarcely able to get a word in, even when he confessed that he had come to believe that religious faith deserved more serious consideration than he had once thought as a younger man. The bishop was an even better talker than he was a laugher.

Sam Beer later summed up our experiment in exploring disagreements agreeably: "For us on the Harvard side it was an invaluable experience to learn at firsthand that there is no truth in the old bromide about the Catholic Church being a monolithic community in which the priests hand down a stereotyped set of opinions to the laity. We learned that once beyond the area of dogma there is plenty of freedom for Catholics to disagree and criticize each other on questions of social and political policy. We heard them doing it."

Mark DeWolfe Howe of the Harvard Law School, who became one of our most faithful members, commented, "I was trained in the tradition that says you never talk about religious differences, so I found it unusual and refreshing to find a group of people who come right out and say what they think, and still like each other afterward." He thought that the question of religion in the public schools was the one that had yielded least to our search for common ground.

Bill Daly of Boston College had this reaction: "I was surprised to see how much we agreed, especially on social and political questions. John Cogley once wrote in *Commonweal* that the millennium would arrive when Arthur Schlesinger Jr. was invited to speak at Holy Cross. We didn't swing that, but it was a result of our meetings that Schlesinger was invited by the Faculty Club to speak at Boston College. And a fine talk it was, well attended and well received by students and faculty, lay and cleric."

CONVERSATION WITH KENNEDY, DEBATE WITH BUCKLEY

I doubt if our experiment was very significant nationally, but perhaps it helped to create a better atmosphere for the Kennedy presidential campaign in 1960. In 1959 I had spent a semester at Brandeis as a Florina Lasker Fellow, and I did a study of Al Smith's campaign for president in 1928. Just as now, in the year 2003, some of the topics discussed by our Harvard–Boston College group seem a little old-fashioned and irrelevant, so the anti-Catholic arguments printed in 1928 by such sophisticated journals as the *Atlantic Monthly* struck me in 1959 as something out of the nineteenth century. But even in 1959 anti-Catholic prejudice was strong, and the 1928 arguments, however outdated, retained widespread currency.

During the 1960 campaign I had a conversation with Kennedy that demonstrated how conscious he was of this factor and how touchy about it. At the Harvard commencement that year, as a member of the twenty-fifth reunion class, dressed in capitalist top hat and tails, I was acting as an usher at the VIP lunch in Fogg Museum. Kennedy was there as a member of the board of overseers. I was stationed at the door to greet the guests and show them to their seats. Kennedy came up the steps alone and greeted me like a long lost brother, which was surprising because we had never been that friendly. I think he felt a little ill at ease among the Boston Brahmins and was simply glad to see another Catholic and Democratic face.

We talked for a bit. He said he thought Nixon would be tough to beat, and I tried to reassure him that Nixon would be easy to beat. He was upset because the Vatican newspaper, *L'Osservatore Romano*, had just published an editorial telling Catholics not to vote for certain candidates in the Italian elections. He thought it was pretty stupid of *L'Osservatore* to print a piece that could be used by anti-

Catholic types in the United States who were saying again, as in 1928, that if a Catholic were elected president, the pope would always be interfering in U.S. politics, telling the president what to do and the people how to vote.

As he went on about this issue, I thought that it was a little arrogant on his part to argue that the pope's paper should tailor its editorial policy to fit his campaign. In retrospect I am not so sure he wasn't right.

After he was elected, but before the inauguration, I went to a debate between William F. Buckley and Schlesinger sponsored by Newton College of the Sacred Heart, a women's college attended by daughters of a group of people sometimes called "the Venetian blind Irish." Also attending the debate were friends and parents, many of whom thought Buckley was great and Schlesinger no more than a dirty Red. But others there were proud and glad that Kennedy, one of their own, had been elected president. The day before the debate it had been announced that Kennedy had named Schlesinger one of his personal assistants. This news created an interesting kind of schizophrenia in the crowd, with Republican prejudices straining against tribal Irish Catholic instinct.

In any event, however, Schlesinger demolished Buckley. Many of the students, not so many of the parents, applauded this victory, which seemed to speak well for the future.

A few days before the presidential election of 1956 I myself had debated Buckley before the Catholic Women's College Club of Lowell, an organization consisting mainly of middle-class Irish American ladies, on the topic, "Should a Catholic Be a Liberal or a Conservative?"—which at that point in time was another way of saying, "Should a Catholic vote for Eisenhower or Stevenson?"

I armed myself with quotations from the Bible and the encyclicals that fell off Buckley and the nice ladies like so much water off the proverbial duck. Buckley was smarter. He appealed directly to their pocketbooks, and they loved him. The only time his knees buckled slightly was when I asked him how to handle the problem of poor workers who became too old to work, considering that he opposed Social Security as well as the whole panoply of New Deal legislation.

In response he said that the solution was to have the more well-to-do families take these poor old men and women into their homes on a voluntary basis, more or less as members of their own families.

Personal Christian charity and all that. Looking down at the ladies, I could see their eyes glaze over as they imagined what life would be like with a couple of old Italian textile workers in their homes. For a moment they walked with him no more, but I did not have the instinct or the weapons to move in for the kill. Schlesinger was more effective.

After my debate a friend suggested that I should have asked Buckley if he was in favor of public schools. I thought it a foolish fancy to suppose that he was opposed to public education, but, sure enough, I later discovered that he was, and if I had studied the *National Review* more closely instead of being satisfied with a quick review of *God and Man at Yale,* I would have known this.

Buckley himself I found charming. The brightness of his mind is a pleasure to see, like watching a well-made machine, even when you feel an accompanying distress that the machine is being driven by a Neanderthal primitive.

My First Hurrah

In the spring of 1958 a seat opened up in the two-seat Ward 22 in Brighton, an area several miles long running along the Charles River from Harvard Stadium to the Newton line and including the northern sections of Allston and Brighton, and I decided to run for state representative from that ward. The population was mostly working-class Irish with some Italians, Poles, Jews, and miscellaneous groups, including a few home-owning blacks.

The ward was solidly Democratic, and the whole goal was to win in the primary, which was "tantamount"—that wonderful word—to election. I was a relative newcomer, and this ward was the kind where in order to get elected a candidate had to have been born in the ward, raised in the ward, gone to school in the ward, played on the football team, played well on the football team, sung in the parish variety show, sung well in the parish variety show, belonged to the Knights of Columbus, attended all the wakes and weddings, etc., etc.

I had not done any of these things except join the Knights and sing in the parish variety show. At one point in my brief political career I found myself on the stage of John Hancock Hall in Boston, in front of two thousand Brighton neighbors, a straw hat on my head and a cane in my hand, imitating Maurice Chevalier as he listened to every little breeze whispering "Louise," with two cute girls doing a soft-shoe behind me. When you consider that Chevalier was the only man in the world who could smile and curl his lower lip at the same time, it is possible to see how imitation presented problems. I got by on the strength of the girls and my mastery of that sexy guttural growl that Chevalier throws in just before the last reprise. In fact, to be truthful, we brought the house down.

To be even more truthful, that moment was probably the pinnacle of my political career. As I left the stage, I could see my principal rival, the incumbent rep and future state treasurer, Robert Q. Crane, turning a slight shade of green. The green was appropriate because he had built his more substantial career on his own mastery of the art of singing Irish songs. He was the perennial MC at the variety shows of Our Lady of Presentation Parish, and that night when he saw the house explode at my imitation of the great Maurice, he recognized a serious rival for his seat.

I was filled with energy and ambition and set out to ring every doorbell in the ward. That was about eight thousand doorbells. Starting in the spring, I worked evenings and weekends, and then spent my three-week vacation in August finishing the job. It was quite an experience. And I made mistakes.

Among them was the day early in the campaign when I approached a group sitting on the lawn in the sun and handed out cards. An elderly lady said, "Sorry, but we're committed to Paul Kinsella."

"But you have two votes. You can always give me the other one."

"No," she said, "Joe Cusack's relatives live down the street."

Confronted by this hopeless situation, for which I had not yet formulated a suitable reply, I said the first thing that came into my head, "Well, if either one of them drops dead, remember me." The reaction was not good.

In time I developed a set of stock answers for almost any situation. None of them, however, was a match for the old Polish lady who said she could not vote for me because I had too many children. "Too much money," she kept repeating. Her accent was heavy, and for a while I could not make out what she meant.

Finally I said, "You mean I'd have to take too much graft to support our children?"

"That's right."

"Do I look dishonest?" I said, a little indignant, and then, in reference to a local scandal involving one of my opponents, "After all, I don't believe in one hundred and forty dollars a week for a station wagon."

"What's the matter?" she said, "Not enough?"

That I should lose one vote because of the children was only fair. I certainly got enough because of them, and I used the family picture shamelessly on my cards and literature. I discovered that it is an article of faith among many Boston Irish that a man who has a large family must be a good man. Sometimes, when some nice old lady would talk like this and I was sure of her vote, I would kid her and say, "Well, you know a man with a big family could still be a terrible scoundrel," and she would protest that it could not be. Quite a different scenario played out at my liberal friends' cocktail parties, however, when I would meet a woman who had enough to drink to dispense with courtesy and, on learning of all those children, would give me a verbal karate chop to the effect that I must be some kind of an animal.

On another occasion, when a friend was trying to sell me to one of her friends, the other woman said, "I'm going to vote for Vin Shanley because he has eight kids."

My friend said, "Look at John Cort. He has nine."

"Yes, but John Cort can support his kids. Shanley can't." She was wrong, actually, at least with regard to Shanley.

To counteract this sympathy vote, the opposition circulated various data, real or imagined. One such "fact" was the glad news that Helen was related to the DuPonts. When confronted with this intelligence, she would confess only to the fact that her cousin sold paint. Another one was that I came from Texas, presumably from a prominent oil or cattle family. Still another was that we came from New York, which being true, hurt us among those who felt that coming from New York was little better than coming from Moscow.

Mostly, though, in going from door to door I was courteously received, especially by the Irish from the old sod, who seemed to have a courtesy and a friendliness that was sometimes missing among their native-born relations. The experience also produced a grudging admiration for politicians. Sometime in their lives, it occurred to me, they must have sweat, unless they never had any serious opposition, which is rare. Those dog days in July and August were rough: climbing the stairs in the three-family houses, ringing the doorbells, standing in the hall, and asking myself, "Why the hell am I doing this?"

I was doing it because boredom had eroded the Newspaper Guild job and politics offered an escape into a more interesting world where one might also do some good. Clearly, plenty needed to be done. In fact, tramping up and down the dank, smelly, unpainted, crumbling stairwells of the poor reminded me that my platform had an important missing plank—namely, a law to compel landlords to have at least the halls and interiors of their houses painted and plastered at reasonable intervals.

Last Hurrah and a Blowout

The best I could do in 1958 was runner-up, but I beat seven opponents to achieve that distinction, so I was not permanently discouraged. In 1960 I tried again. This time no empty seat waited, but I thought Crane was vulnerable. He was in the food brokerage business, and his votes tended to be conservative. He had voted repeatedly for the sales tax, a regressive tax that fell most heavily on the poor. My friends in the labor movement gave me encouragement and support, including a $500 check from the state AFL-CIO.

Because I was the only opposition to the two incumbents, they would have a free ride if I could be gotten out of the race. This was the situation when, early in the campaign, a nice-looking young man came to the house and offered his services. I will call him Mr. X. He said he lived just over the line in Newton, but that he believed in what I stood for and wanted to help. And he did help. He even went house to house with me ringing doorbells and hustling votes. He became for a while my most active worker, a man I looked on as a good and loyal friend.

This time I did not make such a big thing of the doorbell ringing, only a few thousand, not the entire eight. I did make a big thing of persuading about sixty of my friends to circulate nomination papers, which I had learned was an excellent way to get elected. My campaign managers, Leo McCusker and Vin McCarthy, led the way, and by July we had collected 3,235 signatures.

Mr. X offered to take a set of my nomination papers to City Hall and the State House to qualify me for a place on the ballot. I was a little surprised at his offer but could think of no reason to reject it without seeming distrustful. At that time the law provided that only 25 valid signatures were necessary. The first step was to take them to City Hall, where the registrars certified that 30 signatures, 5 more than the required number, corresponded to the names that appeared on the voting list as registered Democrats. They did not certify the validity of the signatures, as I wrongly believed.

Mr. X then returned to City Hall, picked up my papers, and, as he told me later, took them up to the State House to the secretary of state's office. The only hitch was that the papers apparently never reached the secretary of state's office. At the last minute we discovered this fact and rushed in another set of 75 signatures. Unfortunately, that set had been collected by a friend who was even more ignorant of correct procedure than I was and whom I had failed to instruct in correct procedure. Of the 30 signatures certified by City Hall she had accepted 6 written by two wives for their husbands, a son for his mother, a father for his son, and a sister for two sisters. This left me 1 valid signature short. We had collected 3,235 signatures and could not get 25 properly certified.

Crane had a supporter go out and get signatures from the 30 certified on my nomination paper. He then had a handwriting expert determine that 6 of the 30 were invalid and thus challenged my signatures; I was ruled off the ballot and, after an unsuccessful appeal to the courts based on the first missing set of signatures, decided to run on stickers. In the history of Massachusetts politics no one had ever beaten an incumbent running on stickers on voting machines, a much more difficult proposition than to do so on paper ballots. However, we put out a leaflet explaining what had happened and how to vote, and there was a wave of sympathy for this wet-behind-the-ears novice who had been bested by the professionals.

On the first count I received 2,694 votes to Crane's 2,676, with the other incumbent, Shanley, well ahead of both of us. Crane asked for a recount. After one day I was ahead by 33 votes, after five days behind by 93. The Boston Board of Elections counted the ballots with what did not seem to me to be evenhanded fairness. On one sticker the corner had been torn off so that only "hn C. Cort, 64 N. Crescent Cir., Boston" appeared. The chairman, David Lasker, ruled that this sticker could not be counted. When we asked why not, he replied, "The name might have been Kahn C. Cort." I protested, "At the same address? I live in a single-family house." Lasker's answer, "It can't be counted."

The lone Republican on the board, Perlie Dyer Chase, voted for me on this and other points where elementary fairness dictated, but Lasker and the other three Democrats outvoted him. They rejected six other torn stickers plus 47 votes by people who, not having a sticker, had written in my name directly on the paper roll as "Cort," "J.C. Cort," or "J. Cort." Lasker and friends ruled that the sticker had to read "John C. Cort" to qualify. Others were knocked off because stickers were in the wrong place or overlapping, as on one roll where the machine had jammed and there were thirteen stickers in an area with room for only four. We decided an appeal to the courts might regain 50-odd votes, but not enough to win.

The campaign, including legal fees, cost me approximately $4,000. I used to say, "About as educational as a master's degree in government, and only a little more expensive." I was able to raise enough from friends to pay all the bills and even send back the $500 check to the state AFL-CIO. It was a comfort when they voted unanimously to refuse my check.

Since the court appeal on the ballot dispute, we had not seen much of Mr. X, the young man who said he had filed my first set of papers. Suddenly he had become very busy. Suspicion began to grow, but it did not blossom until I learned that he had been active in the Democratic Party in Newton and was known to be strongly against Americans for Democratic Action and also that he had been seen in friendly conversation with Crane. Circumstantial evidence. Inconclusive.

Some years later, when I was working on this book, I decided to check out Mr. X, maybe look him up and ask him about it, see how he reacted. I began calling old friends in Newton. One of them gave me the name of a woman who was a friend of Mr. X. I called her, looking for a lead, but careful not to ask her outright if she thought Mr. X was a spy working on Crane's behalf.

She told me that Mr. X had died some years ago of a nervous disorder. She acknowledged her friendship for him, said that she remembered my campaign very well and had even met me on one occasion, then she added, "There's only one word for what happened to you. You were screwed. [Mr. X] was not only close to Crane. He was very close. I can remember once I had a parking ticket, but he said to me, 'Give me the ticket. Bobby will take care of it.' Whenever

I had any little thing I wanted done in the State House, he would get Crane to take care of it." Still circumstantial evidence. Mr. X might have done the whole thing without Crane ever knowing about it. He might have volunteered to do it without Crane asking him.

This conversation with Mr. X's friend was not very flattering to me, but no less than I deserved. She said, "When I learned that you let him take your nomination papers, I figured you must be crazy—to trust your nomination papers to a stranger!"

"Well," I protested, "he wasn't exactly a stranger. I had known him for a couple of months and believed I could trust him."

"If I knew Jesus Christ for a couple months," she said, "I still wouldn't trust him with my nomination papers."

I laughed. "That's a great line. I'll put that in the book."

Even more years later I got Crane on the phone, read him the paragraphs about Mr. X and the nomination papers, and asked him if he wanted to comment. He said that he did not know Mr. X personally until "long after the event."

No Insurance Against Stupidity

What did I learn? Was my experience in fact as educational as a master's degree in government? Perhaps. A more accurate conclusion might be that it was a painful lesson in self-knowledge. I had not learned the lesson of the Gospel: "Be ye wise as serpents and simple as doves." I was simple as a dove, all right, but about as wise as a dodo. I remember thinking to myself afterward, "When you came to Boston from New York, there were things you could teach them about the labor movement, but, brother, there are things they can teach you here about politics."

It was also evident that I was weak in the matter of detail. I had not read the fine print carefully enough or had passed on what little I knew to all my campaign workers. Crane was simply the professional pol who probed for the weak spots, found them, and drove on through. I really had no reason for cynicism about the political process. Democracy did not provide a built-in insurance policy against stupidity and carelessness, and there was no reason to expect that it should.

I learned other things. I learned something about the cynicism that characterizes the average voter. One young lady whose doorbell I rang was so disgusted with politicians that she told me she intended never to vote again. Again and again I ran into the conviction that politics and dishonesty were synonyms. It was not comforting to me as a Catholic to note that this conviction was held in a district, in a city, where Catholic politicians predominated.

But I do not really believe that the cynicism was justified. Both the district and the city have produced honest officials and even more who were at least as honest as the average voter. Unfortunately, average voters will not accept someone who is only as honest as themselves. They want a candidate who is able to resist the temptations that they know in their hearts they themselves would not be able to resist. In a sense they are right. After all, average voters at least have the honesty not to put themselves forward as objects of trust.

What was more discouraging than the cynicism of the voters was the cynicism of the politicians, many of whom I got to know then and later, when I was working for them. To them, too often, politicians could be divided only between those who were reasonably dishonest and those who were unreasonably dishonest. It was simply a matter of degree.

Again and again they would tell me, as they put an arm over my shoulders and leaned close for the friendly word of advice, "Politics is a dirty game, John," or, in justifying some cute but slightly soiled maneuver, simply, "That's politics." Often the man who said such things was one whom, on overall points, I would consider a man of honor and honesty. His own career may have been evidence that moral carelessness is not essential to the profession, but nevertheless he persisted in believing that he himself was an exception to the general rule that to succeed in the game one must be ready, always, to look the other way.

PANICKED BY THE THREAT OF SUCCESS

Meanwhile, the prospect of another try rose again in 1962. Given my new role in the ward as political martyr, it seemed evident that, failing some new stupidity, I could walk past Crane the next time out. Faced with the threat of success, Helen panicked. Politics and political campaigns drove her crazy: my prolonged absence from home, leaving her with the nine kids, the constant ringing of the telephone, the hassles, the tension, and everybody after me to do something for them. Ward 22 had no one in the City Council, and people went to the state rep, or even to a candidate like myself, when they wanted something done that was really city business, not state business: a sidewalk repaired, a leaky hydrant, a pothole in the street, work for a drunken, unemployed relative. A council member was really a shop steward for the ward, handling grievances and doing favors, and his wife was the answering service. A dog's life. A dog's wife's life. Helen pleaded with me to try something else.

In 1961 Larry Fuchs, a bright, charming friend who was then dean of the faculty at Brandeis, joined the Peace Corps as director of a big educational project in the Philippines and persuaded me to apply for a position on his staff. I went down to Washington, D.C., for interviews with Sargent Shriver, director of the Peace Corps, and some of his aides. I think Crane might have helped me. He had connections in the Kennedy administration, and I know he was aware of my application. I can imagine him on the phone to Washington, telling them, "Get this guy out of my hair. Give him a job."

Shriver was the kind of man who would be more impressed by the fact that a Boston politician was afraid of me than by all the rest of my experience combined. He gave me the job. And so I joined a great staff and a great project, and we made some great friends: among them, Bill and Jay Warren, Harvey and Roberta Pressman, Larry and Betty Howard, Roger and Becky Flather, and John and Virginia Harville.

13

Pursuing Peace in the Philippines

> People here keep asking me, "Is it true? Did we really see
> that on TV? Did the Filipinos really pull off a miracle?" I
> tell them: Yes, it's true, I saw it with my own eyes, and it
> was a miracle. They really did overturn a tyrant and his
> armies, using only faith and prayer and love. For me, I tell
> them, the experience of the Philippine revolution was like
> lifting a corner of the universe to see the way God works.
>
> —Kaa Byington, *People Power: An Eyewitness History of
> the Philippine Revolution of 1986*

WE LANDED at Manila airport on the sunny morning of February 12,
1962, and were met by an explosion of flash bulbs and the effusions
of Filipino reporters. There was something about the combination of
Peace Corps and nine children that appealed to the media. A San
Francisco paper put our photo and arrival there on page 1, and even
a newspaper in Rome took note of our departure.

The combination was not so appealing to Otto Passman, a conservative Democrat who was chairman of a House subcommittee responsible for the Peace Corps budget. He protested that my services
were not worth all the money required to get that large family and
its belongings over to the Philippines. And he had a point. This objection too got widespread circulation in the media. Later, when Julia,
our tenth, was born, a UPI reporter who got wind of it, called me to
confirm. I gave him a smart-alecky confirmation, "Yes," I said, "if it
had been a boy, we would have called it Otto." Then I added hastily,
"That's off the record, of course." But it was too late. You cannot put
something off the record retroactively. The next morning *The Stars
and Stripes,* the international daily published for Americans abroad,
had a news story that opened with the words, "'If it had been a
boy, we would have called it Otto,' John Cort, Peace Corps official,
jested."

Manila was a shock. As we rode in from the airport, we saw garbage lying amid the ruins of World War II and squatters' shacks made of scrap metal and cardboard tied together with string. Many of these shacks were built, with a dramatic sense of contrast, up against the wall of a fine house. All fine houses were surrounded by walls to protect them from the poor people who lived in the shacks. This status quo included the house assigned to us by the Peace Corps, which was in a suburb of Manila called Quezon City on a street called Sacred Heart in an upper-middle-class district known as Theoville, the City of God. Despite the Peace Corps' mistake in choosing such an upper-class setting the religious names were a comforting thought and served to remind us that we were in the only Christian country of Asia.

The local squatters' shacks were about a hundred yards away, over the brook that ran behind the house and served as their water supply, laundry, and bathroom, as well as the upstream depository of poisonous chemicals from a local film company. The squatters were out of sight but close enough to underline the fact that we were also in a country where most of the people were terribly poor, and more than 90 percent of the real wealth was in the hands of 5 percent of the population.

The first night in our Filipino home I stood on the back porch and stared out through the darkness, across the wall beyond our yard, listening to the sounds of the night and oppressed by a strange, unreasoning fear of what and who lay beyond. As we got to know the country and the neighbors, this fear wore off, even after we began to lose clothes, sheets, and towels off the clothesline to thieves who slipped nimbly back and forth over the walls. So we got a dog.

Manila was a big, sprawling, unkempt city still rebuilding from the devastation of the war, when the Japanese made the Americans fight for every block. Filipino architects had designed new buildings of some beauty and distinction, but for real beauty it was necessary to go to the countryside, to the islands and the beaches, active volcanoes, extinct volcanoes, and the terraced, flooded rice fields, which when seen from the air delighted the eye with their green shoots emerging in ordered rows through shimmering veils of water. On one occasion I rode out to a coral island and, snorkeling in shallow water, saw beauty such as I had never seen: multicolored coral, seaweed waving gracefully over bright white sand made brighter by sunlight, and gorgeous tropical fish weaving their way in and out of the coral and the waving weeds. All that and the sobering possibility of man-eating sharks not too far away.

My first duties, however, were in Manila, never too far from the slums and the poverty. At that point there were 222 Peace Corps volunteers, which shortly grew to more than 600, average age twenty-five, evenly divided between men and women, mostly products of liberal arts colleges who had had thirteen weeks of training to teach English as a second language and perhaps science and math. The government was concerned to upgrade the use of English, which was the medium of instruction, or at least supposed to be, and the principal language of commerce and government as well as the main hope for scientific and technical progress. The volunteers were not so much teachers—there were plenty of Filipino teachers—as they were assistants to teachers of English, math, and science, a difficult and ambiguous role, which they pursued mostly out in the barrio (village) schools in southern Luzon and the Visayan Islands.

Shortly after arrival I began work in the Manila office but also was given responsibility for volunteers in one province, Camarines Norte, whom I serviced by occasional plane trips. On one occasion I visited Parker Borg, a Dartmouth graduate, in his school in a seaside barrio. It was a beautiful morning. The school was on a hill overlooking the village and the blue waters of the bay. As I climbed the steep path, a cool breeze came in across the water, and I stopped to admire the white curve of the beach through the palm trees, the row of nipa huts that lined the beach, and the sight of a bronze, bare-legged fisherman out in the bay, his legs spread far apart as he balanced himself in his outrigger *banca* and with a wide, sweeping motion cast his net into the sea.

In the school above I watched Parker teach a class of ragged, bare-foot kids in a primitive dirt-floor classroom. He had divided the class into two teams and was teaching multiplication by involving everybody in a game of arithmetical baseball. The excitement grew intense as the lead swung back and forth. The ratio of strikeouts (mistakes) to runs (correct answers) was pretty high, but Parker told me that only a few months earlier it was much worse. He seemed pleased and encouraged. As I looked at him and the eager faces of his ragged kids and then turned and looked out the window at his gorgeous view, I could understand the attraction of the boondocks for many volunteers.

Walking down the hill, I wondered about the people in the huts along the beach and how much the beauty of the setting could compensate for the less glamorous aspects of existence in a poor village. How much were they attracted to the boondocks? Another volunteer, Sue Johnson, ran into this question when she was teaching her children the words of an old English song: "Meat nor drink nor money have I none / Yet still I will be merry." A small boy rose in the back of the room and said simply, "Why?"

ARGUMENT AT THE EMBASSY

After a time Larry Fuchs established his headquarters in a barrio near Zamboanga, leaving me to run the Manila office. This job involved, among other things, attending the U.S. ambassador's weekly staff meetings at the embassy. The ambassador was William Stevenson, a distant relative of Adlai, a former president of Oberlin College, and a very decent man. Despite his good instincts he could not reverse overnight the basic thrust of the U.S. presence in the Philippines.

At one meeting a question rose regarding the interests of U.S. drug manufacturers, which at that point were in conflict with the Filipinos' interest in developing a drug industry of their own. I suggested that it might be in the long-term interests of the American people to encourage the development of Filipino industry and ignore the complaints of the U.S. drug industry, which was doing very well anyway. The commercial attaché, a dapper man who had a very clear notion of the function of a U.S. embassy, became indignant and suggested that it might be better for the Peace Corps to keep its nose out of matters that did not concern it. I tried to develop a few of the more obvious connections between our concerns and the concerns of the Filipinos. Unfortunately, my Peace Corps superiors told me to stay out of such arguments, and I did not pursue this line at future meetings. Neither did anybody else, though I think it bothered Stevenson.

This argument, however, did highlight a major significance of the Peace Corps, which began to change, if only slightly, the image of the United States in the undeveloped countries of the Southern

Hemisphere, where most of its volunteers were working and continue to work today. The people of these countries had known Americans mainly as rich tourists or rich businessmen interested in securing as much pleasure or money as possible as quickly as possible from those countries. Or, alternately, they knew us as a great military power interested in suppressing any evidence of a left-wing revolt against the rich.

Then Kennedy and the U.S. Congress started sending thousands of attractive, educated, mostly young Americans out into the boondocks and poor communities of those countries to teach their children, to improve their agriculture and their health and their social services. Never mind the motives. I could see that the Filipinos were pleased and touched by this act of friendship and responded with acts of friendship of their own. Even the Filipino intellectuals, traditionally hostile to Americans, were surprised and intrigued to see the Americans going out to live in the barrios, which they themselves had been trying to escape for years. Seeing how the Americans enjoyed it, they were beginning to wonder if the road to fulfillment must necessarily lead to the big city.

Out in the Boondocks

After a year of bureaucratic hassling in Manila I was awarded my own region with 125 volunteers in eighteen provinces of central and southern Luzon and the islands of Palawan, Mindoro, Marinduque, and Catanduanes. This reassignment offered a great improvement. I was on the road most of the time, traveling by plane, train, jeep, jeepney, bus, and bicycle, with occasional rides in boats called *bancas* or *vintas*.

The provincial bus ride was often an experience to strike terror to the heart. Passengers clung to every visible foothold or handhold, including the roof. Pigs and chickens might be under my feet and an old lady beside me chewing betel nut and depositing a layer of nut juice on top of them. The bus lines competed with each other for passengers, racing the competition to the next town, often at fifty miles an hour on a narrow dirt road, around turns, up hill and down dale, in a cloud of choking dust, and amid a chorus of cheers, prayers, and curses from the passengers. After each ride I was grateful for the chance to stop at a volunteer's nipa hut and take a cold shower out of a tin can, wash off the dust and the sweat, have a bottle of San Miguel, the best beer in the world, and enjoy a fine supper of fish, rice, and vegetables.

SEXUAL ANXIETIES

I spent my time visiting volunteers and Filipino school officials, trying desperately to make sure the volunteers were fully employed and, if possible, allowed to have classes of their own, if only for remedial or enrichment work with the worst and best students. Much of our anxiety involved sex, and our policy was Victorian, to match the concerns of our Filipino hosts and hostesses, who had a very conservative and edifying view of the matter. For this and other reasons we urged the volunteers, especially the females, to live with a Filipino family, not only to learn Tagalog or the local dialect more quickly, but also to learn the culture and, above all, to obtain the protection that living with a family could provide.

One of the more unpleasant experiences involved several female volunteers who ignored this advice and lived in their own nipa hut. It had a bamboo floor with narrow spaces between the strips that made the hut cooler but also proved a temptation for young Filipinos who crawled under the hut at night to observe the volunteers as they undressed. The only way the volunteers could stop it finally was to pour boiling water on the peeping Thomases.

At one point I advised my volunteers: "The private life of Peace Corps volunteers is their business up to the point at which it becomes a public scandal. . . . We will say, however, that any volunteer who stays overnight in a house with a member of the opposite sex in an unchaperoned situation has automatically created a public scandal and should not try it unless he or she is prepared to return to the States."

The volunteers, of course, resented this puritanical policy, but I don't recall that any of them ever challenged it or publicly flaunted violations of it, at least not in my region. The Filipino code was just too strong to ignore, and everyone soon came to recognize that as a fact of life. Unflaunted violations certainly occurred, as evidenced by unplanned pregnancies, among both female volunteers and Filipinas, whose loveliness was a constant temptation to the male volunteers. As one of my volunteer leaders, Bill Tucker, put it, "There's all that femininity *throbbing* at you."

BOWING DOWN TO THE THUNDER

How much of an impact a Western view of science and math, taught by a minority of volunteers, had on the Filipino teachers was one of the unresolved questions of my Peace Corps experience. This irresolution featured a visit to a volunteer on the island of Panay who thought he could show the local farmers a better way to grow dry rice. The school where he was teaching let him use some of its land, and he planted the best seed and used his own money to buy fertilizer. He used so much fertilizer that the plants grew unusually tall. A storm came along and blew most of his rice flat to the ground. As we stood there looking mournfully at his little experiment, the Filipina science teacher with us explained the disaster with a knowing air and complete seriousness. "The rice," she said, "bowed down to the thunder."

I had been in her classroom only a few minutes earlier and, impressed, had noted the mottoes that she had hung on the walls and their ambitious claims for science, "Science conquers all" and "There are no mysteries in life that cannot be explained by science"— mottoes that I thought might be a little difficult to reconcile with either common sense or the Christian faith of the people. But here she was explaining a perfectly simple scientific phenomenon in terms of the deeper and darker faith of her pagan ancestors.

A JAPANESE QUESTION

One day I was sitting in our regional office in Quezon City talking to a group of visiting Japanese officials who were studying our operation so that they could make recommendations toward the setting up of a Japanese equivalent of the Peace Corps. I had invited several volunteers to be present, and one of them was a remarkable young man named Al Bradford who had been unusually happy and successful in his work. One of his gifts was that he could improvise flute accompaniments to Vivaldi concerti even as he heard them in our house for the first time, but a greater gift was that he could teach kids, make friends, and influence people without even seeming to try.

The visitors were asking the volunteers what they found to be their principal difficulty. Al said, "My main difficulty was teaching myself to accept the Filipinos as human beings like myself." I winced and thought to myself, "Al, couldn't you have thought of a more original way to put that?"

But the visitors were more impressed. Perhaps it was the way Al said it, the feeling he conveyed that for him this ancient cliché had real meaning, that for him the Peace Corps was neither a weapon in the Cold War nor an inexpensive ticket to see the world and enjoy "a meaningful experience," but rather a basic encounter of one human being with other human beings in the spirit of complete friendship.

At any rate, an old Japanese man who had seemed to be dozing while I was talking suddenly was wide-awake. He looked sharply at Al and through the interpreter asked, "Where did you get your humanism?"

Al's answer was discursive, involving his growing up in the South and his awareness of racial conflict, his experiences at a particularly good college (Antioch), and, finally, the most interesting part, "the songs my mother taught me." It did not include any mention of religious faith, but what do I know? I should have asked him what was in those songs.

I thought to myself then and pondered afterward, "This is a wise old Japanese and also a wise young American. But what is amazing is that the young American states a rather simple, obvious tenet of both the Christian tradition and the supposedly more enlightened Western tradition, and the old Japanese is so surprised to see that the young American really means it that he immediately wants to know where the American learned it. How many phony Christians this old Japanese must have met, how many disappointing Westerners!"

A LOOK BACK

In June 1964, after I had been on the job longer than any of my fellow staff—the Peace Corps policy was short assignments for both staff and volunteers—my family and I returned to the United States by boat at twenty knots, not much faster than a clipper ship. I liked to stand by the taffrail and watch the albatrosses gliding behind the ship on scimitar wings, waiting for garbage. And while I watched, I thought about our experiences over the past couple of years and tried to put them in perspective.

We had gone to the Philippines with some of the very best of young America. They had worked in small barrio schools and large universities. They had lived in remote island villages, eaten fish and rice, slept in nipa huts, were burned by the sun and drenched by the rain. Some had lived in the cities, disappointed to discover that they had all the comforts of home, including television. Some had taught students who were going to be leaders and thinkers; others had worn themselves out teaching children who were going nowhere, who would be planting rice and watching cockfights for the rest of their lives. There were the Al Bradfords, the Sue Johnsons, the Parker Borgs, the Jerry Poznaks, the Jennifer Grants, the Tom Dines, the Marjorie Pfankuchs, the Dave Lewises—the obvious successes. Lewis was a volunteer who invented a bamboo and sawali windmill that any farmer could put together for 150 pesos, about $38, as compared with 3,000 pesos for a manufactured one—a thing that could supply cheap power for irrigating rice fields, a thing that could make a real, practical economic difference.

And there were some who quit and went home; others who had to be sent home; others who wanted to quit but stuck it out because they had too much pride and guts to quit; and still others, the majority, who just went on from day to day and did a solid, unspectacular job, making their act of faith that some day one of these Filipino students, because of what he or she had learned, might do something that would move that country a little closer to the goal of justice, prosperity, and freedom.

All the polls and surveys told us that most Filipinos, including those who worked most closely with the volunteers, believed that the volunteers had made a valuable contribution to the teaching of English, math, and science. The Philippine government, like the governments in almost all the countries where Peace Corps volunteers have worked, has continued to ask for more volunteers than the Peace Corps can supply. Since 1961 some 152,000 young, middle-aged, and old American volunteers have served in 134 countries, some 8,800 in the Philippines, including our daughter Susan, who stayed three years and dazzled us with her facility in the Cebuano dialect. Daughter Barbara went back to teach Muslim students in a little Protestant college in Mindanao, married a Filipino American, and got a doctorate, writing a thesis titled "The Politics and Pedagogy of Language Use at the University of the Philippines."

To some of us the Peace Corps was even more than the sum of such things, even more than a new departure in U.S. foreign policy. Nick Royal, another bright, successful volunteer, got excited by Teilhard de Chardin's *The Phenomenon of Man* and urged Helen and me to organize a book discussion group for volunteers, which we did. We concluded that the Peace Corps may be part of what the French Jesuit anthropologist was talking about—the process he describes by which the world is contracting, by which the tension and the speed and the ingenuity of human thought is increasing. Teilhard put it this way:

> Essentially, in the twofold irresistible embrace of a planet that is visibly shrinking, and thought that is more and more rapidly coiling in upon itself, the dust of human units finds itself subjected to a formidable pressure of coalescence, far stronger than the individual or national repulsions that so alarm us. . . . Humankind, the spirit of the earth, the synthesis of individuals and peoples, the paradoxical conciliation of the elements with the whole, and of unity with multiples—all these are called Utopian and yet they are biologically necessary. And for them to be incarnated in the world all we may well need is to imagine our power of loving developing until it embraces the total of people and of the earth.

A bit cloudy that, but food for thought.

THE MARTYRDOM OF BENIGNO AQUINO

I first met Benigno (Ninoy) Aquino when I went north to visit him in Tarlac in central Luzon, where he was serving as one of the youngest provincial governors in the Philippines. We had no volunteers that far north, and my job was to determine if Tarlac would be a good place to assign some.

We had lunch and a good talk. I had met impressive Filipino politicians previously—men such as Vice President Pelaez, Senators Manahan, Manglapus, and Diokno—but Aquino was the most impressive, a man of extraordinary charm and intelligence. He came from an elite family of sugar plantation owners, and his wife Corazon (Cory) was from an even wealthier family. He took some obvious pride in telling us how as an even younger man of twenty-one he had traveled to New York and gone before the board of directors of one of the big banks and persuaded them to lend his family a million dollars to develop their plantation.

Aquino urged us to send volunteers to Tarlac. His reason was interesting: "I don't care if they aren't the best teachers in the world. [They weren't.] We need them here as catalysts, to make our teachers and our children think, to stimulate their minds and imaginations, to give them some idea of the infinite possibilities that lie beyond their own barrio or *población* [town]."

Some years later, after Tarlac did get volunteers, he told me that they were the best possible investment the United States could make in foreign aid "because they show the people of our country what America and Americans are really like at their best." On that first day at Tarlac, however, the more interesting question was, "Did Aquino himself imagine at that time the possibility that waited for him beyond the walls of his governor's office?" In the early 1960s the Philippines was a functioning democracy under President Macapagal, tilted toward the rich elite—not the most progressive democracy in the world, but still a democracy. Then Ferdinand Marcos succeeded Macapagal, declared martial law in 1972, and turned the Philippines into an oppressive dictatorship. Aquino had become a popular senator and was almost certain to be the opposition candidate to Marcos and the next president if an honest election were held. Instead, Marcos had him tried on fictional charges of murder and treason and condemned him to death. For seven years Aquino sat in prison under that sentence of death while Marcos tried to decide if he could afford to kill Aquino in the face of protests from the United States and other nations around the world. Finally, in response to such protests, he released Aquino to come to the United States for heart surgery on condition that he not return.

I met with Aquino several times after he had successful surgery and acquired a fellowship at Harvard. I arranged for him to speak to a group of religious socialists at a Jesuit school of theology in Cambridge. I knew that while he was in prison, he had written a 145-page defense to present before the military tribunal that condemned him to death. In response to the Marcos charge that he was a Communist, he wrote: "If I must be labeled I think that I will fit the label of a Christian socialist best. My ideology flows with the mainstream of Christian democratic socialism as presently practiced in Austria, West Germany and the Scandinavian countries. . . . It grieves me profoundly to be carelessly branded a Communist by those who never bothered to understand the difference between communism and Christian socialism."

At that Cambridge meeting Aquino told us of the terrible years he spent in the Marcos prison—how he had fought against the sin of despair and asked the Virgin Mary to pray to the Lord for him, how he had a kind of mystical experience in which she appeared to him, and how the next day his family was allowed to visit him for the first time in several years.

He told us that he had resolved to go back to the Philippines, even though it might mean his death. Several years went by, and he did not go back, so I thought that perhaps his resolve had weakened. Then he did go back, and as he got off the plane on August 21, 1983, a Marcos assassin, a convicted criminal, shot and killed him and then was himself shot and killed by other Marcos assassins in an effort to conceal who was in fact responsible for Aquino's murder.

This clumsy effort fooled no one. It took several years for the universal indignation to reach boiling point. Cory Aquino ran for president against Marcos in February 1986 and was officially declared the loser, but the election was so obviously fraudulent that the people rose in almost unanimous protest. Defense Minister Juan Enrile and General Fidel Ramos, deputy chief of staff of the armed forces, swept along by the tidal wave of protest, announced that they were leading a revolution against the Marcos regime, although they controlled only a handful of soldiers equipped with small arms and faced overwhelming Marcos superiority in men, tanks, and armed helicopters.

What they did was to make a radio appeal to the Catholic bishops and other religious leaders to mobilize priests, nuns, seminarians, ministers, rabbis, and laymen and women of all faiths to surround their headquarters in Camp Crame and form a human shield against the expected attack. The religious leaders responded, and so did the people. Several hundred thousand massed before the camp. For whatever reasons the armed forces did not attack, Marcos fled the country, and Mrs. Aquino took office as president.

A good Christian woman with no political experience, Corazon Aquino was no Christian socialist, nor did she have her husband's extraordinary abilities. What she had was the courage to put herself forward as a symbol of rebellion against the Marcos corruption, a symbol around which the people could rally. Her administration was not a great success, but she did manage to get the Philippines back on some sort of democratic track.

I am not so foolish as to suggest that the Peace Corps was responsible for the restoration of some measure of democracy to the Philippines. You are reading about it here because the Peace Corps gave me an opportunity to meet Aquino and to be deeply moved by his martyrdom and by the peaceful, nonviolent revolution that his martyrdom inspired.

Dorothy Day never convinced me that nonviolence was always and everywhere the answer to tyranny, aggression, and injustice. I don't think, as noted previously, that she entirely convinced herself. But she and the Philippine revolution certainly convinced me that nonviolent revolution is possible and infinitely preferable whenever and wherever it may be possible.

To prove that point I refer the reader to a marvelous book of photos and personal accounts of the revolution entitled *People Power: An Eyewitness History of the Philippine Revolution of 1986*. It features some of the best and funniest reporting I have ever read, done by a Filipino American journalist named Kaa Byington, whose conclusion I have placed at the beginning of this chapter. May the Filipino people always be true to the religious vision contained in that conclusion, and may the Peace Corps as well, for I believe that the vision behind the Peace Corps also has its origins in the best of religious faith.

A WORD OF ADVICE

One final word of advice to any future or current members of the Peace Corps staff in the Philippines. As you tramp the steamy streets of Manila, you may look out at the blue waters of Manila Bay from time to time and see sailboats sailing. You are a sailor yourself, and you long to be out there with the wind in your hair and a tiller in your hand. A departing American offers you a small sailboat very cheap, but to sail it you must join the Manila Yacht Club. You try to justify the purchase on the ground that your children can get sailing instruction and you can take visiting volunteers out for a ride. Under no circumstances fall for this insidious temptation. I speak as a repentant sinner.

14

Making War on Poverty I

> Power just goes to two poles—to those who've got money,
> and those who've got people. You haven't got money, so
> your own fellow men and women are your only source of
> strength. Now the minute you can do something about it
> you've got a problem. Should I handle it this way or that
> way? You're active. And all of a sudden you stand up.
>
> —Saul Alinsky

AFTER LANDING in San Francisco, we bought a nine-passenger van
to hold twelve big and little Corts and drove it across the country, a
pressure cooker that never quite exploded. The dealer swore the
motor was broken in, and there would be no problem climbing the
mountains, but the dealer lied.

We had to be towed up the first serious mountain we faced so that
we could coast down into Yosemite Valley. We rented a cabin and
woke in the morning to find a bear up in a neighboring tree. All day
I drove the van around and around the beautiful valley, dear Becky
keeping me company, so that we could get the engine in shape to
pull us up and out of the valley. And thank God the valley was so
beautiful that the driving was almost a pleasure.

We did make it up and over and coasted down the Great Plains,
thrilling to the sight of prong-horned antelope bounding across the
endless prairie and feeling suddenly the wildness and wonder of the
American West. The Grand Canyon was predictably grand. As we got
out of the van and walked to the edge, I said to Paul, age fourteen,
"Wow, isn't that terrific?" or something equally banal. Paul said, "It's
interesting," with a bored, falling inflection. But later in life he went
back twice to see it and to camp at its floor, so the boredom must
have been more surface than real.

As we crossed the Navajo Reservation in Arizona, we were struck
by the generosity of the white man in leaving to the Navajos some of

the most desolate, godforsaken land in the country. At a trading post another white man sold us a handsome Navajo blanket for a substantial sum, and we wondered how much of that sum ever reached the Navajo who made the blanket.

If you approach it from the West, Little Rock, Arkansas, with its tree-lined streets and handsome houses, strikes you as the first eastern city. There we visited my aunt Mildred and uncle Hugh, a retired general and member of MacArthur's staff in the invasion of the Philippines. Continuing eastward, I wanted to go out of our way to cut across the northwest corner of Mississippi, just to say we had been there. That state was in the news for outbreaks of racist terrorism, and so bad was its reputation that Helen protested that it would be an unnecessary risk. She was afraid that somebody might resent our out-of-state license plates and do something violent, like the rednecks in the movie *Easy Rider*. She is ordinarily a reasonable woman, so I had to defer to her fears, thinking, "Mississippi, you better do something about that reputation."

The War on Poverty

In Washington, D.C., I stopped in to see Sargent Shriver. Though still head of the Peace Corps, he was by then deeply involved in the War on Poverty and the creation of the war's staff headquarters, the Office of Economic Opportunity (OEO). He told me, "Mike Harrington says that it's badly underfunded, but I don't know. I never had a billion dollars to spend, and I find the prospect pretty exciting."

As he was seeing me out of the office, he opened the door for me, and I noticed on the back of the door two mottoes whose fame had reached us in the Philippines. In fact, I had resolved that if the occasion ever presented itself, I was going to say something about them, although I had no clear idea what. The mottoes were: "There is no room for losers on this ball team" and "Nice guys don't win ball games." I resented the gratuitous and inaccurate slap at nice guys, and I had also tasted the sour wine of a loser and didn't appreciate that slap either.

I saw the mottoes, remembered my resolution, and said the first thing that came to mind: "The thought occurred to me that Jesus Christ was the greatest loser of all time."

Shriver's whole manner changed abruptly. He closed the door. "Oh no," he protested, "He won a great victory over death." "Not as the world saw it," I said. "As the world saw it, he was wiped out." We sparred briefly, he pointing out that idealism is no excuse for incompetence, and I lamenting the fact that the mottoes could be interpreted to mean that winning is all and that any kind of tactic is justified in order to win. Many years later I was reading Hans Küng's *On Being a Christian*. Küng's theology is too free and easy for my taste, but I liked what he wrote on p. 410: "It is not indeed as risen, exalted, living, divine, but as crucified that this Jesus Christ is distinguished unmistakably from the many risen, exalted living gods and deified founders of religion, from the Caesars, geniuses and heroes of world history. . . . Without faith in the cross, faith in the risen Christ lacks its distinctive character and decisiveness."

I suspect that now, after Shriver's several brushes with failure and defeat, his respect for losers and the cross may well be stronger. One must, however, take nothing from his accomplishment in putting the Peace Corps on the map of the world. He was no loser there. As for the War on Poverty, he gave it his best shot with the weapons and the money that Lyndon Johnson and Congress were willing to spare from the war in Vietnam. If he was a loser there, it wasn't his fault, and in any case it is by no means certain that the loss was clear-cut.

A DOMESTIC PEACE CORPS

We headed north to Helen's parents' home in upstate New York, and visions of Grandma's roast beef, corn on the cob, and apple pie à la mode began to dance in the children's heads. I ordered a stop to visit the battlefield at Gettysburg and found myself with another battle on my hands. So close to the Promised Land, they would brook no further delays, but they were smaller then, and I was bigger. I was able to make them brook.

A few weeks later we were sitting around the supper table at my brother David's camp in the beloved Thousand Islands when a small boy in a rowboat came around the point with a telephone message. It seemed that Massachusetts governor Endicott Peabody wanted to see me. Larry Fuchs, back at Brandeis, had persuaded Peabody and the state legislature to appropriate $500,000 to organize a domestic

234 DREADFUL CONVERSIONS

corps of volunteers "to meet the critical human needs of the citizens of the commonwealth in the areas of health, education, and social service." It was to be called the Commonwealth Service Corps, and the governor was asking me to run it. The notion that one could meet those needs with that kind of money and volunteer labor was the stuff of dreams, but to minimize Shriver's remark, I had never had half a million dollars to spend, and I found the prospect pretty exciting.

Within a few months we were designated the state antipoverty agency and started receiving grants from Shriver's OEO. As such, we had to help organize and assist the twenty-five antipoverty agencies in the state, otherwise known as Community Action Programs. We also received money to recruit, train, and assign workers from Volunteers in Service to America (VISTA), the national domestic Peace Corps, and we were among the first to change VISTA policy: we stopped recruiting exclusively white, middle-class volunteers and began recruiting both black and white poor folks to work among black and white poor folks. Our first VISTA grant was the work of Dan Fox, a brilliant recruit from the Harvard faculty.

We operated an education project for migrant Puerto Rican farmworkers. We helped small businessmen obtain loans and training in management skills. The State Department gave us money to train and assign foreign volunteers working with antipoverty agencies up and down the East Coast, a reverse Peace Corps that gave me particular pleasure and satisfaction. We supplied volunteers to a wide variety of projects: childcare centers, welfare programs, senior citizen centers, settlement houses. At our peak we had an annual budget of $1.5 million, a staff of sixty, more than five hundred full-time volunteers, one hundred VISTA volunteers, and several hundred part-time student interns assigned to public agencies. Not a giant operation, but not small either. In any case we were up to our necks in the War on Poverty.

What was the justification for this war? Did the United States really need it? The 1960s were considered a prosperous time. Even John Kenneth Galbraith had written *The Affluent Society*, whose major thesis was that the poor in the United States were mainly minority groups: blacks, Native Americans, the elderly, migrants, Chicanos. But then Michael Harrington wrote *The Other America*, and Dwight Macdonald did a long review of it in *The New Yorker*, and people began to realize that poverty in this country was more than a minority problem. It was also, as Harrington, Macdonald, and Saul Alinsky pointed out, a problem of power—that is, an almost total lack of power on the part of the poor, who, though numerous, were so fragmented, disorganized, leaderless, and alienated from the political scene that they did not even bother to vote.

It was a problem affecting vast numbers of our population. Approximately 30 million were living below the poverty line, and another 15 million in "near poverty." In Massachusetts, one of the more prosperous states, 15 percent of whites were poor, and nearly 50 percent of blacks were poor. And the figures today, in an even more prosperous time, are not so very different.

On Being Good and Bad

One of my first hires was Dan Murrow, who had been a social worker in New York City working with teenage gangs in the Bronx and running a home for juvenile delinquents in Spanish Harlem. He was a warm, friendly guy who tended to hug everybody he liked, male and female. He had some interesting stories. "One time," he said,

I was walking along the street one night when I saw about twenty kids a block away dragging this black kid along the sidewalk. I thought I recognized one of the gangs I was working with at the time. They were dragging this kid into a dark schoolyard next to a Catholic church. They had a .45 revolver and a sawed-off shotgun, and they intended to kill the kid.

As they passed in front of the church, the black kid, believing that he was going to die, asked for permission to say a prayer before a statue of the Virgin Mary. They stopped for a few seconds to let him say a prayer and then went into the yard. They kicked him a few times and then fired the .45 at him, but it misfired. They were just about to finish him with the shotgun when I caught up with them. Recognizing me, they all scattered and ran, all but one, a guy named Cosimo Micalone, who started to run, but then stopped, picked up a shoe that had fallen off the black kid, and threw it toward me.

"Hey, Dan," he said. "Here's a shoe." Then he ran off. The black kid was lying face down on the ground, bleeding but not seriously hurt. I took him home, bandaged him, and we had a good talk. He was a member of a rival gang. Afterward I went to find the other kids in the poolroom where I knew they hung out. They were sitting around feeling shitty and ashamed of themselves. I chewed them out, told them it was a chicken thing to do, and treated them to Cokes.

I'm not sure they deserved those Cokes, but that was Dan. A very warmhearted guy. I liked the part about Cosimo Micalone, who decided not only to let the black kid live, but to give him back his shoe. Was he more compassionate than the rest or just an archetype of the guy who swings with the wind? Dan was convinced that kids wanted to be good if somehow it could be arranged. He quoted one of them: "When I was in Puerto Rico, everybody was friendly, I was good. But in New York, people insult you; you have to be bad."

Dan was successful in turning around one outstanding gang leader, a big handsome Puerto Rican named Johnny Torres. This young man's conversion started in jail when he found himself in the same cell with a member of the Dragons, a rival gang. He told Dan, "When you live with a guy day in and day out, and he gives you smiles and cigarettes, man, he ain't your enemy. It was then I realized the Dragons ain't my enemy. The enemy was something inside myself."

This reminded me of a speech I heard Reinhold Niebuhr give during World War II. He said, "An even more dangerous enemy than Hitler is the Hitler inside ourselves." The famous theologian and the Puerto Rican gang leader had come to similar conclusions about original sin.

Murrow was effective with most of our volunteers. Sometimes his bear hugs turned off the cooler types, and sometimes I thought his heart interfered with his head in recruiting volunteers. Sometimes I was wrong. He once described to me a scene in which one of his volunteers, a blind man, was helping another of his volunteers, a paraplegic woman, up the steps of our regional office in Fall River.

"There they were," Dan said to me in his warm, emotional way, "the blind man helping the woman, and the woman guiding the blind man. It was beautiful, man, just beautiful!"

And I replied in my cold, unemotional way, "Yeah, great, but are they doing anything for anybody else besides each other?"

Actually, the paraplegic woman, Eugenia Farnyaz, turned out to be a very effective volunteer, teaching arts and crafts to other disabled adults in a sheltered workshop. The blind man didn't last, but Dan recruited another blind man, Ed Driscoll, who became an organizer of senior citizen centers and so competent that he was elected chairman of both the volunteers Regional Advisory Council and their State Council. In that capacity he didn't hesitate to tell me off from time to time and did the same to any other state bureaucrats who he thought were not giving the volunteers a fair shake.

We were slow getting started. Our first big splash was the summer of 1965. Belden Daniels, a Phi Beta Kappa from Dartmouth who rebelled against the prospect of a successful career in a Boston bank, led the effort. We recruited nearly six hundred high school and college students and put them out in the field, working with mentally disabled children, running playgrounds, tutoring, working in day camps, painting houses in the ghettos, fixing up parks and housing projects.

At our short training program I invited Bill Saltonstall, former headmaster of Exeter, to speak. He had just returned from directing the Peace Corps effort in Nigeria. Many of our recruits were white middle-class kids from the suburbs, and because some were going into Roxbury to work in the black community, I thought it appropriate, when I introduced Saltonstall, to draw a parallel between American volunteers going into Nigeria and white suburban volunteers going into a place like Roxbury, which to many of them was just as strange and foreign as Nigeria. Some of our black staff and black volunteers, who lived in Roxbury themselves, did not appreciate this analogy, however valid.

One of our staff, Joanne Ross, made me understand pretty quickly that I better develop a little sensitivity to the feelings of black people. A Cape Verdean, Joanne had been a welfare mother herself and led a demonstration of mothers at Columbia Point, where they lay down in the road to block access to dump trucks, one of which had run over and killed a small child. She then organized a citywide group called Mothers for Adequate Welfare (MAW). Joanne was so competent and articulate that within a few years she was hired away from us at a salary that exceeded mine.

IN THE BEGINNING WAS THE WORD

In a dusty playground set in a grove of pine trees beside a lake I watched thirty college and high school students work with ninety mentally disabled children from the Paul Dever School in Taunton. Of the ninety children, about sixty had Down's syndrome. The sheer number of this group, seen together, was unnerving.

A high school girl described to me her experience in teaching a ten-year-old boy to say his first word, the word *ball*. As she told me about it, I was struck by the pleasure and excitement reflected in her face. She had been able to raise this boy one step upward toward human communication, toward a more complete fulfillment of human personality, and the experience was for her clearly intoxicating.

Afterward, when the children had been loaded onto their buses and taken back to the school, I gathered the volunteers together under a tree and talked to them. I asked them how many would like to make this kind of work a career. About half raised their hands. I doubt that any of them would ever have given it a thought before that summer. I am sorry to say that I cannot tell you how many actually did make this work their career.

From LSD to SDG

Timothy Leary got us involved in another project, which started as a bit of personal volunteering by Larry Fuchs; Walter Clark, a theologian from Newton-Andover Seminary; Pat Menton, a retired member of the state parole board; a few others; and me. The project was something called the Self-Development Group (SDG). Leary, at that point still a respectable psychologist at Harvard, had persuaded the warden of Concord Prison to let him try hallucinogenic drugs on a dozen of the tougher convicts. Leary was just looking for human guinea pigs, but the warden thought the drugs might shake the convicts up and out of their criminal habits, so he let Leary go ahead. After a few months of controlled experimentation one of the men, Don Painten, was having religious visions. In one vision he saw himself helping Christ carry his cross. A number of the men were shaken up and began asking themselves and each other, "What the hell are we doing here? This is crazy."

Led by Painten and Jim Kerrigan, a fast-talking veteran of the Massachusetts prison system and a natural leader, the men organized SDG as a kind of group meeting that would do for convicts what

Alcoholics Anonymous was doing for alcoholics. Leary passed out of the picture, almost literally, but Kerrigan wrote to Larry Fuchs, and Larry put together a board of respectable types who got permission from the Corrections Department for the men to meet together without guards present as long as one of us was also present. We used to go to Concord every few weeks and meet with our own groups of SDG members. I enjoyed the meetings. Years earlier Helen and I had run a religious discussion group in a home for unwed mothers in Brighton. I used to tell people that some of the most innocent women I ever knew I met in a home for unwed mothers and some of the nicest guys I ever knew I met in jail.

More Powerful than LSD

It was in this capacity that I got to know Kenny Abramson, a tough type who had spent too much of his life in a series of jails. He had been involved in a prison break that failed, and he told me that at one point he was under indictments that could have kept him in jail for several hundred years. He said the turning point in his life came one day when he was sitting in a cell in solitary as the result of some prison infraction. In the cell next to him the prison psychologist was arguing with another con, and Kenny heard the psychologist say to the con, "Well, you do your thinking, and I'll do my thinking."

Something about the statement, the way the psychologist said it, and the context triggered the realization in Kenny that he had been allowing other people, and especially his fellow convicts, to do his thinking for him. He started to do his own thinking. Eventually, along with other Concord inmates, most of whom were SDG members, Kenny became a Commonwealth Service Corps volunteer in a project that involved going out on release time to work with some of the most severely mentally and physically disabled patients at the Fernald School in Waltham.

He told me about working with George, twenty-four, who was not only deaf and dumb, but blind as well, and believed to be mentally disabled. For seven years George had lived worse than an animal, locked up in an isolated room whose walls and ceiling were spotted with excrement that George had flung about. This was incredible—

not that he had flung the excrement, but that it was not cleaned up. I saw it with my own eyes.

Kenny worked with George long enough to establish a relationship of trust and friendship and to convince himself that George was not mentally disabled at all but an intelligent human being. He taught him to dress and undress himself, to find his way to the shower room, and to adjust the hot and cold water. He tried him on manual puzzles, things like concentric eggs that you take apart and put together again, and found that George could solve them without difficulty. With more work George improved to the point where he was admitted to a school for the blind and was on his way to making it as a functioning adult, and the whole thing happened because a hopeless convict started to do his own thinking.

Working with George speeded up the change in Kenny. It was a case of finding a personality change agent that was even more powerful than LSD—namely, helping other people. He told me: "You can't do nice things for people very long without feeling nicer about yourself. First I was doing negative things for positive reasons, like stealing clothes and food for George. But gradually I worked my way out of that. I enjoyed the good feelings that helping George gave me enough so that I could do without the paranoid, old screw-everybody feelings that had put me in the can and kept me there for so long."

Kenny got out of Concord a few years later and within a few more years worked his way into the directorship of a similar program involving Service Corps, Norfolk Prison, and Medfield State Hospital. At one point the convicts he worked with had a recidivism rate of zero, as contrasted with a statewide rate of 78 percent. Kenny eventually became an assistant regional director of the state's Youth Service Board and, last I knew, was doing well.

Down on the Farms

Our education project for Puerto Rican migrants on fruit, vegetable, and tobacco farms attracted some of our more lively and militant volunteers. In addition to English, they taught the migrants health and citizenship, and under these rubrics we thought it proper that the volunteers should remind the migrants of whatever few and meager rights and privileges our society provides to migrant farmworkers.

Sometimes our volunteers even whispered a word about the superior wages and conditions migrants were enjoying in other parts of the state.

Some farmers naturally took this advice amiss, so amiss that they refused us entry to their farms. Because the workers lived on the farms, often in miserable shacks, this refusal meant that our people could not talk to them. One of our staff, a Puerto Rican named Alfredo de Jesus, was so persistent that a farmer threatened to shoot him. "That's all right," Alfredo told him, "I've been shot before."

When Alfredo told me this story, I told him that I admired his courage, but I did not think we needed a dead Puerto Rican at that point and urged him to wait for less-painful remedies, which we set out to win by legislative means. The farmers legally had the right to prevent people from visiting employees on their property. With the help of some good progressives like Joe Bradley, Paul Menton (Pat Menton's son), and Mike Dukakis in the state House of Representatives and Mario Umana in the Senate, plus good media coverage of a press conference in which we likened the conditions of the migrants to serfdom and slavery, we won passage of a bill that gave anyone the right to visit employees who live on an employer's property.

To my knowledge, this bill was the first such legislation, either state or federal, ever enacted in this country and broke new legal ground. California later provided a similar right of visitation, which the powerful enemies of Cesar Chávez and the United Farm Workers continued to challenge and deny.

STRANGE REPUBLICANS AND DEMOCRATS

I was sitting in the state Senate gallery one day waiting for a Service Corps bill to come to the floor when an incredible scene unfolded before my eyes. They were debating the question of public regulation of the new cable TV industry, a business loaded with potential profits for the lucky ones who got in on the ground floor.

I was surprised to see that the Republicans, led by Brahmins like William Weeks and another Bill Saltonstall, were arguing for a statewide regulatory system that would protect the public interest, and it was the Democrats, led by Joe Ward, who were arguing for a chaotic form of regulation by individual cities and towns, one that would be a piece of chocolate cake for the cable TV people. A complete reversal of the usual party roles.

This reversal was shocking enough to a cradle Democrat like myself, but what was even more unsettling was the argument made by Joe Ward, the only man in the Senate who had the oratorical skills to make everybody listen. Addressing his remarks to Senators Saltonstall and Weeks, he said: "You Yankee Brahmins can afford to be idealistic about this thing because your Puritan ancestors made their pile running slaves from Africa and rum from Jamaica and exploiting the workers in the textile mills. So now why should you want to spoil the chances of the poor Johnny-come-latelies who only want the same opportunity your great grandfathers had to improve themselves?"

Moreover, the lobbyist for the cable TV companies just happened to be Gerry Doherty, former chairman of the Democratic State Committee. All this shook me up so much that I checked the voting records in the House and Senate against the standards set by Americans for Democratic Action. I found that in both houses the Republicans had the more progressive records.

Of course, it was easy to conclude that what protected the Republicans in their liberalism, besides the wealth of their ancestors, was a certain absence of temptation—namely, a realization in the business community that they didn't have the votes. True, they were able to elect a Republican governor from time to time, largely because of the fact reflected in the proverb, "In Massachusetts the Republicans are a band of well-organized mice in a room full of chaotic cats."

Lieutenant Governor Frank Belotti spectacularly demonstrated feline chaos when he decided to run against Governor Peabody, another Yankee Brahmin in Democratic clothing, for the Democratic nomination in 1964, for no better reason than that he thought he could beat him. Which he did. For this unfriendly act he received his just deserts and was defeated by the Republican John Volpe, who was not a Yankee Brahmin but a very decent man who gave us all the support we deserved. He departed for Washington, D.C., leaving us with another Republican Brahmin, Frank Sargent, also a decent man but one who presided over a reorganization that folded us into a department run by hard-nosed bureaucrats who looked upon the Service Corps as a bunch of dreamy do-gooders with vine leaves in their hair.

The hard noses made life so difficult that I was forced to resign in

1970 and take a job with the Boston Red Feather agency United Community Services, working out of the city of Lynn, from which I shortly moved into the job of director of the Lynn Model Cities project, a new federal antipoverty program. I will leave this story for chapter 16, which will include some comment on Daniel Patrick Moynihan's and Saul Alinsky's critiques of the War on Poverty.

In 1976 I went back to the Service Corps office to see what had happened to it as it approached the twelfth anniversary of its birth. It was still alive, with 305 volunteers out in the field and another 100 transferred to the Office of Elder Affairs, a new agency. The projects were much the same.

As I came in, I saw a sign pasted up: "RAC [Regional Advisory Council] Meeting Here." Maureen Maher and Ed Donnelly were about all that was left of the original staff, but I also saw Barbara Strothers, a black volunteer who used to run a senior citizens' center and had since become the Boston regional director. She and her assistant, Nina Saunders, another volunteer face from the old days, were sitting in her office discussing the RAC meeting, which had just adjourned.

I asked them what the volunteer delegates had been talking about at the meeting. Nina said, "The same old thing: how to get the eighty dollar stipend raised."

Later I checked the rise in the cost of living since the legislature had set that monthly stipend back in 1964. The Bureau of Labor Statistics told me that the $80 was in 1976 worth $46 in 1964 money—$46 a month for thirty hours of work a week, and that did not include expenses.

How could the Commonwealth of Massachusetts be so tight-fisted? A few years later it proved to be even more tight-fisted as it eliminated the program entirely. This decision simultaneously eliminated the question: Was the $80 a month, added to whatever psychic income could be derived from the title "volunteer," enough to justify a program built largely on getting a great deal of cheap labor out of poor folks?

That question, too, I will defer to a later chapter.

15

The Black Experience

If ever the colored question comes up again as long as I
live, I will be counted in with the black men.

—John Boyle O'Reilly, editor of the *Boston Pilot,* a
Catholic newspaper, 1885

ON ELECTION DAY in 1965 I was standing in front of the polls at the
firehouse in Oak Square, Brighton, handing out fliers in support of
the school committee slate endorsed by an organization called Citizens for the Boston Schools.

At the time Helen, the kids, and I were living in Newton, a more
affluent suburb adjacent to Brighton. We had sold our Boston home
when we left for the Philippines, and then when we returned we
could not find a house in Brighton large enough to house our family,
so we bought this big old house in Newton.

We had been members of the Citizens back in the 1950s and had
once given a campaign house party for Citizen candidates, including
Mel King, who was a black member of the 1965 slate and had run
several times previously. The slate also included a good friend, Arthur
Gartland, the only member of the incumbent school committee who
had the head, heart, and guts to stand up to Louise Day Hicks, leader
of the racist forces that controlled the committee and dominated the
city.

The Citizens were an interracial group, mainly white, who were
concerned to do something about the disgrace that masqueraded
under the appearance of a public school system. At that time black
children made up nearly 30 percent of the student body, although
blacks were only 13 percent of the population. It seemed reasonable
to elect at least one black member to represent them. The members
of the school committee were elected at large rather than by district
and had always been white and usually Irish.

The Citizens slate also supported the idea that the city should pay for busing so that black and white children could attend better schools outside their immediate neighborhoods in the event that those schools had vacant seats. This busing was to be strictly voluntary.

All the other candidates, taking their lead from Mrs. Hicks, expressed their strong opposition to this idea under a banner that read, "SAVE THE NEIGHBORHOOD SCHOOLS!" This was the big issue. Some years later, when mandatory busing was the issue, Mrs. Hicks protested that she opposed only *forced* busing, but the truth is that her original antibusing campaign was directed at *voluntary* busing. She actually went so far as to oppose the city expenditure of $200,000 for voluntary busing, even though the failure to spend that money would sacrifice $25 million in state and federal funds for new schools that Boston desperately needed. Fortunately, she did not get her way on that one.

It seems clear that opposition to voluntary busing, especially when illuminated by the slogan "Save the Neighborhood Schools," has its roots in racism. I know I turned the slogan over and over in my mind for years, chewing on it, masticating slowly like a cow on its cud, rolling it round on the tongue, exposing it to the taste buds and the palate, searching for every possible suggestion of flavor and meaning. I could find only one basic meaning, expressed in its least crude form about as follows: "Keep the black kids out of our neighborhood because they are inferior, and if they are permitted to go to school with our kids, they will drag down the quality of the school. Besides, our kids might like some of them. Yes, there are good kids among them, but would you want your daughter to marry one?"

In any case there I was standing in front of the polls in Oak Square handing out these leaflets. Although I was no longer a Boston resident, I thought I could be helpful at the polls because Oak Square was our old neighborhood, and I retained, I thought, some aura of martyrdom from the 1960 campaign for state rep.

Not for long. As a woman who used to be my strong supporter went by, not stopping, she tossed her head and yelled, "What's the matter, John? Are you trying to keep them out of Newton?" I realize that people don't toss their heads much anymore, but I can vouch for the fact that this lady tossed hers.

As it happened, we had an African exchange student living with us at the time, but in a sense this woman had me. I was not only not a

Boston voter, as still other former friends that day reminded me, but I lived even farther than they did from the point where turf met turf. Her comment kind of struck home.

Before she got out of range, she tossed another one: "When I saw where you let your daughter go to Selma, I said to myself, 'If that's all he cares for his own flesh and blood—.'" The conclusion of that sentence was apparently too awful for utterance. It was true that we had permitted our oldest daughter, Barbara, then eighteen, to join Martin Luther King Jr. in the civil rights marches in Selma, Alabama, entrusting her to the protection of an older friend.

An old man came out of the polls and stopped to talk. "If only they would stay in their place," he said. "I have property in Dorchester [a section of Boston next to Roxbury], and now they're moving into the neighborhood, and the property values are going down. They should stay where they belong."

He spoke with a foreign accent, and I couldn't help thinking, "How long ago was it, old man, that native-born Americans were saying about you, 'These immigrants are dragging down the neighborhood and our property values. They should stay where they belong.'" But I didn't say it.

The election itself was a disaster. Even Gartland was knocked off the committee in a clean sweep for antibusing. He was defeated by a political newcomer who had only the following visible qualifications as far as I could tell: (1) he was opposed to voluntary busing; (2) he was the brother of a city councilor; (3) he had the same last name as a popular governor's councilor to whom he was unrelated; (4) he was white; and (5) he was Irish. These "qualifications" proved to be enough to beat Gartland.

I am not certain at what point on that miserable day I made up my mind that we should move to Roxbury. I think it started with the former supporter's tossed taunts. It certainly ended that night with the returns on TV and the news that Gartland had been defeated. Helen had already decided that we ought to move. Then there was also the added factor that I was directing an antipoverty agency and living in a neighborhood where poverty was invisible. Dorothy Day would not have liked that. But Nicholas was a senior at Newton High and the twins, Paul and Becky, were juniors, and they asked us to wait until they graduated. Because we had already bounced around so much, honoring their request seemed only fair.

It wasn't until May 1967 that we actually signed papers that gave us ownership of a dilapidated but handsome old house on Winthrop Street near Dudley Station in the heart of Roxbury. Everything we realized from the sale of the Newton house, about $7,500, we spent to fix up the new one. It had once been the elegant home of rich white folks in the days when Roxbury was a fashionable place to live, around 1865. It had parquet floors and four fireplaces with inlaid marble. From the second floor we could see over the wall of the Carmelite convent next door, where flowering trees and shrubs bloomed in a pleasant field. A charming part of the ghetto.

BAPTISM BY RIOT

After we bought the house but before we could move in, a riot broke out in Roxbury. It was early evening of June 2, 1967, when I heard about it. I was home. Mary Berger picked me up, and we drove in to the office of Operation Exodus on Blue Hill Avenue, where we were both known to Ellen Jackson, the dynamic young black woman who directed that project.

The riot started when several husky black welfare mothers, led by Service Corps volunteers assigned to MAW, had that afternoon locked the front door of the Grove Hall welfare office and chained themselves to it in a demonstration designed to call attention to their grievances. The cops came, and a predictable fracas ensued, particularly in view of the MAW representatives' size and strength. Reports of police brutality swept through the area, and the riot was on.

That night I stood in the Operation Exodus office doorway and from a safe distance watched the fires and the looting up and down Blue Hill Avenue. The stores were owned mostly by whites. Those that weren't had "SOUL" chalked or painted on their windows. Of eighty-nine members of the Dudley Station Merchants Association at that time only three were black. Many of the white-owned stores would not hire black clerks.

The streets were full of police, but I don't remember seeing a single black one. At one point the riot police came marching up the middle of the street in force, firing their carbines at random into the air that by this time was as thick and crackling with racial hatred as it was with smoke and fire. As I stood there watching them go by, a black man standing beside me crumpled to the ground. I thought for a moment a stray police bullet had hit him, but apparently he had been felled by either booze or a stroke. They took him away in an ambulance, and I thanked God that nobody took a shot at the police or at me in retaliation for an imagined homicide.

Jim Bishop, the governor's black aide, came by, and he and I walked up to the police command post at Grove Hall and persuaded Deputy Superintendent Saia that the riot squad was doing more harm than good. He gave orders that they be put back in their buses and driven out, leaving the field to less-warlike regulars.

Reports began coming back from the police stations that the kids arrested for looting were being beaten up and denied their legal rights. Tom Atkins, a black lawyer soon to be elected a city councilor, was beaten by police for trying to protect another man from a similar beating. I talked to Atkins in Station 9 as he sat holding his bleeding head and broken glasses. I complained to a lieutenant, but he denied everything.

As the riot continued, leaders of the community held a meeting in the Exodus office to decide what they should do. Because I was a state agency head and seemed sympathetic, they invited me to join them. I was surprised to see the bitterness of some of the more radical leaders toward the older, more conservative men whom we thought of as representing the community. One of the radicals, a blind man who was murdered about a year later in a fight over control of a heavily funded antipoverty project, was determined, for example, that the current National Association for the Advancement of Colored People (NAACP) president should not be allowed to speak for the people of Roxbury. The man who emerged as the strongest and most respected leader was Jim Breeden, a gentle, soft-spoken Episcopal minister.

The meeting named a committee to go to police headquarters and meet with Commissioner McNamara, and they asked me to go along. We went, and the black leaders stated their complaints to McNamara about the conduct of the police and about the failure to establish any kind of communication with the leadership of the community. At one point I asked McNamara how many black policemen he had on the force, pointing out that the black-white aspect of the riot was an obvious irritant in driving a bad situation toward violence.

McNamara told us that out of a total force of 2,500 he had only 54 blacks. That's 2.16 percent in a population that was then 13 percent black. The curious thing was that none of these 54 black police officers, as far as I could see, were used that night in the black sections of the city.

The next day Breeden invited me to join him, Archie Williams, and Noel Day on a committee to sit down with Mayor Collins to discuss the situation. It was a Saturday, and we had to go around to the back entrance of City Hall. As we went in, the others ahead of me, we could hear a cop in an anteroom off the hall announce to others in the room, "Here are the niggers arriving."

The mayor, however, was more cordial. The city was still in turmoil, and Collins was obviously in the mood to make concessions to the black community, to cool it off before nightfall. Breeden's committee wanted especially to get some concessions for the welfare mothers. Unfortunately, among the young white members of MAW were some New Left types, and these women were able to persuade their black sisters to tell the mayor that (1) he must come out to Roxbury to talk to them, and (2) they needed more time to prepare their demands.

I tried to get into a MAW meeting to urge them to hurry it up, to strike while the iron was hot, but no luck. The best I could do was pass in a note. The effort was fruitless. By the time, three days later, that they had their demands ready, the iron, the city, and the mayor had cooled off. Very little came of the negotiations. The New Lefties no doubt enjoyed their brief illusion of power, but the welfare mothers were left about the same as when they chained themselves to that door in Grove Hall.

Years later I heard a story about this riot, one of those rare stories that are at once funny and illuminating. A white man named Jack Williams, one of Sargent Shriver's assistants up from Washington, D.C., was driving his car through Roxbury at the height of the riot. He had worked in Roxbury with young folks in years past and was popular in the community. As he drove along that night, a young black man threw a rock and shattered his windshield.

As Williams stopped the car, the black youth shouted at him, "That will fix you, Whitey!" Then, as he recognized Williams, he added in a completely different tone, "Oh, hiya, Jack."

CAT AND DOG IN THE CONVENT

The boys and I started working on the Roxbury house. One evening I went out on the porch roof to cool off. From the roof I could see into the convent grounds. A Great Dane and a boxer dog could see me over the wall, which was topped with barbed wire and broken glass to protect the nuns from their black neighbors. The dogs came charging and barking up to the wall, and I thought for a moment they were coming right over it.

Some time later, after we moved in, our cat Murray (not named for Phil Murray) climbed a tree, got over the wall, and was chewed up by the boxer dog. Helen heard the cat's cries for help and ran around to the front door of the convent. It was a cloistered convent, and the nuns did not speak to visitors face to face. After Helen had rung the bell and secured entrance to the lobby, a disembodied voice came out of the wall, saying by way of greeting, "Blesséd be our Lord Jesus Christ."

I told Helen later she should have responded, "And curséd be your boxer dog," but you couldn't blame her for being somewhat taken aback. Ordinarily she is quick with the riposte. Instead she said, "Uh, yes, I'm Helen Cort. I live next door, and your boxer dog is killing our cat."

"Oh," said the voice. "Yes, we know about that. Wait just a moment." In a minute or two an opening appeared in the wall, and a sort of Lazy Susan swung around and delivered a dead Murray.

"Gee," said Helen, further traumatized, "have you got something to put it in?" The Lazy Susan swung around again and delivered Murray in a shoebox, ready for burial.

We got to know the nuns through one of their number, a highly intelligent and dedicated Christian who was the daughter of a prominent Boston physician and the sister of Vincent Stanton, one of our Newton friends. She called me on the phone and asked me to visit. I did so and then asked Jim Breeden and John Harmon, a white Episcopal priest who lived in the neighborhood, to come with me and tell the nuns something about the place in which they lived.

The mother superior couldn't bring herself to let three men talk to her nuns face-to-face at that point, but we were able to talk to her and Sister Elizabeth through a grill. And changes did occur. The Great Dane and boxer dog disappeared, giving place to a smaller, less ferocious animal. The barbed wire and jagged glass came off the wall. The nuns gave over part of their yard to a playground for the neighborhood children. They opened up their chapel for community folk masses, and at one memorable mass Brother Blue, a delightful black minstrel, did a graceful and reverent dance right in the sanctuary. The convent even acquired a black sister, and Helen suggested, but not to them, that they put her in a window so all the neighbors could see.

One of the surprising things about Roxbury then was the number of white people who still lived in it. Irish bars still stood on Dudley Street, and within a quarter mile the neighborhood had five convents and several Catholic churches, including our parish church, St. Patrick's, which had its own grammar school as well as a girls' high school, with mostly white students. The number of white residents in the area was probably as much as 30 percent. Just across the street from us was Packard Manse, an ecumenical movement presided over by John Harmon, his wife Nikky, and their lovely daughters. It was nice to go over on Sunday evenings and sing hymns, the great Sarah Small at the piano, and take part in interesting discussions.

Learning to Understand

Shortly after we moved in, somebody decided to celebrate Labor Day by setting fire to an abandoned house on our street. It blazed merrily and even spread to a church next door. About a dozen fire trucks showed up from stations all over the area. I looked in vain for one black face among the firefighters. It was then I began to understand why there were so many fires and even more fire alarms in Roxbury. It was a way of baiting Whitey. I later learned that in a force of about 2,100 there were just 18 blacks, less than 1 percent.

I began looking around me, trying to see through the eyes of a young black boy growing up, anxious to stay clear of the pimps and the hustlers, the petty thieves and muggers, the gangs and dope, anxious to find some kind of honest work that would pay him enough to get married and lead a decent life. It was clear that the police and fire departments were not very promising places to look for such work. They were part of the white world, the Man's world, foreign territory.

After the riots that had broken out all over the country around that time, President Johnson appointed a commission to explore the causes of such violent outbreaks. The commission reported that the black ghettoes had at least twelve deeply held grievances. Number one was police practices, number two was bad housing, and number three was unemployment and underemployment.

Too many of the young men and boys looked upon the police as the enemy, the White Enemy. To be a police officer was for a black man too often a kind of treason, a going over to the enemy. Later, when that man married and maybe even bought a home, he would be griping that there weren't enough police officers, white or black, to protect his home, himself, and his family because it was also clear that most of the victims of black crime were black themselves.

ONE POLICE PRACTICE

I did not really learn to understand why "police practices" were number one on black people's list of grievances until the night of October 7, 1969. I was driving home that night around 7:30, going south on Northampton Street, when my car was forced to stop near the corner of Washington Street in the South End, another black section of Boston that lay next to Roxbury. Just ahead of me a squad car had stopped in the middle of the street, and just ahead of the squad car was a police wagon. I saw several white policemen put a short black man into the wagon. About fifteen or twenty spectators, mostly black, stood by watching.

At this point one of the spectators, a tall, husky man, said something to the cops as they were getting back in the squad car. I could not hear what he said, but I assumed he was protesting the arrest. His manner was not aggressive, and his voice was not loud enough to carry to my ears although I was only twenty feet away and had the car window open. One of the officers got out of the car and, yelling, advanced on the spectator, who had retreated to the opposite sidewalk and was standing there alone, with his hands down, when the officer, two other cops right behind, hit the mans hard across the left side of the face with an overhand blow of his blackjack.

The officers grabbed the man and rushed him into the wagon. As he was stooping to get into the wagon, one of the cops, from behind, hit him a hard whack over the head with a nightstick. As the police drove off, I turned on Washington Street and continued homeward, but after driving a few blocks I decided I could not go home. I turned around and drove to the police station and asked to see the captain. The captain was not in, but a lieutenant agreed to see me in the office. When I told him what I had seen, he said that nobody had been brought in and that he knew nothing about it. I went outside and waited across the street. After a few minutes, a squad car pulled up, and several officers got out.

I thought I recognized one of them as the man who had hit the spectator with his blackjack. I followed him into the station. In the lobby I said to him, "Did you just have an altercation with two black guys at the corner of Northampton and Washington Streets?"

He said, "I sure did." The way he said it, I had the feeling he thought I was about to congratulate him for exemplary behavior.

I said, "I want to bring charges against you." I asked his name. When he gave it to me, I went back into the office and told the lieutenant that I was bringing charges against the officer for unjustified assault. I also told the lieutenant that if I could identify the other officer who struck the man from behind with his stick, I would have brought charges against him also, but I could not do so.

The lieutenant suggested that I come back in the morning and see Captain Russell. I went home and wrote out my complaint in the form of a letter to the captain. I added the information that on the way home I had stopped at the same corner and found three witnesses who were willing to testify to what had happened. One of them said that he heard what the man said to the officers and that it was merely a question as to why they were arresting the other fellow for what seemed to be no apparent reason. I gave their names and addresses and then added the following:

> I am concerned about this incident because I live in the black community and because my job as director of the state's antipoverty program compels me to be concerned about the bitterness that many black people feel toward white people and particularly white policemen. Just this morning a Black Panther gave me a leaflet outside Dudley Station. It included the usual reference to the police as "racist fascist pigs." From my knowledge of the people in Roxbury, I do not believe that many of them accept this crazy doctrine that all policemen are pigs, even though many of them have had unpleasant experiences with indi-

vidual officers. But incidents such as the one I witnessed are going to make it very hard for people like myself to persuade our black friends that there are plenty of decent policemen. The actions of men like [this officer] are simply going to increase the bitterness and spread it around until I can see nothing ahead but violence and bloodshed.

I returned to the station in the morning and gave the complaint to Captain Russell. He told me that he had already heard about the matter and read from a report that he had on his desk. He said the officer in question reported that he had hit the man only after the man had first hit him and that he, the officer, had been hit so hard that he had to go to City Hospital to be treated for abrasions of the ribs. I expressed my disbelief that the spectator had caused any abrasions, real or imaginary, because I was certain that he had not struck the officer.

Captain Russell said, "I'm aware of the poor image that the police have in the black community, and I want to reverse that image. I assure you that I will give this incident a full investigation." He spoke with apparent sincerity.

He also told me that at that very moment the case was in municipal court, where both men were charged with gaming—taking part in a dice game—and the spectator, a man named Miller, additionally with assault and battery. It is an interesting side note that on the night the arrest took place, when the lieutenant asked the officer what he was charging the two men with, he answered, "Resisting arrest, assault and battery, gaming and drunkenness."

I figured Miller would need a lawyer, and I called one of our staff at the Service Corps, Jim Farrell, and asked him if he would take the case without fee. He readily agreed. Farrell and I went up to the courthouse where Judge Elijah Adlow, an eccentric character who was known for eccentric decisions, was holding his eccentric court.

When Miller was brought out, I said to Jim, "That's the man." The judge asked Miller if he had a lawyer, and he said "no," but Jim stood up and said, "Yes, he does." He asked for time to consult and went into an antechamber with Miller and his short friend while Judge Adlow went on to other cases.

When our turn came, the officer testified that he had seen the two men in a dice game in the alley and presented two one-dollar bills and a pair of dice, which he said he had found on the ground after the men scattered and ran. He said that Miller had punched him in the ribs and presented a doctor's statement that he had been treated at City Hospital.

Miller testified that he and his friend, the small black man, had not been in any dice game but had just come out of a bar and were crossing the street when the latter was arrested. He confirmed that the two officers had hit him twice, without provocation, and said further that the officers had not informed them of their rights, as required by law, and that in the police station his repeated requests to make a phone call were ignored. I was impressed by his testimony. He spoke with force and intelligence. I knew the arresting officer was lying like hell, and I was inclined to believe Miller's statement that he had not been in a dice game.

I testified to what I had seen. In the end Adlow ruled that Miller was not guilty of assault and battery, but declared both men guilty of gaming, although he said, "The charge should have been present at a game, which is the same thing." He fined them $10 each but put the fines on file, which means that they did not have to pay them—in short, the next best thing to being declared not guilty. Adlow then added, "This is just another case of a small matter mushrooming into something else because of indiscreet performance of duty." I interpreted these words as a slap on the officer's wrist. "Indiscreet performance" yes, but "duty" no.

Some time later a detective came to the house and quizzed me at length about the incident. After several weeks I called Captain Russell. He informed me that because Miller did not want to pursue the matter, he was letting it drop. But Miller had no need to pursue the matter because Russell had enough in my testimony and in Judge Adlow's rebuke, mild as it was. It would have been simple to transfer the officer to another precinct outside the black community, but Captain Russell—sincere-sounding, image-conscious Captain Russell—couldn't even bring himself to recommend that. He said it would be a black mark on the officer's record. So a violent young officer with clear racist tendencies was permitted to remain where he could go on beating up on black people. Not an encouraging sign.

An ironic postscript: after the trial, I gave Miller and his friend a ride back to the South End. I told them about the Black Panther leaflet and asked Miller if he agreed with the Panthers' evaluation of cops. He said, "No, I don't agree with that shit. One of my best

friends is an Irish detective." An encouraging sign, even if this incident did not justify it.

In case someone accuses me of personal bias let me quote from
the 1968 report of President Johnson's Riot Commission, an item
included after "extensive studies in one city":

> In predominantly Negro precincts over three fourths of the white po-
> licemen expressed prejudiced, or highly prejudiced, attitudes towards
> Negroes. Only one percent of the officers expressed attitudes which
> could be described as sympathetic towards Negroes. Indeed, close to
> one half of all the police officers in predominantly Negro high crime
> areas showed extreme prejudice against Negroes. What do I mean by
> extreme racial prejudice? I mean that they describe Negroes in terms
> that are not people terms. They describe them in terms of the animal
> kingdom.

I did not look into grievance number two, the lack of decent housing, but I did do some personal checking on number three, the lack
of employment opportunities. I have mentioned the police and fire
departments and the absence of black owners *and* clerks in the Roxbury stores. When I read a news story about trouble in one of the
Roxbury schools, I decided to check it out. Although the student
enrollment in that school was more than 90 percent black, there were
only two black teachers in a faculty of seventy-eight men and women.
I checked further. In the whole school system only 2 percent of the
teachers were black, though the student enrollment was nearly 30
percent black. I noticed that in the Roxbury schools even the janitors
were white.

Twice a day I passed through Dudley Station, a large bus terminal,
and for several months I failed to see a single black bus driver. I
learned that applicants for driver jobs had to take a test in algebra—
not very useful for testing driving skills, but probably helpful in weed-
ing out blacks.

The final irony was that the men doing the really dirty public jobs
in the heart of Roxbury, street cleaning and trash and garbage removal, the kind of jobs usually reserved for blacks, were exclusively
white men.

I began looking at the building projects in Roxbury, the good jobs,
the ones that paid good money. At the end of our street the Boys'
Club was putting up a handsome new building to serve the black

community. And to whom did they give the contract, this well-meaning, philanthropic organization of white do-gooders? To a firm that hired almost exclusively white labor. I checked the site every day as I walked to Dudley Station. Out of approximately sixty or more men working on it, over the months I saw only one or two black faces.

Ironies multiplied. Lyndon Johnson appointed a black man to his cabinet—a first, I believe—heading up the Department of Housing and Urban Development, and the man gave contracts to white contractors who hired mainly whites to build and renovate housing in Roxbury. Mel King and the Urban League had to organize picket lines and demonstrations to put a stop to it. Marty Gopen, a white man, did a great job with the Urban League, kicking and screaming, digging and fighting, to find jobs for blacks in the construction industry, where the unions, much to my shame and regret, had a long history of racial discrimination.

Once at a public meeting I had the bad judgment to commend Marty's work just after I had called attention to the black cabinet officer's behavior. A black speaker followed me on the platform and denounced me as a racist. I learned from that experience as well.

But mostly I learned that our society was telling the young black boy, "Get yourself a hustle, snatch yourself a bag, mug yourself an old lady, rip off a home, pimp for a whore, pedal some drugs, steal, kill if necessary—it's the only way you're ever going to make it in this white man's world."

After the assassination of Martin Luther King Jr. on April 4, 1968, more riots broke out around the country, including Boston. A wave of panic, an actual fear of impending slaughter of blacks by whites, swept through the ghetto. Two responsible organizations, Operation Exodus and the Urban League, put out a leaflet. In large letters the first page instructed the people to "COOL IT" and added, "Defend your home and family, but don't start anything." On the second page were these words: "Next time *they* will turn off all utilities, gas, water, lights, phone, and plan to murder *all* black people. . . . When the riot starts, you can expect martial law, which will confine you to your home for as long as a month or more. Start your survival plans NOW. If you wait for the riot to begin, you will be too late." The first suggested precaution was: "Have a gun and plenty of ammunition. Nothing wrong with a bow and arrow."

Another page was headed, "As of April 4, 1968, Non-Violence Is

Dead—the Black Community Faces Extermination." Other pages detailed the kinds of food and other items that should be stored in the people's homes and the phone numbers of doctors, nurses, hospitals, friendly organizations, and churches. One Catholic church, St. Joseph's, where Monsignor Russell Collins and Father Michael Groden had already built a center of interracial friendship, was included in this list.

HOW TO SELL DOG FOOD

Certain elements in the white community began to respond. A Boston chapter of the Urban Coalition was organized, and many of us in Roxbury—black and white, radical, liberal, and conservative—were invited to a meeting in the John Hancock Building. More than one hundred attended. When the organizers read off a list of black and white people who had been chosen to serve on committees to study various aspects of the race problem and to make recommendations, some of the radicals rose to protest that the organizers of the coalition were going about it the wrong way, that they should first allow the black community to select its own representatives and not try to impose them on the community from outside.

The chairman, who was the president of a large insurance company, rose to his feet in what was a sincere attempt to be conciliatory. He agreed that the speakers had a point and that perhaps the black members of the group should be given an opportunity to name their own representatives. Then he added, "After all, as they say in the advertising business, 'You may have the best dog food in the world, but if the dogs won't eat it, what good is it?'"

That analogy just about killed that meeting, and the Boston chapter of the Urban Coalition faded away shortly thereafter. I tried to start a discussion group of black and white leaders, receiving some favorable responses from white leaders, but no interest from the black leaders unless we were going to talk about specific ways and means to do something. At this point Mel King was director of the Urban League of Boston and had converted it into a militant and active organization. He suggested that we talk about "jobs for black workers and contractors in housing construction and housing rehab."

We held two meetings at the house. Attending were eight black men involved in construction or housing rehab; ten key executives from the banking, insurance, and real estate fields; and a few interested bystanders like city councilor Jock Saltonstall, Bob McKay, Marty Gopen, and I. Among the companies represented were John Hancock, New England Life, New England Merchants Bank, Fiduciary Trust, First Realty, and the Boston Banks Urban Renewal Program, plus an expression of interest from First National. One banker came to the first meeting but complained that his wife didn't want him to drive into Roxbury at night. He didn't show again.

Nothing much came of these meetings at the time. Actually, the white types had more interest than the blacks. I got the feeling that the blacks just couldn't believe that white bankers and insurance executives would really put money on the line to help blacks. Also, when it came time for specific plans, the plans advanced by the blacks were weak on detail but strong on total and unquestioned black control with a minimum of accountability to anyone. Once again it appeared that the time was not ripe for solutions. Suspicion and distrust still hung too heavy in the air.

THE POOR PEOPLE MARCH ON WASHINGTON

June 1968: A convoy of seventeen buses takes off from Boston around 11:00 P.M. to join the Poor People's March on Washington. About half the passengers in our bus are black, half white; about half appear poor, half middle class. Not necessarily the same halves. These are roughly the same ratios for the marchers as a whole. We are a microcosmic busload, not purely poor perhaps, but surely pro-poor. With me is Wally Bither from the Service Corps staff.

5:00 A.M.: We stop at a roadside restaurant in New Jersey. Twenty-five other buses are already there, most of them from Massachusetts, but some from upstate New York. After fifteen minutes searching through the crowd, I find my daughter Lydia. Somebody says that Bishop Harrington is on one of the Catholic Charities buses from Worcester. The dawn is breaking, and there is a growing air of excitement.

9:15 A.M.: We are entering the District of Columbia. The thought occurs that we should organize a delegation to visit our Congressman, John W. McCormack, Speaker of the House and possibly the second most powerful man in the country. I ask the organizer on our bus if he agrees and would like to go along. He does and would. I suggest we keep our own bus together so we will have a representative delegation. He says, "No, no problem. Just meet me at the entrance to Resurrection City after you make the appointment with McCormack, and I'll organize the delegation." His self-confidence is disarming.

9:35 A.M.: Our bus parks along the tidal basin with all the other buses in the world, and we start walking toward Resurrection City, where the poor have been encamped for the past month. The sun is shining; Washington, D.C., is beautiful; and the people in power seem to have loaned the poor the most beautiful part of it, as if to disarm them. It is all water, trees, and grass, and the sun shines on it. Plywood cabins are in among the trees, like a summer campsite.

9:55 A.M.: We find the entrance and a public pay phone. I call McCormack's office and tell an assistant that a group of Boston constituents from the Poor People's March would like to see the Speaker. He says, "I'll call you back." We hug the pay phone, and in three minutes it is ringing. The Speaker will see us at 10:45. Amazing. We couldn't get a meeting with the Speaker of the Massachusetts House that easily.

10:20 A.M.: The organizer still hasn't showed up. We pick up a few friends from the passing crowd, including Joe Bradley, who is running for Congress. I see several black friends and urge them to join us in the Speaker's office. They agree. Still no organizer. I pick my way through the mud to Resurrection City Hall and plead with the Reverend Hosea Williams to make an announcement on the loudspeaker. He reluctantly agrees. Six of us take off in a taxi for the Capitol. Later four others join us, but unfortunately all of us are white.

10:50 A.M.: The Speaker greets us warmly. We explain our visit, emphasizing that this march was the last dream of Martin Luther King Jr., who may have been the last great apostle of nonviolence, and that if the march fails to move Congress to right the wrongs suffered by the poor, then things are going to be very tough in the ghetto.

"When I was growing up in South Boston," the Speaker says, "we never called it a ghetto, but we were poor. We paid a dollar and fifty cents a month rent for our flat, but only because we couldn't get one for a dollar and twenty-five cents."

As in previous meetings with the Speaker, the conversation tends toward reminiscence. We finally get into a discussion of the Poor People's Campaign: bills to ensure more and better jobs, housing, improved education, and so on. The Speaker indicates his general support but complains about the Republicans, who replaced forty-seven Democrats at the midterm election in 1966.

Several members of our group raise the question of Vietnam, a dubious strategy, for the atmosphere grows edgy. "If we pull out of Vietnam," the Speaker says, his voice rising, "without an agreement that provides for peace with justice, then the Communists will have won their greatest victory in fifty years." Fifty years. That would take us back to the Russian Revolution. We are getting nowhere on Vietnam, and somebody drags the discussion back to the other war, the War on Poverty.

The Speaker calls attention to several signs that Congress is softening up: the rent supplement bill, more money for food stamps, a bill on decent housing. "As Election Day approaches," he says, "even the coldhearted Republicans warm up." We are in there almost an hour and could probably have stayed longer, but there seems no purpose. As we go out into the hall, saying good-bye, reporters ask the Speaker if he supports the Poor People's Campaign, but the most he will say is that "they are exercising their constitutional right" and "at least it stirs up public opinion."

A few days later he will be pledging full support to the police who are breaking up Resurrection City and arresting its inhabitants. He also has given us an excellent demonstration of how and why Johnson and later Nixon are able to persuade Congress to neglect the War on Poverty while they pour billions into the war in Vietnam.

1:00 P.M.: We join the crowd just south of the Washington Monument, waiting for the march to start toward the Lincoln Memorial. The Reverend Jesse Jackson, a militant-looking young man in the preferred blue denim, is having trouble getting the march started but seems to be enjoying it. He urges the crowd to chant "Soul Power!" whenever he pumps the air with his right fist. Fists go up, the chant rings out, and suddenly it is a little clearer why Bayard Rustin resigned as national coordinator of the march. The ambivalence of this performance against the background of confusion and disorganization would stagger less-particular men than Rustin. Consider how moderation and militancy are blended here. We don't chant "Black

Power!" because that would be too militant, but *soul* means "black," so it comes to the same thing; *soul* also means "spiritual," but then, lest anybody think we are getting too pious, we hold up the clenched fist, just like in Russia. Something for everybody. Ambivalent, but also ingenious. Jackson will go far.

2:05 P.M.: Bending to the iron law of live television, the speaking program starts almost on time. Somewhere between fifty thousand and one hundred thousand people stand in the hot sunshine, lie or sit beneath the trees, and even wade in the pool. Numerically the march is a success, and everybody feels better. There are *thirty* speakers, and the program goes on for more than five hours.

3:00 P.M.: Senator Eugene McCarthy, who has discouraged Lyndon Johnson from seeking reelection, is introduced and gets a sustained ovation that seems to belie the report that he is not popular with the lower classes. Or are just us middle-class types applauding? Vice President Humphrey is introduced and is greeted by a loud burst of booing. Neither is permitted to speak.

3:30 P.M.: Walter Reuther comes closer than anybody to galvanizing the crowd with one of his better performances. He makes me think of the young Reuther of the 1930s and 1940s when the CIO was attracting the same kind of young militants now flocking to the Black Revolution, the War on Poverty, and the anti-Vietnam movement.

5:00 P.M.: Coretta Scott King finally gets to speak and impresses everyone with the force of her delivery. She is clearly a strong personality and a potential leader in her own right. She points out that "poverty can produce the most deadly kinds of violence: starving a child is violence, discrimination against the workingman is violence, ignoring medical needs is violence."

No politicians are permitted to speak except the only black U.S. senator, Edward Brooke, a Republican from Massachusetts. He gives a speech that would sound radical back home but here seems only routine. Most of the oratory is angry and bitter. Even moderates like Roy Wilkins of the NAACP and Whitney Young of the Urban League give speeches that sound like Stokely Carmichael and Rap Brown. But we also get hymns, prayers, and invocations from religious leaders, including Cardinal Patrick O'Boyle, archbishop of Washington, D.C. The atmosphere is somewhere between a religious revival meeting and a Black Power rally.

5:40 P.M.: Ralph Abernathy, saving himself for last, has waited too long and lost the crowd, but of all the speakers he is still most nearly in the mold of his master, the dead King. For almost an hour the indictments roll out: "The rich and mighty of the land are gorged on luxury, the affluent indulge every appetite; the plantation owners feed on the government; the prosperous, the complacent, and the satisfied drink from the full cup of contentment."

By this time Wally and I have fled the scene in pursuit of an air-conditioned bar and a full cup of cold beer. As we walk back across the littered field, picking our way between the National Guardsmen and a crowd gathered around a barbecue pit, Abernathy is still going strong, afflicting the comfortable: "Most Americans inhabit the household of comfort and warmth, but poor Americans face rats and roaches, high rents and miserable apartments, slave wages and crowded shanties." Abernathy vows to stay on in Resurrection City or go to jail until Congress heeds the cry of the poor. A few days later he goes to jail.

6:30 P.M.: Back at the buses people sit on the grass listening to Abernathy on transistor radios. We sit with a group that includes an old friend, a moderate-militant black man from the Congress of Racial Equality. He says, "This won't do much good. We should have marched on the Capitol, violated the law, and confronted Congress directly, physically."

Later on the bus I ask a smart-looking young black woman what she thought of the march. "Pleasant enough," she says, "but there should have been more poor people. Too many of you middle-class types taking up the seats on the buses." Judging from her clothes and speech, she seems pretty middle-class herself, so I gather that what she really means is white types. I ask her if more poor people would have come if we had contributed our $20 fares. She says, "Yes, everybody enjoys a free ride." But later I learn that this is untrue. Boston could have sent more buses if more poor people had accepted the offer of free rides.

She is another one who is not happy with the religious, nonviolent quality of the march. "I didn't go to Washington," she says, "to join in a lot of praying and singing." She too feels that we should have confronted Congress directly, even if it meant charging the police lines.

I'm a peace-loving type myself, but as the days go by I have to admit that the march has not done much perceptible good. And a few months later Hubert Humphrey, the man who was booed, is narrowly defeated for the presidency by someone who (I think) is much worse, Richard Nixon.

POLITICS AT THE LOCAL LEVEL

I have described the school committee fiasco of 1965, but in 1967 a bright young man, Tom Atkins, came along with a Phi Beta Kappa key from Indiana University as well as master's and law degrees from Harvard and got himself elected to the city council, the first black person to be elected under the new city charter, which in 1950 had replaced election by districts. In 1969, however, it looked as though Tom would have only one term. With nine elected at large, Tom finished thirteenth in the primary. Mrs. Hicks, moving up from the school committee, finished first. In those wards where she did well the turnout was 30 to 40 percent. In those where Atkins did well it was only 15 to 20 percent. The problem was to persuade black voters that the democratic game was a game worth playing. Because the black vote would be little more than 10 percent, however, an even greater problem was to persuade white people to vote for a black candidate.

In preparation for the final vote we ran a house party for Tom and used the occasion to organize the Committee to Re-Elect Tom Atkins, with Arthur Gartland as chairman. We raised money for ads in the Boston papers and got 135 signatures on them, including three monsignori and twenty-five priests, most of them Irish Americans. Our headline was "Tom Atkins Makes Sense for All of Boston."

The work paid off. Tom finished second, after Hicks, in the November finals, probably the strongest comeback after a poor primary showing in the history of Boston politics. Unfortunately, the showing was so strong that in 1971 he was encouraged to run for mayor and dropped down to defeat at 12 percent, leaving the city council with no black members. In the finals of that race incumbent mayor Kevin White defeated Hicks by a margin of roughly three to two, proving either that the race issue had not totally conquered Boston or that the men, in particular the Italian men, distrusted a woman mayor even more than they distrusted White.

WHAT ABOUT OUR CHILDREN?

A good friend living on the Upper West Side of New York, not far from Harlem, read one version of this chapter and wrote a critique in which he expressed disbelief that Helen and I could have been so positive about life in a black ghetto, so apparently indifferent to the threat of physical, psychological, and educational damage to our children. He included the following: "How far does one implicate the lives of one's children in one's own quest for social justice, democracy, and equality? Also, how does one decide these things within the family—by patriarchy, consensus, matriarchy, by the person deciding who will bear the greatest burden of the decision, by the children having a say, etc.?"

I wrote to all of our children and asked for their reactions to this critique as to Roxbury and the Philippines. Only three seemed concerned enough to respond in writing. One other responded verbally that the move to Roxbury was "unforgivable," but that he still loved his parents who had made that unforgivable decision. Another complained bitterly in writing that we had not consulted with the children before making the move, forgetting that we not only had consulted with him and two siblings about the move, but at their request had deferred the move for two years so that they could graduate from Newton High School.

As to the move itself, however, his criticism was justified. Helen and I made the decision, she even before the electoral disaster of 1965, and her support was a great comfort, but we should have discussed it first with the children, listened to their views, and responded as best we could. We were operating still in the most ancient tradition of unquestioned and unquestioning parental authority.

Why did we feel so right, so righteous, about it? I have given some of the answers: the deplorable state of racism in Boston, my position as head of the antipoverty agency, the desperate need for some commitments by the white community to solidarity with the black community. Also, Roxbury did not seem so very threatening. A number of our white friends, notably ministers and their wives and children, the Coxes, the Harmons, the Hasties, the Blackmans, the Kelleys, were all living in Roxbury or the South End already. The white presence, as mentioned, was about 30 percent. In the event, however, we did not escape unscathed. Several of the younger children were hassled and physically molested. As I was coming home from Dudley Station foolishly by an untraveled shortcut, four men jumped me, knocked me to the ground, verbally abused me within an inch of my self-esteem, and relieved me of a cheap watch, a few dollars, and my previous confidence that there was no danger on the streets of Roxbury. It was not Harlem, but it was still a black ghetto, with more danger for parents and children than one would expect in a white suburb or a whiter section of the city.

Ultimately, it came down to an act of faith that we were doing something that God would approve and that God would protect us from serious harm. And for the most part, we were protected.

The most interesting letter came from Susan, who was three years old when we moved to the Philippines and nine when we moved to Roxbury:

> Even though I was very young in the Philippines, I still have very vivid memories, most of them positive and exciting: Peace Corps parties, wonderful travels around the islands, our loving maid Rosario, native dance lessons, the incredible trip back to Boston on the *SS Roosevelt* and driving across the country. Those were terrific adventures. . . .
>
> Roxbury was, uh, interesting. Everything that was happening in the late sixties—the Black Pride movement, the antiwar movement, the hippie movement—it was all there, and we were all swept up by those intense times. It was not an easy time for us as a family. . . . It was not an easy time for me. St. Patrick's was a nightmare of a school. Classes were huge—about forty kids for every teacher. Learning was all by rote. . . . [We learned] about the new experimental parent-run school, Highland Park, and after two years of St. Patrick's hell, I was able to transfer.
>
> It was a very noble experiment. . . . There were ugly problems and the biggest was discipline. . . . One of my classmates was raped in the back hall restroom. I was attacked on a couple of occasions by . . . a boy who had a crush on me but a weird way of showing his affection. During one incident he came up behind me and started choking me with a wire. . . . In spite of the ever-present fear of physical harm, things were not all bad. I had some of the most dedicated and caring teachers ever. Even though I was one of only five white kids, most of the time I felt like I wanted to be there, like I was really learning something, in both traditional and nontraditional ways. Our history teacher even took us to one of the big antiwar rallies on Boston Common. We felt like we were a part of things.

What can I say? You made some difficult choices and exposed us to a wide variety of stuff. . . . To be honest, my most miserable years were in Nahant [a lily-white, seaside suburb to which we moved in 1970]. Moving to such an insular, narrow-minded town was the worst, most unpleasant culture shock I have ever known. The verbal abuse and emotional isolation I faced for being an outsider were horrible. Looking back, I would much prefer to relive my year at Highland Park, choking incident and all, versus going through the hell that was my life in seventh grade at Nahant Junior High. . . . Those kids just didn't see the big picture. And, I guess, thanks to you and Mom, I do.

What can you conclude? Dangers and blessings are everywhere; they come in every conceivable package, and who can say which are the most dangerous or the most blessed? We all depend on God's protection. Incidentally, Nahant has become much more diverse since the 1970s. In those days some kids in Nahant had never been to Boston, which was only a half-hour ride away by car or bus.

Our oldest, Barbara, made some thoughtful comments:

I can't be of much help on the Roxbury experience since I was in college and only lived there during the summers. My recollection is that crime didn't seem to be as much of an issue as [our critic] assumes. I certainly was never mugged coming and going from Dudley Station or anywhere else, for that matter. . . .

The fact that moving to Roxbury was preceded by living in the Philippines was important for the adjustment process. In the Philippines we were constantly being stared at, pointed at, and commented on as being foreigners. I found this disconcerting but eventually came to grips with it. I adjusted. One of the ways I adjusted was to view myself as part of a larger historical process. This helped to spur my interest in history as a field.

Although I suffered from "reverse culture shock" on my return and was very critical of American materialism, foreign policy, etc., one thing I enjoyed very much was the feeling that I could walk down the street and blend in physically and linguistically. So even though Roxbury was a different milieu from Brighton or Newton, it was definitely America and therefore much more "home" than the Philippines had been. Perhaps if we had moved to Roxbury direct from Brighton we would have experienced the original "culture shock" we encountered when we went to the Philippines. . . . But Roxbury was nothing after our plunge into the Philippines, and I for one was able to appreciate the difference.

An important difference was the knowledge that this was my country and I was entitled to have a say in what went on. Participation in the civil rights movement was also important in this regard—part of my seeing myself as part of the larger whole. You may recall that I was involved in civil rights activities when we lived in Newton. I helped to found the Civil Rights Club at Newton High. I went to the big Selma, Alabama, march that Mom couldn't attend, and I picketed the Boston School Committee regularly in the company of local blacks to protest its racist activities. So moving to Roxbury wasn't my first exposure to African Americans. I was able to see it in a much larger context and to feel that I was part of the struggle as well. I guess I would say that the Philippine experience broke me out of my white middle-class cocoon and made the Roxbury experience just one of a series of life stages that empowered me to participate in world affairs.

THE PANTHERS, FATHER BERRIGAN, AND ROBERT COLES

Father Dan Berrigan, poet, prophet, and anti-Vietnam martyr, appeared in 1968 at a meeting in a Catholic church in the South End to raise money for the Black Panthers defense fund. The Boston headquarters of the Panthers was only a hundred yards down the street from our house. We could see them filling bags with sand to protect themselves against a police raid that fortunately never came. A white friend once, in a friendly mood, had knocked on their door. There was no answer, but the next day two FBI agents knocked on her door in Cambridge and asked her why. Thinking fast, she said that she was looking for a place to go to the bathroom.

On the one hand, I had to agree that the tactics the police used to harass and shoot down Panthers were beyond contempt. On the other, I could not agree with Panthers like Huey Newton that "the basic tool of liberation is the gun" or Virgil Morrell's belief that "The only way we can do this is to pick up the gun. We are gonna walk all across this motherfucking government and say, 'Stick 'em up, motherfuckers, this is a holdup. We come to get everything that belongs to us.'"

There was the minor difficulty of black people being outgunned, but in any case I agreed with Lewis Coser when, after conceding the need for guns in certain extreme situations, he wrote: "Recourse to guns always corrupts, absolute reliance on guns corrupts absolutely, and those who make a mystique out of guns are already corrupted in advance."

Father Berrigan disagreed with me about the Panthers. At the meeting he said that we should support them because they were fighting "a defensive war." I was at the meeting with Helen and Becky. A priest friend from Packard Manse saw us come in and asked me to help take up the collection. I agreed, but then, after watching the Panthers in their fascist-type uniforms making their fascist-type salutes and mouthing their fascist-type rhetoric, I said I didn't want to take up a collection for them.

Helen and Becky were disgusted with me, and it was true that the main purpose of the collection was to be sure that the Panthers got a fair trial. It was also true, however, that off to the side TV cameras were trained on the scene, and it might be newsworthy that the head of a controversial state agency was caught taking up a collection for the Black Panthers. Common sense or cowardice? I will never know, but I suspect cowardice.

After the meeting there was a gathering over at the Jesuits' Warwick House. I said hello to Father Berrigan and expressed some of my reservations about the Panthers. He cut me off with, "That's a typical white man's reaction." End of conversation.

Then there was Robert Coles, the wise and perceptive sociologist, who said, after busing had gone from being voluntary to being involuntary, "I think the busing is a scandal. Busing should not be imposed like this on working-class people exclusively. It should cross these lines, and people in the suburbs should share it. And if people in the suburbs won't share it, then there should be legislation to make that possible."

Unfortunately, passing such legislation was impossible because, as Coles also said, "all the laws are being written for the wealthy and the powerful." How then to secure for black children their constitutional right to a decent education? Judge Arthur Garrity concluded that it was possible only by involuntary busing, thus creating a volatile situation.

A VISIT TO SOUTH BOSTON

Several hundred white kids were standing on the front steps of South Boston High facing out as the two yellow buses drove up with the black kids from Roxbury. Cops were ringing the building like an armed camp. I saw Mel King, now a state representative, on one of the buses and yelled to him. The man always seemed to be where the action was.

Some of the white kids applauded as the buses drove up. I turned to a reporter, "What do you suppose the applause meant? Was it friendly or ironic?"

A young woman beside me said, "We can't do anything to please you people, can we?"

"What do you think should please me?

"The kids are going to school, aren't they? And maybe some of them are glad to see the black kids."

The school was being reopened—January 8, 1975—after a prolonged closing occasioned by the stabbing of a white boy by a black boy on December 11, 1974. Community leaders were urging parents in South Boston to keep their children home, to boycott the schools until the busing was stopped.

I said to the young woman, "I was just asking questions. I want to know what the kids really think, what they feel, what the community feels."

"Why don't you go down to the South Boston Information Center and find out?"

Earlier I had talked to three white boys on the street. What they felt was that the black kids should be kept out of the school "because in this country we have a patriotic right to have free schools."

After all the students had entered the school without incident, I walked to my car and passed three white girls of obvious high school age. I said, "Aren't you going to school today?" Two said, "No." The third said, "Yes," then a few words I couldn't catch, then "keep the niggers out." I tried to think of intervening words that might defuse that part, but no luck.

As I drove down Broadway toward the South Boston Information Center, I noticed signs in many of the store windows: "WE SUPPORT THE SOUTH BOSTON SCHOOL BOYCOTT." At the bottom was the name of the center.

When I got there, I said I was covering the busing story for *Commonweal,* a national Catholic magazine. A long, mostly friendly conversation followed with several members of the Home and School Association, which runs the place. One was a tall, handsome fellow in a green beret whom I recognized as the man who had figured in a fracas in front of the school. He asked if I was a member of the John Birch Society or perhaps a priest in plain clothes. I said I had ten children, and he said, "The way things are going, that doesn't prove a thing."

I asked about the boycott signs. A lady who seemed to be in charge said, "Well, we're not telling anybody what to do. We leave it to them to make up their own minds." I was rude and said, "Don't kid me. Of course you're telling people what to do." She didn't like that and later quizzed me sharply as to whether I was really a practicing Catholic.

Green Beret said, "The Catholic Church is falling apart. The real story for you is not here but in West Roxbury [a white middle-class area of Boston], where the archdiocese told the pastor of St. Thomas Aquinas that he must take 50 percent black kids, give them free tuition and free uniforms. He closed down the school rather than go along." Another man said he didn't think I had the guts to write that story. I said I would check it out.

The next day I called St. Thomas Aquinas Church, which was in Jamaica Plain. The pastor said his school had closed two years ago, but it had nothing to do with black students. They didn't have the nuns to run it. I called St. Theresa's in West Roxbury, just to be sure. The pastor said their school was still open, and the only instructions he had received from Cardinal Medeiros were that parochial schools should not be used as a refuge for parents trying to escape integration in the public schools.

Before I had left the Information Center, I also had asked if any priests in South Boston agreed or disagreed with the members' position. They mentioned one who was "fair-minded." I went to see him. He said that all the priests in South Boston were opposed to forced busing. He generally agreed with the people at the center. He was particularly disgusted by a case of four black boys raping a white girl in Roxbury. He said that the boys had bitten her breasts off, a detail I didn't remember reading, and characterized the act as "animal."

I mentioned the more recent incident of two black men pulled from their car in South Boston and beaten up for no reason other than their blackness. He said this was the act of "a few crazy people" and should not be laid at the door of an entire community. I tried to make the obvious parallel. No luck again. So many more bad actors apparently lived in Roxbury than in South Boston. When I spoke of the lack of job opportunities for blacks and how in Roxbury even the men on the city garbage trucks were white, he asked me, "Well, did the black people apply?"

As I left the rectory, I walked across the street and visited the basement of the imposing church. The Christmas crib was still in place before a side altar. I checked to see if the usual black Wise Man was present. His back was to the congregation, and I had to lean over the communion rail and peer sideways to authenticate the black skin. He had a more humble, subdued look than the others. On my way out I picked up a parish bulletin. Thought for the Week: "Live for today, dream of tomorrow, and learn from yesterday."

I remembered from my antipoverty days that some "fair-minded" people were also at the Community Action Center in South Boston. I went there and spoke to one of the top staff, a youngish graduate of Boston College. He said that ten years earlier he would have been for integrated education, but after raising three children in South Boston, he had changed his mind because he "wanted them to have a decent chance." He was disenchanted with the Catholic Church, which he thought was doing too little too late to help the urban poor, both white and black.

I asked him if he knew anybody in South Boston who really believed in integrated education. He mentioned a nun at Cardinal Hayes High School. Before I left, he complained that none of the media had mentioned that a black woman had been elected president of the Home and School Association at the D Street housing project. I said I would mention it.

I went to see the nun. She was very nice and really seemed to believe in integrated education. She said that for five years she and eight other Notre Dame nuns had been living in the D Street project, a very poor housing project in more ways than one, so as to identify with the community. I asked her about the black president of the Home and School Association.

"Mrs. Bridgewater," she said, "who was an excellent president, was forced out of the project a few months ago. Some of her neighbors feel very badly about it. She had to move to Roslindale. One of her daughters started the year at South Boston High, but because she lived so close, she could not qualify for a bus ride and had to walk to school. She was pelted so much by white kids going to and from school that she had to quit. I'm surprised that they don't know that up at the Community Action Center."

I asked her if she would tell our mutual friend at the center because if she didn't, I most certainly would. She promised to tell him. She also said that two priests had been outspoken and gone out on the street to keep peace and try to make integration work, but both had recently left South Boston.

I asked her about the high school. She said it was a school of six hundred girls who came from all over the city. When she first came in 1963, there had been only two black girls and very few girls from South Boston. Now there were one hundred black girls and two hundred from South Boston. When black girls first became a sizeable percentage of the school population, there had been some "serious problems," but now things were going smoothly, and the black girls were accepted and recognized as making a very positive contribution to the school. This story made me feel better.

She was very sympathetic to the people of South Boston, who she felt were largely misled and exploited by their elected officials and shortchanged on city services. She mentioned the chronic failure to get a separate road for truck traffic, which regularly caused the deaths of little children.

At one point she said that she thought that all white people were racist, either consciously or unconsciously, because we all considered ourselves superior to black people. As I got up to leave, she expressed the fear, as the others had, that my report would be biased against the people of South Boston.

To cover my retreat I said, "Sister, I'm like you. I'm prejudiced against all white people, including myself."

I could have mentioned that as a young man I had rooted for Max Schmeling, the German heavyweight, to defeat Joe Louis. You can't get more racist than that.

16

Making War on Poverty II

> To manage those minor affairs in which good sense is all
> that is wanted, the people are held to be unequal to the
> task; but when the government of the country is at stake,
> the people are invested with immense powers; they are
> alternately made the playthings of the ruler and his master,
> more than kings and less than men.
>
> —Alexis de Toqueville

ONCE AGAIN, in 1970, I was in charge of organizing and directing a federal antipoverty program, this time the Model Cities Program in the city of Lynn, a somewhat depressed remnant of the shoe industry, mainly dependent on a steadily diminishing General Electric plant making marine turbines and airplane engines.

Model Cities differed from Community Action, Shriver's OEO, in limiting itself to one particular section of a city, the Model Neighborhood. The idea was to go for greater impact than was possible in a program that spread limited funds over a much larger area. For me it also had the advantage of getting closer to the front lines of the war because it was necessary to win approval of our projects from the Model Neighborhood Citizens Council (MNCC) elected by residents of the neighborhood.

As may be evident by now, I was fascinated, and still am, by the notion that democratic process should be extended from the strictly political realm to the realms of work, industry, and the delivery of social services.

We also had the problem of winning approval from three different mayors during the three years I held the job and the further problem of winning approval from one of the more erratic city councils in the country. One of its more erratic members was a woman who was opposed to every single program we proposed, even though the federal government funded them all. She judged every program on the basis of the city's experience with the federal Department of Housing and Urban Development (HUD), which had torn down scores of residential buildings and then left vacant lots for several years in their place. A legitimate beef.

This neglect had given rise to demonstrations by a militant organization called Citizens for a Better Lynn, whose signs read, "HUD Spelled Backwards Is DUH." They were convinced that a bulldozer was hidden behind every federal program. I called the woman to ask if I could visit and explain how our programs differed from urban development. She said, "Don't bother to come and see me, Mr. Cort. I will never again vote for a federal program in the city of Lynn."

Fortunately, most of her fellow councilors disagreed with her. The mayor, Warren Cassidy, was a somewhat humorous type who told me, "As long as the federal government is paying for it, I don't care if you paint the streets purple over there." A colonel in the Marine Reserve, he once confessed to me that his ambition was to "organize the city like a Marine battalion, complete with short haircuts."

We did not paint the streets of the Model Neighborhood purple. We funded sixteen different projects, including Meals on Wheels for shut-ins, a senior citizens' center, the first free mental health facility in the Greater Lynn area, three child daycare centers, an adult education center, a housing rehab project, a sewage disposal study, an employment office, a minority cultural center serving mainly blacks and Hispanics. One project planted 270 trees along the streets of the Model Neighborhood and remodeled parks and playgrounds. (Warning: If you remodel a playground, don't put the swings or seesaws next to the wall of somebody's home.) We funded a teen center, but a cheerful arsonist burned down its new facility before the teens could even move in. One of Lynn's depressed conditions was that somebody always seemed to be working off his or her frustrations by setting fire to something.

We also funded a facility for teenage delinquents. Various public and private agencies ran our projects; the Lynn Council of Churches ran this particular program. These good people bought the revolutionary idea of a Yale psychologist who proposed that there be no hierarchical structure, no boss, no reformatory atmosphere, but a staff of nine, all of whom had equal salaries and equal authority and who operated by consensus. Consensus was elusive. Before the project could get going, five of the nine threatened to resign if one of the other four, a black resident of the Model Neighborhood, was not fired. The Lynn Council of Churches said, "Resign." Five more were hired; the project predictably sank into chaos; the teens predictably spun out of control; the neighbors predictably complained to the city council; the council predictably voted to terminate the project.

This experience served to fortify my prejudice against all notions of operating an organization by consensus without a clear executive authority—Yale psychologists notwithstanding.

ADVICE OR VETO

Ours was one of the few Model Cities projects in the country that gave the citizens' council the power of veto over the projects rather than simply an advisory role. I preferred it that way myself, even though it made the job more difficult—one, because I had an intellectual interest in the democratic process, and, two, because I believed it meant better programs and stronger support for them in the community.

True, the operation of the council and its deliberations were sometimes crude and lacking in sophistication. One group of observers came away from a council meeting with the complaint that the discussions "bordered on the ridiculous." I heard discussions that ran rampant all over the ridiculous, but you cannot judge a group or a process on the basis of one meeting. I must have attended several hundred meetings of that council and its committees. The thought occurs that over the course of my life I must have attended thousands of meetings, including those of the U.S. House and Senate; the Massachusetts House and Senate; religious, political, fraternal, and labor organizations of various kinds, with both middle and working class, as well as some of the sharpest wise guys employed by the U.S. press.

I would sum them all up in the ancient aphorism: "Never overestimate the knowledge of ordinary citizens and never underestimate their intelligence."

The MNCC meetings were basically no different from the meetings of any of the other groups I mentioned, including the U.S. Senate. Some of the idiocy was perhaps a little less refined, some more so. Knowledge was sometimes less in evidence, so intelligence was sometimes more difficult to discern. But it was there, bright and shining, appearing often when I least expected it. If democratic process is valid for anybody, it is also valid and workable for the poor.

Two Different Views

In the mid-1970s Model Cities was replaced by Community Development, another federal program that continued to fund some of our more successful projects, at least until the Reagan cuts. The program was no longer restricted to the Model Neighborhood, and the old citizens council was no more. In its place was the citywide Community Development Advisory Council, consisting of members appointed by the mayor and city councilors. It had no staff.

In an effort to get some feel for the new setup I paid a visit to friends who had served on both programs. I first went to see Abner Darby, a big black man who had been a service station operator in the Model Neighborhood and on one occasion had given me hell at a meeting as I tried to sell the mayor's insistence that the center for delinquent teens should have a director. He carried the council with him, and the mayor gave way, with the aforementioned unhappy denouement. Abner later became director of the community cultural center that we established with Model Cities funds.

Abner greeted me warmly. He told me that the cultural center, with a paid staff of six, was running a successful credit union and a full program of counseling, training, and classes in art, crafts, music, dancing, history, judo, and so on. He had come a long way from the Big Black Rebel of 1971. Responsibility had tempered rebellion. He clearly preferred the advisory council setup to the MNCC.

"It's dangerous," he told me, "to give power to untrained people who have never had it. They don't know how to use it. Take, for example, that residential center that I was yelling at you about. If we hadn't had a veto, that center might still be going today."

I said, "Do you think the MNCC voted against the idea of having a director just because the mayor was in favor of it?"

"Well, we were tired of people telling us what to do. We wanted a chance to make our own mistakes. There was a kind of automatic reaction. We were like a primitive country that isn't ready yet for democracy."

"You mean that you needed a colonial power like England or France to train you first?"

"No, not them, but maybe the United States. With all its faults there's a lot of good here. For people like us the advisory role is much better. When you're only advisory, you have to work harder to sell your program to the power structure. At the MNCC we could just sit on our veto and make the power structure come to us. On the advisory council we still got what we wanted. We wanted a program that was only this far off what the mayor and the city council approved." He held up two fingers to indicate a very small distance.

"Abner," I said, "it sounds like you've become part of the power structure yourself."

He laughed. "Maybe you're right."

"If the MNCC hadn't had meaningful power," I asked him, "would you have become so active in it? Would you have developed the qualities of leadership or the contacts that qualified you for this job at the cultural center?"

He didn't know, and neither did I. I might also have asked if without that power there would have been any cultural center for blacks and Hispanics for him to direct. But neither of us knew the answer to that question either.

The next day I talked to Jim Bollen, a white man who had been a member of the MNCC, had done a good job on my staff later, and was now a member of the Community Development Advisory Council.

Jim disagreed sharply with Abner. "You learn pretty quick that the advisory council has no real power and no real impact. If you raise questions, even members of the council remind you that we're only advisory, so what's the use of raising so many questions? At our first meeting they brought in the application for a whole year's funding, a whole package of projects, and expected us to approve it right away. They look on us as just a rubber stamp."

That struck a chord. I remembered how often when there was a deadline to meet, we bureaucrats demanded action right away.

I asked Jim how he would respond to Abner's points. "The best way," he said, "is to remind Abner of black people in the South after the Civil War. A lot of people said they weren't ready for democracy either."

Jim is an old union man. He said, "They used to tell us at Colonial

Meat that working people couldn't run their own union. But we did, and it was a good union. On the advisory council you find a better-educated class of people than we had on the old MNCC. There's not so much profanity or dirty language. But the principles are the same. Give me the group with real power every time."

So there you are: Abner Darby and Jim Bollen, two very different views. Take your choice. I was grateful to Jim for the union reference. It matched my own judgment that really no difference exists between working people who are running a trade union, on the one hand, and neighborhood people who, if not actually running publicly funded projects, at least have a meaningful say in the running of those projects. I would agree with Jim that all power in these matters need not be left to political officeholders like mayors and city councilors. Being closer to the people affected, neighborhood councils tend to care more and know more about such programs than the politicians who not only are farther removed but are deluged with problems affecting the entire city.

The best way to learn how to handle power is to have real power to handle. You don't learn how to drive a car by giving advice to the driver, and as Abner Darby might remind us, you don't turn a man loose behind the wheel without training him first. There *is* a middle way.

FINALLY, WE LOST THE WAR

As for the War on Poverty in general, whether Johnson's war or what was left of it after Nixon, Ford, Reagan, and the Congress got through with it, the conclusion has to be that we lost it—at least more lost than won. We had small victories in minor skirmishes; we did good work in training antipoverty soldiers to fight more effectively in future wars; and the battles themselves afforded opportunities for poor people and black people to get the training and experience that helped them put their feet on the rungs of the ladder up. Many on my two staffs, black and white, poor and middle class, went on to influential careers in both private nonprofit and public service. I have mentioned Joanne Ross already. Two black men, Ivan Ashley and Harold Thompson, who were languishing in low-level jobs, got a chance on our staff at Commonwealth Service Corps to showcase their abilities and went on to top jobs in the regional offices of federal agencies. Others did go on to become city councilors, state and federal legislators, mayors, and governors. Who knows, maybe one of them will be president some day. The war has made a difference and will continue to make a difference.

At the lower rungs of the ladder we gave welfare mothers a chance to help run childcare centers or senior citizens centers or neighborhood centers, until they were expert enough to qualify for regular-paying jobs in such projects.

And some of our projects involved just plain trouble making—that is, making trouble that cried out for the making. We recruited eight Service Corps volunteers in the South End of Boston, then a poverty area that since has been largely gentrified, to help organize the South End Tenants Council. Tenants themselves, they ran meetings to discuss conditions in their buildings. The more serious grievances they referred to their own legal counsel, who brought landlords into court or in one case before the Rabbinical Court, which ruled that a Jewish landlord should pay $28,000 for rehabilitation of his slum property. Sometimes they organized rent strikes.

Many of our volunteers worked for MAW, the welfare mothers' group, or the National Welfare Rights Organization, which, by processing the mothers' grievances, made trouble for our sister state agency, the Welfare Department, or for various city departments, agitating for better welfare, better trash removal, better parks, better playgrounds, better schools.

This practice of making trouble raised interesting questions of policy. Should a state agency supply money to organize the poor to make trouble for other state agencies, for cities and public agencies within the state, for all sorts of establishment types: mayors, governors, legislatures, city councils? We were bringing the whole power structure under attack, using not only state but also federal money to "rub raw the sores of discontent," to use Saul Alinsky's phrase.

Some people denied that we had the right to do this. They claimed it was a sign of decadence and degeneration in our society—the society helping to destroy itself. I preferred to say that it was a sign that our society was still healthy enough to create agencies that could challenge it, test it, and preserve it from dry rot.

ALINSKY ON "POLITICAL PORNOGRAPHY"

Saul Alinsky once came to Boston and spoke at a big meeting at the Copley Hotel. He said: "The poverty program is turning into a prize piece of political pornography. It's a huge political pork barrel and a feeding trough for the welfare industry, surrounded by sanctimonious, hypocritical, phony, moralistic crap."

My reaction was that the statement itself was moralistic crap surrounding a kernel of truth, and I still believe that. Alinsky was an organizational genius who had been fighting his own war on poverty in Chicago for years with very little money. Suddenly the federal government comes along and starts paying people, including a certain number of lightweights and phonies, more money than they sometimes deserved to do what Alinsky had been doing for almost nothing. No wonder he was bitter.

But if what Alinsky was doing with scarce private funds was worth doing, then it was still worth doing when the feds began paying people to do it. There was no question that private funds and private people, even with Alinsky's genius, could not begin to do the job that needed to be done.

MOYNIHAN'S MISUNDERSTANDING

Former Senator Daniel Moynihan is a bright, good-hearted man who has more gut feeling for poor people than most senators. He was one of the few Democrats who fought with passion against President Clinton's dismantling of the federal welfare program. Coming out of the Harvard faculty in the early 1960s, he went to work for Kennedy and Johnson and helped plan the War on Poverty. He and Michael Harrington pushed unsuccessfully for the inclusion of a $1.25 billion provision to create jobs, a most commendable effort. That failure probably colored his mostly negative comments in his 1969 book *Maximum Feasible Misunderstanding*, a title that played on a requirement that the program should provide for "maximum feasible participation" by poor people in Community Action Programs.

I remember going over to Cambridge in the 1960s to hear Moynihan speak about the War on Poverty and tell us how it combined and confused four different functions: (1) organizing the power structure, (2) expanding the power structure, (3) confronting the power structure (à la Saul Alinsky and our own Service Corps), and (4) assisting the power structure.

Under the last heading he mentioned the Peace Corps and "putting tin roofs on the huts of the natives." I remember thinking at the time, "Gee, I wish I was clever enough to put down a program with a neat phrase like that."

Rereading his book recently, I came away with the impression that Moynihan was himself a tad confused and ambivalent about the whole antipoverty program. He ends the book with a reference to "the traumas of the 1960's. Not least of these shocks has been the debacle of the community action programs of the war on poverty: the soaring rhetoric, the minimum performance, the feigned constancy, the private betrayal." But earlier he praises Alinsky's strategy of confronting the power structure, a strategy that many of us copied, as a necessary prelude to developing a power structure of the poor that could wrest benefits, wrest justice in effect, from the power structure of the rich and the indifferent.

He also predicted the eventual demise of the Community Action Programs or their absorption by city government or both. To learn how accurate Moynihan's analysis and predictions were I recently visited Action for Boston Community Development (ABCD), where my old friend Bob Coard was in his thirty-fourth year as CEO. ABCD dates from 1962, two years before the OEO existed, but then became Boston's Community Action Program in 1964.

I learned that ABCD, operating from a ten-story building on Tremont Street in the heart of town, is still pursuing its original mandate "to promote self-help for people and neighborhoods," assisting more than eighty thousand low-income individuals and families, with a citywide network of Area Planning Action Councils, twenty-six Head Start centers, health services, job and job-training programs, youth programs, housing services, services for the elderly, fuel assistance, and a two-year college right there on the eighth floor. Their 1999 budget was $76 million plus, mostly in federal funds.

I also learned that far from disappearing or being absorbed by city government, 995 Community Action Programs still exist in all fifty states, Puerto Rico, and the territories. Of these programs only 12 percent have been absorbed by city or other governments.

I saw no "debacle ... minimum performance ... feigned constancy
... private betrayal." I didn't even hear any "soaring rhetoric," only
facts and figures about work in the poor neighborhoods of Boston.
So it seems that there was "maximum feasible misunderstanding,"
Mr. Moynihan—namely, yours.

THE IMPORTANCE OF PAPERWORK

One year in the 1960s the Service Corps organized an antipoverty
convention at Boston College. One of our panel speakers was an
OEO veteran named Miles Hollister, a wise and perceptive man. In
his remarks Hollister quoted a resident activist from a poverty area:
"I think the pros should take care of the paperwork and let us do the
rest."

The hall was full of poor folks who were active in various antipoverty programs around the state, either in a volunteer or a paid capacity. The reaction to Hollister's quote was loud and prolonged
applause, but he rebuked those who applauded. He said, "You may
think that is a great idea, but I tell you it is a lousy idea. Paperwork
is control, and unless you are willing to develop the competence to
handle the paperwork, you are never going to gain control of your
own programs."

That was a lesson whose truth I recognized but was never entirely
able to master. I did not have to gain control. I was given control, but
sooner or later the paperwork wore me down, bored the pants off
me, exposed my administrative weaknesses. I was okay at riding the
first waves of enthusiasm for a new program, but when those waves
subsided, I was not one for the long trip. Given an unfriendly mayor
and a firm push, I departed Model Cities in 1973.

So ended my career as a social activist, and so began my new career
as an amateur scholar, a man trying to figure out the meaning of his
own life and his own experience, and how that life and that experience, enriched by Christian faith and the reading of many books,
dictated certain conclusions about the life of the world. This new
career led to a second "dreadful conversion" to socialism; the coediting of a small periodical entitled *Religious Socialism;* the publication
of a history of Christian socialism; and the writing of a history of the
philosophy of justice and how it relates to the right to decent, paid
work, one of the most fundamental of all human rights.

17

How the Females Put an End to Male Oppression

The first half of this chapter is for the most part a reprint (with some minor editorial changes) of an article that appeared under the same title in the July 3, 1981, issue of Commonweal. *I reprint it here to offer (1) some relief from the heavier material that has preceded it, (2) some insight into the workings of our extraordinary family, who have not gotten the attention they deserve heretofore, and (3) a reminder of how families like ours thought in the year 1973, the year of the meeting I describe in the chapter. I also make a point of printing it just as it first appeared because I see things somewhat differently in the year 2003, and it provides a useful device to introduce and highlight the difference. For those who have not noticed what a conservative, even reactionary Catholic I really am, this chapter should be the clincher and make it even more puzzling and perhaps intriguing that such a conservative Catholic could ever become a socialist, as I describe later in chapter 18.*

> What I find oppressive is the fact that a faction of this family is doing the bulk of the domestic work, and a few individuals have removed themselves completely from this domestic work, which has to be done daily.
>
> —Mary Liz Cort

IT HAS SOMETIMES BEEN SAID that the patriarchal structure of the family has a crippling effect on the development of democratic structures at other levels of life. This is a big subject, and I am not going to exhaust it in this article, but it might be interesting to relate how one family tried an experiment in democratic process and what came of it. The year was 1973.

As I first looked back on The Meeting, my unaided recollection was that the females simply outvoted the males. After all, they outnumbered us two to one. But my recollection was wrong. Becky, Lydia, and Susan were absent, and Julia was too young to care. All the males were present, so actually the count was even, four against four.

Unknown to most of us, Mary Liz taped the meeting—at least the first forty-five minutes or so.

DAD: What do we want to put on the agenda? One, method of voting—

PAUL: No, no, no, no, no, no. We're not going to have any votes. This is a consensus gathering. In matters of importance we want to achieve consensus. If you have a voting system, people are not going to be willing to negotiate or compromise, figuring they can win by voting.

MARY LIZ: Paul's running scared already.

DAD: Let's try consensus first.

BARBARA: I object. What if it doesn't work? I prefer voting.

A consensus developed that consensus should be tried first, but a wrangle followed immediately on setting the agenda.

MARY LIZ: I'd like to suggest a system of recognizing the speaker. Three people are talking at once.

DAD: Yes, I think that's necessary. This is a very aggressive group.

BARBARA: Who's recognizing?

DAD: I'm recognizing. I'm the chairman.

PAUL: Who voted you the chairman?

DAD: Well, do we have a consensus that I'm the chairman?

CHORUS: NO!

ALICE (Radcliffe freshman home for the weekend): I think I'm the least involved, and I would like . . . uh . . .

BARBARA: Yes, I think it's a very good idea. I vote for Alice for chairman.

PAUL: I vote for Alice.

DAD: Do we have a consensus that Alice should be chairman?

We did. Alice assumed the chair. We further agreed that people need not raise their hands to be recognized, but that there would be "a free exchange unless it comes to a donnybrook," in which case

Alice would intervene. Alice had to intervene a few times. Part of the problem was that nobody thought to remove the parakeets, who tended to get very stimulated when there was lively conversation, and between the people and the parakeets interrupting each other, it was difficult to keep the discussion on an even keel.

The most interesting part of the tape revolved around the following issue:

BARBARA: I want to throw something out for consideration on a basic statement of goals and policies of the family. We should subscribe to the idea that *(a)* it is good to support the family financially as long as you're living here, *and (b)* it's good to help with household work as long as you're living here.

Four of the older kids—Barbara, Nick, Paul, and Mary Liz—were working but still living at home. Most of them were contributing money to the family exchequer, but virtually all of the household work (cooking meals, washing dishes, laundry, cleaning) was being done by the females, mostly by my wife Helen, who at that point was working at an outside job half-time.

NICK: I suggest that we substitute the words *and/or* for the word *and* between *(a)* and *(b)*.
BARBARA and MARY LIZ (simultaneously): No.
BARBARA: The word *and* is very important.
PAUL: Why is it important?
BARBARA: I find it extremely oppressive to live in any situation where I feel dominated by either money or work, where I'm either paying all the money or doing all the work, and somebody else is paying all the money.
PAUL: So who is paying all the money or doing all the work?
MARY LIZ: What I find oppressive is the fact that a faction of this family—
PAUL: *Oppressive* now. That's the word you used.
MARY LIZ: Shut up. Exactly, exactly. A faction of this family is doing the bulk of the work—
PAUL: As you see it.
MARY LIZ: As I see it. And a few individuals have removed themselves completely from this domestic work, which has to be done daily.

PAUL (unaware meeting is being taped):   I just want to be sure those words appear in the record.

MARY LIZ: They will. (Laughter from those in the know.)

PAUL: What you said is obviously untrue. I assume you're speaking of the boys. They clean their rooms, for one thing.

MARY LIZ: I'm talking about the daily upkeep of this house.

BARBARA: It's good to contribute both financially *and* in terms of work. It's a very healthy way to relate in a household. If people feel oppressed by having to pay a lot or do a lot of work, then that's very bad.

PAUL: But if some people want to pay instead of work, what's wrong with that? Where is the injustice? We're talking about injustice, not about ideal family life.

BARBARA: We're talking about ideal family life *as well as* injustice.

MARY LIZ (addressing Paul):   You're talking about a situation that doesn't apply here. You're not going to find people who are willing to share the entire workload of this house, and to discuss that is ridiculous.

PAUL: You haven't established that. The point is that you can attach a monetary value to the work that is done—

MARY LIZ: It would be very hard to place a value or price on the work that is being done in this family.

ALICE: I think that's what you're arguing more about—the price.

There followed a rundown of each working person's take-home pay. It didn't actually get into each one's financial contribution to the family. Nevertheless:

MOTHER: Papa's financial contribution being so overwhelmingly large at this point sort of backs up his reluctance to take on—

BARBARA: Only if you have that horrible attitude that your whole life is experienced in terms of building up your earning power, and this completely relieves you of any responsibility in your personal relationships at home. I reject that.

MOTHER: I sort of reject it, too, but in Daddy's case, considering the extreme pressure in his job and the number of evening meetings, the long hours, plus the health problem—

MARY LIZ: I agree with Mother.

BARBARA: I disagree.

MOTHER: I don't think he should be forced to take on a daily job like cooking or dishes.

BARBARA: I didn't say that. All I said was that I think Daddy should subscribe to the ideal, that for a pleasant home relationship it is important to have people *committed* to helping at home however they can.

PAUL: But he does help in many ways.

NICK: He's helping all he can. Right now. [Note how the males stick together.]

DAD: I'm willing to agree that maybe I could do a little more about dishes and things like that. [He thought he was going to get off that easy, the poor schnook.]

MARY LIZ (smelling victory):   Okay, we've agreed about that. Let's get down to some real distribution of jobs.

But Paul was able to put off the awful hour for a while yet. The meeting got sidetracked in a long discussion about the family budget and economizing (PAUL: This family is spending too much on food; NICK: I'm losing weight), about how much electricity TVs use up, about Mary Liz's suggestion that all food eaten between meals be contributed by people out of their own pockets (BARBARA: I don't like it—it makes everybody uptight and individualistic), and about whether David, a high school senior who was very quiet all afternoon, rated an allowance of $5 a week.

Eventually, long after the tape ran out and partly as the result of exhaustion, but mostly, I think, as the result of the triumph of reason over self-interest and of justice over the inertia of history, we agreed by consensus that there should be a more equitable distribution of household work. A few months later, when Helen went full-time and I left my work at Model Cities and started writing, it was further agreed that everybody, including the oldest and the youngest (excepting only Doc, the grandfather) would take turns cooking dinner, cleaning up after dinner, and doing the daily laundry; plus, there would be an equitable split of the remaining maintenance chores. The result was that I cooked my first family dinner in more than twenty-six years of married life and have been turning them out ever since, more or less edible. Ditto for washing dishes and doing laundry, also more or less passable. Some of the boys discovered that they were pretty good gourmet cooks.

The significance of The Meeting: it was the first time in our family that we had really faced up to the fact that the conditions of modern life have profoundly altered the relationship between men and women living in the same household.

I was one of five boys, and I don't remember ever seeing my father do a thing inside the house other than fix or paint something. There were no sisters, so the boys had to share the housework, and we hated and resented it as a symbol of our lack of manhood, largely, I think, as a result of Father's example.

I can remember few more depressing times of my entire life than the moments I spent, when I was about ten, slumped in a kitchen chair, crippled with self-pity, staring at a table and sink piled high with dirty dishes, bowls, platters, glasses, forks, knives, spoons, pots, pans, and garbage, the greasy remnants of some Thanksgiving or Christmas feast, while the sound of distant laughter floated in from the living room, where the rest of the family and guests had repaired for conversation, music, fun, and games.

Eight years ago, at age fifty-nine, I found myself at the sink again, and I thought to myself, "What the hell is happening? Here I am back to square one. I've lost nearly fifty years of hard-earned ground. It ain't right."

But it was right. And I knew it. I learned to accept it and live with it and managed not to get stuck with it on feast days.

A CHANGE IN MY THINKING

Now, at age eighty-nine, I no longer cook dinner and rarely wash dishes, though I sometimes dry. I am still encouraged to vacuum and dust our bedroom, make the bed, and do a slapdash job of cleaning the bathroom from time to time.

All of the children left home, and most acquired their own families, but two have returned. Weekends and summers the house is usually crowded with children, in-laws, and grandchildren. I mentioned a change in my thinking since 1973. It does not involve any quarrel with the results of The Meeting. There was indeed an unfair distribution of labor, and The Meeting corrected that. Nor does it involve any disagreement that a family meeting is a good idea now and then to clarify family rules, regulations, and administration. It involves the whole question of patriarchy, probably the most politically incorrect idea among the better-educated, most with-it citizens of this country.

The first sentence of the article includes the words "the patriarchal structure of the family." In 1973, strange as it may seem only thirty years later, it was still possible to assume that structure as a given. Not so many years before that, I could get away unchallenged with the statement that everybody had a vote in making family decisions, but I had twelve votes, even though it might be accompanied by a chorus of protesting groans.

At The Meeting, you may recall, when it came to the question of who was the chairman, I said, "I'm the chairman," and Paul said, "Who voted you the chairman?" I said, "Do we have a consensus that I'm the chairman?" and there was a chorus of "NO!"

Based on my current thinking, assuming I had the guts, I would not have asked for a consensus but would have answered Paul's question as follows: "God voted me the chairman—God, speaking through the Bible and the church, but speaking more universally through reason and human experience, a combination that we call common sense. So if you want to have a meeting without me, that's fine. I'll be glad to consider any recommendations you may agree on." And I would have upped and left the room. What would they have done then? I have no idea.

So what is this common sense I speak of, this combination of reason and human experience? Very simple. Just try to wipe your mind clear of all sophisticated preconceptions, make it a tabula rasa, as the philosophers call it, a clean slate, and follow the argument step by step:

1. Every family, but in particular every family with children, is a small community, what the ancient Greeks called a *polis,* and requires a polity or form of government.

2. Governments have three major functions: *(a)* the legislative function, determining the basic rules and regulations, *(b)* the executive function, running the community and making sure the rules are faithfully and fairly applied and obeyed, and *(c)* the judicial function, which would involve appeals as to the fairness of the rules, rewards, punishments, and the distribution of goodies.

3. From the beginning of recorded time, in every culture, it has been accepted that children owe their parents obedience, unless the parents are guilty of patently unjust or irrational behavior. Therefore,

the parents have the authority to govern. Children might well be encouraged to make recommendations, and parents should certainly listen to such advice, but the advice cannot be binding.

4. Wherever there are children, and even where there are none, disagreements will arise between father and mother, husband and wife. Sometimes these disagreements occur at times of crisis, when questions of justice and injustice are flying around the room at full volume and full throttle, when decisions must be made and made firmly and quickly. The situation then is like a ship at sea in a storm. If there are two captains with equal authority, the chances of shipwreck are greatly increased.

5. If father and mother, husband and wife have equal authority and veto power, deadlock will occur sooner or later, thereby increasing the volume and bitterness of the disagreement, sometimes leading to physical abuse and nearly always leading to some kind of damage to the children.

6. In the long history of government, legislative, judicial, and executive bodies have consisted mostly of an odd number in order to avoid such deadlocks. The main exception that comes to mind is the Roman consuls, elected every year, which worked for a time only because one of them was usually at the front fighting the barbarians, leaving the other in Rome to run the government.

7. If one person must head the family government, why not the woman? Why not matriarchy rather than patriarchy? Answer: the idea that men and women must be equal in all things is pure fantasy. They are certainly equal in the eyes of God. They certainly should be equal in the eyes of the law, in the eyes of employers, in the eyes of voters if running for office, whether for president or CEO. But wives cannot be equal to husbands or husbands to wives in all things. In many things wives are clearly superior. They are infinitely superior in the ability to bear children, to nurse children at the breast, to nurture, care for, and comfort children, especially in the early years of childhood. Researchers tell us that doctors, nurses, teachers—anyone who has to instruct or advise parents of small children—invariably directs their remarks to the mother, even when the father is present. Usually they don't even bother to make eye contact with the father. These professionals know that it is the mother, not the father, who can be counted on to follow through with the necessary action.

Women are programmed physically, emotionally, and psychologically for this function or functions and have been for hundreds of thousands of years. Not that men cannot share some of these functions. They can and should. By all means.

For this superiority, however, women pay a price. They pay a price in objectivity, in impartiality. They identify so strongly with the children that the *usual* thing (always here we are speaking of the generality, not every woman) is for the mother to side with the children, particularly when there is a disagreement with the father over what behavior should be allowed or punished and, if punished, what that punishment should be.

Men, on the other hand, have been programmed for hundreds of thousands of years to leave the nursing, nurturing mother in the home and go out to hunt, to work, to bring home enough bacon to support wife and children. This programming has provided the man, *usually*, with a more impartial, objective view of domestic matters. Therefore, the father, the husband, should be the necessary head of the family government.

The conditions of modern life have changed since this kind of reasoning was generally accepted. Many more women are working outside the home, contribute to support of the family, and therefore feel reluctant to submit to their husbands' authority. There are other reasons why the divorce rate in the United States has increased since the 1960s from one in ten marriages to one in two, but, I submit, the feminist notion of perfect equality between husband and wife is one of the major reasons.

THE BIBLE AND THE CHURCH

When Helen and I were married in 1946, the epistle read at the mass was from St. Paul's Epistle to the Ephesians (5:22–23). We were not asked to choose an epistle because the Catholic Church assigned this same epistle for all nuptial masses. It included these sentences: "Brethren: Let wives be subject to their husbands as to the Lord. . . . Husbands, love your wives, just as Christ also loved the Church. . . . Even thus ought husbands also to love their wives as their own bodies."

In 1970 a new edition of the Catholic marriage rite came out, containing eleven possible epistles, one being the epistle from Ephesians and another a similar passage from Paul's Epistle to the Colossians. (Paul includes the same admonition in his epistles to Titus and to the Corinthians. There is similar language in Peter's first epistle and in Genesis in the Old Testament.)

Until 1998 the church's lectionary, the book containing the readings for Sunday mass, included the Colossians passage for Holy Family Sunday, but in that year a new lectionary was published in which alternative versions of the passage appeared, one with the submissions language and one without. The pastor was free to choose either alternative. Ours chose the "without" language, as I imagine many other pastors did as well, for who wants to stir up trouble if it can be avoided? Pastoral authority in the parish, male authority in the church—that's a different question. But male authority in the home? That's expendable.

What is extraordinary and most significant about the "without" version of the Colossians passage is the other language that is omitted in addition to "Wives, be subordinate to your husbands, as is proper in the Lord," which is: "Husbands, love your wives, and avoid any bitterness toward them. Children, obey your parents in everything, for this is pleasing to the Lord. Fathers, do not provoke your children, so they may not become discouraged."

Few Christians would object to this language, which remains acceptable even to the most liberal, but it would have been too obvious to omit just one sentence, so some excellent and essential admonitions go down the drain in order to placate the opposition to patriarchy.

The lectionary for daily masses still contains the Ephesians passage for Tuesday of the Thirtieth Week of the Year. And so it was that, doing lector duty on that day, I found myself reading in our parish church, much to Helen's dismay, these words, "Defer to one another out of reverence for Christ. Wives should be submissive to their husbands," and so on. Note that this selection is unusual in that it includes a sentence about mutual submission, presumably as the ideal situation when possible.

The obvious conflict between the lectionary for daily masses and the lectionary for Sunday masses got me thinking. What seems to have happened is that the feminist revolution has now succeeded in persuading the bishops to back away from the traditional teaching, thereby abandoning us poor husbands and fathers to our individual fates. Whether or not my argument has merit, it does seem that before the Vatican and the bishops abandon us entirely, we ought to have an opportunity to state our case because we have had—let's be frank—even more experience with the problems raised than have the Vatican and the bishops. And, after all, this problem involves more people—men, women, and children—than abortion and birth control combined.

Spurred on by these troubling thoughts, I went to a meeting of our Holy Name Society, a men's organization, and proposed that we discuss the question before a general meeting of the congregation. Reactions ranged from sarcastic indifference to strong support for the feminist position. I think there was silent agreement for the patriarchal position, but no one expressed it. I said I would speak for the affirmative on the question, "Should the traditional teaching be retained?" and suggested that we invite the Women's Sodality to provide a speaker or speakers for the negative.

I approached the chair of the Women's Sodality with an invitation. Its executive committee met, but, with what sounded like righteous indignation, the chair told me that the Sodality declined the invitation. However, the Holy Name chairman agreed to argue the negative, and the pastor reluctantly agreed to the meeting but then changed his mind and vetoed the idea. When I asked him why, his only explanation was that I was "determined to stir up trouble in the parish." To non-Catholics it may seem strange that a Catholic pastor has the authority to veto a congregational meeting on a legitimate question of this sort, but the fact is that in the government of most Catholic parishes, patriarchy still rules.

Is This Issue Important?

Yes, this issue *is* important. We are in the midst of a revolution that ranks right up there with the more important revolutions in history, and the better-educated men, those best qualified to defend male authority in the home, are giving up with scarcely a word. They seem paralyzed, brain-dead, when confronted by the single word *equality*. The evidence also shows that the Catholic hierarchy and our pastors as well, who over the years have been champions of male authority in the home, are abandoning us husbands and fathers while clinging tenaciously to their own male authority in the church.

Helen disagrees with my analysis of this question, and I invited her to contribute her own analysis to this chapter. She declined the invitation except to provide a flattering quote from *Hamlet:* "O, what a noble mind is here o'erthrown." Our difference of opinion, however, did have consequences, which, fortunately, our love and our marriage were able to survive.

In 1985 Doc Haye, Helen's father, age ninety-four, died. All the children had left home by then, and Helen was still working as deputy director of the hearings division of the state welfare department so that, before he died, I was needed at home to be available when he required help.

Freed from that obligation when he died, I decided that we should return to Roxbury. Helen disagreed. Her conscience told her that we should remain in our seaside home in Nahant to make a weekend and summer retreat for the children and grandchildren. My conscience told me to renew the commitment to identify with the black community, so I took some surplus furniture and moved into a small apartment on the third floor of a three-family house on Thornton Street in Roxbury. For the next six years I lived and worked there, mostly on my history of Christian socialism, coediting and publishing *Religious Socialism,* and doing some volunteer work in a soup kitchen and a shelter for homeless families. I returned home only on weekends. This state of affairs continued until 1991, when Helen's old roommate, Rachel Meltzer, whom she had invited to move in after I left, was dying of cancer. I went back to Nahant to take care of Rachel while Helen continued working, and when Rachel died, I did not return to Roxbury. By that time I was seventy-eight years old and running out of perverse energy. About once a month now I go in to Roxbury and attend mass with old friends at St. Francis de Sales/ Saint Philip's, which is a mainly black Catholic parish.

18

The Second Conversion

> Far from working against it, let us learn to embrace social-
> ism with joy as a way of life better adapted to our time and
> more in accordance with the spirit of the Gospel.
>
> —Dom Helder Camara, archbishop of Recife, Brazil, in
> "a pastoral letter from the Third World" also signed
> in 1967 by fourteen other Catholic bishops and two
> apostolic vicars from Brazil, Colombia, Algeria, China,
> Egypt, Indonesia, Laos, Lebanon, Oceania, and
> Yugoslavia

I THREADED MY WAY down the corridor, through the beards and the tables piled high with radical literature, registered with the young lady at the door, and found a seat in the lecture hall. Having grown a beard myself, I was ready either to tango or to tangle. A young man in the next row gazed out the window at the sun shining on the snow and remarked cheerfully to his companion, "What a great day to smash the state!"

So began the first international conference of People for Self-Management (PSM) at MIT in January 1974, bringing together approximately three hundred supporters and some critics of the idea that democracy should be extended to the workplace, the same idea that Albert Gallatin, Jefferson's secretary of the Treasury, had advocated in 1797. Also present were a few loony leftists whose four-letter rhetoric and wide-ranging abuse were directed without prejudice at anything that moved. And so, having left Model Cities and found myself with time to think, I entered on the path to a second conversion, the conversion to a state of mind in which I became proud to call myself a socialist.

Of course, if I were really smart, I would never have started this chapter by mentioning that the young man sitting in the next row exclaimed, "What a great day to smash the state!"—amusing as it may have seemed to me at the time. That remark would simply confirm many Americans' reaction to the word *socialist* as hopelessly wedded to a kind of crazy radicalism. Instead, I should have noted that democratically elected Socialist Parties run most of the countries in western Europe, countries that we look to as custodians of the best in Western civilization. Are they so wrong about socialism, or are we? I should have mentioned that Tony Blair, approximately half of his cabinet, and more than fifty Labour members of Parliament are also members of the Christian Socialist Movement, which traces its ancestry back to 1848, the year two anti-Christians, Karl Marx and Friedrich Engels, published the *Communist Manifesto* and began to hijack the movement and switch it onto a track that would lead to the Great Train Wreck of 1989. And I should have asked, "Isn't it about time that we look at this movement with calm deliberation and try to sort out the good from the bad, the sane from the insane, the logical from the mythical, the true from the false?"

In any case there I was at this conference at MIT. Most of those present were sober academics from universities in the Boston area, but there was also an enthusiastic group from Cornell, led by Professor Jaroslav Vanek, who had founded PSM nine months earlier.

Vanek (a cheerful, middle-aged man in full suit and tie, with a smooth face, not even sideburns) explained: "We live in a period of serious crisis . . . the logical result of two hundred years of assimilation of the workingman to the machine and his use and manipulation for profit."

The meeting included an interesting speech by Walter Kendall, English socialist and director of the Institute for Workers Control at Oxford (full mutton chops, glasses, working-class accent and Oxford don's vocabulary): "Affluence is important but not the whole life of man. Economic gains can be eroded, but control in the workplace remains forever. . . . State ownership and control don't equal socialism."

The most impressive speaker was Irving Bluestone, vice president of the UAW, director of its General Motors Division, and the man most responsible for the UAW's leadership in the whole area of joint production and quality-of-working-life committees described in an earlier chapter. He said:

> We've got to make jobs more complex, more interesting, so that they are soul satisfying and self-satisfying to the workers, so that the workers

feel they are a piece of the action. . . . They are not interested, usually, in sharing management of the entire company, even though decisions made at the company level, such as the failure to develop a small car sooner, clearly affect what happens to them where they work. . . .

Managing the job where they work is something that our members care about. After we have done something about that, then we must move on to having something to say about managing the enterprise, about the big decisions on prices, sales, the nature of the product, financing, plant distribution, and contracting.

CRAZY CRIES OF *"FASCISM!"*

At that point some of the crazies began to hurl barnyard abuse, and cries of *"Fascism!"* troubled the air. One of them said we were engaged in "an idiotic child's discussion." But to me it was neither idiotic nor childish. To me there began to dawn the possibility of a new concept of socialism, which turned out to be a very old concept, and of a way in which this new/old concept might realize the promise Eric Gill expressed in my CW youth: "People work best when they own and control their own tools and materials."

I joined PSM and began attending the monthly gatherings of the Boston chapter, which usually consisted of a dozen academics meeting in somebody's living room. Some of them were Marxists, but they were mostly young, bright, and open to new ideas and new approaches. They stimulated my mind and my imagination. About the same time the country was sinking into a swamp of unemployment, inflation, and aggravated poverty that persuaded me that capitalism had failed again to produce a society that was either just or compatible with the teachings of Christ.

I also went to a meeting of the Boston chapter of the Democratic Socialist Organizing Committee (DSOC), a body founded in 1973 by Michael Harrington and others out of the old Socialist Party of Norman Thomas. (In 1982 DSOC merged with the New American Movement and became the Democratic Socialists of America [DSA]. Up to now DSA, like DSOC, has operated within the Democratic Party on what Harrington called "the left wing of the possible.")

The meeting was at the Paulist Center and obviously beamed at Catholics. The speakers were Peter Steinfels of *Commonweal* and

David O'Brien, the Holy Cross historian. I remember raising some questions substantially along the same line as the question I raised when Norman Thomas had spoken at Harvard some forty years earlier to a large meeting in the New Lecture Hall. The blood pounding up the back of my undergraduate neck, I had risen to my feet and asked Thomas how he would reconcile the demands of freedom with the vast concentration of power represented by state ownership of the means of production. I don't recall the precise answers Thomas gave, but he did not persuade me to be a socialist at the time, nor did Steinfels and O'Brien at the DSOC meeting.

I did, however, begin reading the *Newsletter of the Democratic Left*, the DSOC periodical edited by Harrington, my fellow CW graduate who had left the church and become the most persuasive apostle of democratic socialism in the United States. I read his book *Socialism* and noted that he seemed to be more attracted to Marx than was Norman Thomas, who once wrote, "For me the outstanding fact about [Marxism], despite its proven power, is its inadequacy for our time under any interpretation." I could also see that Harrington's devotion to democracy was above question, as was his rejection of Stalinism, Maoism, Castroism, and all other forms of Marxist dictatorship. His intelligence was of a high order, and he had the gift of writing about the gloomy complexities of capitalist chicanery with clarity, force, and humor.

"ANY FOOL CAN NATIONALIZE"

Harrington agreed with Walter Kendall, the British Labourite, that socialism neither could nor should be equated with nationalization or state ownership. As Harrington put it, "Any fool can nationalize." He thereby distanced himself and DSOC from that monstrous error of Marx, who in the *Manifesto* called for "the concentration of all instruments of production in the hands of the state." Harrington's socialism was much more pragmatic and pluralist and was concerned with what actually happens in either private or publicly owned enterprises—namely the question, Are the relationships within labor, the divisions of labor, and the distribution of the fruits of that labor consistent with justice and equity?

So I went into Boston one day in September 1975 and signed up as a member of DSOC with Julie Bernstein, the late beloved director of the Jewish Labor Committee, who had maintained a socialist presence in Boston over the years and now gathered around him an expanding DSOC local.

I began to think that perhaps I had been a socialist all along, ever since I joined the CW in 1936, or, better, since I got involved with the ACTU and realized that government also has responsibility for the works of mercy and justice. I simultaneously began to realize that my socialism was related directly to and fed by my Catholicism and the teachings of the church. In fact, I wrote an article, "Why I Became a Socialist," for *Commonweal,* and the editors added a subhead quote, "I Have Always Been Inclined to Take the Papal Encyclicals Seriously."

I could at this point pursue that line: why somebody who takes the papal encyclicals seriously should logically be a socialist, even though some papal encyclicals have condemned socialism. Or I could widen the argument to include Jews and Protestants by demonstrating that anyone who takes the Bible seriously should be a socialist, which would be a similar argument.

ALASDAIR MACINTYRE IS WRONG

The line I prefer at this point, however, is that any ordinary, rational, decent human being should be a socialist simply by reason of his or her rationality and decency. So I pursue that line, and the first thing I must do is to question a subversive idea promoted by Alasdair MacIntyre, a prestigious moralist, in his book *After Virtue:* that our society cannot hope to achieve moral consensus. MacIntyre denies that human rights have any real existence: "There are no such rights, and belief in them is one with belief in witches and demons." Further: "No one could have known that there were . . . rights" before, roughly, 1400 C.E.

Check a dictionary, any dictionary. I have checked five, and in all five a *human right,* as distinguished from a *legal right,* is defined as "a moral claim" or similar words—words that are related to the virtue of justice. The classic definition of *justice* common to the ancient Greeks and Romans is that contained in the Justinian Code (534 C.E.): "Justice is the constant and perpetual will to render to everyone his [or her] due"—that is, everything to which he or she has a valid moral claim. Long before the year 1400 our forebears knew that they had valid moral claims that other forebears were obligated to satisfy. They knew that they had rights, even if they didn't use that word.

Let us go back to Adam and Eve, or to whoever our first ancestors were, and to that awful moment when they ate the Apple and came to knowledge of good and evil. If you wish, substitute a metaphor of your own to stand for the moment when some original male and female, products of a gradual evolution or a sudden creation, arrived at the point where they could reason, draw reasonable conclusions from experience, and, important, imagine how they would think and feel if he (Adam) were Eve and she (Eve) were Adam. Without that facility to imagine neither one could be said to be human.

THE ORIGINAL APPLE SAUCE

After they have eaten the Apple and learned to distinguish good from evil, but before they have been expelled from the Garden, Eve plucks another apple and makes a baked apple or perhaps a tasty dish of apple sauce. She gives this to Adam, and he likes it, but because he is in a rotten mood, he swears at her and gives her a slap. She is hurt, not just physically but deep down within her soul because she knows that she had a moral claim, a *right*, not to be treated cruelly in response to her kindness. Adam, when he gets over his rotten mood, realizes that he has been cruel and feels guilty because he can imagine how he would feel if the same treatment were given to him. In other words, human rights existed from the very first moment of human reason and imagination. Alastair MacIntyre is all wrong.

Now we must consider a slightly more difficult case. A rich man is eating dinner, and his table is piled high with food, far more than he could ever eat. A starving child enters and collapses beside his table. A little food will save her life. If the rich man has the most elementary decency, he will give the child a little food. Question: Does he do so out of charity or justice? Can it be said that he owes this food to the starving child because the child needs it and he does not? I think not only can it be said, but it must be said. The child has a moral claim, a *right*, to that food in justice, not simply in charity.

This is not fanciful speculation. Recorded history reveals that from the time of the ancient Egyptians up through the time of Zoroaster, the Buddhists and the Hindus, the Confucian Chinese, the Jews and Christians, the Muslims, the Greeks and Romans, on and up to modern times in the writings of such diverse thinkers as Hobbes, Locke, Voltaire, Kant, Max Weber, and Malcolm X, the Golden Rule and its negative form, sometimes called the Silver Rule—"Do not do to others what you don't want them to do to you"—have dictated a universal standard of behavior, a moral consensus. Differences abound, of course, in the application of the rules. Other factors—historical, political, personal, and emotional—obscure, distort, or even conceal the rules for a time, but the rules remain because they are engraved in the minds and hearts of normal human beings. They are the laws of human nature, the natural law. "Upon them," as Jesus said, "hang all the law and the prophets."

POOR CHILDREN AND RICH MEN

The hungry child lying by the rich man's table is a most appropriate image to describe our situation here in the wealthy United States of America. According to the U.S. Bureau of the Census in 1998, 18.9 percent of our children under the age of six were still living in poverty. For black and Hispanic children the figure was just under 40 percent, a percentage approximately four times that of white children. The averages for the countries of western Europe, excluding England, were around 5 percent, despite higher unemployment, because of their superior welfare provisions.

Meanwhile, the rich Americans were increasing their riches by record figures. *Business Week* reported the average annual income of our top CEOs as $10.6 million in 1998, up 442 percent over their annual income of $2 million in 1992. In 1979 CEO income in such companies averaged 29 times that of the average employees. By 1999 it had ballooned to 475 times that of the employees. In Japan the ratio was 11 to 1, in the United Kingdom 24 to 1.

You can bet that the worldwide economic slowdown beginning in 2000 has had a negative impact on the 1998 poverty and unemployment rates—greater numbers of poor people and the poor much poorer. But I doubt that it has affected the obscenely rich.

Some employees have won modest increases, but many have not, and many others have been downsized onto the street. According to William Julius Wilson, the Harvard sociologist, more than half the adult population is unemployed in the black poverty ghettoes, defined as inner-city communities where more than 40 percent are living in poverty. Why are they unemployed? Because the jobs—and especially the blue-collar jobs—have emigrated to the suburbs, the South, and all the low-wage sweatshops of the undeveloped world. Drug dealing and homicide have become major occupations, and most of those who still can do so have fled the scene.

As for general U.S. poverty, the most recent figures compiled by the United Nations also show the United States as the worst of seventeen industrial nations, at a 19.1 percent poverty rate as against a 6.7 percent rate for the Scandinavians. U.S. poverty figures have improved somewhat lately, but there is no evidence that we have climbed out of last place. Some 35 million Americans are still stuck there.

What does all this prove? That the capitalist system we have here in the United States and the very rich people who control it are trampling on basic human rights. It proves further that some more decent, human, equitable system should replace that system.

THE CONVERGENCE OF SOCIALISM AND CATHOLICISM

I return now to my claim that any Catholic who takes the papal encyclicals seriously should logically be a socialist. Let me support this outrageous statement by a brief history of the Socialist International and the teachings of the Catholic Church in the twentieth century and by an analysis of the lack of a significant difference in the policies of those two bodies as regards political and economic affairs by the end of that century. And let me describe how Michael Harrington, the CW graduate who described himself as "a Catholic atheist," contributed to that extraordinary convergence in my thinking.

The Socialist International traces its ancestry back to the International Workingmen's Association, which originated at a mass meeting in London in 1864. Almost immediately Marx became its dominant figure, although he was not without rivals for leadership, in particular the Frenchmen Pierre-Joseph Proudhon and Auguste Blanqui and the Russian anarchist Mikhail Bakunin. That same year an even more dangerous German rival, Ferdinand Lassalle, had eliminated himself by getting killed in a duel over a foolish young woman.

If Lassalle had not died in that duel, the whole history of socialism might have been radically different, for his socialism was a socialism of worker cooperatives, not state ownership, of tolerance for both religion and private property, of a preference for peaceful rather than violent change. He was much admired by Bishop Wilhelm von Ketteler of Mainz, the first prominent Catholic socialist, whom Pope Leo XIII once called "my great predecessor."

Marx's success in establishing his leadership followed not only from his powerful intellect but from the force of his personality. That force is revealed in a Russian participant's vivid description of a socialist earlier meeting, which can be found in Edmund Wilson's *To the Finland Station:* "Marx was a type of man all compact of energy, force of character and unshakable conviction. . . . He never spoke at all except in judgments that brooked no denial. . . . This tone expressed the firm conviction of his mission to impress himself on men's minds, to dominate their wills and to compel them to follow in his train."

Bakunin, however, was not one to be dominated or compelled. Rather than let the International be taken over by the anarchists, Marx arranged in 1872 to move the headquarters to New York City, where it quietly expired in 1876. It never had more than thirty thousand members.

The Second Socialist International dates from an 1889 meeting in Paris. Although Marx had died six years earlier, his disciples had wrested control of the German Social Democratic Party from followers of the dead Lassalle. This party was by far the largest in the International and had had enough success in electoral politics to commit the International to parliamentary democracy despite its Marxist bias.

The Second International, which expelled the anarchists in 1896, came to have affiliates in Europe, the United States, Canada, and Japan, and a membership of 9 million. In its leadership Rosa Luxemburg and Vladimir Lenin represented the opposing tendencies. Luxemburg insisted, "there can be no socialism without democracy," whereas Lenin, more faithful to the authentic teachings of Marx, a man whom he much resembled in charismatic style, seized his chance in World War I, led the Russian Revolution, crushed all opposition and imposed a one-party dictatorship.

The Second International died in World War I, with socialists filling the trenches on both sides of No Man's Land. Lenin founded the Comintern, or Third Socialist International, in 1919 as a vehicle for world revolution, but Stalin dissolved it in 1943, convinced that it was more important to conciliate his democratic allies in the war against Hitler.

THE SOCIALISTS DENOUNCE COMMUNISM

An effort to revive the Second International as a home for democratic socialists failed in 1920, but another effort in 1951 in Frankfurt, Germany, was more successful. And here is where this little history lesson begins to have relevance for Catholics, Christians, and religious folk of every conceivable faith and for democrats of every faith or none. The statutes of the new Socialist International, known as the Frankfurt Declaration, include a strong, extended denunciation of communism as irreconcilable with socialism: "Communism falsely claims a share in the Socialist tradition. . . . Wherever it has achieved power it has destroyed freedom or the chance of gaining freedom."

Although the declaration includes several dubious references to Marxism, it for the first time welcomes to the socialist movement non-Marxists who are "inspired by religious or humanitarian principles." Its most basic and clarifying statement, however, is: "While the guiding principle of capitalism is private profit, the guiding principle of Socialism is the satisfaction of human needs." It does not condemn private profit. It simply states that "the satisfaction of human needs" must enjoy priority over the accumulation of private profit.

In that one sentence the Socialist International aligned itself with the social teaching of the Catholic Church and, from my observation, with the thinking of most Americans, whether members of the Democratic Party or, even, of the more progressive wing of the Republican Party. To the extent that we believe that idea, we are all closet socialists and, fundamentally, anticapitalist.

CONSIDER THE ROOTS

Consider the two words *capitalism* and *socialism*. The root of *capitalism* is capital—that is, the system of economy that places first the interests of those who control capital, as distinguished from those who own capital, namely, the larger chunks of money and productive property that dominate our economy. The root of *socialism* is the Latin word *socius,* which means, and I quote from my Latin dictionary, "*adj* joint, allied, confederate; held in common, common; *n* associate, companion, ally, partner."

The issue comes down to this question: Which system of economy corresponds more accurately with the better elements in human nature—capitalism, which places first the interests of capitalists and their private profit, or democratic socialism, which places first the satisfaction of *common* human needs—namely, food, clothing, shelter, health, education, respect, and the good jobs at decent wages that make possible all these good and necessary things?

Are we all just self-centered egotists demanding a chance to become billionaires? Or are we more fundamentally self-centered egotists who have this extraordinary gift to see beyond our self-centered egotism and recognize that we cannot be really happy unless we suppress that egotism from time to time and think about the satisfaction of other people's human needs?

Enough of that for now. I return to the intriguing subject of socialist Republicans further on.

In 1989 the Socialist International met again in Stockholm and revised the Frankfurt Declaration, replacing it with the Stockholm Declaration. One of its authors was Michael Harrington, who was dying of cancer at the time. Despite a modest DSA membership Harrington had not only won the affection and confidence of the leaders of the International, but was recognized as being the best writer in the organization. The International was then on its way to representing both parties and nonparty organizations like DSA in 134 countries, bringing together what must now be well more than 100 million members or voters or both.

The Stockholm Declaration makes no references at all to Marxism. Improving still further on the Frankfurt Declaration, it incorporates Harrington's view that both private and public ownership are possible options, but "neither private nor state ownership by themselves guarantee either economic efficiency or social justice."

Tony Blair duplicated this clean break with the Marxist past at the 1995 convention of the British Labour Party. He persuaded the convention to abandon clause 4 of the party constitution, which called for "the common ownership of the means of production, distribution and exchange." This action was largely responsible for Labour's landslide victory in 1997.

Sections 62, 63, 64, and 76 of the Stockholm Declaration affirm its faith in a market economy but insist that "the State must regulate the economy in the interests of the people and obtain for all workers the benefits of technology." The more doctrinaire Marxists in the Socialist International have attacked this concession to common sense as a surrender to Thatcherite/Reaganite economics, a ridiculous charge that only reveals their panic at the realization that Marxism is no longer a major influence in the International.

Another significant feature of the Stockholm Declaration is its failure to mention any aspect of sexual relations other than "dissemination of information and practical assistance for family planning." This gratifying reticence on the explosive subject of abortion indicates that important affiliates of the International still hold to a traditional view of the matter or at least prefer to avoid divisive controversy in the interests of maximum unity in the fight for *common* human needs.

THE DEVELOPMENT OF CATHOLIC SOCIAL TEACHING

Except for the work of outstanding bishops and cardinals like Ketteler in Germany, Manning in England, and Gibbons in the United States, the church's record during most of the nineteenth century would not qualify as anything remotely resembling socialism. Gregory XVI and Pius IX were reactionary popes who showed little interest in the poor and ignored all the Christian and Catholic elements in the socialist movement, simply lumping socialism and communism into one mindless anathema.

Leo XIII, pope from 1878 to 1903, was a different story. The encyclical he wrote in 1891, *Rerum Novarum* (English title: *On the Condition of Labor*), also condemned socialism because he began where the International wound up a century later—that is, with an affirmation of the right to own private property. The Socialist International had been revived two years earlier, in 1889, and the Marxists who dominated it not only were opposed to that right, but were repeating Marxist dogma about how religion was "witchery" and "an opiate" and ought to be abolished.

As noted, but worth repeating, Leo wrote things in *Rerum* that sounded as radical as anything in the *Communist Manifesto:* "The present age [has] handed over the workers, each alone and defenseless, to the inhumanity of employers and the unbridled greed of competitors. . . . In addition the whole process of production as well as trade in every kind of goods has been brought almost entirely under the power of a few, so that a very few rich, and exceedingly rich, men have laid a yoke almost of slavery itself on the unnumbered masses of nonowning workers."

I would not venture to say that this passage is a perfect description of U.S. labor relations in the year 2003, but aspects of our current downsizing scene—its burgeoning crop of ENRON-style billionaires and abject poor, as well as its virulent antiunionism—suggest some similarities.

In addition Leo set out with indisputable clarity the right and duty of government to protect and promote the workers' right to work for a living wage because "only a wage earned by his labor gives a poor man the means to acquire . . . those things [necessary] to sustain life."

Leo went further. He established this fundamental principle of government, which underlies both socialist and Catholic theory, in these words: "If, therefore, any injury has been done to or threatens either the common good or the interests of individual groups, which injury cannot in any other way be repaired or prevented, it is necessary for public authority to intervene."

Elsewhere in *Rerum Novarum* Leo notes that such injury would include the exploitation of child labor, oppressive conditions imposed on female workers and miners, Sunday work, and denial of the workers' right to organize in trade unions, for, quoting Proverbs, "A brother that is helped by his brother is like a strong city."

Such statements were not a bad beginning. In 1931, forty years later, as the Latin title reminds us, Pius XI wrote *Quadragesimo Anno,* the encyclical I was teaching in that CW storefront at 115 Mott Street in Little Italy in 1937. In it he too condemned socialism and went so far as to say that "Religious Socialism, Christian Socialism are expressions implying a contradiction in terms. No one can be at the same time a sincere Catholic and a true Socialist." However, only two pages earlier he also wrote that the socialist movement had split into two opposing camps: the violent, atheistic Communists and a more moderate, reasonable camp, "which has retained the name of

Socialism" and has been relinquishing its adherence to "class warfare and the abolition of private property." Then he says: "If these changes continue, it may well come about that gradually the tenets of mitigated Socialism will no longer be different from the program of those who seek to reform human society according to Christian principles."

<h2 style="text-align:center">PRECISELY WHAT HAPPENED</h2>

And that is precisely what happened, with both sides converging, for Pius XI immediately contributed a new addition to the teaching of Leo XIII: "For it is rightly contended that certain forms of property must be reserved to the state, since they carry with them an opportunity of domination too great to be left to private individuals without injury to the community at large."

In short, private ownership is the rule, and public ownership is the exception, but it is a perfectly legitimate exception in the case of "certain forms of property." Another firm step was taken toward socialism.

Actually, the man who wrote most of *Quadragesimo Anno* was not Pius XI, but a German Jesuit priest, Oswald von Nell-Breuning. And later, in 1970, in *Sacramentum Mundi*, an encyclopedia of Catholic theology, Father Nell-Breuning wrote: "It is certain that forms of socialism existed in 1931 which did not exhibit the features described in the encyclical [*Quadragesimo Anno*] and accordingly were not affected by the papal condemnation—the British Labour Party for one, which the Archbishop of Westminster hastened to reassure on this point, and probably Scandinavian socialism as well."

John XXIII, that wise and perceptive man, was in 1963 able to see the sound elements in the socialist movement, and he made this understanding clear in *Pacem in Terris*. Finally, Paul VI, writing in *Octogesima Adveniens* in 1971, went so far as to say that if "careful judgment" were exercised, Catholics might understandably "wish to play a part within" the socialist movement. The bars were down once and for all.

By 1975 I had read all these papal statements, together with the solidly progressive stands of the world's bishops at Vatican Council II. Having noted also DSOC's and the International's strong repudia-

310   DREADFUL CONVERSIONS

tions of communism, I saw no obstacle in the teachings of my church to membership in a socialist organization.

THE ROAD LIES OPEN

Since 1975 I have come to focus more and more on that one sentence from the Frankfurt Declaration of 1951: "While the guiding principle of capitalism is private profit, the guiding principle of Socialism is the satisfaction of human needs." I would insert only one word, *common,* before "human needs." This word provides a necessary qualification that helps distinguish "needs" from "wants." Many people convince themselves that they need drugs, mink coats, yachts, and a third home on the Riviera.

The road to a socialist society lies open very clearly before us. It is not required that the workers "own and control" all business enterprises, as Eric Gill and I dreamed back in the 1930s. Worker-owned cooperatives are the ideal, and we should continue to work toward that ideal, but it is not essential. First things first. What is essential and much easier to obtain is that the federal government guarantee decent jobs at decent pay for every last man, young and old, and every last woman, married or single, who needs one. As St. Paul said, "He [or she] who will not work, neither let him [or her] eat." For those who cannot work the government should provide adequate welfare, health, and child care programs.

WE HAVE THE MONEY—NO QUESTION

Not so long ago the federal government enjoyed a surplus so large that it was embarrassing. What did the Republicans and too many Democrats decide to do with it? Give it to the rich in tax cuts. And this, incidentally, is how you tell a closet socialist from a capitalist: their reactions to tax cuts. The closet socialist opposes the tax cut because he wants the money for the satisfaction of unmet human needs. The capitalist favors the tax cut because he wants the money for himself and his friends. "Tax and spend," the phrase that turns a politician's backbone to jelly, is actually a three-word summary of Christian political theory as long as the taxing is on those who can afford it and the spending is on those who need it. We will never have a just society until this simple truth is accepted more widely.

What would the unemployed do if put to work by the federal government or by the state, county, and city governments funded by the federal government? Make work? Never. All kinds of work are crying out to be done: construction, renovation, maintenance, and staffing of public schools, hospitals, libraries, health care centers, and child care centers; construction, renovation, and maintenance of roads, parks, recreation facilities; protection and improvement of the environment; construction, renovation, maintenance, and staffing of improved public transportation; construction, renovation, maintenance, and staffing of low-income housing.

WELFARE OR JOBS

Another way to satisfy common human needs is to restore and expand the welfare state, which has been the approach in western Europe, excluding Great Britain. Although Sweden, a consistently socialist and low-unemployment country, slipped to double-digit unemployment in the early 1990s, only 3 percent of its children lived in poverty as opposed to our 24.5 percent at that time. This was because Sweden was spending more than 14 percent of its gross domestic product (GDP) for disability, job training and development, unemployment insurance, health insurance, child care, family allowances, and other welfare benefits, whereas the fabulously wealthy United States of America was spending less than 4 percent of GDP for the same, making it the third poorest performer of all industrial nations in the employment and care of its citizens.

Sweden does not drive single mothers out into the street unless it can provide jobs for them. The eminent economist Lester Thurow, in his book *The Zero-Sum Society*, made a similar point when he wrote: "We consistently preach that work is the only 'ethical' way to receive income. We cast aspersions on the 'welfare society.' Therefore we have a moral responsibility to guarantee full employment. *Not to do so is like locking the church door and then saying that people are not virtuous if they do not go to church*" (emphasis added).

Then there is the Japanese approach. Japan has a poor welfare system, in part because Japanese families take care of their own. What they have is a great employment system, even without a federal guarantee, even under a conservative government, even in the midst of what blind Western pundits have called a serious recession. As the new millennium began, their unemployment rate was 4.6 percent, only half of one percent higher than our oh-so-proud 4.1 percent and without our yawning gaps of high unemployment for minorities. For the twenty-five years from 1973 to 1998 the Japanese averaged 2.3 percent unemployment to our 6.6 percent, with good wages, minimal inflation, much better job security, and much better distribution of wealth and income. The Japanese would call their economy a capitalist economy, but by our definitions it is clearly a socialist society.

One reason they have done so well, among too many to go into here, is that they are smart and, without knowing it, have taken a leaf out of Pius XI's *Quadragesimo Anno*. They have a system of industry councils, including representatives of government, management, and union as well as representatives of consumers, academia, and the media. These councils meet regularly to confer on how their industry can produce better products at a more competitive price and, for example, grab giant shares of various U.S. markets.

Back to the Shocker

Back aways I made the shocking statement that most Americans, including even the more progressive Republicans, were, in my opinion, already closet socialists inasmuch as they probably would agree with the statement in the Frankfurt Declaration that "the satisfaction of human needs" should have priority over the accumulation of private profit.

Before I get to the Republicans, however, let me deal with the Democrats. Although this national party has been losing support because of its fixation on abortion and its failure to fight for what it stands for, it does still stand for most of the better causes on the current political scene.

Outside of the Progressive Caucus in the House, Democratic Party leaders have, however, mostly forgotten that part of Roosevelt's State of the Union Message of 1944 in which he called for "A second Bill of Rights under which a new basis of security and prosperity can be established for all—regardless of station, race, or creed. Among these are the right to a useful and remunerative job in the industries or shops or farms or mines of the nation."

The horrors of the Great Depression, highlighted in chapter 1 of this book, were still fresh in people's minds in 1944. *Fortune* magazine conducted a poll that year and found that 67 percent of those polled supported the proposition that the federal government should assure jobs for everyone seeking employment.

That same year Governor Thomas E. Dewey of New York, the Republican candidate for president, said, *"If at anytime there are not sufficient jobs in private enterprise to go around, the government can and must create job opportunities because there must be jobs for all in this country of ours."*

Assuming Dewey meant it, that statement, on the face of it, would make him a closet socialist in the sense that socialism has been defined in this book and in the Frankfurt and Stockholm Declarations of the Socialist International.

But consider a more recent example. On the evening of November 7, 1991, I was watching the *MacNeil/Lehrer News Hour.* As Nicholas Brady, a Republican banker and secretary of the U.S. Treasury in Bush I's cabinet, was being interviewed, he said, "The worst thing in the world is a guy without a job." A few moments later he repeated that opinion, but this time he worded it, "The most unfair thing in the world is a guy without a job." He did not say how he felt about a woman without a job, but even so I suspect that beneath that Republican/banker/cabinet member's pinstriped vest there may well have beat the heart of a closet socialist. What Brady or Dewey would have been willing to do to provide jobs is, of course, another question— and an important one.

AN OLD TORY'S INDICTMENT

Samuel Johnson—a hopeless Tory, but a faithful Christian and one of the few world-class Christian intellectuals of the eighteenth century—once said, "a decent provision for the poor is the true test of civilization." By that test the United States is an uncivilized country, one of the most uncivilized of all the industrial nations, as the figures cited earlier clearly show. A few seconds of rational thought should

persuade anyone that the only really decent provisions for the poor
are decent jobs for those who can work and decent welfare for those
who can't.

Some will no doubt object that we unfortunately must give priority
to private profit for the rich and the not so rich because that is the
only way to satisfy the needs of the poor. To repeat Aristotle's phrase,
however, the facts are otherwise. We have been giving priority to
private profit for years and years, and the needs of the poor still have
not been satisfied, as all competent authority has proved and clearly
revealed.

Is There Any Hope?

Given the smug, monumental self-satisfaction that seems to smother
us, given the callous indifference to the sufferings of others that
seems sometimes to paralyze our better natures, is there any hope?

I think so. I see it in the awakening of the young from their long
sleep in the lotus lands of sex and drugs, drugs and sex. It finally
dawned on the college students of the 1990s that great, greedy corporations were exploiting little children working for starvation wages in
the wideflung sweatshops of the Third World as they made the sneak-
ers, sweatshirts, jackets, and a dozen other products emblazoned either with the names of the colleges or of the greedy corporations or
both.

Awakened from their long sleep, these students began to take action. They began to make a difference. They forced the greedy corporations to listen and to improve wages and conditions in the
sweatshops.

Not only that, but many of these young folks are going to work in
the labor movement to improve wages and conditions in our own
sweatshops, to spread the blessings of democracy from the political
process to the industrial process, just as Albert Gallatin advised in
1797. In this pursuit these young folks will not find perfect joy, but
over the long haul, I would guess, they will find more joy and more
fun than is likely to be found in the lotus lands of sex and drugs.

This realization may be the most important, the most significant
development of them all. Today, for the first time in many years, the
decline of the trade union movement has been arrested and reversed.

The AFL-CIO is well into a vigorous organizing campaign and a more militant plan of action. More union members and in particular more militant union members will mean that presidents, senators, and congressional representatives of all parties or none will have to take notice and face the much more serious threat that unless they start voting for "the satisfaction of human needs" and start giving that satisfaction priority over private profit and tax cuts, they may not be presidents, senators, or representatives much longer.

This is what our political pundits have aptly called "the vision thing."

WHAT ABOUT THE OTHER POOR?

Mention of the sweatshops of the Third World brings to mind a neglected question: What about the needs of the poor beyond our borders? This question, too, should embarrass us, citizens of a supposedly civilized and certainly rich country. Private citizens do give generously to agencies that try to improve the miserable conditions that exist in most of the undeveloped world. But our government, which is supposed to represent us, has the very worst record of all the industrial nations of the world.

Less than one percent of our gross national product (GNP) is devoted to foreign aid, and much of this amount is military aid, which doesn't count.

Why do young Muslims kill themselves in acts of terrorism that kill innocent people and move the Israeli and U.S. governments to kill innocent people in return? We will never—*never*—learn the answer to this question until we give serious thought to the other question: What is the relation between acts of terrorism and the shameful fact that less than one percent of our GNP goes to foreign aid? As the Fathers, doctors, and popes of the Catholic Church have said, "Superfluous wealth belongs to the poor." It is not a question of charity. It is a question of justice.

Again we must go back to the analogy of the rich man sitting at the table piled high with food and drink, the starving child dying at his feet. Is charity or justice involved here? Surely it is justice. The superfluous wealth of the rich man, before it disappears in tax cuts, is owed to the starving child. Our government, whether Republican or

Democrat, is that rich man, and all of us share in the guilt of his injustice.

What about Bush II's War on Terrorism and Evil?

The terrorist attacks on September 11, 2001, caused a major loss of innocent lives and created a situation that justified military response. In my opinion. That opinion assumes the belief, on the evidence, that Osama bin Laden, Al Qaeda, and the Taliban rulers of Afghanistan either were responsible for these attacks or were complicit in protecting those who were responsible.

The George W. Bush administration, overriding some efforts of restraint by Colin Powell, is now using the situation to promote a global war against anyone and everyone who is perceived as dangerous to U.S. interests. Bush's former isolationism has now been replaced by a virulent interventionism. In the closing paragraph of an insightful article in *Commonweal* (May 17, 2002) William Pfaff, political columnist for the *International Herald Tribune* in Paris, admirably summarizes where this trend is headed:

> The final obligation is to comprehend that American nationalism, wedded to American messianism, has currently acquired overpowering force in American life, in that it drives a military program of total military domination everywhere, among allies and neutrals as well as enemies, and a political program of suppressing any resistance to perceived American interest in any matter at all, whatever the cost to allied interests, international community, or international law or precedent. Behind this seems to lie what I would describe as an unarticulated, unintended, yet culpable denial that any sovereign interest exists, beyond American interest—which is an implicit blasphemy.

Over against this "implicit blasphemy" I would pose a "sovereign interest"—namely that embodied in the words of Isaiah (32:17): "Peace is the work of justice."

Of necessity we are learning something about the misery of the Muslim world and the oppression that Muslims suffer even under their own Muslim rulers, not to mention under the attentions of Israeli tanks, helicopters, and heavy artillery.

Is the connection between misery and terrorism, between and among security, peace, and justice, beginning to sink in? Has it occurred to anyone in Washington that there will likely be no peace, no security, no freedom from the fear of terrorism until we have spent a significant amount of our superfluous resources, pelf, power, and brains not to impose a *Pax Americana* of military might and economic domination, but to bring justice to all—Muslim, Buddhist, Hindu, Israeli, Palestinian, Christian, Jew, atheist, white, black, brown, red, yellow, rich, and poor—both here at home and around the world? Not with unilateral arrogance, but in reasonably humble collaboration with our allies and the United Nations.

Shortly after the end of World War II one of our French friends, a journalist who was covering the conflict between Israel and the Palestinians, summed up that conflict again and again with the gloomy conclusion, "The situation is hopeless."

The situation has not improved much since then. If anything, it is worse. But accepting the idea that anything good is hopeless runs contrary to my religion.

19

Final Conversations
and Quotations

> Human nature is transfixed in the sacred words, "The
> imagination of man's heart is evil from his youth". . . . Yes,
> yes, humanity—its injustice, malice, cruelty, its average
> stupidity and blindness are amply demonstrated, its ego-
> ism is crass, its deceitfulness, cowardice, its anti-social in-
> stincts constitute our everyday experience. . . . And yet . . .
> despite so much ridiculous depravity, we cannot forget the
> great and honorable in humanity, which manifest them-
> selves as art and science, as passion for truth, creation of
> beauty, and the idea of justice.
>
> —Thomas Mann, *The Coming Victory of Democracy*

IN MARCH 1976, as noted, I wrote a piece entitled "Why I Became
a Socialist," which came to the attention of a wonderfully wise
woman, Sister Mary Emil Penet, I.H.M., who was teaching social
ethics at the Weston School of Theology, a Jesuit seminary in Cambridge, Massachusetts. A socialist herself, she wrote to me, and I
went to see her.

She persuaded me to write a history of Christian socialism, and to
help me on my way she secured a spot for me at Weston as a visiting
scholar and use of the great library that the Jesuits shared with St.
John's Episcopal Seminary across the street. She also invited me to
join her seminar and learn something about social justice as taught
by Thomas Aquinas and by the other Fathers and doctors of the
church.

So I entered on the life of a scholar, but being who I was, I could
not give up entirely on the active life, which I have continued, though
it grows more difficult to make all the meetings, the picket lines, and
demonstrations. Only once did I manage to get myself arrested and
incarcerated, a record that pales beside Dorothy's multiple arrests

and imprisonments. Mine came as the climax to a series of demonstrations against U.S. support for the Contras in Nicaragua. Most of these demonstrations involved lying down on something: a street, a sidewalk, a lobby floor. One time I did manage to get myself pulled by a cop through horse manure and on another occasion barely escaped a mounted policeman's horse's attack by urine. The incarceration followed a lie-down at a U.S. army camp. For a few hours we were held in the camp squash court for purposes of arraignment. Our punishment was having to travel every few weeks to a courthouse on Cape Cod to hear that the case had been held over and then eventually dismissed.

It was comforting to see some of our children out there in demos or on union picket lines. Lydia and David have been especially active in union support and organizing, Lydia in the Teachers Union and David at Harvard. Fair portions of the children, not necessarily the same ones, are also regulars at church on Sunday.

On several union picket lines I talked to John Sweeney, the new and more militant president of the AFL-CIO, who remembered me from the New York ACTU. It was good to see him out on the street in support of striking workers and good to learn that he had joined DSA shortly after being elected.

I got myself elected a delegate to the Chicago convention of DSOC in 1977 and at this time came to know Michael Harrington better, a most attractive man, and Irving Howe, one of the best of the Old Left, who surprised me one day by telling me that "the religious community is probably the best recruiting ground for socialism." At this time I also began a long struggle over abortion with my fellow socialists and my fellow Democrats.

At the convention about a score of delegates met off the floor and organized the Religion and Socialism Committee (later Commission) of DSOC. They elected me coordinator and editor of the newsletter, which we called *Religious Socialism.* Among early leaders, coeditors, and contributors to the quarterly were Peter Steinfels, Sister Mary Emil, Rosemary Ruether, Harvey Cox, Cornel West, Arthur Waskow, Joe Holland, James Luther Adams, Jim Gorman, Maxine Phillips, and Jim Wallace. In one interesting three-way exchange Mike Harrington, Rosemary Ruether, and Monsignor George Higgins sparred over Mike's claim that "the political and social, Judeo-Christian God of the West is dying," over Rosemary's claim that Mike did not appreciate the vitality of liberation Christianity in Poland and among the Sandinistas in Nicaragua, and over Monsignor Higgins's protest that the Sandinistas weren't all that great and that the Brazilian bishops did not fit Rosemary's dismissal of the institutional church in Latin America.

In 1983 Maxine Phillips, then national director of DSA, organized a successful Religion and Socialism Committee conference in a Franciscan monastery in the Catskills. Many of those listed in the previous paragraph spoke there, as did Dorothee Sölle, the German poet-theologian. Approximately 140 religious socialists attended, including a sizeable Jewish contingent attracted by Arthur Waskow. All attendees showed high enthusiasm.

For eleven years I carried the main responsibility of putting out the magazine, but burned out in 1988. Then Jack Spooner took it over and kept it going for ten more years, ably assisted by Curt Sanders. In 1998 Jack resigned, and I, now rested, picked it up again with noble support from coeditors Maxine Phillips, the young Anglo-American and graphic genius Andrew Hammer, the Reverend Norm Faramelli, and Alex Mikulich, plus an editorial team that still includes Harvey Cox, David O'Brien, Cornel West, Jack Clark, the Reverend Judy Deutsch, and the Reverends Michael Dyson and Marcia Dyson.

Thanks to these good folks *Religious Socialism* and the vision it embodies remain alive and well. The magazine has long outlived *The Christian Socialist,* published from 1903 to 1922 by Edward Ellis Carr in the Midwest, and the various Christian socialist publications edited by Walter Rauschenbusch and Reinhold Niebuhr (subscription $10; 536 W. 111th St. #37, NY 10025).

In 1983 and 1986 Jack Spooner and I attended congresses of the International League of Religious Socialists, with which our Religion and Socialism Commission had affiliated, the first in Stockholm and the second in Managua, Nicaragua, where we were the guests of the Sandinistas. I had difficulties with some of the delegates over their reluctance to criticize the Soviet Union's aggressive policies in Poland and Afghanistan, but eventually we achieved a sort of uneasy consensus. In any case that is all history, and our disagreements are almost as dead as the Soviet Union.

In 1990 Helen and I visited our daughter Susan's in-laws in Yugoslavia. When Helen went home, I, carrying a Eurail pass and a pack on my back, went off to meet with Christian socialists in Austria,

Switzerland, Germany, Sweden, Finland, Belgium, Ireland, England, Italy, and Spain, with a side trip to admire the great Mondragon co-operative movement in the Basque country.

VISITS TO DOROTHY

Sometime in the 1970s I went back to the New York House of Hospitality, then on East First Street, to visit Dorothy. Life at the CW was still full of drama. On the sidewalk two young Catholic Workers, Pat Jordan and Mike Kirwan, were interposing their nonviolent bodies between two violent guests, both quite drunk. One of the latter was bleeding badly from a head wound. As Pat tried to restrain the more aggressive drunk, the latter pulled a knife and held it a few inches from Pat's throat. "Up against the wall," he said, but Pat did not move.

I was in no hurry to intervene physically, but always a good man for questions at a safe distance, I asked the knife man, "What's your problem?"

He was at a loss for an answer, or, more likely, he saw something in Pat's eyes that gave him pause. In a few seconds the threat was over; he had put away his knife and had his arm around Pat's shoulder in a gesture of obvious affection. Nonviolence had triumphed again. They walked down the street together, arm in arm.

A little later, when Dorothy and I returned from mass, the Catholic Workers had got the bleeder bandaged and were feeding him supper, still there on the sidewalk, in front of an equally bandaged little gingko tree that he had broken in another drunken fit several weeks earlier. Someone had called for an ambulance, and the police had come along, their squad car parked at the curb. Dorothy was clearly fed up with the bleeder, and I could see she was particularly annoyed by his assault on the gingko tree, which was almost the only tree on the block.

Bellevue Hospital had already refused to take the man. The diagnosis was "insane but not dangerous" or something equally unhelpful. One of the Workers said to Dorothy, "He didn't start the fight. The other guy started it."

I could see her hesitate, torn between her desire to get rid of him and some inner voice that said, "Give him the benefit of the doubt.

If a man take your gingko tree, give him your weeping willow also."
She let the police drive off without a word.

Still later, as I walked to the subway on Houston Street, past the
bodies of three drunks who lay like casualties on the battlefield of
life, I stopped at a traffic light, and there the bleeder with his bandaged head was energetically wiping the windshield of a motorist who
waited for the light—cadging money for another drink. So it went, so
it goes.

DEMOCRACY AND THE CW?

During that visit Dorothy and I argued a bit about pacifism and democracy, sitting in her little book-lined bedroom-office on the third
floor. I was doing a study of democratic process at the time and trying, with some difficulty, to figure out a relation between democracy
and the CW. Dorothy was well into her seventies by then, her figure
more stooped, her face more lined, her hair whiter, but she still had
the same contagious laugh, the same warmth, the same sense of in-
domitable will.

Actually, there was no relation between democracy and the CW,
not as I knew the CW. I recalled the incident of my posting the three
rules at the Mott Street House and her ordering me to take them
down. I added, "It was not until a few months ago that the question
occurred to me, 'Why didn't I call the guys together, explain the
situation, and see if I could get an agreement or at least a majority
vote?' That would have been the most personalist thing I could have
done, not to mention democratic. It would have demonstrated that I
had enough respect for them as persons to give them a chance to
discuss the question and, if they agreed, to give their personal assent
to the decision. The thought also occurred to me that we never had
a staff meeting or a house meeting during the years I spent at the
CW. Why not?"

"No," she replied, "because Peter Maurin said you have to run it
like an abbey. If people don't like what the abbot decides, they leave.
If the abbot is wrong, then he changes his policy. Voting and such
just leads to the creation of factions and cliques."

So that's what it was: an abbey without any rules. No wonder we
called her the Abbess. I had forgotten the rationale.

I protested, "But even an abbey has chapter meetings where the monks have a chance to criticize, complain, and contribute something to the decision-making process. Even the pope has his college of cardinals, councils, and now the synod of bishops." I made concessions for the fact that the CW had to deal with people who were often more sick than sane. No, Peter said you ran it like an abbey.

I later discovered that she had written in her journal, back in my time, "I feel bitterly oppressed. I am in the position of a dictator trying to legislate himself out of existence. They all complain that there is no boss. Today I happened to read Dostoyevsky on the Grand Inquisitor. Most apropos. Freedom—how men hate it and chafe under it, how unhappy they are with it!"

It also occurred to me that there was a parallel here between my reservations about democratic process in the family and Dorothy's reservations about it in the CW family, but with one difference: she ruled out the idea of an advisory council. She was an absolute monarch, a supreme matriarch. Who am I to say that this approach was not the most practical solution for the CW in those years? Democracy is not always and everywhere the answer.

No, Dorothy was neither a democrat nor a socialist. Although she first went to jail for picketing the White House in 1917 for women's suffrage, she never voted. Personal responsibility for our neighbors, not government responsibility, was her gospel and Peter's gospel— Peter's gospel before it was hers. On this they agreed, and on this every socialist must disagree. None of us can escape our personal responsibility for the poor and those who suffer, but as far as I can tell, the verdict is in as to beating poverty with personal acts of charity and "a thousand points of light." It will never happen.

A few months later I spent five days and nights at the CW house on First Street, trying to get a feel before I wrote about it. The food was better than it had been thirty-five years earlier. Personalism seemed to be working better, too. More people took it seriously. The house seemed to be in better shape. I picked up a few lice but no bedbugs. And they were feeding several hundred a day and giving shelter to about thirty more.

Problem guests still abounded. One old lady, swathed in multiple overcoats and ballasted with shopping bags, was so determined to be insulted that when somebody said to her, "God bless you," she shouted back, "You lying hypocrite, you don't mean 'God bless you,'

you mean, 'God damn you.'" I wrote home to Helen, "You hear an awful lot of ragtime, and the problem is to figure out the point where you have listened long enough to be kind but not long enough to lose your own mind."

THE LAST VISIT

A few months before her death in 1980 I visited Dorothy again. She had had several heart attacks and was propped up in bed watching John Paul II making his first trip to the United States as pope. I could see she was excited and proud that he was getting such an enthusiastic reception. She was actually rather negative about the nun who made a public protest to the pope about the church's refusal to allow the ordination of women.

She said, "I don't know what they're complaining about. I was always able to do anything I wanted to do."

"But Dorothy," I said, "You never wanted to be a priest."

At this point Frank Donovan, the CW's *éminence grise*, came in and told me firmly that my twenty minutes was up. I never did get a response to my objection, but later I learned that she had in fact signed a petition favoring women's ordination that was sent to the Vatican.

Peter Maurin, who Dorothy believed was a saint, died in 1949. Dorothy herself, who almost everybody believes was a saint, died on November 29, 1980, just three weeks after her eighty-third birthday. It was a peaceful death in her room at Maryhouse, the new addition to the House of Hospitality two blocks north. At the end she was still worrying about somebody else, telling her daughter Tamar that "we must do something to help the poor people in Italy" who had been decimated by earthquakes.

They laid her out, the noble face gaunt and wasted, in a plain wood coffin in the chapel at Maryhouse. There were no cosmetics—one last lesson in honesty and realism. The wake and funeral were a gathering of CW alumni, friends, and admirers from all over the country. I saw former Workers, some whom I hadn't seen for more than forty years: Joe Zarella, Gerry Griffin, Tom Sullivan, Jim O'Gara, Nina Polcyn, Tom Cornell, George and Maggie Donahue. Also there were Mike Harrington, Cardinal Terence Cooke, Cesar Chávez, Frank

Sheed, David Dellinger, and Abbie Hoffman. I. F. Stone came in by bus and told a fellow mourner, "Of all the journalists of our generation, she wrote the best."

Although the funeral was supposed to be private, the church was packed. Father Geoffrey Gneuhs, the CW chaplain, gave a moving eulogy. We sang an ecumenical assortment of hymns: "Amazing Grace," "A Mighty Fortress Is Our God," and "Salve Regina" in Latin. A group of fine musicians led us. During the singing of a free-verse version of the Twenty-third Psalm a young man with a voice of haunting beauty sang the third verse as a solo:

> I nothing fear; for Thou, O Lord,
> Art with me night and day,
> In tent, with shepherd's staff and rod,
> To guide me when I stray,
> And in the fold Thou dost uphold
> My fainting heart alway.

It was difficult to think of Dorothy in terms of a "fainting heart," but the beauty of the song struck me as a most appropriate tribute. She loved good music, she loved beauty in all its forms, and especially did she love the beauty of the Good Shepherd, who must certainly have received and upheld her in his fold.

On a Sunday morning in 1997, close to the one hundredth anniversary of Dorothy's birth, Cardinal John O'Connor, the successor to Cooke as archbishop of New York, announced from the pulpit of St. Patrick's Cathedral that he intended to initiate the process that could lead to her canonization. Later he was quoted as saying, "If anybody can be called a saint, she can." Despite his own service as admiral chaplain of the U.S. Navy he saw nothing incongruous in making this claim about one of America's foremost pacifists. Still later, after making his own investigation, he journeyed to Rome for the express purpose of promoting her cause.

When your "way of life has fall'n into the sere, the yellow leaf" and you are getting into the end game, you look for someone, a Shakespeare, a Thomas Mann, someone having a better way with words, to lend some distinction to what you are thinking and feeling. I like the Mann quote that starts this chapter and the optimistic bent with which it concludes. I also like the optimistic bent of the title of the book from which it comes, written after Mann fled Hitler's Germany.

I started this book many years ago with a sub-subtitle: "Being Also an Autobiographical Study of the Extension of Democratic Process." That sub-subtitle fits in with Mann's quote. He was not a religious man, and so his optimism can encourage those who do not think they can look to God for strength and encouragement but only to exclusively human resources.

For us religious types I have picked two quotes. One is from Sigrid Undset's *Kristin Lavransdatter*, which some think the best Christian novel after *The Brothers Karamazov*. It is also appropriate because written by a woman: it was a woman, Dorothy Day, who, despite serious disagreements, inspired, motivated, and changed my life more than any other human being, simply by the force of her response to Christ's appeal for the works of justice and mercy. And a third woman, Helen, rescued me from the grip of the TB bacillus and raised ten wonderful children.

> So at last she was come so far that she deemed she could look on her own life as from the uppermost step of a glen. Now did her road lead down into the darkling valley, but ere she took that road she had been given grace to understand that, in the loneliness of the cloister and at the gates of death, there waited for her one who had ever beheld the life of mankind as men's parishes look, seen from the mountain brow. He had seen the sin and sorrow, the love and hate, in the hearts of men, as one sees the rich manors and the humble cots, the teeming cornfields and the abandoned wastes, all born on the bosom of the same countryside. And He had descended. His feet had trodden the peopled lands, and stood in palaces and in huts. He had gathered up the sorrows and the sins of rich and poor, and lifted them aloft with Him upon a cross. *Not my happiness and my pride, but my sin and my sorrow, O my sweet Lord.* She looked up where the crucifix stood, uplifted high over the triumphal arch.

My last quote is from Pope John XXIII, who perhaps more than any other human being, despite the brevity of his reign, confirmed my faith in the papacy. It is what he said in 1962 to the opening session of Vatican Council II, that watershed event that proved that the spirit of democracy could penetrate even the formidable battlements of the Catholic Church. In a real sense it also serves to bring together the humanism of Thomas Mann and the Christian faith of Dorothy Day, Sigrid Undset, and Helen Haye Cort:

> In the daily exercise of our pastoral office, we sometimes have to listen, much to our regret, to voices of persons who, though burning with

zeal, are not endowed with too much sense of discretion or measure. In these modern times they can see nothing but prevarication and ruin. They say that our era, in comparison with past eras, is getting worse, and they behave as though they had learned nothing from history, which is nonetheless the teacher of life. They behave as though at the time of former councils everything was a full triumph for the Christian idea and life and for proper religious liberty.

We feel we must disagree with these prophets of gloom, who are always forecasting disaster, as though the end of the world were at hand.

In the present order of things divine providence is leading us to a new order of human relations which, by men and women's own efforts and even beyond their very expectations, are directed toward the fulfillment of God's superior and inscrutable designs.

My brother David used to say, "The Corts are all optimists in an insane kind of way." But John XXIII was not insane, and he made this extraordinary statement when the twentieth century already had witnessed more death, destruction, and disaster than any of its predecessors. He must have seen something that most of us could not see, and I am willing to let his statement stand as a conclusion to this tangled tale. To me those words and the unusual appearance and performance of the man who said them symbolize the hope and the mystery of democracy, the hope and the mystery of the socialist movement, the hope and the mystery of human life, the hope and the mystery of Jesus Christ.

APPENDIX

Can Good Come from Evil? Yes

JULY 9, 2002

In chapter 11, "The Miracle of Good Pope John," I describe some correspondence with Cardinal John Wright, then a member of the Vatican Curia, about democracy and the Catholic Church. Since the sex abuse scandal in the United States in 2001–2002 there has been a great deal of such talk, in particular about the need for more democratic structures that would make it possible for the laity and the lower clergy to participate in the setting of policy.

To put it bluntly, those sex scandals and the complicity of the hierarchy in those scandals have stripped away the veil of infallibility and unaccountability that have concealed much of what happens in our church, and the folks in the pews at least, who up to now have been expected only to "pray, pay, and obey," seem determined to do something about that concealment.

So I include here this brief report of some documents and structures that presently exist regarding participation, the possible reform of those structures, and the proposed creation of new structures to make this reform even more possible.

Vatican Council II

One of the major documents of Vatican Council II was *Lumen Gentium,* "Dogmatic Constitution of the Church." In section 37 of that document, about the role of the laity, the bishops said (with some slight changes in wording to make it gender inclusive):

> Every layman and laywoman should openly reveal to [their sacred pastors] their needs and desires with that freedom and confidence that befits a son or daughter of God and a brother or sister of Christ. An

individual layman or laywoman, by reason of the knowledge, competence, or outstanding ability which they may enjoy, is permitted, and sometimes even obliged to express their opinion on things that concern the good of the church. When occasion arises, let this be done through the agencies set up by the Church for this purpose.

Pope Paul VI approved these words on November 18, 1965, at which time the church had no agencies set up for this purpose, at least not on a formal, functioning, mandatory, democratically elected basis, at least not in the United States. The words were later strengthened in Canon Law (no. 212) to read: "Laypeople have the *right*" to express their needs and desires, etc.

Parish Councils

After some years Cardinal Humberto Medeiros, archbishop of Boston, urged his pastors to create parish councils, elected by the people, to advise and assist them in the operation of their parishes. They were voluntary, not mandatory. In 1988 Cardinal Bernard Law convened the Eighth Synod of the Archdiocese of Boston, and this synod made the creation of elected parish councils mandatory. The synod itself did have some representation of the laity, 60 laymen and 63 laywomen out of a total of 340 members, but all were appointed by the cardinal. Out of 147 priests only 17 were elected by their fellow priests.

There is also an ongoing Archdiocesan Pastoral Council that includes 48 laymen and laywomen, but they are appointed.

On March 9, 2002, after the sex scandal had broke and begun to expand like a mushroom cloud, Cardinal Law called an all-day convocation in Boston's World Trade Center, with an open invitation to priests and laity to attend. Approximately 2,500 did so. Part of the program was a one-hour session during which we could speak for two minutes each to our five regional bishops. Several of us suggested that there should be mandatory regional councils as well as parish councils on which clergy and laity, elected by their peers, could sit and meet regularly with our regional bishops. These councils could then elect priests and laity to sit on the Archdioicesan Pastoral Council so that the whole structure of the church in the Boston area would truly and honestly represent both laity and lower clergy. Then, and only then, could we say that we were in compliance with Vatican Council II, "reveal[ing] to [our sacred pastors our] needs and desires with that freedom and confidence that befits a son or daughter of God and a brother or sister of Christ."

In our parishes both priests and people began meeting and giving vent to their anger and determination that things must change. One parish council in the western suburbs tried to start an association of parish councils. Cardinal Law made a statement forbidding the priests to approve or encourage such an association, indicating that he intended to stonewall the entire situation, including the many demands for his resignation.

Personal note: I have been on friendly terms with the cardinal since his arrival in Boston in 1984. He remembered me from his undergraduate days at Harvard when I used to lecture at the Catholic club there. I have found him to be very good on the subjects of labor unions, the poor in general, and the Hispanic poor in particular. He has an excellent command of Spanish. Despite, or because of, our friendship I wrote to him early on and urged him to resign and take a pastoral assignment in a Hispanic parish or country. He did not respond.

Our parish is part of a triparish cluster that includes churches in Swampscott and Marblehead. On July 7, 2002, our parish council voted unanimously for a motion that reads as follows:

> THAT we invite the parish councils of St. John's, Swampscott, and Our Lady of the Sea, Marblehead, to meet with us and discuss the creation of elected committees or councils representing the laity and clergy of the Salem Vicariate, the North Region and the Archdiocese, to serve as advisory bodies to Monsignor Garrity [the vicar of the Salem Vicariate, which includes twenty-three parishes], Bishop Irwin [our regional bishop], and Cardinal Law. It is understood that a committee, if created, would start by requesting a meeting with the Vicar.

It is summer, and I do not expect action very soon in response to this motion and the invitations that will go out to the other parish councils. But it is a start. And many of us, both here and around the archdiocese, are determined that it shall be more than just a start. There will be changes in the structures of our church. Good *can* come from evil. Yes!

JANUARY 10, 2003

In the words of the shopworn but useful cliché there is good news and bad news.

The Good News

1. Cardinal Law has resigned.

2. The Voice of the Faithful (VOTF), an organization dominated by sensible laymen and laywomen, is alive and well and continues to put pressure on our priests and bishops to be more responsive to the laity's demands for greater participation in the formation and implementation of church policy.

3. The VOTF Structural Change Working Group voted unanimously on September 26, 2002, to adopt a version of our proposal for "the creation of parallel Lay Councils on intermediate levels such as the vicariate and region, if a diocese is so divided and if decisions affecting the laity are made at those levels." Our proposal differs in that lower clergy and religious (nuns and ordered priests and brothers) would also elect representatives on such "pastoral councils," culminating in an *elected* archdiocesan council.

4. A meeting of parishioners of the three churches of our triparish cluster voted overwhelmingly to affiliate with the VOTF and organized study groups to deal with major aspects of our problem. One study group on church structures voted unanimously to endorse our proposal for extending pastoral councils upward to vicariates, regions, and the archdiocese.

The Bad News

1. A regional bishop, Richard Lennon, has replaced Cardinal Law, at least temporarily, and has squandered the good feeling that greeted his appointment by declining, so far, to meet with VOTF leaders and by retaining Law's veto on VOTF meetings on church property. Cardinal Law made a strange compromise, allowing meetings where they already existed, but forbidding new ones. Some parish pastors have ignored this veto.

2. The pastor in our neighboring parish in Swampscott has not delivered our invitation to his parish council to meet with our council

to discuss our proposal, although it is now more than five months since he received it and several council meetings have been held in the interim.

3. The parish council in Marblehead declined our invitation to meet on the ground that "meeting with the three councils at large would be too cumbersome and counterproductive at this time." Earlier the pastor there had told me that "there's no harm in talking." Apparently there is harm in talking.

4. Six bishops in other dioceses, as of last count, also have forbidden VOTF meetings on church property. This number includes our old friend Bishop William Murphy of Rockville Centre, New York. Sad.

Meanwhile, I remain an optimist. The trauma of the sex abuse scandal has been too deep, too wide, too terrible to be ignored. Despite such scandals, despite such serious losses in faith and commitment, the Roman Catholic Church remains the oldest organization in the history of the world. It has one billion adherents who in widely different degrees of faith and commitment still confess some fidelity. I do believe, as promised, that the gates of hell—and the events in Boston have provided a fair look at those gates—shall not prevail against it.

BIBLIOGRAPHICAL ESSAY

The ACTU

A labor historian tells me that the academic community will be, or should be, most interested in the chapters about the ACTU. A superficial check reveals that there is a sizeable literature on the subject, including books, articles, and doctoral dissertations. I list and comment on only the most notable. If you have read the ACTU chapters, you should be able to evaluate these efforts yourself—but not necessarily, as I have learned from bitter experience.

The surest and most reliable sources of information are microfilm copies of *The Labor Leader,* ACTU's national newspaper, published in New York, and *The Wage Earner,* originally *The Michigan Labor Leader,* published by the Detroit ACTU under the excellent editorship of Paul Weber. They ran from 1937 and 1939, respectively, to around 1960. The New York and Boston public libraries have microfilm of both. The Detroit library might have microfilm of *The Michigan Labor Leader* and *The Wage Earner* at least.

Non-ACTU sources, in chronological order from 1948 to 2001, include:

1. John F. Cronin, *Catholic Social Action* (Milwaukee: Bruce, 1948). Father Cronin, like Father George Higgins at that time, was an assistant director of the Social Action Department of the National Catholic Welfare Conference (NCWC) under Monsignor John A. Ryan. His work is a textbook and devotes only two pages to ACTU in the edition I saw, but it was enough to set off a rather angry protest in an article in *Commonweal* by a New York ACTU chaplain, Father George A. Kelly, entitled "The ACTU and Its Critics" (December 31, 1948). Father Kelly seems to have read a different, slightly more critical edition of Father Cronin's book. The key statement in the edition I read was, "Many Catholic leaders . . . fear the divisive effects of any religious organization working formally within the labor movement." Not exactly a devastating criticism.

Father Kelly's article led to a lengthy defense of Father Cronin by Father Higgins in a letter to *Commonweal* (January 21, 1949), which I am sure did nothing to allay the hypersensitivities of Actists such as Father Kelly, who thought that they weren't getting the kind of wholehearted support they deserved from NCWC headquarters. Monsignor Charles Owen Rice, an ACTU chaplain even feistier than Father Kelly, chimed in with a letter defending Father Cronin from the charge of lacking wholeheartedness, which proved once again that ACTU chaplains and ACTU chapters frequently disagreed with each other.

2. Philip Taft, "The Association of Catholic Trade Unionists," *Industrial Labor Relations Review* (January 1949): 210–18. Taft was a highly respected labor historian at Brown, author of *Economics and Problems of Labor* (2d ed., 1948). With a grant from the American Philosophical Society no less he made a study of the ACTU and concluded that it was not guilty of "splitting labor unions on religious lines." His final sentence: "By espousing decent and progressive unionism and by opposing racketeers and abuses within unions, ACTU is helping to give leadership to the forces that believe in more intelligent and better administered unions—leadership that would not subordinate union functions to ulterior political ends."

3. Irving Howe and B. J. Widick, *The UAW and Walter Reuther* (New York: Random House, 1949). Irving Howe was one of the men, besides Mike Harrington, whom I most liked and admired in DSOC and in its successor DSA. As I mention in chapter 19, he once told me that in his opinion "The religious community is probably the most fertile ground for recruiting socialists." In *The UAW and Walter Reuther,* however, he and Widick offer a negative judgment about the ACTU, despite the fact that the ACTU was an important ally in support of their hero Walter Reuther and despite further that ten pages prior to making this negative judgment they make the positive judgment that "only two groups, the Catholic unionists and the Socialists, tried to examine the Reuther program in terms of its ultimate, underlying meanings." They then support this second judgment with favorable comment on Paul Weber's praise for Reuther's challenge to General Motor's monopoly over decisions as to prices and profits, similar to my praise in *Commonweal.*

In Howe and Widick's negative judgment, "The ACTU people supported Reuther against the Stalinists because they would like to root all radicals, genuine or false, from power." Howe could not then accept the notion that Catholics could be radicals unless they embraced some form of explicit socialism. And we were certainly not socialists at that time, although we were often their allies and on the basis of program might be called closet socialists.

In the previous pages, to save space I have not given a complete account of ACTU activity in this crucial campaign for control of the UAW. It is available in the pages of *The Wage Earner* and also in a piece I wrote entitled "The Association of Catholic Trade Unionists and the Auto Workers," *U.S. Catholic Historian* (fall 1990): 335–51.

This fuller account is essential as a corrective to the Howe and Widick book as well as to the Betten, Cochran, Seaton, Rosswurm, and Buhle books that I list later in this bibliography. It includes several important facts not mentioned in my text here—namely, that *The Labor Leader* opposed the deportation of Harry Bridges as a subversive alien and criticized the constitution of the CIO Utility Workers for barring Communists from membership. *The Wage Earner* also criticized this disbarment.

A quote from Wilfrid Sheed in the *Atlantic Monthly* (July 1973) is also relevant to this recurring charge that the ACTU was antiradical: "By the late Forties . . . the closest thing to a coherent radicalism was Walter Reuther." The ACTU, however, was clearly to the left of Reuther in proposals to change the U.S. economy.

4. Michael Harrington, "Catholics in the Labor Movement: A Case History," *Labor History* (fall 1960): 241–63. Harrington, a fellow CW graduate who left the church and became America's foremost socialist, did a much more detailed study than Philip Taft, focusing mainly on the campaign against Communist leadership of the UE, CIO. I discuss this article in chapter 9 in connection with my visit to Father Rice and also quote from it at the beginning of that chapter. The quote supports Taft's conclusion that the ACTU did not act in a religiously partisan, divisive manner. Harrington also notes that ACTU protested the expulsion of twenty-seven members of a Bridgeport UE local on the grounds of "communism." His general conclusion echoes Father Rice's wry admission, "We battle the UE and strike a blow for progress every once in a while, but we are not the men the Commies think we are." Harrington is especially effective in showing the lack of cohesive, unified ACTU organization and communication, noting also that the Communists exaggerated

338 BIBLIOGRAPHICAL ESSAY

the ACTU influence to discredit their opposition, but the ACTU exaggerated it out of "organizational pride." A valid pair of points.

5. Neil Betten, *Catholic Activism and the Industrial Worker* (Gainesville: University Press of Florida, 1976). Betten, an associate professor of history at Florida State University, was also an official in the American Federation of Teachers, AFL-CIO. He does a mostly competent, scholarly job and does not try to conceal either his sympathy for the Communist faction in the CIO or his antipathy for the ACTU.

He admits that the ACTU supported "several hundred strikes" (I'm not sure that it was that many), but he holds that this activity mostly ended around 1939, about the time of the Hitler-Stalin pact, after which the "dominant concern" became the campaign to drive Communists out of the labor movement. His scholarly competence dissolves over this insupportable thesis, which, thanks in part to his book, became a standard smear when the smoke cleared after World War II.

Betten's closing paragraph reveals his bias: "With the expulsion of the communist unions from the CIO came the weakening of progressive idealism in organized labor."

6. Bert Cochran, *Labor and Communism: The Conflict That Shaped American Unionism* (Princeton, N.J.: Princeton University Press, 1977). Cochran gives a detailed, largely objective account of the key conflict between the Communist Party and the Reuther coalition in the UAW. He is more impartially critical than Betten. He agrees with Kermit Eby's "a plague on both your houses" (see chapter 6), describing the ACTU and the Communist Party as "two extreme poles of power attraction" engaged in "the larger struggle for control of the world."

7. Ronald W. Schatz, *The Electrical Workers: A History of Labor at General Electric and Westinghouse 1923–60* (Urbana and Chicago: University of Illinois Press, 1983). At time of publication Schatz was a member of the history department at Wesleyan University. This book is a fairly impartial, straightforward account of union organization and disorganization resulting from conflicts between anti-Communists and the leadership of the UE, CIO, with special attention to the Westinghouse local in East Pittsburgh and the General Electric local in Erie, Pennsylvania. Schatz barely mentions the national ACTU, although Father Rice, Pittsburgh ACTU chaplain, was a

major player in both Erie and East Pittsburgh. The UE, once the Communist Party's major possession at five hundred thousand members, was reduced to fifty-eight thousand members by 1960 after separation from the CIO and was replaced mainly by the IUE, CIO.

8. Douglas Seaton, *Catholics and Radicals: The Association of Catholic Trade Unionists and the American Labor Movement from Depression to Cold War* (Lewisburg, Penn.: Bucknell University Press, 1983). Seaton was a member of the Rutgers faculty. His book is an outrageous hatchet job, identifying the Communists as the good guys and the Actists as the bad guys, leaders of the conservative forces that prevented the CIO and the Communist Party from spawning a strong socialist movement in the United States. When Seaton is at loss for a fact to prove his case, he simply invents one. I reviewed the book in *Commonweal* (August 12, 1983), singling out eleven such inventions.

9. Steve Rosswurm, "The Catholic Church and the Left-Led Unions: Labor Priests, Labor Schools, and the ACTU," in *The CIO's Left-Led Unions*, edited by Steve Rosswurm (New Brunswick, N.J.: Rutgers University Press, 1992). Rosswurm is a professor of history at Lake Forest College. Although he doesn't invent facts, for mysterious reasons of his own he arrives at the same conclusions as Seaton. For example, "The Catholic Church, both clerics and laity, played a central role in isolating, defeating and ultimately destroying the CIO left, both Communist and non-Communist." Rosswurm places the ACTU at the core of that effort. The truth is, however, that the ACTU itself was part of the non-Communist left, a part it had won with blood, sweat, and tears on picket lines, in union halls, and in labor school classrooms. Let us analyze those words *left* and *right*. The entire CIO constituted the left of the labor movement. The anti-Communist wing included almost every variety of Marxist except the Stalinist brand, democratic socialists, radical Catholics, run-of-the-mill trade unionists. And what did the Communist Party represent? What right did it have to claim the label *left?* Whatever the illusions and delusions many of its zealous, hardworking members clung to, they had pledged their allegiance to one of the most reactionary, dictatorial, homicidal governments in the history of the world. So it was left against right, yes, and the real right lost, and the real left won.

10. Charles McCollester, ed., *Fighter with a Heart: Writings of Charles Owen Rice, Pittsburgh Labor Priest* (Pittsburgh: University

340 BIBLIOGRAPHICAL ESSAY

of Pittsburgh Press, 1996). This work is a handsome, copiously illustrated compilation of Monsignor Rice's writings, mainly in *The Pittsburgh Catholic*, from the founding of the Catholic Radical Alliance (later the Pittsburgh ACTU) in 1937 until 1993, through his support of a hundred good causes. The collection also includes final tributes on the deaths of two ancient Stalinist adversaries, Steve Nelson and Harry Bridges, and contains the famous pamphlet Father Rice wrote in 1947 and distributed widely: "How to De-Control Your Union of Communists." In one good sample of his writing Father Rice tells his readers: "Remember, if you push for something and the union gets it, then you claim credit and claim that you pushed the opposition into going after it. If the union does not get it, yell, 'sell out,' 'double cross,' 'ineffective,' 'stumble bum,' etc. . . . Train your. . . . people to yell 'boo, sit down, back to Moscow, etc.'" A little difficult to reconcile this advice with either the Old or New Testaments, not to mention *Roberts Rules of Order*.

Perhaps remorse over such tactics and his own cooperation with the House Un-American Activities Committee and the FBI led him in 1977, as revealed in chapter 9, to reevaluate this effort and to write, "I think I wasted a lot of time on a crusade that did more harm than good." See also his "Confessions of an Anti-Communist" (pp. 99–106 in *Fighter with a Heart*), first printed in *Labor History* (summer 1989): 449–62.

The key passage in "Confessions" is: "I was sincerely convinced that they [the Communists] had a chance to take over America's entire labor movement or, at least the major portion of it, as they had in France and, after WWII in Italy, and that would have been pure disaster . . . but there was no chance, absolutely no chance, of that happening." Was there not? They came within a few votes of taking over the UAW, and control of the UAW probably would have meant control of the CIO. But control of the UAW or the CIO was not necessary to spell disaster. Control of just one UAW local at North American Aviation almost spelled disaster in 1941, and control of Henry Wallace and the Progressive Party came close to spelling a fair amount of disaster in 1948. Perhaps the New York and Detroit ACTU members, with a better perspective on the big picture, were in a better position than Father Rice to make a judgment.

11. Symposium on *Fighter with a Heart* in *Labor History* (February 1999): 53–68. This symposium was put together by Steve Ross-

wurm (see number 9) and includes contributions by Ronald Schatz (see number 7); David Rosenberg, curator of labor collections, University of Pittsburgh; Ellen Schrecker, professor of history at Yeshiva University; John C. Cort; and a response by Monsignor Rice. The fact that Rosswurm put together this symposium, invited me to participate, and participated in the tribute to Father Higgins (see number 14) seem to indicate a certain mellowing of the harsh opinions he expressed seven years earlier.

The symposium is a valuable collection of multiple takes on Father Rice's extraordinary and overall admirable and valuable career, despite all.

12. Paul Buhle, *Taking Care of Business: Samuel Gompers, George Meany, Lane Kirkland, and the Tragedy of* American Labor (New York: Monthly Review Press, 1999). Buhle teaches American Civilization at Brown and is a fellow DSA member.

This book is a highly negative history of the U.S. labor movement up until the election of John Sweeney in 1995, for whom Buhle expresses some hope. Even Walter Reuther comes off looking bad, and George Meany seems to be the personification of pure evil. I loaned Paul the manuscript of my book before he published his, but about the ACTU all he wrote was:

> The Association of Catholic Trade Unionists (ACTU), earlier engaged in what they considered democratic struggles against minority Communist leadership of union headquarters and locals, turned swiftly to the right after the war. Demanding the expulsion of Communists and the dismemberment of unions which could not be brought into line, their local members joined local businessmen and the tabloid press, placing labor leftists within their crosshairs, working with local FBI branches and the tabloid press on what might be called counter-insurgency campaigns of dirty tricks and libel.

He writes further that "the purge of left-led unions from the CIO in 1949–50 is now understood to have been a disaster for labor by all but a few traditionalists." Understood by whom? Academics? Union members? The general public? And what was the count? How many pro, how many con, how many no opinion? No hard feelings, Paul, but you don't really know how many understood what or whether that purge was a disaster, a blessing, or something in between the two, do you?

13. *Religious Socialism* (summer 2001). *Religious Socialism* is the quarterly publication of the DSA Religion and Socialism Commission. This issue, edited by Alex Mikulich, features a lead article about the ACTU by Maurice Isserman, Mike Harrington's biographer and a professor of history at Hamilton College. It also includes comment by Monsignor George G. Higgins and reprinted material about the ACTU from his and coauthor Bole's excellent book *Organized Labor and the Church: Reflections of a Labor Priest* (New York: Paulist Press, 1993). Isserman's defense of the ACTU is most significant, coming from a left-wing, non-Catholic historian.

14. *Social Catholicism: Essays in Honor of Monsignor George Higgins*, special edition of *U.S. Catholic Historian* (fall 2001): 3–118. It was good that this tribute to Father Higgins came out in time for him to read it before he died, at age eighty-six, on May Day, 2002, a day when left-wing labor celebrates its historic day and Catholic labor celebrates a feast in honor of St. Joseph the Worker.

The essay writers include Father Higgins's biographer, William Bole, as well as Andrew Greeley, John Sweeney, Steven Avella, Gerald Costello, Eugene Fisher, Timothy Meagher, John Shepherd, Joseph Turrini, Charles Curran, Steve Rosswurm, John O'Brien, and another great labor priest, Patrick Sullivan, C.S.C.

The collection includes tributes to the splendid work Father Higgins did in helping to win for Cesar Chávez and the United Farm Workers their first real breakthrough in the vineyards of California, a victory that, unfortunately, Republican politicians, with assistance from the Teamsters Union, were able to reverse. Contributors also pay tribute both to Father Higgins's outspoken opposition to so-called—outrageously so-called—antiunion right-to-work laws and to his lay-it-on-the-line rebukes to sister hospital administrators who hire union-busting lawyers and consultants to avoid their moral obligations to bargain with bona fide unions.

Father Sullivan closes the symposium with this reminder about the Bishops' Social Action Department, which Father Higgins headed for so many years: "As more research is conducted, it will become abundantly evident that the NCWC Social Action Department played such an essential part that if Ryan, McGowan, Hayes and Higgins had been absent, it would have been very detrimental to U.S. workers and their unions, the labor priests and the Church."

AFL-CIO president John Sweeney puts it more personally: "For six decades now, no clergy member from any faith has given more energy, effort, vision and wisdom to the American union movement than Monsignor George Higgins."

The story I like best is the one about the out-of-town priest who spent three hours with him the day before Father Higgins was to receive the Presidential Medal of Freedom several years ago. In those three hours Father Higgins never mentioned it. The visitor found out about it only two days later from reading the newspaper. I ask myself, "Could I have done that?" I don't think so. He was not only a great man, but a very good one.

DOROTHY DAY AND THE CW

The literature on Dorothy Day and the CW is too voluminous to list all of it. A good place to start, for those who are not familiar already, is Robert Ellsberg's *Dorothy Day: Selected Writings* (Maryknoll, N.Y.: Orbis, 1992), originally published by Knopf in 1983 under the title *By Little and by Little*, with Tamar Hennessey, Dorothy's daughter.

Ellsberg is the son of the *Pentagon Papers* hero, Daniel Ellsberg. He is a convert from Judaism and spent five years at the New York CW, during two of which he was editing the newspaper. His introduction is one of the best things ever written about Dorothy and the CW.

You also should read at least one of Dorothy's books, such as *From Union Square to Rome, The Long Loneliness, On Pilgrimage, Loaves and Fishes,* and *Thérèse.* In my opinion she is the best writer the American Catholic Church has produced to date, better than Thomas Merton, Daniel Berrigan, J. F. Powers, Flannery O'Connor, Walker Percy, or Garry Wills. She probably is also the best spiritual writer if you separate out her political and economic vagaries, though there I am not entirely qualified to judge.

ACTU AND THE CW

1. Mel Piehl, *Breaking Bread: The Catholic Worker and the Origins of Catholic Radicalism in America* (Philadelphia: Temple University, 1982). Piehl, a professor of humanities at Valparaiso

University, has done the best job of telling the CW-ACTU story. I think he was, or is, a Lutheran, but his Christian sympathy for Catholic movements and his scholarship and fairness are evident throughout.

2. For ten years, from July 1945 to March 1954, as associate editor of *Commonweal*, I wrote a regular column entitled "The Labor Movement." This column is also a good source of information about all the subjects discussed here. On October 1, 1948, *Commonweal* printed one of these articles under the heading "Reform Begins at the Plant Level." This and two subsequent articles headed "Is a Christian Industrialism Possible?" and "Christian Industrialism III" (October 29 and November 26, 1948) produced, as I recall, more letters to the editor than any other subject discussed in *Commonweal* up to that time.

These articles and the letters brought out the differences between the ACTU and the CW, which Robert Ludlow, successor to the ailing Peter Maurin as chief theoretician of the movement, had magnified. Ludlow kicked off the letter barrage in the October 22, 1948, issue. He was an anarchosyndicalist with an agrarian twist. His all-purpose solution to the evils of capitalism was "general strike and take over." With admirable honesty he told me he did not accept Leo XIII's and Pius XI's labor encyclicals. When I asked Dorothy if she agreed with Ludlow's line, she said she did, but that she also agreed with the encyclicals. A difficult pair of agreements. In that first letter of the controversy Ludlow, signing himself as "Associate Editor, *Catholic Worker*," stated:

> The fundamental disagreement between the ACTU and *The Catholic Worker* lies not only in the extent with which we accept industrial methods but also on the question of class collaboration. The Industry Council Plan, on a state or plant basis, which Mr. Cort advocates, assumes class collaboration. This we reject as an impossibility under the capitalist system and as a betrayal of the workers. We advocate the elimination of the capitalist class by non-violent direct action and the cessation of acquisitive class society. Our belief calls therefore for radical non-violent revolution. The procedure advocated by Mr. Cort calls for class collaboration and reformism. We believe the ACTU program to be unrealistic and lacking in vision. It is little more than New Dealism.

Dorothy did not participate in the *Commonweal* give-and-take, but in the November 1949 issue of *The Catholic Worker* she blasted the

Industry Council Plan proposed by the CIO's Phil Murray and endorsed by both the ACTU and the American bishops, all parties agreeing that the plan was based on Pius XI's *Quadragesimo Anno*. Dorothy wrote: "We don't believe in those industrial councils where the heads of United States Steel sit down with the common man in an obscene *agape* of luxury, shared profits, blood money from a thousand battles all over the world." It does seem that she agreed more with Ludlow than with the popes. It is worth noting that the heads of United States Steel showed no interest either then or later in sharing luxury, profits, or blood money with the common man.

Of late *The Catholic Worker* seems much less passionate about its agrarianism and more simpatico to even reformist elements of the labor movement. The 1940s brought out the passion in all of us.

CHRISTIAN SOCIALISM

1. Here I must refer the reader to my own book *Christian Socialism: An Informal History* (Maryknoll, N.Y.: Orbis, 1988), not because it is so great, but because it is the only thing available that is reasonably up-to-date and comprehensive and that is written from an American point of view. Since its publication I have been quietly smoldering at the Orbis insertion of the word *Informal* in the title. The book is lousy with reference notes and other scholarly trappings, but, actually, Orbis's assessment of the scholarly nature of the book is probably my own fault. My style is what somebody called "idiosyncratic." I'm a journalist at heart, and I write journalese. I even used the personal pronoun a few times in the book, a terrible faux pas, as in relating a conversation with Gustavo Guttierez, the liberation theologian. My major error was in misstating the membership of the Christian Social Democrats of Sweden, who are an important source of strength for the Social Democrats of that country. Instead of "a thousand members in 200 groups," it should be "10,000 members in 200 groups," a remarkable achievement.

The book also covers the subject of liberation theology, which has been one important expression of Christian socialism. The book is critical of Marxist and Leninist elements in liberation theology, but the liberation theologians, led by Guttierez, deserve everlasting gratitude for their work in shifting the Catholic Church away from a preferential option for the rich and powerful to a "preferential option for the poor."

2. Chris Bryant, an Anglican priest and chair of the Christian Socialist Movement of England, of which Tony Blair and fifty other MPs are also members, has published a fine book entitled *Possible Dreams: A Personal History of the British Christian Socialists* (London: Hodder and Stoughton, 1996). It has much material that my book does not. The Christian Socialist Movement is also an important source of strength for the Labour Party.

3. If you know Italian, you might want to read the monumental, five-volume work by Alfredo Luciani of the University of Verona, founder in 1976 of Azione Socialista Cristiana Europea (ASCE) and at one time an official of the Italian Socialist Party: *Cristianesimo e movimento socialista in Europa 1789–1985* (Venice: n.p., 1986). He also has a one-volume version, *Cristianesimo e socialismo in Europa 1700–1989* (Milan: ASCE, 1989).

INDEX